Approaches to Audiences
A Reader

Also available in this series

Approaches to Media: A Reader
Edited by Oliver Boyd-Barrett and Chris Newbold

Media in Global Context: A Reader
*Edited by Annabelle Sreberny-Mohammadi, Dwayne Winseck,
Jim McKenna and Oliver Boyd-Barrett*

FOUNDATIONS IN MEDIA
General editor: Oliver Boyd-Barrett

Approaches to Audiences
A Reader

Edited by
Roger Dickinson,
Ramaswami Harindranath
and Olga Linné

A member of the Hodder Headline Group
LONDON • NEW YORK • SYDNEY • AUCKLAND

First published in Great Britain 1998 by
Arnold, a member of the Hodder Headline Group,
338 Euston Road, London NW1 3BH

http://www.arnoldpublishers.com

Copublished in the United States of America by
Oxford University Press Inc.
198 Madison Avenue, New York, NY 10016

British Library Cataloguing in Publication Data
A catalogue record for this book is available from the British Library

Library of Congress Cataloging-in-Publication Data
Approaches to audiences: a reader/edited by Roger Dickinson,
   Ramaswami Harindranath, and Olga Linné.
      p.   cm. — (Foundations in media)
   Includes bibliographical references and indexes.
   ISBN 0-340-69224-3. — ISBN 0-340-69225-1 (pbk.)
   1. Mass media—Audiences.   2. Mass media and culture.   3. Mass
   media—Social aspects.   I. Dickinson, Roger, 1956–.   II. Harindranath,
   Ramaswami, 1959–.   III. Linné, Olga, 1941–.   IV. Series.
PS.A83A68   1998   98–8038
302.23–dc21   CIP

Production Editor: Liz Gooster
Production Controller: Helen Whitehorn
Cover Design: Terry Griffiths

ISBN 0 340 69225 1 (pb)
ISBN 0 340 69224 3 (hb)

1 2 3 4 5 6 7 8 9 10

Typeset in 10/11 Palatino by AFS Imagesetters Ltd, Glasgow
Printed and bound in Great Britain by MPG Books Ltd, Bodmin, Cornwall

What do you think about this book? Or any other Arnold title?
Please send your comments to feedback.arnold@hodder.co.uk

Contents

List of contributors   vii

General editor's preface   ix

Editors' introduction: approaching audience studies   xi

Acknowledgements   xvii

Section 1. Societies, masses and publics

1 American pop culture sweeps the world   2
   Herbert I. Schiller
2 Up close from a distance: media and the culture of cricket   14
   Aggrey Brown
3 News influence on our pictures of the world   25
   Maxwell McCombs
4 Toward a critical theory of television   36
   Douglas Kellner
5 Unpopular messages in an age of popularity   50
   Sut Jhally and Justin Lewis
6 Cultural Indicators: European reflections on a research paradigm   61
   J. Mallory Wober
7 Critique: meaning, the media and the market   74
   Michael Tracey

Section 2. Individuals, impacts and influences

8 Media violence – four research perspectives   88
   Cecilia von Feilitzen
9 Research about violence in the media: different traditions
   and changing paradigms   104
   Olga Linné and Ellen Wartella
10 Ten things wrong with the 'effects' model   120
   David Gauntlett
11 Children and television: a critical overview of the research   131
   David Buckingham
12 Ten theses on children and television   146
   Bob Hodge and David Tripp
13 With the benefit of hindsight: reflections on uses and
   gratifications research   151
   Denis McQuail
14 Social psychological perspectives in reception analysis   166
   Birgitta Höijer
15 Critique: audiences 'Я' us   184
   Martin Barker

Section 3.   Cultures, communities and families

16 Television: polysemy and popularity   194
        John Fiske
17 Mass communication and the construction of meaning   205
        Graham Murdock
18 On looking into Bourdieu's black box   218
        Martin Barker and Kate Brooks
19 Domestic relations: the framework of family viewing in
        Great Britain   233
        David Morley
20 Television and everyday life: towards an anthropology
        of the television audience   245
        Roger Silverstone
21 Modernity, consumption and anxiety: television audiences
        and food choice   257
        Roger Dickinson
22 Cultural differences in the retelling of television fiction   272
        Tamar Liebes
23 Documentary meanings and interpretive contexts: observations
        on Indian 'repertoires'   283
        Ramaswami Harindranath
24 Critique: elusive audiences   298
        Peter Dahlgren

Author index   311

Subject index   315

List of contributors

Martin Barker is Reader in Media Studies at the School of Cultural and Community Studies, University of Sussex.

Kate Brooks was Research Assistant on the Judge Dredd Project in the School of Cultural Studies at the University of the West of England.

Aggrey Brown is Professor of Communication and Director of the Caribbean Institute of Mass Communication, University of the West Indies.

David Buckingham is Lecturer in Media Studies, Institute of Education, University of London.

Peter Dahlgren is Professor of Sociology in the Department of Media and Communication Studies, University of Lund.

Roger Dickinson is Lecturer at the Centre for Mass Communication Research and Sub-Dean of Graduate Studies, University of Leicester.

Cecilia von Feilitzen is Senior Lecturer in the Department of Journalism, Media and Communication, University of Stockholm.

John Fiske is Professor of Communication Arts, University of Wisconsin-Madison.

David Gauntlett is Lecturer in Social Communications at the Institute of Communication Studies, University of Leeds.

Ramaswami Harindranath is Lecturer in the School of Cultural Studies at the University of the West of England.

Bob Hodge is Professor and Dean of the Faculty of Humanities, University of Western Sydney.

Birgitta Höijer is Senior Lecturer in the Department of Media and Communications, Oslo University.

Sut Jhally is Professor of Communication in the Department of Communications, University of Massachusetts, Amherst.

Douglas Kellner is Professor of Philosophy at the University of Texas at Austin.

Justin Lewis is Professor of Communication in the Department of Communications, University of Massachusetts, Amherst.

Tamar Liebes is Director of the Smart Institute of Communications at the Hebrew University of Jerusalem.

Olga Linné is Senior Lecturer and Postgraduate Research Tutor at the Centre for Mass Communication Research, University of Leicester.

Maxwell McCombs is Chair, Department of Journalism, University of Texas at Austin.

Denis McQuail is Emeritus Professor of Mass Communication, University of Amsterdam.

David Morley is Professor of Communications, Department of Media and Communications, Goldsmiths' College, University of London.

Graham Murdock is Reader in the Sociology of Culture, Loughborough University.

Herbert I. Schiller is Professor of Communication, University of California at San Diego.

Roger Silverstone is Professor of Media and Communication, London School of Economics and Political Science.

Michael Tracey is Director of the Center for Media Research, University of Colorado, Boulder.

David Tripp is Associate Professor in the School of Education, Murdoch University, Australia.

Ellen Wartella is Dean and Walter Cronkite Regents Chair in Communication Studies, College of Communication, University of Texas at Austin.

J. Mallory Wober is Principal Lecturer, Department of Media Production at Bournemouth University.

General editor's preface

This volume is one of a series of five readers which aim to provide a comprehensive set of resources for media study courses. Other volumes of the series address the following themes: approaches to media; media in global context; media industries and professions; and media texts. Each volume of the series is intended to stand alone for the benefit of individual students or course organizers of courses at both undergraduate and postgraduate levels in media, journalism and broadcasting, communications, culture and literary studies, and, more generally, of courses in sociology, politics, and literature and education. Taken together, the volumes provide a broad introduction to the study of media, and they cover each of the major issues, topics, themes, approaches and methodologies encountered in the study of media. They are also intended to provide an international inflection both in source and topic, which is in line with the process of globalization of the media industries and with world-wide interests in the study of the media.

Oliver Boyd-Barrett

Editors' introduction: approaching audience studies

Roger Dickinson, Ramaswami Harindranath and Olga Linné

Our purpose in assembling this volume is to bring together a very wide range of work which, in some way or other, has made its focus the impacts, influences, effects on or uses made of mass media outputs by audiences. As such, it will, we hope, be of value to students on general communications and media studies degrees (both at graduate and undergraduate level), as well as to others with a special interest in the study of media audiences.

The usual reason offered by editors for publishing a reader is the need to bring together in a single volume the key elements of a widely scattered literature. Justifiable as this is, the result is all too often a bafflingly disparate collection of chapters and extracts which seem important or useful, often essential, for an understanding of a discipline, field or area of study, but one which lacks coherence. We hope the present volume is different. We feel it is the job of the editors to offer some sense of connectedness to their collections and this is what we have attempted to do in designing the structure into which the chapters of this book are placed.

When we began to think about what a 'Reader on Audiences' might look like we quickly realized that the attractions of a kind of, as it were, undisciplined discipline-defining collection are almost irresistible. In our research and teaching we had often found it difficult to define what was meant by the term 'audience research' but we felt we knew it when we saw it. Faced with the challenge of compiling this collection, we began to see a case for the inclusion of a vast array of different pieces which could illustrate the variety of approaches that the field exhibits and an assortment of material which we ourselves had found useful, stimulating and sometimes indispensable at various times in our work. This poses a conceptual as well as a logistical problem and it arises because in some sense, of course, all media research contains or draws from, explicitly or not, some theory of media influence. This is a point we want to make particularly strongly because we feel such a perspective can not only help newcomers to the field get their bearings, but should also remind those who are more experienced just why the study of audiences is important. All research which takes media processes as central to its analysis stems from an interest or concern with the *consequences* of the media for society, communities, publics, readers, listeners, viewers, consumers – audiences. The difference between approaches is, essentially, to do with the scale of analysis or the length of focus – micro or macro – chosen by the researchers in question.

One of the decisions necessary while editing this volume was how to restrict our selections to those contributions which made an explicit case for the audience. Even then we had to leave out, mostly for practical reasons, essays which would otherwise fit within the rubric of audience research. Space is a severe constraint on attempts to compile an 'ideal' Reader.

Clearly, we have had to be selective, but we have also tried to offer some coherence to our selection. So, as a way of representing the breadth of the field and as an aid to making sense of the range of research and theory on the audience, we have divided the book into three sections: 1. Societies, masses and publics; 2. Individuals, impacts and influences; and 3. Cultures, communities and families. This division is made to show how research on the audience has reflected and continues to reflect a range of concerns about media influence that require theorization at different levels. The contents of each section also show that these different foci involve different disciplines from within the social sciences and humanities.

The prime objective is to provide illustrations of the major traditions and approaches to the study of mass media audiences. While there is an obvious historical dimension to the selection, the intention is to demonstrate that many of these traditions are still very much alive and that each continues to contribute to the sum total of our understanding – and, importantly, to pose further research questions – about the processes of media influence, whether considered at the cultural, national, societal, individual or small group level. To illustrate this point, alongside extracts from important previously published texts in audience research and media influence, the volume contains original chapters from authors currently working in the field. In fact these make up more than half the book. We feel this is an important contribution of this Reader – the inclusion of new material indicates that the different traditions of research, the questions they pose, and their epistemological assumptions and concerns continue to have significance for those who are active media and communication scholars.

The diversity of approaches to audiences this represents not only reflects the abiding concerns which characterize this area of study, but also points to the continuing debates which have been refining methodologies, rethinking research questions and reflecting on theoretical bases. One of the outcomes of these developments can be seen in the increasingly interdisciplinary nature of audience studies. We have come a long way from the rather simple stimulus–response model of the relationship between media and their audience which was prevalent in the 1940s and 1950s. The different approaches and the debates and conversations which have been going on between them suggest a growing acceptance of the complexity of this relationship.

Our selections are sometimes widely divergent and include work by authors that some readers might not readily associate with 'audience research'. In recognition of this, and in anticipation of the need to draw together the arguments in each of the broad areas of work we have identified, we close each section of the book with a specially commissioned chapter which offers an appraisal and critique of the various approaches and contributions included.

Section 1, 'Societies, masses and publics' contains examples of research and theory on the impact and influence of the media which tackle these questions at the 'macro' level of analysis or which deal with the audience conceived as an aggregate of individuals, typically identified or character-ized as 'the public' (perhaps more helpfully, 'publics') or 'society'.

Discussions of the media's influence on national cultures which have led to debates about 'media imperialism' and the erosion of national or indigenous cultures inevitably boil down to questions of media consump-tion, and there is continuing and lively debate as to whether Western media forms and media content can be successfully 'resisted' by those living in nations and regions which are seen increasingly as markets for Western media products. While much of the debate on these issues has focused on the dominance of Western media in Third World media indus-tries, research is increasingly being conducted on the actual impacts, uses and consumption of media products among Third World audiences. The two chapters in this section – an extract from a recent statement in the American critical tradition by Schiller, and Brown's original contribution to the volume – represent both ends of this particular spectrum.

A significant step forward in the history of the theory of media influ-ence was the shift from a powerful, direct effects model to a model which posited mediated effects. The concept of agenda-setting, which drew from Cohen's intuitively persuasive assertion about the press's 'stunning' success in telling us what to think about, symbolizes a further shift towards a more complicated (though by no means complex) notion of media influence. The near contemporary extract from a review by McCombs, one of the tradition's founding exponents, demonstrates how the agenda-setting concept continues to thrive and be developed in studies of audience behaviour, particularly as it relates to 'public opinion' and media and political processes.

From the late 1960s to the present, a great deal of theorizing about the role of the media in society has been dominated by the debate about ideology and the notion that the media are best understood as part of a system of domination. The media are thought of as bearers of ideas that serve to support and maintain the existing structure of society, which can be characterized as materially divided and unequal. This reflects the influ-ence of Marxist thought on the social sciences in general, and on the study of the media in particular. Indeed, it was because the media were impli-cated in the theory of the dominant ideology that they became a focus for study among Marxist theorists. The nature of the impact of the media on the audience is implied rather than explored in this work, but the approach can be thought of as being 'about audiences' because its concern is with societal level media effects in the broadest sense. The extracts by Kellner and Jhally and Lewis offer very bold representations of this strand of work.

A dissatisfaction with the notion of direct media effects, coupled none the less with a continuing belief in the notion of powerful mass media gave rise in the 1960s to George Gerbner's theory of cultivation and the study of media products, specifically television, as indicative of prevailing cultural values. Gerbner's work represents an attempt to show how television functions as part of the social order to maintain and reinforce patterns of power relations in society. Here, in a chapter written specially for this volume, Wober, whose many years of experience as an academic and professional audience researcher provides a unique vantage point, evaluates Gerbner's work from a European perspective.

In sharp contrast, Section 2 deals with research which has a much tighter focus, being concerned primarily with the individual. This work has been influenced significantly by, and has drawn deeply on, theoretical perspectives in social psychology.

The issue of causality lies at the root of many attempts to study the individual in the audience. Arguments and assertions regarding the media and violence as well as more general questions about the impact of the media on children and young people have given rise to a search for empirical verification of a causal relationship between the media and individual behaviour. The media themselves regularly take up the issue of the relationship between media violence and the individual. However, proof of a causal relationship between media violence and violent behaviour has been difficult to come by. Never the less, research on the issue has flourished throughout the industrialized world and continues to do so. We have commissioned three original contributions from scholars who trace the history of this work, and provide an appraisal of it, from different perspectives: Linné and Wartella, von Feilitzen, and Gauntlett all offer overviews but address different facets of the long-standing debate.

Research on children has often focused on attitudinal and behavioural effects, cognitive effects, 'pro-social' effects, on identification and fear, and on children's use of advertisements and video games. Within the field of mass communications and media studies a great many resources have been invested in studies of the effects on children of fictional, entertainment, and factual programmes. Two overviews of the key issues in the various debates associated with this work are included here: Buckingham's original chapter offering a comprehensive review of the field, and an extract from Hodge and Tripp's important study of young Australian viewers in which they outline some key hypotheses for research on children and television.

The Uses and Gratifications model has been the theoretical framework for many studies of children and young people, as well as other groups, varying from fans of specific programmes to different gender and ethnic groups. Several scholars continue to argue for its utility to our understanding of media consumption. Here we include a classic statement of the Uses and Gratifications case, written by McQuail, one of its foremost proponents, as the model was reaching the peak of its popularity in the field.

Researchers working within the social psychological tradition of audience research have focused on audiences as active interpreters of the message rather than as active readers of the text. The understanding of sense-making can be based on the reader's *interpretation* of the text or the reader's *comprehension* of the message. Most media researchers from the humanities focus on the interpretation of the text because they are interested in cultural and contextual factors, while psychologists tend to find comprehension more useful because it reveals the reader's dependence on knowledge structures. In an original contribution, Höijer provides an overview of this theoretical position and makes a case for its application in contemporary research.

Recent debates concerning media audiences emphasize the conception of the audience as socially and culturally situated but none the less active participants in the process of mediation. This reconceptualization of the nature of audiences and their viewing practices, which requires a more sophisticated theorizing of audience participation than before, is characteristic of what have been called the New Audience Studies. Section 3 of the book brings together examples from the various strands that feed into this debate, highlighting the different areas of focus within the active audience concept.

The extract by Fiske deals directly with the concept of the active audience and the idea of 'reception analysis' as the method for examining audience's interaction with mediated texts. In some ways the chapter represents the radical extreme of the continuum, granting the audience complete control over the construction of meaning from the text, and texts are consequently taken to be polysemic, affording the viewer any number of possible interpretations. The focus is on the way in which this process of meaning construction occurs, but positing the audience as impervious to the influences of the media not only presents a challenge to the 'powerful media' theory, but also questions the idea that social contexts might affect interpretive practices.

Murdock's chapter covers the conceptualization of audience activity as occurring within specific social contexts. Here audience members are still active in their reception of media content, but their signifying practices are defined by the socio-cultural environment to which they belong, and which constrains their power as interpreters. Members of an audience function as members of 'interpretive communities' that are assumed to correlate with divisions of economic class and culture and decoding procedures therefore correspond to the community to which audience members belong. Conceptualizing the audience in this way enables researchers to examine the ideological control of the media, whose power can no longer be assumed to rest solely with textual content, while at the same time the number of possible interpretations is also limited by audiences functioning as members of communities.

In their contribution, based on some recent original research, Barker and Brooks argue that the understanding and enjoyment of film can be usefully linked to the notion of 'investment', a concept which they use to illuminate a particularly interesting aspect of their data. These authors are interested in what audiences might bring to the 'cinema experience' in terms of their expectations, knowledge, and interest. Barker and Brooks suggest that an exploration of investment via an engagement with the work of Pierre Bourdieu may offer a way of studying more accurately the determining impact of hierarchies of taste and social class.

Isolating the practice of media consumption from other everyday practices has been considered problematic by some researchers for whom the study of audience activity includes the investigation of media use (usually television viewing habits) within the household. Meaning emerges not as the result of solitary activity, but from the dynamics of family viewing, and therefore the examination of interpretive activity involves an ethnographic analysis of the use of the media in everyday, 'normal' settings. The chapters by Morley and Dickinson draw our attention to the domestic sphere as a site for the consumption of non-media as well as media products. Though acknowledged in the other chapters here and elsewhere in the Reader, Silverstone's insistence on the importance of the everyday raises specifically methodological issues, making his chapter an important contribution.

The final part of Section 3 contains two chapters examining the audience in a larger setting, as members of national or regional cultures. Liebes demonstrates the ways in which differently situated audiences interpret well-travelled series like *Dallas*. Harindranath's chapter investigates the links between culture, knowledge and signifying practices by posing the question, how do collectivities like cultures or nations affect interpretive activity?

What we have tried to offer in this Reader, then, is a collection of work which represents the full range of scholarship in media and communications research which can be characterized as being preoccupied, to a greater or lesser degree, with audiences. We hope that by defining the field widely and locating such a range of studies on this broad terrain we will have helped to provide some orientation for readers so that they may navigate their way more smoothly and confidently through what remains for us a most stimulating and challenging area of study.

An enterprise like this inevitably involves a large number of people and is simply impossible to complete without the skills, insights and encouragement of others. Many people deserve our thanks. We must, above all of course, express our deepest gratitude to the authors of the original chapters appearing in the book. We have been greatly impressed by their enthusiasm for our ideas, their excellent contributions and for their patience in seeing the project through to a successful conclusion. Special mention must be made of our critique authors, Professors Michael Tracey, Martin Barker and Peter Dahlgren, who were set difficult tasks but executed them with rare skill and accomplishment. We must also thank our friends and colleagues at CMCR, Leicester and the Faculty of Humanities at Bristol for their support throughout, in particular Corin Flint, Cathy Melia, Zahira Ahmad and Heidi Jennings for clerical assistance; Jim McKenna for valuable advice on the editorial process, and Oliver Boyd-Barrett, not only for inviting us to take on the project in the first place but also for his wise counsel in its early stages. We are grateful to them all. Finally, we must thank Lesley Riddle, Elena Seymenliyska and Liz Gooster at Arnold for their support and great forbearance during the many months of preparation, and Susan Dunsmore and Vanessa Mitchell for their expert technical assistance in the final stages.

Acknowledgements

Blackwell Publishers, Oxford for the extract from *Children and Television: A Semiotic Approach*, pp. 213–18 © 1986 by B. Hodge and D. Tripp.

Lawrence Erlbaum, Hove for the extract from J. Bryant and D. Zillmann (eds), *Media Effects: Advances in Theory and Research*: News influence on our pictures of the world, pp. 1–16 © 1994 by M. McCombs.

Penguin, Harmondsworth for the extract from *Reconstructing Social Psychology*: Mass communication and the construction of meaning, pp. 205–220 © 1974 by G. Murdock.

Routledge, Inc. for the extract from *Information Inequality: The Deepening Social Crisis in America*, pp. 111–21; 123–8 © 1996 by H. Schiller.

Sage, Inc. for the extract from *World Families Watch Television*: Domestic relations: the framework of family viewing in Great Britain, pp. 22–48 © 1988 by D. Morley.

Sage, London for the extract from *Public Communication: The New Imperatives. Future Directions for Media Research:* Television and everyday life: Towards an ethnography of the television audience, pp. 173–89 © 1990 by R. Silverstone.

Speech Communication Association, USA for the extract from *Critical Studies in Mass Communication*: Television: polysemy and popularity, Vol. 3, No. 4, pp. 391–408 © 1986 by J. Fiske.

Speech Communication Association, USA for the extract from *Critical Studies in Mass Communication:* Cultural differences in the retelling of television fiction, Vol. 5, No. 4 pp. 277–92 © 1988 by T. Liebes.

Speech Communication Association, USA for the extract from *Critical Studies in Mass Communication:* With the benefit of hindsight: reflections on uses and gratifications research, Vol. 1, No. 2, pp. 177–93 © 1984 by D. McQuail.

Westview Press, Colorado for the extract from *Enlightened Racism: the Cosby Show, Audiences and the Myth of the American Dream*, pp. 131–46 © 1994 by S. Jhally and J. Lewis.

Westview Press, Colorado for the extract from *Television and the Crisis of Democracy*, pp. 1–10; 14–24 © 1990 by D. Kellner.

Section 1

Societies, masses and publics

1

American pop culture sweeps the world

Herbert I. Schiller

From Schiller, Herbert I. (1996) *Information Inequality: The Deepening Social Crisis in America*, London: Routledge, pp. 111–21, 123–8.

Governability and economic stability, for most states, are increasingly problematic. The far-ranging activities of essentially stateless businesses undercut local decision making everywhere, a phenomenon some like to call 'globalization'. The central player in this process, one writer notes, 'is the international corporation. The primary driving force is the revolution in information and communication technologies.'[1]

The new information and communication technologies are indeed at the centre of the current changes, providing the technological means for world businesses to conduct their operations. Equally important, they supply the cultural industries with the instrumentation for reaching global markets with their media-cultural product. Dense worldwide communication networks are now available for corporate (and other) use. The proposed global information infrastructure [...] intends to extend the capacity and accelerate the speed of these linkages.

In these onrushing developments, meaningful input from the public sector is being foreclosed by a rash of corporately organized initiatives that are creating a de facto commercial framework for global communication. In 1993 and 1994, for example, in the space of months, the three major United States long-distance telecommunications carriers signed agreements with powerful European partners to stake out shares of the world communications business.[2]

These arrangements do not in themselves constitute a completed global information infrastructure. They supplement networks already in place. Their significance is that they underline the prioritization of private interests in the unfolding global system. 'Industry experts', writes one knowledgeable telecommunications reporter, 'say that all long-distance carriers are chasing a market of only about 2,000 corporate customers, most of which are either based in the United States or have some operations there.'[3] Whatever the number of companies in this market, they represent a minute, but spectacularly influential fraction, of the global community.

Which particular telecommunications consortium will command the future global communications system remains to be seen. What is not in doubt is that whichever specific groups come to dominate the field, the steady erosion of national power will continue. Contrary to the view that anticipates global civil society emerging – featuring diversity, and roughly equalitarian roles for participants – the evidence overwhelmingly points to a world order organized by, and in the interests of, large-scale private economic enterprises.[4]

The electronic communication infrastructure now being created is intended to serve these interests in two important ways: the information flows that are, and will be, transported over the network serve to command and rationalize economic activity, and to extend the reach of corporate marketing to every corner of the earth. The second, equally vital function of the communication infrastructure, is to provide the circuitry for the already immense, and still increasing, flow of the product of the (mostly but not exclusively) US cultural industries. This flow circles the world. Its impact, in ways to be described, further weakens the influence of local leaderships, and thereby creates additional national and global instability. [...]

The political role of the global media industries

The consequences of global information mastery were strikingly on display throughout the Persian Gulf War. During the actual hostilities, one account – that of the transnational, US-based and owned Cable News Network (CNN) – dominated television screens around the world.[5] One definition and one account of this momentous geopolitical event was given to global audiences. For the national public, it served as a chilling signal of how orchestrated and concentrated the information supply had become. Though press interpretations of the war may have varied from country to country, the vivid broadcast images of high technology combat were identical worldwide.

This particular demonstration of information monopoly was remarkable but barely suggests the full dimensions of the capability to define reality now at the disposal of the largely US-owned cultural industries, and by the BBC's World Television Service and France's Euronews. International broadcasting, and CNN's output in particular, are but one kind of image, sound and symbol production. Such output also comes in the familiar forms of film, television programs, video games, video cassettes, newscasts, recordings, CD ROMs, books and magazines, multimedia offerings, and, not least, electronic on-line data and computer software itself.

The special significance of the transmission of this diverse and rapidly growing production is succinctly explained by Walter Wriston, former chief executive officer of Citicorp, one of the global banking giants:

> The single most powerful development in global communities has been the satellite, born a mere thirty-one years ago ... Satellites now bind the world for better or worse, in an electronic infrastructure that carries news, money and data anywhere on the planet at the the speed of light. Satellites have made borders utterly porous to information.[6]

Wriston properly makes no distinction between news, money, and data: '[H]undreds of millions of people around the world are plugged into what has become essentially a single network ... of popular communication.'[7]

Those global corporations and media-cultural conglomerates that have the capability to use the global satellite systems are indifferent to formal communication boundaries. Digitized electronic communication transforms all messages and images into a uniform information stream. This globalization of communication since the 1960s is represented in the phenomenal growth of transnational media-information corporations such as Time Warner, Disney, Reuters, SONY, Murdoch's News Corporation, and Bertelsman. They are based mostly in the developed economies but their activity is worldwide.

While state, non-governmental, and non-corporate organizations have made use of the new electronic networks, their utilization is dwarfed by that of the transnational companies. The capability of the private, resource-rich conglomerates to transmit or shift messages and images, capital, currency, production, and data – almost at will – constitutes the true levers of contemporary power. For example, a world-class cultural history corporation such as Time Warner or Disney, or one of Murdoch's enterprises, can combine a rich mix of informational, pop-cultural activities, synergistically spinning one product off another, or promoting one item by incorporating it in another format. Novels, in some instances, become movies. Movies wind up as TV series. TV programs and movies are retailed as video cassettes and their sound tracks move out into their own orbits as records and tapes. [...]

The net effect of such total cultural packages on the human senses is impossible to assess but it would be folly to ignore. For example, transnational polling companies, also mostly US-owned, make surveys of audiences that have been exposed to transnational advertising and commercial programming. In one poll, data was assembled and tables constructed on 'What People Think They Need.' The North American Free Trade Agreement (NAFTA) received some of its support in Mexico, this survey indicated, from the people's 'Hunger for US Goods,' seen 'on imported television programs and in movies.'[8]

The worldwide impact of the transnational cultural industries, it can be argued, may be as influential as other, more familiar, forms of (US) power: industrial, military, scientific. In recent years it has actively abetted the transformation of broadcasting and telecommunications systems around the world. People everywhere are consumers of (mostly) American images, sounds, ideas, products and services.

Walter Wriston enthusiastically makes clear that national efforts to protect and insulate a community from these stimuli have been futile. Not unexpectedly, therefore, global notions of what constitutes freedom, individual choice, a good life, and a desirable future come largely from these sources. Institutional infrastructures in country after country have been recast to facilitate the transmission of the informational and cultural products that pour mainly from American cultural enterprises. Inexorably, from the initial conception and the first design, to the ultimate product, market criteria and imperatives prevail in the cultural factories and their outputs.

Media analyst Edward Herman describes the integration of broadcasting into a global market in recent decades, achieved largely through 'cross border acquisition of interests in and control of program production and rights, cable and broadcasting facilities and the sale and rental of program stocks, technology, and equipment.'[9] These are practices and activities that duplicate the expansion programs and financial legerdemain of other manufacturing or service enterprises in the global market place.

However, there is at least one critical difference in the media-informational sphere that distinguishes it from the rest of the for-profit industrial system. This is its direct, though immeasurable, impact on human consciousness. What is standard economic behavior for media-cultural companies, therefore, rarely fails to have considerable socio-cultural impact as well. For example, the international economic expansion in broadcasting that Herman writes about, '[has] tended to increase the strength of commercial broadcasting and reduce that of public systems.'[10] Herman concludes that 'The strength and momentum of the forces of the market in the last decade of the twentieth century are formidable. It therefore seems likely that the US patterns of commercial hegemony over broadcasting will be gradually extended over the entire globe.'[11] This is no minor change! Half a century's experience demonstrates that commercial broadcasting transmits images and messages vastly different from those produced by a public service broadcasting system.

Herman's predictions have been validated with astonishing rapidity and singular effect. While American cultural product – film, television, fashions, and tapes – still dominate screens, homes, and shops throughout the world, local and regional outputs are also increasing. Invariably, however, they are fashioned on the American model and service the identical objectives of the original. They are commercial products designed as bait with which to snare the potential consumer. French TV dramas, for example, repeat worn US formulae; British producers are no less compelled than their American counterparts to concentrate on audience ratings; Brazil's powerful television production industry is at the beck and call of the same transnational advertisers who dominate North American television screens.[12]

The American pop cultural product has obviously attractive features that can be attributed to a century of marketing experience and the rapid utilization of state-of-the-art technologies to achieve compelling special effects. These developments, coming at the end of the twentieth century, should serve as an alarm signal. The globalization that many find such a promising prospect can be viewed more realistically as the phenomenally successful extension of marketing and consumerism to the world community. A world communication infrastructure, heavily dependent on the new information technologies – satellite, computer, fiberoptic cable – is being put in place. It serves largely the needs of global business, engaged in producing and marketing its outputs worldwide.

Other constituencies, to be sure, also use these new electronic networks. Non-governmental organizations, professionals, social groups, and individuals, each have some access to the instrumentation. Clearly, this global and local 'civil society' has had its expression and activities enhanced and facilitated with such facilities as the Internet. Yet the balance of advantage in the utilization of these networks is hardly equal. The efforts of the noncorporate users remain puny and relatively marginal. The Internet itself is all too likely to be transformed into a commercial and pay-for-use system in the near future.

The flattening of public debate

In one respect especially – access to the media – the disparity in influence is overwhelming. For many years this has been particularly observable in the United States. Now it has become characteristic of global affairs.

In the United States, despite a seemingly thick network of organizations and social groups that make up a rich civil society, the voice of the corporate speaker has succeeded in dominating the national discourse. Although the corporate perspective has for generations held a privileged place in American society, it was balanced in earlier times by the opposing voices of farmers' movements, organized labor, and civil rights organizations on the national stage. Since the end of World War II, powerful structural changes have transformed the American economy and weakened, if not eliminated, most of these dissenting voices. Additionally, the arrival of television in the same period, has also contributed to the near-disappearance from the American scene of a national and comprehensive adversarial view.[13]

Single-issue constituencies have emerged and their oppositional voices occasionally receive prominence, and from time to time some issues do generate a modicum of excitement. For the most part, however, consensuality prevails on the essential features of the social order. The main business of corporate America, money-making, proceeds uninterruptedly. So, too, fundamental institutions have been reshaped to accommodate the dominant presence of the corporation in American life, offering thereby, seeming confirmation of the claim that what exists must be the outcome of inescapable natural forces.

Corporations not only enjoy the protection of the law. For more than a century they have been regarded and treated as *individuals*.[14] In the post-World War II period, the corporation has had its status further up-graded. Now it is granted substantial First Amendment rights.[15] These judicial interpretations have legitimized the preeminent role of corporate expression in the contemporary cultural landscape. Given the near-total dependency of American radio and television on commercial advertising, the domestic informational system has become, in effect, a marketing and ideological apparatus of hard-to-exaggerate influence. Only the largest national companies can afford to pay for prime time commercial messages and the programming that accompanies them. Corporate expression has no competition – literally.

Public broadcasting, which was supposed to be a non-commercial alternative to advertiser-supported television has been co-opted by sponsorship. This development has progressed to the point where the editor of *Harper's Magazine*, unqualifiedly, has called for the plug to be pulled on public television.[16] Paradoxically, despite its present conservative character, congressional rightwingers are doing their utmost to do just that – eliminate the system entirely. Cable television, while still receiving most of its revenues from paid subscriptions, is steadily drawing more support from advertisers as well.

In this political economy of communication, where revenues come exclusively from advertising, the quality of television programming, with some notable exceptions, falls far short of its informational-cultural potential. The commercial broadcasters' seemingly unlimited greed, expressed in their efforts to capture as large as possible a share of an increasingly fractionated audience, is a guarantee of cultural default – all too frequently in evidence. The absence of programming that might shed some light on the country's deepening general social crisis does not seem to concern the industry's owners. Instead, the audience is regaled with endless hours of sports spectaculars, fortuitous human tragedies, and infomercials.

In sum, with numerous non-dramatic institutional changes, the economy, and cultural expression itself, have become the private domain of a highly concentrated transnational corporate power. As might be expected from this state of affairs, the realm of permissible debate has narrowed appreciably in recent decades. In the medium that really matters, television, there has been a proliferation of talk shows, call-in-shows and personal witness programs.

Though there are more television channels than ever and a large number of computer bulletin boards have been created where views are easily expressed and exchanged, for all this, the *national* discourse, where it exists at all, is astonishingly bland, where it is not raucously conservative. Scrutiny and debate about the structural determinants of American existence are nowhere to be found, at least not in the national media.

It follows that the rich fabric of history from colonial days to Clinton's presidency, with its never ceasing struggles against plutocratic privilege, and its strivings for social dignity and equality for working people (including women and African- and Mexican- and Native-Americans), rarely if ever, is brought to the attention of the national audience. Generally what little that does get noted is either decontextualized or fragmented.

Globalization of commercial messages and images

This thin and largely expurgated presentation of the national experience is the underside of the daily retailing of corporate images and messages and endless affirmations of commercial culture. In recent years these highly selective accounts no longer are confined within national boundaries. With the phenomenal growth of the transnational business system, and its utilization of the computer and the communication satellite, what used to be national in form and content has become transnational or, as some prefer to describe it, global. Additionally, the collapse of the former Soviet Union and the Eastern European political systems and the market 'reforms' in China have opened a vast new terrain to transnational marketing and the corporate voice. The media-cultural conquest of these areas, for the moment at least, appears to be unconditional.

As early as September 1991, it was reported that in Moscow, 'most of the fare at the movie theaters is now American ... more than twenty American films are now showing in the city ... [and] the brooding statue of Pushkin is bathed in the neon glow of a Coca-Cola billboard and the lights from the world's largest McDonald's restaurant.'[17] Since this was reported, the Moscovites have lost their ranking as the site of the largest McDonald's. This status now is held in Beijing. Where it will be located next depends on the rapidity and breadth of the transnational corporate global envelopment.

With no significant oppositional pole to the transnational system now in existence, the poorer and weaker countries are almost defenseless against the economic and cultural maneuvers of the world business system. In fact, many of these countries' leaders have jumped enthusiastically on board, expecting to extract some marginal benefits for a tiny stratum (including themselves, of course) of their societies.

Mexico serves as an exemplary, though not unique, case of a country whose material and nonmaterial substance are being appropriated. The plans of one of Mexico's current big investors are described:

> Call it Pepsi's Latin invasion. And it's not just tacos, and not just Mexico. Last month the company [Pepsico] announced a $750 million five-year assault in Mexico, including plans to buy interests in big bottlers, big distribution routes and advertise heavily. The company is opening Pizza Hut, Taco Bell and KFC (Kentucky Fried Chicken) franchises throughout Latin America, and selling Fritos, Ruggles, and Doritos as far south as Tierra del Fuego. And it will soon announce that later this year it will spend tens of millions of dollars to sponsor Michael Jackson on an eight-city tour of Latin America.[18]

What is not in doubt in this account is the powerful media-economic interlock that now characterizes the global corporate dynamic. Saturation advertising follows (sometimes precedes?) the corporate investment. What are the long-term effects of this particular case; unhealthful changes in the national diet; likelihood of a non-reversible shift away from a self-reliant agriculture; the bathing of the public's senses in commercial imagery receive scant concern and certainly are not subjects for debate on Mexican television, which is more commercially dominated, if imaginable, than the US model.

Mexico's economic collapse in the winter of 1994–95 in no small way can be attributed to the (largely US-produced) advertising that led to extravagant expenditures on, also largely American-made, consumer goods, financed by short-term foreign loans. Pepsico's strategies to penetrate the Mexican and Latin American markets are replicated by hundreds, if not thousands of other companies, striving for their shares of the world market.

The efforts of these companies contribute to the current global environment of transnational corporate capitalism, which follows similar marketing formulas and voices a uniform rhetoric.[19] This includes the espousal and protection of corporate speech. It justifies whatever programming is produced and transmitted as the proof of consumer choice and sovereignty. International efforts to combat or counter the now-pervasive condition of corporate dominance have been defeated by the counterattack of the transnational corporate order and its national surrogates. [...]

The weakening of international structures of information accountability

The pursuit of American global information dominance has resulted in additional initiatives that have crippled or eliminated several national and international agencies and structures that once served as partial shields against unlimited transnational corporate power. In Europe, for example, there has been unrelenting pressure to eliminate or marginalize the Post, Telephone, and Telecommunications entities (PTTs). These governmental bureaucracies, for all their faults and rigidities, at least represented in part, *national* public communication interests. [...]

Having neutralized or eliminated international and state institutions of oversight, the communication super companies can carry on their world-wide operations, almost completely relieved of scrutiny. Domestically, their overseas activities are mostly ignored. Rare is the politician who mentions transnational corporate matters. International organizations like the United Nations, the ITU, UNESCO and the former UN Center on Transnational Corporations have either been bypassed, restructured, weakened, or neutered. The fate of the former UN Center on Transnational Corporations is especially illuminating. Established largely as a result of Third World insistence, the Center devoted its energies to making studies and issuing reports on the activities of transnational corporations. Apparently even this mild informational responsibility was too disturbing to the transnational corporate sector. In 1992, in one of its last newsletters, the Center announced its new status:

> The Center on Transnational Corporations and the United Nations Division of Development Administration will now work together as the Transnational Corporations and Management Division. One of eight units in the United Nations Department of Public Economic and Social Development, the new Division will build on existing complementarities to strengthen *the move to market forces*.[20]

No authority in the international arena now exists to question, much less check, the actions of the prevailing transnational corporate order. In individual nation-states, the information and communication terrain has been made fully accessible to corporate messages, images, and data. These are protected under the expanded definition of free speech.

How have these developments affected the private international media organizations that now produce and manage the worldwide message and image flow? Are these powerful cultural–industrial conglomerates independent and free standing? Do they pursue their own agendas, exclusive of other interests' How do these agendas relate to the interests of generalized transnational corporate power?

The main transnational media-information players today are not a second string team of corporate actors. Time Warner, Disney, Microsoft, Reuters, SONY, Murdoch, Bertelsman, to name just a few, are multibillion-dollar enterprises, whose activities and outputs span all spheres of communication and popular culture. Though each transnational company has its own specific interests, requirements and history, which defy generalization, *there are still fundamental commonalities* that sometimes unite them.

For example, the demand for a new international information order was a prominent issue in the 1970s, the treatment of that issue in the United States media, *without exception*, was uniformly hostile.[21] Again, when the United States Government put half a million troops in the Persian Gulf region in 1991, the national informational system closed its ranks – there were a few marginal dissenting voices – and unqualifiedly accepted and endorsed that decision.[22]

The record suggests that issues of high systemic importance receive immediate attention and support from the media combines. No less well protected and defended are the media's own interests, as they interpret them, i.e., to delegitimate the call for a new international (or national) information order; to protest as denials of free speech and free flow of information, the European Community's limited effort to reserve some screen time for the region's own film and television production. Most events and policies, however, are not of high urgency, demanding systemic attention and priority. Countless unremarkable developments transpire daily and fall within the general routines and permissible boundaries of 'independent' interpretation. Crisis periods excluded, the international flow of messages and images, therefore, is not a systematically coordinated stream that receives approval from some transnational corporate oversight board. Actually, such detailed supervision is hardly feasible or necessary.

The standard procedures for selecting and removing individuals who make the daily (hourly) news and programming decisions are not foolproof but they are reliable enough. [...] The education of journalists, their on-the-job training, and the recruitment and apprenticeship of cultural taste-makers are not random processes. Large-scale media-cultural organizations, like other big enterprises, do not hire and assign personnel willy nilly. The main newspapers, for example, in the Cold War years, did not send correspondents to Moscow without prior vetting. Similarly, high-level political appointments are automatically preceded by an FBI check.

The machinery of information control may not perform perfectly, but it works quite well. In the 1990s the production, processing, and dissemination of information have become remarkably concentrated operations, mostly privately administered.[23] The major producers and distributors are key players in the domestic and transnational corporate worlds. Major television anchors, highly visible national correspondents, and top editors and publishers of the 'quality' press turn up regularly as guests at White House dinners and other social functions. They are well aware of their individual company interests and are no less alive to the general stakes in the global corporate game.

Media and cultural power, awesome already, is further enhanced by its capability to define and present its own role to the public. This self-constructed picture never fails to emphasize the objectivity, dedication to the public interest, and alleged vulnerability of the cultural industries' activities. It does not follow that the general public accepts these media self-portraits. Still, does it really make any difference in most people's lives that one national cultural-informational institution after another is privatized and commercialized and that transnational media take over individual, national, and regional space?

The first, and most direct cost may be to the cultural work force itself. Reducing and sometimes eliminating, state support for film, broadcasting, telecommunications and the arts in general, means less work in some cultural fields and more carefully monitored work in others. The plight of drama in the United States is suggestive of what may be expected of privatized arts activity, left to the play of market forces. In 1988 and 1989, for example, only 38 per cent of the members of Actors Equity, the actors' union, worked at all during the year. Actors worked an average of seventeen weeks. Average salaries for actors were at poverty levels. Taking these grim conditions into account, one drama critic advised: 'If you want to act, learn to type.'[24]

The employment situation is not very different in other creative fields. Driven by the market, commercially-supported arts, sports, and entertainment produce poverty levels of existence for a majority of the creative and performance work force, alongside super salaries for a relatively few 'stars'. Much more difficult to estimate are the social costs to the community that accompany sweeping commercialization of the arts and the unrestricted entry of transnational entertainment and media conglomerates to national space. Indigenous creative forces are swamped and inevitably crippled by the relatively cheap cultural products offered by the big producers. The production quality of the material is also difficult to match because the producers allocate huge resources to the packaging side of the product – the sound, color, music, special effects, photography, and so on. The substantive component, the content, can be almost negligible alongside such fancy wrapping.

The heaviest cost of transnational corporate-produced culture, however, is that it erodes the priceless idea of the public good and the vital principle of social accountability and the longtime dream of international community. Substituted for these elemental human aspirations is the promise of consumer choice – a choice that is not genuine – and a hopelessly narrow standard of production efficiency.

Can the well-being and the vitality of any community be left to the international business system, especially its powerful media/entertainment sector? Canada's experience is cautionary. The United States' northern neighbor, with whom it shares a 3,000-mile border, has felt the full impact of the US cultural industries. One Canadian, in a position to know, sums it up:

> From my Canadian point of view, [the unrestricted operation of market forces has] delivered a whole nation into cultural bondage, to the point where Canadian voices have been drowned out of their own air.[25]

Canada, we may be reminded, is no less industrialized than most European states.

Publicly unaccountable media-cultural power today constitutes the ultimate Catch-22 situation. The public interest, locally and globally, demands honest messages and images. These, however, are dependent on private media providers, whose own interests are often incompatible with the public's.[26] Private information monopolies are contributing, by their fierce, and to date successful, opposition to social oversight, to the growing global and national crisis of governability. This is the challenge of the time ahead.

Notes

1. Ostry, S. (1992) The domestic domain: the new international policy area, *Transnational Corporations*, 1(1) (February), 7.
2. Andrews, E. S. 'AT&T Finds 3 Partners in Europe,' *New York Times*, June 24, 1994, sec. C, p. 1.
3. Ibid.
4. Featherstone, M. (ed.) (1990) *Global Culture*, Newbury Park, CA: Sage.
5. Mowlana, H., Gerbner, G. and Schiller, H. I. (1992) *Triumph of the Image: The Media's War in the Persian Gulf: A Global Perspective*, Boulder, CO: Westview Press.
6. Wriston, W. B. (1992) *The Twilight of Sovereignty*, New York: Charles Scribner's Sons, 12.
7. Ibid., 130.
8. DePalma, A. 'Mexico's Hunger for U.S. Goods is Helping to Sell the Trade Pact', *New York Times*. November 7, 1993, sec. 4, p. 1.
9. Herman, E. S. (1993) The externalities effects of commercial and public broadcasting. In Nordenstreng, K. and Schiller, H. I. (eds) *Beyond National Sovereignty: International Communications in the 1990s*, Norwood, NJ: Ablex Publishing Corp., 108–109.
10. Ibid., p. 108.
11. Ibid.
12. Oliveira, O. S. (1990) Brazilian soaps outshine Hollywood: is cultural imperialism fading out? Paper presented at the meetings of the Deutsche Gesellschaft für Semiotik (German Society for Semiotics), Internationaler Kongress, Universität Passau, October 8–10, 1990.
13. Schiller, H. I. (1989) *Culture Inc.: The Corporate Takeover of Public Expression*, New York: Oxford University Press.
14. *Santa Clara County v. Southern Pacific Railroad*, 118 US 394 (1886).
15. *First National Bank of Boston et al. v. Bellotti, Attorney General of Massachusetts et al.*, 435 US 765 (1978).
16. Lapham, L. H. (1993) Adieu, big bird, *Harper's Magazine*, December, 1993, 35–43.
17. Schmidt, W. E. 'The Neon Revolution Lights Up Pushkin's World', *New York Times*, September 21, 1991.
18. Nash, N. C. 'A New Rush Into Latin America', *New York Times*, April 11, 1993, sec. 3, p. 1.
19. Sklair, L. (1991) *Sociology of the Global System*, Baltimore, MD: Johns Hopkins University Press.
20. *Transnationals*, Quarterly newsletter of the Center on Transnational Corporations, March 1992, p. 1, italics added, quoted in Colleen Roach, 'Trends in Global Communications,' Paper presented to the annual meeting of the International Association for Mass Communications Research (IAMCR), Guaruja, Brazil, August 20, 1992.

21. Preston, W. Jr., Herman, E. and Schiller, H. I. (1989) *Hope and Folly: The United States and UNESCO, 1945–1985*, Minneapolis, MN: University of Minnesota Press.
22. Mowlana, Gerbner and Schiller, op. cit.
23. Bagdikian, B. (1992) *The Media Monopoly*, 4th edn, Boston: Beacon Press.
24. Sullivan, D. 'Unemployment … ', *Los Angeles Times*, December 23, 1989.
25. Ostry, B.'The risk of going global', *New York Times*, December 31, 1989.
26. Baker, C. E. (1992) Advertising and a democratic press. *University of Pennsylvania Law Review,* **140**(6) (June 1992), 2097–243.

2

Up close from a distance: media and the culture of cricket

Aggrey Brown

Introduction

Technologies are both manifestations of culture as they are a means through which culture is created and expressed. That is to say, technologies are both means and ends. As intellectual and physical tools that we create and use to extend our capacity to relate to our environment, they are means. However, in and of themselves, they are simultaneously manifest expressions of our relationship with our environment. Careful observation and analysis of the relationship between ourselves and the technologies we use to relate to our environment will show that always and everywhere the dialectic of technology and culture is an historical and dynamic one: culture being the symbolic, instrumental and social arrangements that collectivities of people make for living.

The taken-for-grantedness of culture in everyday living invariably obscures the crucial role that technology plays in its creation. It is only in moments of revolutionary technological breakthrough that we tend to reflect on the centrality of technology in the creation of culture; when the tools we use so dramatically alter the way we relate to our environment that it is impossible to ignore their significance in everyday affairs.

Furthermore, those technologies which transform everyday routines by virtue of the fact that they represent radical departures from previous technologies tend to affect all aspects of culture – the symbolic, the instrumental and the social. It is the objective of what follows to show how one such group of technologies – media technologies – have influenced and continue to influence, often quite surreptitiously, the evolution of the game of cricket as an expression of culture.

Play, games and culture

Play is a natural and spontaneous activity of human beings. The seemingly incoherent groping of an infant with physical elements within its reach (including its own body) and its apparent meaningless gestures, would seem to indicate that the idea of play is virtually instinctual in human beings. Indeed, contemporary education theories attribute an important function to play in the lives of the young and their ability to learn.

However, whether or not there is such a relationship, organized play in contemporary societies has both an important social function as well as a significant economic impact. And here, organized play refers to formally structured recreational activities involving multiple actors, clearly defined rules of engagement between them, as well as clearly defined outcomes of competitive encounter; in other words, games that can be understood as sport.

The oldest documented sporting events are said to be the Pan-Hellenic athletic festivals from which the modern Olympics takes its name. (Cummings, 1995) The political, economic and social dimensions of the modern Olympics as well as the quadrennial World Cup of soccer, testify to the complex cultural significance of sport in human affairs.

Colonialism and the spread of cricket

That the game of cricket is now a sport of international repute is directly related to its commercialization; the impact of the media on the game and the game's colonial origins. Indeed, that cricket is played in every continent of the world and is a major cultural activity in countries that collectively have almost a half of the world's population, is a direct result of the fact that it was an elite leisure activity introduced by English colonizers in the height of the mercantile era throughout the then British empire.

While the origins of the game are somewhat obscure, it is thought to have been a game played by rural sheep farmers in South-East England in the mid-seventeenth century (Cummings, 1995). Cricket's early development as a sport was an entirely English phenomenon, the first formal game having been played in London in 1727 (Marqusee, 1994). 'Around the same time, the infant weekly newspapers began to cover cricket. To the early reporters, the attendance of persons of high social status, not the result of the match, was the main item of interest' (Marqusee, 1994).

In the West Indian colonies, cricket was played with gusto by both colonizer and colonized with the sugar plantation providing the initial context within which the game developed. Until well into the twentieth century, the production of sugar was the dominant economic activity in the majority of West Indian colonies.

The recorded history of the game up to this period is to be found in print – the only accessible mass media technology until well into the third decade of the twentieth century. Print, however, is a retrospective technology. That is to say, it is a technology that extends the human capacity for recall of events after their occurrence. It is quintessentially a medium of record keeping. Hence the records of the game; the game's history; its critique and its place within the socio-political arrangements of nations and empire were the concerns of this particular medium and those who controlled and had access to it. Concretely and by way of example, what this meant was that at both national and international levels, the history and critique of the game essentially reflected the perspective and interests of the literate and in particular, of a colonial elite who, as C. L. R. James observes, was not without its socio-cultural biases (James, 1963). That early reportage was more preoccupied with the social aspects of cricket as a sporting event, also reflects that fact.

With the introduction of radio broadcasting and in particular short wave radio in the 1930s, access to and participation in cricket as a spectator sport and particular type of cultural event expanded to include the non-literate as well. Although radio as a technology was novel, its overall impact on both those who played the game as well as on those who participated as spectators, was not radical. However, the broadcasting of cricket resulted in some subtle but important changes. The most significant of these was that followers of the game were able to participate in the unfolding of Test matches stretched over a 5-day period *in real time*. No longer was information regarding the state of play in a Test match delayed, abbreviated and filtered through the reporter's written words. Rather, information was now available and accessible on games in progress, albeit that that information was still filtered through the perspective of the game's commentators, initially virtually all of whom were English. Notwithstanding, the game's mass appeal was extended by the advent of radio broadcasting and the immediacy of unfolding events that it made possible.

Dramatic changes in cricket culture were to occur only after the advent of late twentieth-century information/communication (infocom) technologies to which attention now turns.

Contemporary infocom technologies and cricket

Late twentieth-century developments in infocom technologies have had discernible impact on the game of cricket itself, on players, on spectators, on the game's authorities, on administrators and on media audiences; in short, on every aspect of the culture of cricket.

The use of transistors in the manufacture of radio receivers in the first instance in the 1950s transformed radio broadcasting into a genuine mass medium. Among other things, the transistor allowed radio receivers to be miniaturized and mass produced at costs within the reach of many. Radio also became a genuinely portable mass medium as a result of transistorization. More recently, the convergence of electronic media technologies and computers as well as the digitalization of information and the use of satellites for the delivery of information, have resulted in the globalization of media and media products. But more importantly, this convergence of technologies has resulted in the creation of two competing forms of reality and a shift in our perceptions of the empirical and the analytical. Today, spectators of a Test match, regardless of where the game is being played, can be divided into two categories: those who are physically present on location and those who are not physically present. These are both empirical and analytical categories. But as we shall see, there are singular advantages that the latter have over the former as spectators of and participants in a cultural event.

Impact of infocom technologies on the game of cricket itself

The televized aspects of cricket which are now taken for granted by virtually everyone familiar with the game are relatively recent phenomena that are a direct result of transistorization, miniaturization and digitalization of infocom technologies. And the innovations with the most direct and overt impact on the game are instant replay and stop action. These innovations allow any sequence of play to be recorded and immediately replayed from a variety of camera angles in full motion, slow motion or in a single frozen frame. They also not only permit repetition of recorded, fleeting moments of a game but also accurate observation and instant analysis of such crucial moments. In turn, these technological possibilities have resulted in modifications to the rules of the game itself. The formal introduction to the game in 1993 of a third umpire located away from the field of play and in front of a bank of television monitors to adjudicate decisions involving run-outs and stumpings of players, if requested, is a direct consequence of technological convergence.

Officiating umpires on the field of play no longer have to rely solely on their own fleeting and often impaired visual perceptions and capacity to make their instant and often crucial decisions. Instead they are now able to refer to the third umpire who has access to the more reliable and accurate re-presentations of reality of the twin technological innovations of instant replay and stop action.

The miniaturization of video cameras and microphones as well as remote control of these technologies provide umpires and spectators with unusual perspectives of play . Television viewers at home in the hills overlooking Kingston, Jamaica, 10,000 miles away, can hear the comments of players on the field at the Sydney Cricket Ground, Australia, quite distinctly. And thanks to the wonders of the close-up camera shot, they can also see the ball as it is deflected almost imperceptibly from the batsman's glove into the wicket keeper's hands. What is more, the televiewer in Kingston is able to see all this action much more clearly and distinctly than spectators in the stands at the Sydney Cricket Ground. In fact, crowd noises in the arena of play obliterate the spontaneous banter of the players from the hearing of spectators who are physically present. As a spectator sport, cricket is today equally a media phenomenon as it is a live cultural activity.

The transformation of cricket from a live spectator sport to that of global cultural media event occurred in the 1977 Kerry Packer one-day international cricket competition – World Series Cricket. Even though the one-day version of cricket had been played at English County level since 1963, it was Packer who realized the possibilities that the new media technologies presaged and who, for commercial purposes, applied the technologies to televising the game. The result is that one-day cricket is today an institutionalized form of the game with its own rules of engagement designed to be responsive to the imperatives of television.

The format of the game, including the limited number of overs played by competing sides; the change from all-white dress to the colourful attire worn by players; the parameters governing field placement during an initial specified number of overs, and a guaranteed result that precludes the drawn game, are all modifications brought about directly and indirectly by contemporary infocom technology developments.

The commercialization of the sport that the one-day form of cricket epitomizes is but a logical denouement of these technological breakthroughs. Commercial sponsorship of international cricket in both its one-day and Test match modalities merely extends the access of Cornhill, Cable and Wireless, Sandals International etc. to global markets. In short, the impact of infocom technologies on the game, on its rules, and how it is played extends as well to the commercialization and globalization of cricket as sport.

Impact on players

When the young West Indian batsman Brian Lara broke the 36-year-old Test batting record of 365 not out of Sir Garfield Sobers in the fifth test match between England and the West Indies at the Antigua Recreation Ground in 1994, he attributed the development of his enormous talent to, among other things, the influences of the legendary Sir Garfield himself and the mercurial West Indian batsman, Vivian Richards.

To be sure, the Sobers' influence would not have been possible in the absence of film and VCR technologies. Sobers' record had already been standing for eleven years when Lara was born. The only way therefore that Garfield Sobers' influence on the young Brian Lara could have been registered was through a visual record of Sobers at play. This would have been equally true of the influence of Vivian Richards who had all but retired from play when Lara was emerging as a young batsman. More precisely then, the visual media – film and electronic – have been able to influence directly the development of skills and playing techniques of contemporary players by providing a visual record of past, outstanding role models in action.

Contemporary electronic media technologies also have indirect impacts on players. Reference has already been made to the global commercialization of cricket to which must be added the creation of larger-than-life superstar status of the specially gifted. The multimillion dollar advertising and product-endorsement contracts that young superstars such as Sashin Tendulkar of India and the West Indian, Brian Lara, command, are a direct consequence of the influence of media on the commercialization of the game. Global products are marketed to global audiences and global audiences live vicariously through their sports heroes who endorse and advertise global products.

Having seen Brian Lara execute the stroke that broke Sobers' world record is a qualitatively different phenomenon from reading about it. It is the crucial difference between witnessing history being made and reading about history *having been made*. It is the difference between vicarious but active participation in the unfolding of an event and passive recognition and acceptance of the same event after the fact. It is the difference between the impact of the print medium on perceptions and the impact of convergent infocom technologies on reality and perceptions of reality. It is upon this crucial difference between the print and electronic media that the successful commercialization of the sport rests.

Of course the commercialization and globalization of cricket cannot be separated from heightened competitiveness between contending teams and nations since both commercialization and globalization have been cause and consequence of modern media. Contemporary media technologies have transformed cricket as parochial cultural leisure activity into cricket as a professional global commercial undertaking. It is impossible to separate the evolution of cricket as a professional sport from the revolutionary developments in contemporary media technology. The earnings of the game's global superstars correlate directly with their televised successes on the playing field and with their continued ability to perform successfully and to parlay those successes into revenue-earning, peripheral economic activities such as product endorsements, etc. It is not surprising that Lara and Tendulkar should have emerged as cricket's first multimillionaires. Their enormous talent was complemented by their telegenically stunning good looks. They are the global marketeers' dream.

Of course, the impact of infocom technologies on players is also collective since the visual record of play is also used by teams in post mortems of games when analysis of successes and failures can be assessed and used to inform future competitive strategies. During its ascendancy in world cricket, the West Indies cricket team used this form of media analysis to its great advantage.

Impact on spectators

As noted earlier, spectators can be divided into two categories: those at the cricket location and those elsewhere. While these two categories remain separate and distinct, media technologies blur the distinctions and advantages that the one may have over the other.

In the pre-electronic media era there was no substitute for the cricket aficionado but to be physically present when and where the game was being played. To participate meant witnessing first hand the unfolding of play in the arena of play. And while direct participation continues to distinguish one set of spectators from another, witnessing the actuality of a game of cricket contemporarily is itself becoming a mediated phenomenon that is not unrelated to the global commercialization of the sport.

In the larger and better endowed cricket arenas around the world, computerized, electronic scoreboards with big-screen television, instant replay and stop-action facilities are commonplace. These technologies are expected to add to the spectator's information, knowledge and enjoyment of the game. They are also meant to make attendance at games as enticing as the view from the living room.

While crowd noises drown the banter of players' interactions on the field, the use of big screen television replays provide spectators with visual access to aspects of the game that those who are not physically present have. Instant replays of actualities are now an essential feature of live action for spectators. That is to say, a mediated re-presentation of reality is now an aspect of the reality of live action.

Surreptitiously, the media have transformed the very meaning of what is to be understood as a spectator. The private, air-conditioned, sound-proof boxes that are strategically located in the most preferred positions in modern cricket stadiums – the Mound Stand at Lords, for example – are marketing phenomena made possible by media. The occupants of such facilities, though in the same location as spectators in the bleachers or covered stands, can hardly be said to be participating in the game in the same way. Here there is a real blurring of the distinction between spectator as participant observer and audience member as spectator.

Impact on audience as spectator

The view of a game of cricket from the living room is an enhanced view having much in common with that of the third umpire and the view from the air-conditioned stadium box. In fact, the living room spectator's view is the same as that of the third umpire. Once the third umpire is requested to adjudicate a decision on the field of play, living room spectators who are seeing the same replays on their TV screens, know the outcome even before the players in the game know what the actual decision is. But this particular example of mediated actuality aside, contemporary infocom technologies are having an impact on the audience as spectator that is transforming the traditional understanding and meaning of the spectator as a passive participant in the competitive sport spectacle as entertainment.

The view from a distance is, in fact, a view up close. The facial expressions of players, their gestures, their comments; the sound of the bat on the pitch as the batsman takes guard; the sound of the ball on the bat, or the nick from the edge; the sound of the ball as the batsman is struck on the pad; the sound of the ball shattering stumps; the sight of the ball trickling over the boundary board for a four or being put to ground before reaching the fielder's hand; the ball turning viciously from leg stump to off stump as it is bowled or glancing the batsman's shirt at the shoulder before being caught by the wicket keeper and more, are all details of the game that enhance the view and meaning, and hence understanding, of the spectators occupying the living room. More specifically, the view from the living room made possible by contemporary infocom technologies is a detailed information-rich view that remains inaccessible even to all but a few of the players on the actual field of play.

The view from the global living room is also sharpened by the use of computer graphics showing for example, the difference between silly mid-on and short leg or third slip and gully; by line graphs showing the trajectory of scoring strokes; by tables and instant statistical analyses and correlations that were hitherto impossible, all making for more informed, knowledgeable and sophisticated spectators of the game.

The visual immediacy of the unfolding action on the field of play also has a culturally homogenizing impact on the global audience as spectator. All are seeing the action as it unfolds simultaneously and in the same images, from the same visual perspectives, even though the images may have differing relevance and hence, be interpreted differently by members of that audience. The question of interpretation, however, is a socio-cultural/political matter that is of little concern to advertisers who wish to reach a global audience. For the former, what matters is that as the ball speeds on its way to the boundary from the batsman's bat or as the bowler runs up to the wicket to bowl, the names of the products that are being advertised on the arena's perimeter boards provide a clear back-drop for the action on the field of play and that such background images become foreground stimuli to future consumer action. That is, contemporary infocom technologies deliver the game's increasingly knowledgeable, well-informed and discerning global audiences to global marketers by the millions and multiples thereof.

Impact on authorities

Authorities are both official and unofficial and comprise umpires as participants on and off the field of play, sports commentators and the game's administrators. I have already alluded to the obvious impact of infocom technologies on umpiring with respect to the advent of the third umpire and the change in the rules of the game, or at least on how the game is adjudicated. However, at a more profound level under the glare of the cameras' eyes the performance of the game's adjudicators is itself being adjudicated by the millions of televiewers who comprise the audience. The errors of umpires are now permanently exposed for all to see. Conversely, difficult and close interpretive LBW decisions in particular that are correctly adjudicated, are also used to evaluate the competence of these officials of the game. With so much at stake in the contemporary game, it is not at all surprising that third country umpires – the so-called neutral umpires – are now required to officiate in Test matches in conjunction with a national of the country hosting such matches.

Cricket umpires are perhaps no less competent today than they have been in the past; in fact they may even be more competent. However, in the past their errors went unseen by all but the players on the field of play. Thanks to infocom technologies, today the slightest errors are exposed to informed public scrutiny and opprobrium. The fact that many of the rules governing play and the conduct of players are open and subject to the umpires' interpretation compounds the problems of umpires. Instant replay and stop action give today's audience members a better and more leisurely view of the action from the living room than from the actual field of play. Inevitably, the performance of umpires is judged from that vantage point. That is why in the run-up to the 1995 Test series between Sri Lanka and Australia, the International Cricket Council, the ICC, studied the bowling action of the Sri Lankan spinner Muralitharan, brought to its attention by two match referees of the previous contest between Sri Lanka and New Zealand. Apart from the referees' written reports, '[t]he ICC files also included video footage of the spinner, filmed from different angles' (*Trinidad Guardian*, 6 Dec. 1995). The objective of the ICC's ruling was to inform and guide the umpires in the Australian series who had sole authority for determining and calling illegal deliveries. It is no longer enough to leave the decision entirely to the umpires' discretion.

The umpires' discretion can now be informed by electronically recorded and instantly accessible empirical evidence.

Similarly, media commentators are exposed to global audiences as critics. The biases of commentators are also prone to closer scrutiny and criticism than hitherto, since the view from the living room is no different from the view of the commentator. However, infocom technologies have enhanced the capabilities of professional commentators who have ready access to computer-generated and at times esoteric statistics that add interpretive depth as well as breadth to the images projected in the living room.

Prior to the advent of global television, commentators were compelled to provide running audio commentary describing the unfolding of a game. Most of the commentator's time then was taken up with that description leaving little time for embellishment with statistical details. With the advent of television, the commentator's time is devoted to providing the living room audience with details and information not immediately visible on the television screen. In turn, this has made for more knowledgeable and discerning spectatorship. It has also levelled the intellectual and cultural playing field as far as influencing the global public's perceptions through commentary is concerned. Authority no longer derives from the commentator's accent as much as it does from demonstrated ability to enhance the viewer's appreciation of the game as it unfolds up close from a distance on the television screen.

The third category of authorities to have been affected by contemporary infocom technologies is cricket administrators. As a global media phenomenon, cricket now requires administrators to be more responsive to the public's perceptions and demands than was traditionally the case. The obvious class-bound traditions of the game have inevitably given way to the levelling and homogenizing influences of the mass media and concomitant professionalism of players with global potential earning power.

The politics of cricket as a sport ceased being the parochial politics of the traditional English elite clubs and Marylebone Cricket Club (MCC) administrators the moment the mass media transformed the sport into a global spectator phenomenon. In this connection that transformation can be dated from the advent of the Kerry Packer series in 1977 and its challenge to the then governing status quo (Marqusee, 1994).

The election of the former West Indian cricket great, Sir Clyde Walcott, the first non-Englishman, to the presidency of the International Cricket Council (ICC), the game's governing body, in 1993, reflected the reality of cricket as a multinational spectator sport and popular cultural phenomenon, the administrators of which have to be more responsive to public demands and global market forces wooed into existence by infocom technologies.

The unparalleled dominance of the game by the West Indies cricket team from the mid-1970s to the mid-1990s, which also coincided with the infocom technological revolution, made the election of Walcott inevitable. West Indian ascendancy was also the catalyst for the commercialization and globalization of cricket and for its increasing world-wide popularity.

This popularity is manifested in the proliferation of international competitions, especially of the one-day variety, in such non-traditional places as Sharja, Hong Kong and Toronto.

Conclusions

The national origin of the sport cricket is no longer relevant in the context of the game as a global media spectacle. The game's migration from England via the colonial route established its presence throughout most of the English-speaking world. But as with all competitive sports, a predictable set of rules, fairly adjudicated, permitted the transcendence of such traditional barriers to the achievement of excellence as race, ethnicity, and nationalism.

At the highest levels of the sport, at Test level, national cricket teams have stamped their signature on the game but none so successfully in the modern game as the West Indies cricket team. Its 15 consecutive years without being beaten in a series by any other Test playing country is a world record unsurpassed in any other international sport. Undoubtedly, this prolonged period of dominance by the West Indies cricket team helped to popularize both the game and the West Indies style of play internationally. And in that sense, directly and indirectly, cricket has been heavily influenced symbolically, instrumentally and socially, by the West Indies. More than anything else, however, the media and convergent infocom technologies have had permanent and identifiable effects on the culture of the game globally.

Cricket's global popularity is almost entirely due to the electronic media and, in particular, television. But this popularity is not merely the result of accessibility made possible by infocom technologies. Rather, it is the conscious use of infocom technologies to exploit the game's commercial potential that has led to its globalization. The Kerry Packer challenge to the traditional cricket Establishment in 1977 was technology-led and based entirely on the imperatives of television as an entertainment medium.

One result of that successful challenge was the institutionalization of the one-day international version of the game with its modified rules, which, among other things eliminates the possibility of a draw in the interest of creating excitement as well as a sense of closure for global television audiences. As one commentator observed 'No other sport had to mutate so radically to squeeze itself into a market niche' (Marqusee, 1994). But that mutation also had the long-term effect of raising the professional status of cricketers by, among other things, encouraging the proliferation of one-day competitive versions of the game in a number of non-traditional places. Whereas in its early years the game was played seasonally, it is today a year-round phenomenon. Also, the particularly gifted and telegenic players now share superstardom with other icons of the global entertainment industry.

The infocom technologies brought to bear on exploiting the commercial potential of the game in the first instance have also had intrinsic effects on the game itself, the most notable example of this being the introduction and use of a third umpire to adjudicate certain types of decisions with the assistance of television replays. That the particular decision to use television replays was taken by the ICC over twenty years after the technology had been available is itself an interesting example of culture lag – the resistance of traditional practices to change. However, the dialectic of technology and the culture of cricket is perhaps best exemplified by the integration of infocom technologies into the experience of spectators as participant observers. Big-screen mediated re-presentations of action on the field of play are now an aspect of the spectator's experience as participant observer in the spectacle of the sport. And sound-proof, air-conditioned boxes fitted out with television monitors afford some spectators the opportunity to experience both the live and mediated forms of the game simultaneously, leading in such cases to a blurring of the distinction between the individual as spectator and the individual as audience member.

Paradoxically, these same infocom technologies have simultaneously heightened the distinction between the two – spectator and audience member. Prior to the advent of radio broadcasting, there was no such thing as an audience for the game. There were spectators. With contemporary infocom technologies global audiences have become virtually the *raison d'être* of the game. The bold use of innovative infocom technologies ensures that television audiences command a unique view of the game up close from a distance: a view rich in detail and nuance and otherwise quite inaccessible. However, while it may be a unique and information-rich view, it is also increasingly a homogenized view. And ultimately that might be the most enduring effect of the media on the culture of cricket and cricket as an expression of culture – its transformation from parochial leisure activity to a form of commercially packaged global entertainment.

References

Cummings, C. (1995) Cricket as an element of the superstructure. Unpublished PhD thesis. University of the West Indies, Mona.

James, C. L. R. (1963) *Beyond a Boundary*, London: Hutchinson.

Marqusee, M. (1994) *Anyone but England: Cricket and the National Malaise*, London: Verso.

Trinidad Guardian (6 Dec. 1995) ICC to look at spinner's action, p. 23.

3

News influence on our pictures of the world

Maxwell McCombs

From Bryant, J. and Zillmann, D. (eds) (1994) *Media Effects: Advances in Theory and Research*, Hillsdale, NJ: Lawrence Erlbaum, pp. 1–16.

News impacts many facets of our daily lives! How we dress for work, sometimes the route we take to work, what we plan to do this weekend, our general feelings of well-being or insecurity, the focus of our attention toward the world beyond immediate experience, and our concerns about the issues of the day all are influenced by the daily news.

Occasionally, our total behavior is instantly and completely dictated by the news. Everyone old enough to remember at all remembers where they first heard the news of John F. Kennedy's assassination and how so much of the next three to four days was spent absorbing, and discussing the news. Even on less traumatic occasions, millions of Americans follow the national political conventions, watch the presidential candidates debate, or follow the tabulation and projection of the nation's vote on election night. And daily, millions of citizens dutifully glean their knowledge of politics and public affairs from the pages of their local newspaper.

For the vast majority of Americans, this use of the mass media, coupled with brief visits to the voting booth on election day, represents their total participation in politics. This is one of the reasons why the most enduring and sustained line of scholarly research on mass communication traces the influence of the news media on voter behavior. Beginning with the classic study of Erie County, Ohio, by Columbia University sociologists Lazarsfeld, Berelson, and Gaudet (1944) during the 1940 US presidential election, there has been an ever-widening array of studies exploring the impact of news media on voter behavior. But as sociologists Lang and Lang (1959) noted, the influence of the news media extends far beyond the political campaigns:

> All news that bears on political activity and beliefs – and not only campaign speeches and campaign propaganda – is somehow relevant to the vote. Not only during the campaign, but also in the periods between, the mass media provide perspectives, shape images of candidates and parties, help highlight issues around which a campaign will develop, and define the unique atmosphere and areas of sensitivity which mark any particular campaign.
>
> (p. 226)

Over a half century ago, Lippmann (1922) also noted this role of the news media in defining our world, not just the world of politics during and between elections, but almost all of our world beyond immediate personal and family concerns. The issues, personalities, and situations toward which we hold feelings of endorsement or rejection, those points of attention about which pollsters seek the public pulse, are things about which we depend on the media to inform us.

Lippmann made an important distinction between the *environment* (i.e., the world that is really out there) and the *pseudo-environment* (i.e., our private perceptions of that world). Recall that the opening chapter of his book, *Public Opinion*, is entitled 'The World Outside and the Pictures in Our Heads'. And, as Lippmann eloquently argued, it is the news media that sketch so many of those pictures in our heads. This view of the impact of news was congruent with both scholarly and popular assessment in Lippmann's day of the power of mass communication, views that grew out of experiences with mass communication and propaganda during World War I. But subsequent scholarly investigations, such as the Erie County study, led scholars down another path in later decades.

Focused squarely on the ability of the news media and mass communication to persuade and change voters' attitudes, early empirical studies of mass communication instead discovered the strength of the individual, secure in his or her personal values and social setting and inured from change. The result was the law of minimal consequences, a scientific statement of a limited-effects model for mass communication. Although this law may have been the proper palliative for the sometimes near-hysterical ascription of super persuasive powers to mass communication, such a constrained view of mass communication overlooks many effects that are plausibly ascribed to the mass media, especially to the news media.

After all, it is not the goal of professional journalists to persuade anybody about anything. The canons of objectivity, which have dominated professional journalistic practice and thought for generations, explicitly disavow any effort at persuasion. This is not to say that the news stories of the day are not exactly that, news *stories*. They are indeed! And like all stories, they structure experience for us, filtering out many of the complexities of the environment and offering a polished, perhaps even literary, version in which a few objects and selected attributes are highlighted. Many scholars have shifted their attention to the audience's experience with these stories.

Changing perspectives

Explorations of audience attention and awareness signal a shift to research on the cognitive, long-term implications of daily journalism, research that begins to test empirically the ideas put forward by Lippman in the 1920s. Rather than addressing mass communication from the perspective of a model of limited effects, research in the 1960s began to consider a variety of limited models of effects. [...]

But shifting the perspective to limited models of media effects focuses attention on those situations in which the transfer of functional information of some sort from the mass media to individuals in the audience does take place. Part of the scientific puzzle, of course, is to identify exactly what is transferred – the denotative message and its 'facts', the cultural and individual connotations associated with those facts and the style of their presentation, or some other attribute of the message.

Part of this new look at mass communication has been the discovery that the audience not only learns some facts from exposure to the news media, but that it also learns about the importance of topics in the news from the emphasis placed on them by the news media. Considerable evidence has accumulated that journalists play a key role in shaping our pictures of the world as they go about their daily task of selecting and reporting the news.

Here may lie the most important effect of the mass media: their ability to structure and organize our world for us. As Cohen (1963) remarked, the press may not be very successful in telling us what to think, but it is stunningly successful in telling us what to think about! This ability of the mass media to structure audience cognitions and to effect change among existing cognitions has been labeled the agenda-setting function of mass communication.

Agenda-setting role of news

Initially studied in the traditional context of mass communication and voter behavior, the concept of agenda setting took its metaphorical name from the idea that the mass media have the ability to transfer the salience of items on their news agendas to the public agenda. Through their routine structuring of social and political reality, the news media influence the agenda of public issues around which political campaigns and voter decisions are organized.

Each day journalists deal with the news in several important ways. First, they decide which news to cover and report and which to ignore. Next, all these available reports must be assessed. On the typical daily newspaper, over 75 per cent of the potential news of the day is rejected out of hand and never transmitted to the audience. There is not enough space in the newspapers to print everything that is available. Choices must be made. These are the first steps in the gatekeeping routine. But the items that pass through the gate do not receive equal treatment when presented to the audience. Some are used at length and prominently displayed. Others receive only brief attention. Newspapers, for example, clearly state the journalistic salience of an item through its page placement, headline, and length.

Agenda setting asserts that audiences acquire these saliences from the news media, incorporating similar sets of weights into their own agendas. Even though the communication of these saliences is an incidental and inevitable byproduct of journalistic practice and tradition, these saliences are one of the attributes of the messages transmitted to the audience. Agenda setting singles out the transmission of these saliences as one of the most important aspects of mass communication. Not only do the news media largely determine our awareness of the world at large, supplying the major elements for our pictures of the world, they also influence the prominence of those elements in the picture!

The basic idea of an agenda-setting role of the news media can be traced at least as far back as Lippmann, and a variety of empirical evidence about mass communication influence on voting can be interpreted – post hoc, of course in agenda-setting terms. But the concept of an agenda-setting role for the news media was put to direct empirical test in the 1968 presidential election when McCombs and Shaw (1972) simultaneously collected data on the agenda of the news media and the agenda of the public. Reasoning that any impact of the news media was most likely to be measurable among undecided voters, their study surveyed undecided voters in Chapel Hill, North Carolina, and content analysed the local and national news media, both print and broadcasting, regularly used by these voters. The high degree of correspondence between these two agendas of political and social issues established a central link in what has become a substantial chain of evidence for an agenda-setting role of the press.

This early study also firmly established the viability of the concept of agenda setting, a limited model of media effects, *vis-à-vis* the concept of selective perception, a key explanatory element in the then-prevailing model of limited effects. Although still undecided about their presidential ballot, some of these Chapel Hill voters were leaning toward the Republican or Democratic candidate. Using this preference, comparisons were made between these voters' agendas and two different press agendas (viz., the total agenda of issues reported in the news or only the agenda of issues attributed to the preferred party and its candidates). If the correlation between voters' agenda and the total news agenda is the highest, this is evidence of agenda setting. If the correlation with the preferred party's agenda is higher, there is evidence of selective perception. Out of 24 comparisons, 18 favored an agenda-setting interpretation.

Correlations alone do not establish the causal assertion that the news media influence the public agenda. These correlations might even be spurious, an artifact resulting from a common source for both the news and public agendas. However, the rebuttal to this argument as well as new evidence buttressing the concept of an agenda-setting role for the news media was reported by Funkhouser (1973) from an intensive study of public opinion trends in the 1960s. [...] Funkhouser found substantial correspondence between public opinion and news coverage. But most important, he found little correspondence between either of these and his statistical indicators of reality. For example, press coverage and public concern about Vietnam, campus unrest, and urban riots during the 1960s peaked considerably before the actual trends measured by such indicators as the number of troops committed to Vietnam, number of campus demonstrations, and number of civil disturbances.

More recently, the agenda-setting power of the news media has been established experimentally in the laboratory. In a series of controlled experiments conducted by Iyengar and Kinder (1987), participants viewed television news programs that had been edited to highlight certain issues, such as national defense or pollution of the environment. When the participants' ratings of the importance of these experimentally manipulated issues were compared to the salience for them of other issues of the day, clear agenda-setting effects emerged. The issues emphasized in the experimental versions of the newscasts were perceived as more important. In some experiments, exposure to a single television news program created agenda-setting effects. Usually, agenda-setting effects were found only after viewing a number of newscasts. [...]

Agenda setting is a theory of limited media effects. One goal of contemporary research is to identify the conditions under which this agenda-setting influence of the news media does and does not occur. But the existence of an agenda-setting phenomenon is clear. Findings generated by two kinds of fieldwork methodologies, content analysis and survey research, provide evidence of its external validity, and experiments provide evidence of its internal validity. Additionally, the fact that much of this recent evidence, for example, the Iyengar and Kinder experiments, [...] is based on television news further strengthens support for the basic hypothesis because other evidence in the literature (e.g., Shaw and McCombs, 1977) suggests that television news has weaker agenda-setting effects than newspapers. [...]

Contingent conditions

Because the agenda-setting perspective is a model of limited media effects – unlike earlier views of powerful mass communication effects – Shaw and McCombs (1977) turned their attention in 1972 to simultaneous examination of the basic hypothesis and the contingent conditions that limited that hypothesis. Unlike the small-scale Chapel Hill study, which sought agenda-setting effects among undecided voters during the 1968 presidential election, their study during the next presidential election was a three-wave longitudinal study among the general population of voters in Charlotte, North Carolina. Its search for the contingent conditions limiting agenda setting established a theoretical goal that has prompted researchers to venture in many directions. Some scholars sought to identify the personal characteristics of voters or the content characteristics of news stories that limited or enhanced their influence (Winter, 1981). But the most fruitful examinations have examined not isolated properties of people, issues, or news content, but rather the interaction of issues and individual situations. Whereas broad descriptors, such as the income or level of education for an individual or the emotional content of an issue, are surrogates for this interaction, more explicit conceptualizations of this interaction have been the most valuable. Two examples are considered here in some detail.

Issues can be arrayed along a continuum ranging from obtrusive to unobtrusive. As the term implies, some issues literally obtrude in our daily lives. In 1990, the rapidly rising price of gasoline following Iraq's invasion of Kuwait was such an obtrusive issue. No one depended on television or newspapers to inform them about the existence of this inflation. Daily experience put this issue in conversations and on the national agenda. In contrast, our knowledge of other issues, as Lippmann pointed out in *Public Opinion*, is virtually dependent on the news media. What most Americans knew about the situation in the Middle East and US foreign and military policy came entirely from the news media.

For a great many issues there is considerable similarity in where they fall on the obtrusive/unobtrusive continuum for most Americans. This is true for the two examples just presented, inflated gasoline prices and the Middle East crisis. But there are issues where considerable variation exists among individuals. Unemployment is a good example. For tenured college professors and even for most college students, employment is an unobtrusive issue. The salience of unemployment in our minds is essentially the product of our exposure to the issue in the news media (Shaw and Slater, 1988). But for many industrial workers in declining or cyclical industries, such as steel and automobiles, unemployment is a highly obtrusive issue. Even if it has not been experienced firsthand, these workers are aware of the trends in their industry and most likely have friends or family members who have been unemployed in recent years.

Broad brush portraits of the agenda-setting role of the media reveal strong effects for unobtrusive issues and no effects at all on obtrusive issues (Weaver, Graber, McCombs and Eyal, 1981; Winter and Eyal, 1981; Zucker, 1978). More finely etched portraits, which require knowing where an issue falls on the continuum for each individual, show similar results (Blood, 1981).

The concept of need for orientation is the psychological equivalent of the physical axiom that nature abhors a vacuum. Based on the idea of cognitive mapping, this concept recognizes that individuals who are in an unfamiliar setting will strive to orient themselves. For the voter confronted with the issues of a political campaign, there are two important criteria defining his or her level of need for orientation: the individual's level of interest in the election and the degree of uncertainty in that individual's mind about what the important issues are. Voters characterized by high interest in the election and a high degree of uncertainty about the issues, that is, those voters with a high need for orientation, are open to considerable agenda-setting influence. These individuals are exposed to more news about the campaign and its issues and – in line with the basic agenda-setting hypothesis – have personal agendas that more closely reflect the agenda of the news media. In contrast, voters with a low need for orientation are exposed less to news of the political campaign and show less agreement with the agenda of issues advanced by the news media. For example, among, Charlotte voters with a high need for orientation, the correlation between their agenda and the coverage of issues in the local newspapers was +.68 in October 1972; among voters with a low need for orientation, the correlation was +.29 in October of 1972.

The concept of need for orientation provides a general psychological explanation for the agenda-setting process and subsumes a number of lower-order variables and more limited explanations. For example, research findings based on the distinction between obtrusive and unobtrusive issues can be explained in the more general terms of need for orientation. In most cases, persons should have less uncertainty about obtrusive issues and, hence, a lower need for orientation. Of course, it might be counterargued that individuals sometimes have less interest in more distant, unobtrusive issues, thus lowering their need for orientation. In most cases, persons should have less uncertainty about obtrusive issues and hence, a lower need for orientation. But remember that the role of the news media as defined by its professional traditions and values is, at least in part, to stimulate our interest and involvement in such issues. In any event, the concept of need for orientation provides more specific descriptions and predictions than does the concept of obtrusive/unobtrusive issues.

Shaping the news agenda

Initially, the focus in agenda setting was on the influence of the news agenda on the public agenda. For many persons, the term *agenda setting* is synonymous with the role of mass communication in shaping public opinion and public perceptions of what the most important issues of the day are. But in recent years there has been a broader look at the public opinion process. Early agenda-setting scholars asked who set the public agenda. The empirical answer was that to a considerable degree the news media set the public agenda. More recently, scholars have asked who sets the news agenda. The empirical answer to this question is not quite as parsimonious. In part, as common sense would dictate, the news agenda is set by external sources and events not under the control of journalists. But the news agenda also is set, in part, by the traditions, practices, and values of journalism as a profession. Whereas this newer facet of agenda setting may lack the parsimony of the original hypothesis, it has integrated a substantial sociology of news literature with the agenda-setting literature.

Looking, first at external influences on the news agenda, the president of the United States is the nation's number one news-maker. Does this central role played by the president on the media stage allow the president to be the nation's number one agenda-setter?

Like so many questions about contemporary history, the answer is 'Yes, sometimes' (Gilberg, Eyal, McCombs and Nicholas, 1980; Wanta, Stephenson, Turk and McCombs, 1989). The State of the Union address provides a particularly useful vantage point for observing the president's agenda-setting influence because it is the sole occasion when the president's agenda is laid out in a single document. Richard Nixon's 1970 State of the Union address did influence the subsequent coverage of NBC, *The New York Times*, and, ironically, the *Washington Post*. There also is weak evidence of similar effects following Ronald Reagan's 1982 State of the Union address. [...]

Sources of news

In any event, because the president is the nation's number one news-maker, the media spend considerable energy, time, and money on this coverage. In contrast, much of the daily news report is prepared from materials not just provided, but initiated, by the public information officers and public relations staffs of government agencies, corporations, and interest groups. At the beginning of this century, the president read all his own mail, the Washington press corps literally could gather around his desk to find out what the entire federal establishment was up to, and Ivy Lee was just inventing public relations. In today's corporate and government world, public relations is a key component. Despite professional myths to the contrary, public relations also is necessary to today's news media. As Lippmann (1922) observed, all the reporters in the world could not keep an eye on all the events in the world because there are not that many reporters. Even the largest and best national newspapers with their huge staffs of reporters and editors, newspapers such as *The New York Times* and *Washington Post*, obtain over half their daily material from press releases, press conferences, and other routine channels created by government agencies, corporations, and interest groups. Only a small proportion of the daily news results from the initiative and innovation of the news organizations (Sigal, 1973).

But to contradict another myth, this one especially popular along one stretch of the political continuum, public relations pronouncements on behalf of the establishment do not control the news agenda. Judy Turk (1985, 1986) examined the success of public information officers in six Louisiana state government agencies in placing their press releases in the major newspapers of the state. Their batting average was about .500. What the readers of Louisiana's major dailies knew about their state government was not limited to what the government passed out in press releases nor to those issues emphasized in those press releases.

Because the daily news obviously is rooted in the events and trends of the day, it is hardly surprising that those who are major players in these events and those who can enhance access to many of these events have some impact on the news agenda. But news media are not mirrors that simply reflect the deeds of the president or the pronouncements of public information offices. Journalism is a long-established profession with its own entrenched traditions, practices, and values. These are the filters through which the day's happenings are filtered and refracted for presentation in the newspaper or on television. The news is not a reflection of the day; it is a set of stories constructed by journalists about the events of the day.

Like Molière's gentleman who learned that he had been speaking prose all his life, it sometimes is difficult to assess a situation in which we are immersed as producers and consumers of the news. To better highlight the situation here in the United States, two studies based on European observations are cited as examples of the power that these journalistic traditions, practices, and values have on the daily set of news stories. The first example comes from Sweden, where political parties often have direct connections with, including outright ownership of, daily newspapers. But as journalism increasingly has become professionalized, there is little benefit to the political parties from these affiliations. Although one might regard a party newspaper as a captive mouthpiece for the party line, Asp (1983) found this hardly to be the case when he compared party agendas, as reflected in the acceptance speeches of party leaders, with the news coverage of the major campaign issues. Party leaders fared little better in their own newspaper's coverage than in the coverage afforded by the commercial newspapers and newspapers of other parties. The dominant filters on the political news of the day were journalistic values, not partisan values.

The strength of news values over partisan values also is reflected in *The Formation of Campaign Agendas*, a comparative study of American and British press coverage of national elections (Semetko, Blumler, Gurevitch and Weaver, 1991). Whereas there obviously is variation among the behavior of each nation's news corps, the modal pattern among British journalists during the 1983 general election was to follow the lead of the parties. Television, especially, placed heavy emphasis on the substantial live daily events of the campaign trail, reporting more of the material directly provided by the politicians in their morning press conferences, afternoon walkabouts, and evening rallies. The result is a substantial correlation between the party agendas and the agendas of the news media. In contrast, American journalists covering the 1984 US presidential election followed the lead of the parties far less in determining the issue emphasis in their coverage. The correlations between the two agendas are very weak. In comparison to British journalists, US journalists exercised considerably more professional discretion in the framing of the campaign agenda in the news. This discretionary power of the professional journalist seems to lie largely in the freedom to go beyond the issues and to report other aspects of the campaign, especially its strategic and tactical machinations. [...]

In summary, the question of who sets the news agenda is best pursued through that venerable metaphor of peeling the onion. The core of the onion, the daily news report, is surrounded and shaped by several layers of influence. At the outer layer are the news makers and events, including the pseudo-events arranged for news coverage, that provide much of the grist for the daily news. But all of this is shaped in turn by the values, practices, and traditions of journalism as a profession. And these professional decisions are reaffirmed by the behavior of the news leaders, especially *The New York Times*, who on occasion can set the agenda as firmly as any president or dictator.

Summing up

[In the US] fifty million or more persons read a newspaper each day of the week. About the same number watch the news on television each day. Many Americans do both. One significant result of the audience's experience with these news stories is that over time the public comes to perceive that the important issues of the day are those emphasized in the news. Grounded in ideas first put forward by Lippman in the 1920s, this phenomenon has come to be called the agenda-setting role of the news media. [...]

Initial empirical investigations of this agenda-setting influence of the news media were field studies employing survey research and content analysis to ascertain the degree of correspondence between the news agenda and the public agenda. [...] Other tests of the basic hypothesis have taken agenda setting into the laboratory and verified this phenomenon experimentally (Iyengar & Kinder, 1987).

Almost simultaneously with the initial empirical tests of the agenda-setting hypothesis, scholars began to explore the contingent conditions for this phenomenon. No one contends that the news media influence the salience of all issues for all people. Whereas many different characteristics of people and many characteristics of the news have been identified as contingent conditions affecting the strength of the agenda-setting relationship, two conceptualizations of the interaction between issues and individual situations have proved especially valuable. These are the concepts of need for orientation and obtrusiveness/unobtrusiveness. [...]

Consonant with the effects tradition in mass communication research, the early agenda-setting studies explored the impact of the news agenda on the public agenda. More recently, the news agenda has shifted from being an independent variable to a dependent variable. The central research question has changed from who sets the public agenda to who sets the news agenda. [...] Only a small proportion of the day's events and activities ever make the news, and even fewer are directly observed by journalists. The observations of news sources, especially those organized in the form of press conferences and press releases, are key elements in the construction of the news agenda each day. But even the most powerful of these news sources, the president of the United States, plays a very limited part in setting the news agenda. Journalists' professional values, traditions, and practices shape their judgments about the use of this material. [...]

Who sets the public agenda? For many issues, it is the news media who exert considerable, albeit far from complete, influence on the public agenda. Who sets the news agenda? Of necessity, this is a shared responsibility, but the news media themselves are the dominant influence on the shape of the news agenda for most public issues.

References

Asp, K. (1983) The struggle for the agenda: party agenda, media agenda, and voter agenda in the 1979 Swedish election campaign. *Communication Research*, **10**, 333–55.

Blood, R. W. (1981) Unobtrusive issues in the agenda-setting role of the press. Unpublished doctoral dissertation, Syracuse, NY: Syracuse University.

Cohen, B. C. (1963) *The Press and Foreign Policy*, Princeton, NJ: Princeton University Press.

Eaton, H., Jr. (1989) Agenda-setting with bi-weekly data on content of three national media. *Journalism Quarterly*, **66**, 942–48, 959.

Funkhouser, G. R. (1973) The issues of the sixties: An exploratory study in the dynamics of public opinion. *Public Opinion Quarterly*, **37**, 62–75.

Gilberg, S., Eyal, C. H., McCombs, M. E., and Nicholas, D. (1980) The state of the union address and the press agenda. *Journalism Quarterly*, **57**, 585–8.

Hyman, H. H., and Sheatsley, P. B. (1947) Some reasons why information campaigns fail. *Public Opinion Quarterly*, **11**, 412–23.

Iyengar, S., and Kinder, D. R. (1987) *News that Matters: Agenda-setting and Priming in a Television Age*, Chicago: University of Chicago Press.

Lang, K., and Lang, G. E. (1959) The mass media and voting. In E. Burdick (ed.) *American Voting Behaviour*, Glencoe, IL: Free Press, 217–35.

Lazarsfeld, P., Berelson, B., and Gaudet, H. (1944) *The People's Choice: How the Voter Makes Up his Mind in a Presidential Campaign* (3rd edn), New York and London: Columbia University Press.

Lippmann, W. (1922) *Public Opinion*, New York: MacMillan.

McCombs, M. E., and Shaw, D. L. (1972) The agenda-setting function of mass media. *Public Opinion Quarterly*, **36**, 176–87.

Semetko, H. A., Blumler, J. G., Gurevitch, M., and Weaver, D. H. (1991) *The Formation of Campaign Agendas*, Hillsdale, NJ: Lawrence Erlbaum Associates.

Shaw, D. L., and McCombs, M. E. (1977) *The Emergence of American Political Issues: The Agenda-setting Function of the Press*, St Paul, MN: West Publishing.

Shaw, D. L., and Slater, J. W. (1988). Press puts unemployment on agenda: Richmond community and opinion, 1981–1984. *Journalism Quarterly*, **65**, 407–11.

Sigal, L. V. (1973) *Reporters and Officials: The Organization and Politics of Newsmaking*, Lexington, MA: D. C. Heath.

Smith, K. (1987) Newspaper coverage and public concern about community issues. *Journalism Monographs*, No. 101.

Turk, J. V. (1985) Information subsidies and influence. *Public Relations Review*, **11**(3), 10–25.

Turk, J. V. (1986) Public relation's influence on the news. *Newspaper Research Journal*, **7**, 15–27.

Wanta, W., Stephenson, M. A., Turk, J. V., and McCombs, M. E. (1989) How president's state of the union talk influenced news media agendas. *Journalism Quarterly*, **66**, 537–41.

Weaver, D., Graber, D. A., McCombs, M. E. and Eyal, C. H. (1981) *Media Agenda-setting in a Presidential Election: Issues, Images and Interests*, New York: Praeger.

Winter, J. P. (1981) Contingent conditions in the agenda-setting process. *Mass Communication Review Yearbook*, **2**, Beverly Hills, CA: Sage.

Winter, J. P. and Eyal, C. H. (1981) Agenda-setting for the civil rights issue. *Public Opinion Quarterly*, **45**, 376–83.

Zucker, H. G. (1978) The variable nature of news media influence. In Ruben, B. D. (ed.) *Communication Yearbook, 2*, New Brunswick, NJ: Transaction Books, 225–40.

4

Toward a critical theory of television

Douglas Kellner

From Kellner, D. (1990) *Television and the Crisis of Democracy*, Boulder, Colorado: Westview Press, pp. 1–10; pp. 14–24.

Television will be of no importance in your lifetime or mine.

Bertrand Russell

Once television is truly national it will become the most important medium that exists. Everything that it does or does not do will be important.

Norman Collins

Chewing gum for the eyes.

Frank Lloyd Wright

The luminous screen in the home carries fantastic authority. Viewers everywhere tend to accept it as a window on the world, and to watch it for hours each day. Viewers feel that they understand, from television alone, what is going on in the world. They unconsciously look to it for guidance as to what is important, good, and desirable, and what is not. It has tended to displace or overwhelm other influences such as newspapers, school, church, grandpa, grandma. It has become the definer and transmitter of a society's values.

Erik Barnouw

In excess of 750 million TV sets in more than 160 countries are watched by 2.5 billion people per day. Although there is no consensus regarding television's nature and impact (as the quotes that open this chapter attest), the ubiquity and centrality of television in our everyday lives are obvious. At present, almost every home in the United States has a television set that is turned on for more than seven hours per day. Individuals spend more time watching television than in any other leisure activity and, cumulatively, far more time in front of the television than in school; only work absorbs more waking time. Furthermore, polls reveal that more people depend on television for news and information than on any other source, and that it is the most *trusted* source of news and information.[1]

Given television's penetration into everyday life, the controversy surrounding it is not surprising. The controversy intensifies in the light of debates over its social and political functions Television has been deeply implicated in post-World War II presidential elections, the cold war, the Vietnam War and other struggles of the 1960s, and the major political controversies of its era, sometimes referred to as the Age of Television (Bogart, 1956). There is little agreement, however, concerning television's social and political effects. Some commentators argue that television has overwhelmingly defended conservative economic and political interests. Others have argued that television has a primarily liberal bias, bringing down such conservatives as Joseph McCarthy and Richard Nixon, undermining the US intervention in Vietnam, and promoting a liberal agenda of social reform and change.[2]

A series of equally heated controversies surround television's impact on everyday life. [...]

1.1 Theorizing television

Despite these and other controversies, few attempts have been made to provide a systematic theory of television that articulates its relations with the chief institutions of contemporary capitalist society and defines its impact on social and political life. [...]

The politics of theory

Conservatives frequently criticize new forms of popular culture and mass media that they see as a subversive threat to traditional values and institutions.[3] In the 1960s conservative values were under attack by the new social movements of that era and, [...] some conservatives saw television as a primarily liberal medium. In 1969, for example, Vice President Spiro Agnew carried out an assault against 'Eastern-establishment' news media. Noting that a recent Vietnam speech by Richard Nixon was followed immediately by critical analysis on the television networks, Agnew complained that the president's talk had been 'subjected to instant analysis and querulous criticism ... by a small band of network commentators and self-appointed analysts, the majority of whom expressed in one way or another their hostility to what he had to say'. Agnew claimed that a 'small group of men' decide what the country will learn each day, and that they have acquired the power to make or break politicians or policies. These journalists, Agnew continued, are highly parochial and share the same liberal biases. Such concentration of cultural power is intolerable, he argued, and should be carefully scrutinized by the government (Agnew, cited in Emery and Smythe, 1972, 309ff.).

In later speeches, Agnew referred to this 'Eastern, liberal-based' media establishment as an 'effete corps of impudent snobs' and as 'nattering nabobs of negativism' (Barnouw, 1975, 443ff.). A variety of conservative scholars and commentators have subsequently taken the position that network television has a 'liberal bias'. In a study of the 1968 election, Edith Efron (1972) concluded that television was overwhelmingly prejudiced against Richard Nixon and in favor of Hubert Humphrey, given the positive and negative presentations of the two candidates on the nightly news programs. Ernest Lefever (1974) found that CBS's coverage of defense-related issues in 1972–1973 reflected unfavourably on the US military and was slanted toward detente with the Soviet Union. Still others argue that, according to their research, reporters for the major news media were overwhelmingly liberal in their political orientations (Lichter, Rothman and

Lichter, 1986). (Some of these claims, however, were contested: see Stevenson *et al.*, 1973.)

These conservative critiques have formed part of the ideology of the 'New Right', which emerged in the late 1970s. The New Right became increasingly critical of the 'new class' within the media, claiming that its biases are liberal, 'collectivist', and 'anti-free enterprise'. This position was promoted for several years by *TV Guide*, which employed conservatives such as Edith Efron, Patrick Buchanan, Kevin Phillips, and others who argued that television subverted traditional values and promoted a left-liberal sociopolitical agenda. Efron, for instance, claimed that television became a mouthpiece for 'ecological stop-growth types', 'nuclear Luddites and plutonophobes', and 'Third World and socialist tyrannies', all the while exhibiting hostility toward 'US business, US labor, US military and US technology'. In short, she claimed, it promotes the agenda of the New Left (*TV Guide*, 8 October 1977, pp. A5–A6).

In a series of corporate ads, Mobil oil corporation claimed that 'leading reporters and editors of major newspapers and television networks have distinct hostilities toward businessmen' (cited in Dreier, 1987, 64). A similar position concerning television entertainment was advanced by Ben Stein (1979), who attacked television programming for promoting antibusiness, antimilitary, and antitraditional values. Stein contends that the Hollywood community, which produces TV entertainment, is an 'extremely energetic and military class' that uses its cultural power to attack competing social elites and to propagate its ultraliberal views. Segments of the New Right have focused their critiques on television entertainment as well, claiming that it subverts traditional religious values while promoting 'secular humanism'.

Another group of critiques emerged in the 1970s. For instance, Daniel Bell (1976) argued that television and the mass media have been instrumental in promoting a new consumer ethic and hedonistic life-style that contradict the older capitalist-Protestant production ethic with its emphasis on hard work, saving, delayed gratification, the family, religion, and other traditional values.[4] 'Neoconservative' critics such as Daniel Moynihan, Robert Nisbet, and Samuel Huntington maintain that television has eroded respect for authority by exposing political scandals (as well as business corruption and failures) while fostering cynicism, distrust, and disrespect for the system as a whole. These critics complain that the media have gone too far in their 'adversary' function and have eroded the president's power, thus 'seriously and dangerously' weakening 'the state's ability to govern' (Moynihan, 1973, 315). The neoconservatives claim that television has helped produce 'adversary culture', and Crozier *et al.* (1975) specifically assert that it has promoted a democratic distemper'.

The liberal approach to television and popular culture is divided into two camps. One critical position focuses on television's institutional setting and function within contemporary capitalist democracies (Siepmann, 1950; Friendly, 1967; Skornia, 1965; and Bagdikian, 1987). The other, more pluralist position focuses, often affirmatively, on the cultural and social functions of television. Liberal critics usually document the abuses of television caused by excessive corporate control of television and the placement of profit above all other values and goals. They hold that if television were both more fully competitive and in the service of democratic goals, the medium could be embraced as an important institution in a pluralist, democratic social order.

The liberal pluralist position is detailed, along with some conservative and radical critiques, in the anthology *Mass Culture*, edited by Bernard Rosenberg and David White (1957). White presents television and popular culture as parts of a democratic, pluralistic cultural system that provides a marketplace of ideas and entertainment as well as a diversity of choices. This position is also elaborated in Herbert Gans's (1974) study of 'taste cultures', which celebrates the liberal pluralist view of culture – and television in the United States. The affirmative liberal position is reflected as well in James Carey's (1988) description of television and popular culture as a 'communalistic ritual' in which a culture celebrates its dominant values, institutions, and way of life. This view is elaborated by Paul Hirsch and Horace Newcomb (1987), who present television as a 'cultural forum' in which society presents, debates, and works outs its values, problems, and identity. The liberal position also shapes some of the work being done by members of the Popular Culture Association, which views television positively as an important expression of dominant values in the United States.

Although liberals have not developed a distinct and systematic institutional theory or critique of television, most sociological studies of how news is produced tend to take a liberal bent. These studies see the projection of news as a consequence of complex organizational imperatives, which in turn result from the interplay of economic and ideological constraints by management, professional codes and news values, and the interaction of a variety of reporters. Most of these liberal sociological studies (Epstein, 1973; Altheide, 1976; Gans, 1979) see news in terms of a liberal consensus produced through a series of compromises and complex interactions. They call into question the conservative claim that television has a liberal bias by emphasizing how the allegedly liberal bias of reporters is countered by the processes of gatekeeping and filtering, which tend to exclude socially critical stories and radical points of view. The studies also point to the ways in which the constraints in news production force the news media to rely on establishment sources and, hence, to disproportionately favor pro-business and pro-government points of view.

Radicals have variously conceptualized television as part of 'an ideological state apparatus' (Althusser, 1971), as a 'mind manager' (Schiller, 1973); as 'the cultural arm of the industrial order' (Gerbner, 1976) as an instrument that 'maintains hegemony and legitimates the status quo' (Tuchman, 1974), as a 'looking glass' that provides a distorted and ideological view of social life (Rapping, 1987), as an instrument that 'invents reality' according to the needs and imperatives of corporate capitalism (Parenti, 1986), and as a propaganda machine that 'manufactures consent' to the existing sociopolitical order (Herman and Chomsky, 1988; [...] Chomsky, 1989). In a sense, only the radicals have attempted to provide even a rudimentary account of television's place in the system of institutions established in the United States and to analyse its sociopolitical functions and effects. The conservative critique focuses on television's alleged liberal bias, and I have seen no systematic liberal attempt to theorize television as a key institution within contemporary US society.

The logic of accumulation and exclusion

[...] Television has contradictory social functions and effects: sometimes it reproduces the status quo in a highly conservative manner, and sometimes it promotes (liberal) change and social reforms. Against models of contemporary US society that project a pluralist concept of television as a major institutional force between big business and big government, I argue that, in a capitalist society, the state, media and other major institutions are predominantly controlled by business – that is, by the capitalist class. [...]

The media – one of a series of 'ideological apparatuses' along with the state, the church, schooling, and the family (Althusser, 1971) – produce ideology and thus serve the interests of the ruling class by idealizing existing institutions, practices, and ideas. In this context, ideology refers to a set of ideas that legitimate the existing organization of society and obscure class/gender/race domination, oppression, exploitation, inequality, and the like (Kellner, 1978).

Ideology thus attempts to obscure social antagonisms and conflicts – a function that the media carry out in their entertainment and information programs. In opposition to liberals and others who conceptualize US society as a pluralistic system that maintains a balance and harmony of power, I view US society as a terrrain of struggle, as a terrain contested by various economic, gender, and radical groups and forces that is nevertheless dominated by the state, media, and big business. My working assumption is that the capitalist mode of production structures dominant institutions, technologies, media, social practices, and ideologies into a capitalist system. But I also assume that individuals will struggle against their exploitation and oppression, that the interests of capitalists and workers are fundamentally opposed, and that tension and struggle are thus inherent features of capitalist society.

Capitalism is a system of production of commodities in which private corporations attempt to maximize their profits through accumulation of capital in a system of private enterprise. [...] This involves producing programming that will attract large audiences who support the commercial system of television in the United States. It also involves, like other enterprises, exploitation of producers and consumers, though the process of exploitation is more subtle in the extraction of profit in the television industry. Like other productive enterprises, the television industry will obviously pay their employees cumulatively less than the total amount of value produced by their labor. Yet exploitation in the television industry is highly uneven, as top executives are regularly paid over one million dollars a year and celebrities, ranging from newscast anchors to top-dollar stars, are paid in the millions. Thus exploitation of the labor force concentrates on lower-level employees such as technicians, researchers, secretaries, writers, and the like.

In addition, exploitation takes place through the extraction of higher prices for consumers for the products advertised on television. Networks charge the corporations who purchase advertising time according to how many viewers watch a given ad and, in some cases, which viewers in specific demographic categories are supposedly viewing a given program (e.g., upscale women from 30–45). The corporations in turn pass these charges on to the viewers in the form of higher prices; because businesses can still, incredibly, take tax write-offs from advertising expenses, viewers pay for their 'free' television with both higher taxes and the growing public squalor caused by a system in which corporations have paid a dramatically lower tax rate since the beginning of the reign of the pro-business Republican administration of Reagan and Bush. [...]

Yet the television industry is different from other businesses in that it has the crucial ideological functions of legitimating the capitalist mode of production and delegitimating its opponents (i.e., socialist and communist governments, Third World liberation movements, labor, and various anti-capitalist social movements). [...]

Television's logic of accumulation dictates a logic of exclusion that condemns to silence those voices whose criticisms of the capitalist mode of production go beyond the boundaries allowed by the lords of the media. Although specific politicians, corporations, and business practices can be criticized, television does not undertake criticism of the capitalist system in terms of any positive alternatives (such as socialism) and rarely questions foundational capitalist values (such as the right to accumulate unlimited amounts of wealth and power). The opinion spectrum that dominates television thus includes only those liberals and conservatives who tacitly agree that all discourse must take place within the framework of the existing system of production and representative democracy, from which more radical views are rigorously excluded [...]

To be sure, the logic of exclusion shifts and reflects social struggles and changes. Blacks were excluded from television almost completely during the 1940s and 1950s, in part because television executives feared that affiliates in the South would not play programs featuring blacks or dealing sympathetically with their problems. By the same token, views critical of US policy in Vietnam were excluded until significant cracks had occurred in the consensus and debate over the policy itself, and positive views of the Soviet Union were excluded until Gorbachev provided the impetus for more sympathetic and even positive coverage.

The range of ideas allowed by the media depends on the level of social struggle and crisis. Because television is a ubiquitous eye that focuses on social existence twenty-four hours a day, challenges to existing policies and values will occasionally be aired. Such challenges help legitimate television as an independent voice of criticism, which in turn helps produce a balance of power in a democratic society. In the following pages, however, I shall question this view of television and argue, instead, that television has taken on the function of systems maintenance within the structure and dynamics of corporate capitalism and liberal democracy – that is, within the dominant economic and political institutions that together constitute technocapitalist societies in the present age.[5] Accordingly the development of a theory of television requires one to situate television within a theory of society. [...]

1.2 Contested terrain and the hegemony of capital

[...] According to the first-generation thinkers of the Frankfurt School and many of their followers, the very forms of mass culture are regressive, exemplifying commodification, reification, and ideological manipulation. Commodity culture, from this viewpoint, follows conventional formulas and standardized forms to attract the maximum audience. It serves as a vehicle of ideological domination that reproduces the ideas and ways of life in the established order, but it has neither critical potential nor any progressive political uses.

The classic 'culture industry' analysis focuses on mass culture as a cultural form. Whereas the critical theory of the 1930s developed a model of social analysis rooting all objects of analysis in political economy, the critical theory of mass culture neglects detailed analysis of the political economy of the media, conceptualizing mass culture merely as an instrument of capitalist ideology. My aim, by contrast, is to develop a critical theory that analyses television in terms of its institutional nexus within contemporary US society. Moreover, rather than seeing contemporary US society as a monolithic structure absolutely controlled by corporate capitalism (as the Frankfurt School sometimes did), I shall present it as a contested terrain traversed by conflicting political groups and agendas. In my view, television – far from being the monolithic voice of a liberal or conservative ideology – is a highly conflictual mass medium in which competing economic, political, social, and cultural forces intersect. To be sure, the conflicts take place within well-defined limits, and most radical discourses and voices are rigorously excluded; but the major conflicts of US society over the last several decades have nonetheless been played out over television. Indeed, contrary to those who see the logic of capital as totally dominating and administering contemporary capitalist societies, I contend that US society is highly conflictual and torn by antagonisms and struggles, and that television is caught up in these conflicts, even when it attempts to deny or cover them over, or simply to 'report' them.

My response to the first generation of critical theorists (Adorno, Horkheimer, Marcuse, and so on) is the argument that the capitalist system of production and its culture and society are more riven with conflicts and contradictions than are present in the models of 'one dimensional society' or the 'totally administered society' presented by earlier critical theorists. In addition, I stress that US society is not only a capitalist society but also (in part) a democratic one. *Democracy* is perhaps one of the most loaded and contested terms of the present era. In its broadest signification, democracy refers to economic, political, and cultural forms of self-management. In an 'economic democracy', workers would control the work place, just as citizens would control their polity through elections, referenda, parliaments, and other political processes. 'Cultural democracy' would provide everyone access to education, information, and culture, enabling people to fully develop their individual potentials and to become many-sided and more creative.

'Political democracy' would refer to a constitutional order of guaranteed rights and liberties in a system of political decision making, with governance by rule of law, the consent of the governed, and public participation in elections and referenda. The form of representational democracy operative in the United States approximates some, but not all, of these features of political democracy. (See Barber 1984 for another model of 'strong democracy'.) While I admit that full-fledged democracy does not really exist in the United States [...] conflicts between capitalism and democracy have persisted throughout US history, and that the system of commercial broadcasting in the United States has been produced by a synthesis of capitalist and democratic structures and imperatives and is therefore full of structural conflicts and tensions. [...]

Hegemony, counter-hegemony, and instrumentalist theories

The hegemony model of culture and the media reveals dominant ideological formations and discourses as a shifting terrain of consensus, struggle, and compromise, rather than as an instrument of a monolithic, unidimensional ideology that is forced on the underlying population from above by a unified ruling class.[6] Television is best conceptualized, however, as the terrain of an ever-shifting and evolving hegemony in which consensus is forged around competing ruling-class political positions, values, and views of the world. The hegemony approach analyses television as part of a process of economic, political, social, and cultural struggle. According to this approach, different classes, sectors of capital, and social groups compete for social dominance and attempt to impose their visions, interests, and agendas on society. Hegemony is thus a shifting, complex, and open phenomenon, always subject to contestation and upheaval.

Ruling groups attempt to integrate subordinate classes into the established order and dominant ideologies through a process of ideological manipulation, indoctrination, and control. But ideological hegemony is never fully obtained; and attempts to control subordinate groups sometimes fail. Many individuals do not accept hegemonic ideology and actively resist it. Those who do accept ideological positions, such as US justification for the Vietnam War, may come to question these positions as a result of exposure to counter-discourses, experiences and education. Accordingly, hegemony theories posit an active populace that can always resist domination and thus point to the perpetual possibility of change and upheaval

Hegemony theories of society and culture can therefore be contrasted with instrumentalist theories. The latter tend to assume that both the state and the media are instruments of capital, and to play down the conflicts among the state, the media, and capital. Examples include the structuralist

Marxist theories of Althusser (1971) and Parenti (1986). Instrumentalist theories tend to assume a two-class model of capitalist society divided into a ruling class and a working class. These theories see the state and media as instruments used to advance the interests of the ruling class and to control the subjugated class. The model assumes a unified ruling class with unitary interests. A hegemony model, by contrast, posits divisions within both the working class and the ruling class and sees the terrain of power as a shifting site of struggle, coalitions, and alliances. Instrumentalist theories of television tend to be ahistorical in their assumption that television, under capitalism, has certain essential and unchanging functions. The hegemony model, by contrast, argues that media take on different forms, positions, and functions in different historical conjunctures and that their very constitution and effects are to some degree the result of the balance of power between contending groups and societal forces.

Hegemony itself takes different forms at different historical junctures. After the disruption of the conservative hegemony of the 1950s in the United States by the radical political movements of the 1960s, the 1970s witnessed intense struggles among conservatives, liberals, and radicals. The radicals were eventually marginalized and the liberals defeated with the victory of Ronald Reagan in 1980. During the 1980s it became clear that television had been taken over by some of the most powerful forces of corporate capitalism and was being aggressively used to promote the interests of those forces [...]

Gramsci and hegemony

The term *hegemony* is derived from the work of the Italian Marxist theorist Antonio Gramsci.[7] In analysing power relations, Gramsci (1971) distinguished between 'force' and 'consent', two ways in which the ruling class exercises power and maintains social control. Whereas institutions such as the police, military, and prisons use force to maintain social control, ideology wins consent for the social order without force or coercion. Hegemonic ideology attempts to legitimate the existing society, its institutions, and its ways of life. Ideology becomes hegemonic when it is widely accepted as describing 'the way things are', inducing people to consent to the institutions and practices dominant in their society and its way of life. Hegemony thus involves the social transmission of certain preconceptions, assumptions, notions, and beliefs that structure the view of the world among certain groups in a specific society. The process of hegemony describes the social construction of reality through certain dominant ideological institutions, practices, and discourses. According to this view, experience, perception, language, and discourse are social constructs produced in a complex series of processes. Through ideological mediation, hegemonic ideology is translated into everyday consciousness and serves as a means of 'indirect rule' that is a powerful force for social cohesion and stability. [...]

According to the hegemony model, television thus attempts to engineer consent to the established order; it induces people to conform to established ways of life and patterns of beliefs and behavior. It is important to note that, from the standpoint of this model, media power is *productive power*. Following Foucault (1977), a hegemony model of media power would analyse how the media produce identities, role models, and ideals; how they create new forms of discourse and experience; how they define situations, set agendas, and filter out oppositional ideas; and how they set limits and boundaries beyond which political discourse is not allowed. The media are thus considered by this model to be active, constitutive forces in political life that both produce dominant ideas and positions and exclude oppositional ones.

Media discourse has its own specificity and autonomy. Television, for instance, mobilizes images, forms, style, and ideas to present ideological positions. It draws on and processes social experience, uses familiar generic codes and forms, and employs rhetorical and persuasive devices to attempt to induce consent to certain positions and practices. Yet this process of ideological production and transmission is not a one-dimensional process of indoctrination, but, rather, is an active process of negotiation that can be resisted or transformed by audiences according to their own ends and interests [...]

The concept of *hegemony*, rather than that of *propaganda* better characterizes the specific nature of commercial television in the United States. Whereas propaganda has the connotation of self-conscious, heavy-handed, intentional, and coercive manipulation, *hegemony* has the connotation, more appropriate to television, of induced consent, of a more subtle process of incorporating individuals into patterns of belief and behavior. By the same token, the propaganda model assumes that its subjects are malleable victims, who willy-nilly fall prey to media discourse. The hegemony model, by contrast, describes a more complex and subtle process whereby the media induce consent. It also allows for aberrant readings and individual resistance to media manipulation (Hall *et al.*, 1980) [...].

Critical theory and television

This book provides a more differential model of power, conflict, and structural antagonisms in contemporary capitalist societies than previous radical accounts. Although television can be seen as an electronic ideology machine that services the interests of the dominant economic and political class forces, the ruling class is split among various groups that are often antagonistic and at odds with one another and with contending groups and social movements. Under the guise of 'objectivity' television intervenes in this matrix of struggle and attempts to resolve or obscure conflict and to advance specific agendas that are prevalent within circles of the ruling strata whose positions television shares.

Because television is best conceptualized as a business that also has the function of legitimating and selling corporate capitalism, a theory of television must be part of a theory of capitalist society. Contrary to those who view television as harmless entertainment or as a source of the 'objective' information that maintains a robust democratic society, I interpret it as a 'culture industry' that serves the interests of those who own and control it. Yet, in contrast to Horkheimer and Adorno (1972), whose theory of the culture industry is somewhat abstract and ahistorical, I analyse television's mode of cultural production in terms of its political economy, history, and sociopolitical matrix. In the process, I stress the interaction between political, economic, and cultural determinants. [...]

In short, critical theory criticizes the nature, development, and effects of a given institution, policy, or idea from the standpoint of a normative theory of the 'good society' and the 'good life'. Capitalism defines its consumerist mode of life as the ideal form of everyday life and its economic and political 'marketplace' as the ideal structure for society. Critical theory contests these values from the standpoint of alternative values and models of society. In this way, critical theory provides a synthesis of social theory, philosophy, the sciences, and politics. [...]

Notes

1. The number of TV sets in the world was cited in the documentary 'Television', broadcast in 1989 by the Public Broadcasting Service (PBS). In 1988, 90.4 million homes in the United States (i.e. more than 98 percent of the population) had televisions, with 1.651 viewers per TV home (*Broadcasting/Cable Yearbook* 1989, G16). By the end of the 1980s, televisions were turned on more than 7 hours per day, and the average adult watched television more than 32 hours per week. Eight out of 10 people spent 2 or more hours watching television every night (Gilbert, 1988). The Roper Organization Poll indicated that 64 per cent of the people questioned chose television as their chief source of news; that from 1959 to 1980 there was a dramatic reversal in the number of people who chose television over newspapers (Roper, 1981, 3); and that television was deemed the most 'believable' news medium by a large margin (Roper, 1981, 4). The results are consistent with those reported in Bower (1985). They also concur with Gilbert (1988, 234), who states that 44 per cent of the people polled chose television as their preferred source for local news and 60 per cent chose it as their preferred source for national and international news. A whopping 96 per cent believed that local TV news is 'very or fairly' accurate, while 89 per cent believed that network news was 'very or fairly' accurate (ibid.).

2. For some characteristic conservative attacks on television's 'liberal bias', see Efron (1972), Lefever (1974), Phillips (1975), Herschensohn (1976), and Lichter, Rothman, and Lichter (1986). The terms *conservative* and *liberal* are constantly being redefined. Whereas conservatives were once allied with state institutions against the emerging capitalist economy and liberals defended a laissez-faire political economy and criticized state regulation, conservatives today tend to be critical of big government and liberals defend government programs and state intervention in the economy. Previous US conservatives were isolationist in their foreign policy, but since World War II they have been generally interventionist. [...] I characterize 'conservatives' as those individuals who criticize big government and liberal welfare state measures while championing deregulation, a relatively unrestricted free market, an interventionist foreign policy, and traditional social values. By contrast, I identify 'liberals' with welfare state reform measures, redistribution of wealth, less interventionist foreign policy (although this often shifts), egalitarian reform of

social values, and more permissive attitudes toward social and cultural change. And, finally, I describe 'radicals' as those who champion more extensive social transformation, ranging from socialist attempts to reform the capitalist economy to feminist attempts to dismantle the institutions of male dominance.

3. For discussions of earlier conservative critiques of popular culture, see Swingewood (1977) and Brantlinger (1983).

4. On 'neoconservatism' and the New Right, see Crawford (1980). Bell (1976) is sometimes labeled a neoconservative because he defends traditional values against the movements of the 1960s and new cultural forms such as television; Bell himself admits that he is a cultural conservative but also a liberal in politics and a socialist in economics (1978, xi). Still, his critique of television and of contemporary hedonist, 'sensate' culture parallels the neoconservative critique.

5. By 'technocapitalism' I mean contemporary, transnational, corporate capitalism in which the capitalist mode of production and new technologies are creating new products, a new organization and structure of labor, and new forms of society, culture, and experience. For preliminary delineation of the concept of technocapital, see Kellner (1989). As the television industry is a crucial component of technocapitalism, the present book can be read as an attempt to theorize the nature, form, and structure of contemporary capitalist societies via the perspective of television.

6. This position is elaborated in Kellner (1979, 1980, 1982), in Best and Kellner (1987), and in Kellner and Ryan (1988). By contrast, the present book provides a more critical/institutional analysis of television. (I shall later devote a separate book to analysis of television as a cultural form.)

7. On hegemony see Gramsci (1971) and Boggs (1986), and on ideology and hegemony see Kellner (1978, 1979). Among those others who utilize a hegemony approach as opposed to a capital logic or instrumental approach to conceptualizing the media in relation to the economy and society are Stuart Hall and the Birmingham school (see Hall *et al.*, 1980) as well as Gitlin (1980), and Rapping (1987).

References

Altheide, D. L. (1976) *Creating Reality*, Beverly Hills and London: Sage.

Althusser, L. (1971) *Lenin and Philosophy*, New York: Monthly Review Press.

Bagdikian, B. (1987) *The Media Monopoly*. 2nd edn, Boston: Beacon Press.

Barber, B. (1984) *Strong Democracy*, Berkeley: University of California Press.

Barnouw, E. (1975) *Tube of Plenty*, New York: Oxford University Press.

Bell, D. (1973) *The Coming of Post-Industrial Society*, New York: Basic Books.

Bell, D. (1976) *The Cultural Contradictions of Capitalism*, New York: Basic Books.

Best, S. and Kellner, D. (1987) (Re)Watching television: notes toward a political criticism. *Diacritics* (Summer), 97–113.

Bogart, L. (1956) *The Age of Television*. New York: Ungar.

Boggs, C. (1986) *Social Movements and Political Power*, Philadelphia: Temple University Press.

Bower, R. T. (1985) *The Changing Television Audience in America*, New York: Columbia University Press.

Brantlinger, P. (1983) *Bread and Circuses*, Ithaca: Cornell University Press.

Carey, J. (1988) *Media, Myths and Narratives*, Beverly Hills: Sage.

Chomsky, N. (1989) *Necessary Illusions*, Boston: South End Press.

Crawford, A. (1980) *Thunder on the Right*, New York: Pantheon.

Crozier, M., Huntington, S. and Watanuki, J. (1975) *The Crisis of Democracy*, New York: New York University Press.
Dreier, P. (1987) The corporate complaint against the media. In Lazere, D. (ed.) *American Media and Mass Culture*, Berkeley: University of California Press.
Efron, E. (1972) *The News Twisters*, New York: Manor Books.
Emery, M. C., and Curtis Smythe, T. (1972) *Readings in Mass Communication*, Dubuque, Iowa: Wm. C. Brown Company.
Epstein, E. (1973) *News from Nowhere*, New York: Random House.
Foucault, M. (1977) *Discipline and Punish*, New York: Pantheon.
Friendly, F. (1967) *Due to Circumstances Beyond Our Control*, New York: Random House.
Gans, H. (1974) *Popular Culture and High Culture*, New York: Basic Books.
Gans, H. (1979) *Deciding What's News*, New York: Random House.
Gerbner, G. (1976) Television: the new state religion. *et cetera* (June), 3–13.
Gilbert, D. (1988) *Compendium of Public Opinion*, New York: Facts on File.
Gitlin, T. (1980) *The Whole World's Watching*, Berkeley: University of California Press.
Gramsci, A. (1971) *Prison Notebooks*, New York: International Publishers.
Hall, S., *et al.* (1980) *Culture, Media, Language*, London: Hutchinson.
Herman, E. and Chomsky, N. (1988) *Manufacturing Consent*, New York: Pantheon.
Herschensohn, B. (1976) *The Gods of Antenna*, New Rochelle, NY: Arlington House.
Hirsch, P. and Newcomb, H. (1987) Television as a cultural form. In Newcomb, H. (ed.) *Television: The Critical View*, New York: Oxford University Press.
Horkheimer, M. and Adorno, T. (1972; orig. 1947) *Dialectic of Enlightenment*, New York: Seabury.
Kellner, D. (1978) Ideology, Marxism and advanced capitalism. *Socialist Review*, **42**, 37–65.
Kellner, D. (1979) TV, ideology, and emancipatory popular culture. *Socialist Review*, **45**, 13–53.
Kellner, D. (1980) Television research and the fair use of media images. In Lawrence, J. and Timberg, B. (eds) (1989) *Fair Use and Free Enquiry*, Norwood, NJ: Ablex, 146–64.
Kellner, D. (1982) Television myth and ritual. *Praxis*, **6**, 133–55.
Kellner, D. (1989) *Critical Theory, Marxism and Modernity*, London and Baltimore: Polity Press and Johns Hopkins University Press.
Kellner, D. and Ryan, M. (1988) *Camera Political: The Politics and Ideology of Contemporary Hollywood Film*, Bloomington: Indiana University Press.
Lawrence, J. and Timberg, B. (1989) *Fair Use and Free Enquiry*, Norwood, NJ: Ablex.
Lefever, E. W. (1974) *TV and National Defense*, Boston, VA: Institute for American Strategy.
Lichter, S. R., Rothman, S. and Lichter, L. S. (1986) *The Media Elite*, Bethesda, MD: Adler & Adler.
Moynihan, D. (1973) *Coping: On the Practice of Government*, New York: Vintage.
Newcomb, H. (ed.) (1987) *Television: The Critical View*, New York: Oxford University Press.
Parenti, M. (1986) *Inventing Reality*, New York: St Martin's Press.
Phillips, K. (1975) *Mediacracy*, New York: Doubleday.
Rapping, E. (1987) *The Looking Glass World of Nonfiction TV*, Boston: South End Press.
Roper, B. (1981) *Evolving Public Attitudes Toward Television and Other Mass Media 1959–1980*, New York: Television Information Office.
Rosenberg, B., and White, D. (1957) *Mass Culture*, Glencoe, IL: Free Press.
Schiller, H. (1973) *The Mind Managers*, Boston: Beacon Press.
Siepmann, C. A. (1946) *Radio's Second Chance*, Boston: Little, Brown.

Siepmann, C. A. (1950) *Radio, Television and Society*, New York: Oxford University Press.

Skornia, H. (1965) *Television and Society*, New York: McGraw-Hill.

Stein, B. (1979) *The View from Sunset Boulevard*, New York: Basic Books.

Stevenson, R. L. *et al.* (1973) Untwisting the news twisters: a replication of Efron's study. *Journalism Quarterly*, **50**, 211–19.

Swingewood, A. (1977) *The Myth of Mass Culture*, London: Macmillan.

Tuchman, G. (1974) *The TV Establishment*, Englewood Cliffs, NJ: Prentice-Hall.

5

Unpopular messages in an age of popularity

Sut Jhally and Justin Lewis

From Jhally, S. and Lewis, J. (1994) *Enlightened Racism: The Cosby Show, Audiences and the Myth of the American Dream*, Boulder, Colorado: West-view Press, pp. 131–46.

> *It is not enough to cater to the nation's whims, you must also serve the nation's needs.*
>
> Newton Minnow, FCC Commissioner to the
> National Association of Broadcasters in 1961

The Cosby Show has in many ways changed the way TV producers think about portraying black people. Just as *The Cosby Show* has gone from being innovative to institutional, so African Americans have become a fairly common sight on network television in the United States. And not just any African Americans: many middle- and upper-middle-class black characters now populate our screens. Bill Cosby can be credited with spurring a move toward racial equality on television. Characters on US television were always inclined to be middle or upper-middle class; now, in the 1990s, black people have become an equal and everyday part of this upwardly mobile world.

The Cosby Show is, in this connection, more than just another sitcom. It has become a symbol of a new age in popular culture, an age in which black actors no longer have to suffer the indignities of playing a crudely limited array of black stereotypes, an age in which white audiences can accept TV programs with more than just a token black character, an age in which blacks appear increasingly confident of mastering the art of the possible. There is, it seems, much to thank Bill Cosby for.

For these reasons, we began our research genuinely well disposed toward *The Cosby Show* and the trend it represents. Some criticisms of the show seemed to us a little churlish, chiding the series for not meeting a set of standards that nearly everything on network television fails to meet. For all its flaws, Bill Cosby's series, we were inclined to think, had pushed popular culture ever so gently in a positive direction. Our detailed, qualitative, audience research study has dramatically changed this optimistic view. Our conclusions regarding the show's effects on racism are, as the reader will now be aware, profoundly pessimistic.

[...] The problems generated by *The Cosby Show*'s celebration of black upward mobility cannot all be laid upon Bill Cosby's shoulders. The show is full of good intentions. On one level, it succeeds admirably in promoting an attitude of racial tolerance among white viewers and in generating a feeling of intense pride among black viewers. The fact that these achievements are superficial is not entirely Bill Cosby's fault. The show is caught up in cultural assumptions that go well beyond the responsibility of any one program maker, no matter how influential. What we discovered, in essence, was that the social and cultural context that gives the show its meaning turns its good intentions upside down.

The social success of black TV characters in the wake of *The Cosby Show* does not reflect a trend toward black prosperity in the big, wide world beyond television. On the contrary, the Cosby era has witnessed a comparative decline in the fortunes of most African Americans in the United States. The racial inequities that scarred the United States before the Civil Rights movement can only be rectified by instituting major structural changes in the nation's social, political, and economic life. The White House has, since 1980, withdrawn from any notion of intervention against an iniquitous system, committing itself to promoting a freewheeling capitalist economy. This *laissez-faire* approach has been responsible for the gradual erosion of advances made by black people following the Civil Rights movement. For all the gains made in the fictional world of television, the United States remains a racially divided society.

Maintaining these racial divisions is a class system that keeps most people in their place. The American dream is just that, a fantasy that few can or ever will realize. It is a fantasy sustained by anecdotes and success stories that focus on exceptions, rather than the norm. If we are to begin any kind of serious analysis of racial divisions in the United States, we must acknowledge the existence of the class barriers that confine the majority of black people.

The economic laws of free market capitalism keep these class barriers in place with cavalier efficiency. Our society has declared itself officially non-racist and invited its black citizens to compete alongside everyone else. The game of Monopoly is instructive here. If three white people begin a game of Monopoly, a black player who is invited to join them halfway through enters the game with a serious disadvantage. Unless blessed by an unlikely combination of good luck and good sense, the black player is held back by the constant need to pay rent to the other players, forestalling any chance of equal competition for capital accumulation. The United States has treated most of its black citizens in that way. It offers the promise of equal opportunity without providing the means to make use of it. It is the perfect empty promise.

There is a wealth of evidence about the operation of these structural inequalities. What is remarkable about our culture is that it refuses to acknowledge the existence of class structures, let alone understand how they influence racial inequities. And yet, at certain moments we do accept these things as obvious. We expect rich, white children to do better than poor, black children. We expect it because we know that they will go to better schools, be brought up in more comfortable surroundings, and be offered more opportunities. And our expectations would usually prove to be right. The poor, black children who succeed in spite of these odds are glamorous figures in our culture precisely because they have confounded these expectations. Unfortunately, when we are asked to be analytical, we seem to forget these things. Our culture teaches us to ignore these class structures in a naïve obsession with individual endeavor.

US television fiction is directly culpable for this mass incomprehension. It has helped to create a world that shifts the class boundaries upward so that the definition of what is normal no longer includes the working class. It then behaves as if nothing has happened, and, the class barriers that divide working-class viewers from upper middle-class TV characters simply melt away. It displays the American dream come true, paraded in front of us in sitcoms and drama series night after night. In TV land, everybody, or everybody with an ounce of merit, is making it.

But surely, it's only television, isn't it? Most people realize that the real world is different, don't they? Well, yes and no. Our study suggests that the line between the TV world and the world beyond the screen has, for most people, become exceedingly hazy. We watch at one moment with credulity, at another with disbelief. We mix skepticism with an extraordinary faith in television's capacity to tell us the truth. We know that the Huxtables are not real, yet we continually think about them as if they were. We are seduced by television's fictions to believe partly that this is how the world is but mostly to believe that this is how it could be. We learn to live in the dreams sold by network executives.

Characters like Roseanne, as the viewers in our study repeatedly confirmed, become noticeable because they defy this norm. Simply by being working class, she stands out. [...]

The prosperous, comfortable surroundings in which most TV characters live is much more welcoming, and into this less disconcerting world *The Cosby Show* snugly fits. In order to be normal on television, the show's characters had to be middle or upper-middle class. What, after all, could be more routine than a lawyer and a doctor, two of television's favorite types of professionals? It also had to look normal, to portray these wealthy professionals as a regular, everyday family. The show has succeeded in absorbing this contradiction brilliantly. The Huxtables' popularity depends upon this combination of accessibility and affluence. Professionals and blue-collar workers can both watch the show and see themselves reflected in it. Social barriers, like class or race, are absent from this world. They have to be. To acknowledge such barriers would make too many viewers uncomfortable. Television has thereby imposed a set of cultural rules that give us certain expectations about the way the TV world should be.

This makes it very difficult for people schooled in the evasive language of North American television to seriously comprehend the world around them. Any analysis of class structures is simply absent from our popular vocabulary. When respondents tried to make sense of class issues arising in discussions of *The Cosby Show*, many were forced to displace the idea of class onto a set of racial categories. This was particularly the case for black respondents who got enmeshed in the debate about whether the show was 'too white'. The truth is, the Huxtable family does not belong to a 'white' culture but to an upper middle-class culture. In the stilted discourse of US television, many respondents found it difficult to make this distinction.

We cannot blame Bill Cosby for playing by the rules of network television. Only by conforming to these cultural limitations was he able to make a black family so widely acceptable – and respected – among the majority of TV viewers (who are white). The consequence of this intervention, however, this 'readjustment of the rules' to include black people, is to foster damaging delusions. Television, having confused people about class, becomes incomprehensible about race.

Affirming inaction in white viewers

Among white people, the admission of black characters to television's upwardly mobile world gives credence to the idea that racial divisions, whether perpetuated by class barriers or by racism, do not exist. Most white people are extremely receptive to such a message. Like Ronald Reagan's folksy feelgood patriotism, the idea allows them to feel good about themselves and about the society they are part of. The Cosby–Huxtable persona (along with the many other black professionals it has brought forth in the TV world) tells viewers that, as one respondent put it, 'there really is room in the United States for minorities to get ahead, without affirmative action'.

The whole notion of affirmative action has become a hot issue in contemporary politics. Republicans (with a few exceptions) use their opposition to it, as Jesse Helms showed during his 1990 senatorial campaign, as a way of mobilizing white voters. Our study is good news for these Republicans. It reveals that the opposition to affirmative action among white respondents was overwhelming. What was particularly notable was that although most white people are prepared to acknowledge that such a policy was once necessary, the prevailing feeling was that this was no longer so. [...] The positive effects of the affirmative action policy have been confined almost exclusively to middle-class blacks, a fact that no one in our sample discussed. The assumption was that affirmative action is something that *all* black people have benefited from.

There are, of course, circumstances in which a well-qualified black person will receive a warm reception from employers concerned to acquire an 'equal opportunity' image. Any cursory glance at social statistics, however, will show that this is because employers are embarrassed by current levels of inequality in the workplace. Almost any social index will show that we live in a society in which black and white people as groups are not equal – not in education, health, housing, employment, or wealth. So why is affirmative action suddenly thought to be no longer necessary? Partly, we would suggest, because our popular culture tells us so.

During our analysis of the content of three major networks' programing, we came across only one program, *Quantum Leap*, that offered a glimpse of these racial divisions. What was significant about this program, however, was that the story took place not in the present but in the past, during the early days of the Civil Rights movement. *Quantum Leap* was only able to show us racial divisions in the United States by traveling back in time to the 'bad old days'. All black characters in stories set in the present seemed blissfully free of racial impediments. Recent attempts by Hollywood to deal with racial inequality adopt the same strategy. Racism, whether in *Mississippi Burning, Driving Miss Daisy*, or *The Long Walk Home*, is safely confined to history. There are, of course, some exceptions (notably the work of Spike Lee), but the general impression is clear: racial inequality is behind us; we now live in Bill Cosby's brave new world, where anyone can make it.

Television, despite the liberal intentions of many of its writers, has pushed our culture backward. White people are not prepared to deal with the problem of racial inequality because they no longer see that there is a problem. *The Cosby Show*, our study showed, is an integral part of this process of public disenlightenment. Commercial television becomes Dr. Feelgood, indulging its white viewers so that their response to racial inequality becomes a guilt-free, self-righteous inactivity. Television performs an ideological conjuring trick that plays neatly into the hands of free market proponents in the Republican party, with their irresistible recipe of 'don't worry, be happy'.

This retrograde development has burdened us with a new, repressed form of racism. Although television portrays a world of equal opportunity, most white people know that in the world at large, black people achieve less material success, on the whole, than white people. They know that black people are disproportionately likely to live in poor neighborhoods and drop out of school. How can this knowledge be reconciled with the smiling faces of the Huxtables? If we are blind to the roots of racial inequality embedded in our society's class structure, then there *is* only one way to reconcile this paradoxical state of affairs. If white people are disproportionately successful, then they must be disproportionately smarter or more willing to work hard. The face of Cliff Huxtable begins to fade into the more sinister and threatening face of Willie Horton. Although few respondents were prepared to be this explicit (although a number came close), their failure to acknowledge class or racial barriers means that this is the only other explanation that makes any sense.

This explanation for black poverty underlies the increasingly influential analysis of urban poverty put forward by conservative policy-makers. Commenting on this, William Julius Wilson in *The Truly Disadvantaged* (1987) argues that whereas a few years ago liberal perspectives (based upon highlighting racial discrimination and social class oppression) were most influential in shaping how the government thought about dealing with urban poverty, conservative spokespeople are most listened to now. The main thrust of the conservatives' analysis is that the problems of the ghetto underclass originate from the culture of that class itself and that the solution is to change their values. If the underclass members do not succeed, in other words, then it is all their own fault.

The culture of poverty thesis has been lurking in the wings for over a hundred years. The growth of social science in the twentieth century has led to a dismissal of such an intellectually feeble and sociologically naïve notion as quaint – something we used to believe before we knew any better. To see such a reactionary notion become fashionable once again would be ludicrous if it were not so serious. As we approach the twenty-first century, we seem content to abandon all we have learned since the early days of social reform only to embrace an idea that allows our political leaders to pay tribute to a sprinkling of missionaries (a thousand points of light) while abandoning social reform altogether.

Television is partly responsible for this lurch backward. The Huxtables are examples of blacks who have changed their culture and thus their socioeconomic status. Without being able to see the Huxtables and the black ghetto underclass separated by class, television (and the rest of popular culture) stresses instead their unity. If there are families like the Huxtables (which, of course, there are), then the inadequacies of ghetto underclass members themselves explain their social position. That more blacks are in this disadvantaged position than whites further indicates a racial pathology in which the culture of black people keeps them in their place. Sociologist Herman Gray (in Riggs, 1991) comments that *The Cosby Show* plays a role in mediating the polarization between rich and poor that characterized the 1980s: 'We come away with the sense in which the society is fine, there's no problem, you just have to work hard, you just have to have the right kind of values, have the right kind of desires and aspirations, and it'll be alright.'

Wilson is concerned to put forward policies that will be not only effective but able to capture the support and imagination of the general population. Our evidence suggests that liberal policies focused on the historical effects of racism and the contemporary effects of economic deprivation will now be very difficult to sell.

What we end up with, in the apparently enlightened welcome that white viewers extend to the Huxtables, is a new, sophisticated form of racism. The Huxtables' success implies the failure of a majority of black people who, by these standards, have not achieved similar professional or material success. Television, which tells us nothing about the structures behind success or failure, leaves white viewers to assume that black people who do not measure up to their television counterparts have only themselves to blame. In this regard, notes cultural critic Patricia Turner, *The Cosby Show* 'is very appealing to white audiences because it reinforces the notion that the Civil Rights movement took care of all the racial inequalities in the society' (in Riggs, 1991).

Rethinking stereotypes

In a rather different way, the effect of *The Cosby Show* on its black audience is also one of flattering to deceive. The dominant reaction of black respondents to the series was 'for this relief much thanks'. After suffering years of negative media stereotyping, most black viewers were delighted by a show that portrayed African Americans as intelligent, sensitive, and *successful*.

The problem with this response is that it accepts the assumption that, on television, a positive image is a prosperous image. This dubious equation means that African Americans are trapped in a position where any reflection of a more typical black experience – which is certainly *not* upper-middle class – is 'stereotypical'. As one black respondent said, even though he was aware that *The Cosby Show* presented a misleading picture of what life was like for most black Americans, 'There's part of me that says, in a way, I don't want white America to see us, you know, struggling or whatever.' Among white Americans, the feeling, as we have seen, is mutual.

This analysis of stereotyping of black people dominates contemporary thought. It is the consequence of a TV world that has told us that to be working class is to be marginal. To be normal on network television in the United States, our popular culture tells us, you have to be middle or upper-middle class. Viewers are therefore able to see the Huxtable family as both regular, average, and everyday *and* as successful, well-heeled professionals. This may be Orwellian doublethink, and it is encouraged by television.

For black viewers, this duplicity amounts to a form of cultural blackmail. It leaves them two choices. Either they are complicit partners in an image system that masks deep racial divisions in the United States, or they are forced to buy into the fiction that 'there are black millionaires all over the place', thereby accepting *The Cosby Show* as a legitimate portrayal of ordinary African-American life. After years of resentment at television's portrayal of black people, to end up with such a choice is a cruel injustice to most black people.

As we have suggested, it doesn't have to be this way. There is no reason why TV characters cannot be working class and dignified, admirable, or even just plain normal. Other TV cultures have managed to avoid distorting and suppressing the class structure of their societies; why can't we manage it in the United States? There are, we suggest, two main obstacles, the first ideological, the second economic.

Moving beyond the American dream

It is now about four decades since Arthur Miller wrote *Death of a Salesman*. The Pulitzer prizewinning play tells the story of an ordinary middle-class family trapped within the aspirations of the American dream, a story that becomes tragic as the gap between the family's actual life and the dream becomes increasingly evident. The play's frustrated protagonist, Willy Loman, becoming desperate with the ordinariness of his own life, finally loses his grip on reality altogether. It is a sobering lesson that the United States has failed utterly to learn.

The American dream is much more than a gentle fantasy; it is a cultural doctrine that encompasses vast tracts of American life. No politician would dare to question our belief in it any more than they would publicly question the existence of God. Even though politicians of many different persuasions pay lip service to the dream (it is, in conventional wisdom, 'what's great about America'), it is no longer a politically neutral idea. It favors persons on the political right who say that anyone, regardless of circumstance or background, can make it if they try. In such an egalitarian world, the free market can reign unrestrained. For government to intervene to eradicate the enormous social problems in the United States would be to defy the logic of the dream. Intervention would imply, after all, that the world is not naturally fair and that opportunity is not universal.

The American dream is insidious, not innocent. It is part of a belief system that allows people in the United States to disregard the inequities that generate the nation's appalling record (by comparison with almost any other industrially developed nation) on poverty, crime, health, homelessness, and education. It is to be expected, perhaps, that more fortunate persons cling to the self-justifying individualism that the dream promotes. One of the strangest things about the United States is that less fortunate persons do so too.

The ideological dominance of the American dream is sustained by its massive presence in popular culture. The TV and film industries churn out fable after fable reducing us to spellbound passivity. The success we are encouraged to strive for is always linked to the acquisition of goods. This whole materialistic charade is fueled by the most influential cultural industry in the United States: advertising.

Advertising is everywhere in the United States. Billboards loom over us whether we're in the city or the country, and posters and handbills decorate nearly every public place. Shopping areas from downtown districts to suburban malls to the ubiquitous small-town strip are littered with logos and commercial messages. Television, radio, newspapers, and magazines are saturated with advertising. It clutters our mailboxes and even our clothing. With commercial slogans emblazoned across baseball caps, T-shirts and sneakers, we become walking advertisements.

Though such artifacts are not unique to the United States, this nation carries advertising to an unmatched excess. And what do these advertising messages say to us? Consume; then aspire to a level where we can consume more. Our contentment is anathema to the advertising industry: we have to be encouraged to be in a state of constant material desire. The economic logic of the industry requires that we never be happy. We can exist only on the verge of happiness, always at least one more consumer item away from contentment.

The key word in this acquisitive lexicon is *aspiration*. Consumers do not usually see themselves in commercials; they see a vision of a glamorous and affluent world they aspire to be part of. Underlying the preponderance of middle- and upper-middle-class characters on display is the relentless message that the world of happiness and contentment looks like their world. It is not surprising, then, that we assume that more ordinary settings are necessarily gloomy or depressing. As a middle-class white woman in our study put it, 'Nobody wants to see repeats of what they're living ... The everyday struggle of living, I don't think people really want to see all that ... they say, "Please give me something extra funny and special", and "Oh, look at those gorgeous sweaters".' In other words, we expect television to be more dramatic than everyday life, and, in the United States, we also expect it to be more affluent. We don't just want a good story, we want a 'classy' setting. This is the language of advertising. It is now also the discourse of the American dream. This language is now so important in our culture that these attitudes seem perfectly natural. Only when we look at other TV cultures can we see that they are not.

This discourse of aspiration permeates our popular culture. Few other industrial nations allow their cultural industries to be as dependent upon advertising revenue as does the United States. Little happens in the popular culture of the United States without a commercial sponsor. In this lightly regulated free-market economy, cultural industries are not accountable to a notion of public service, only to the bottom line of profitability. Unlike most other Western governments, the United States spends little public money on art and culture. In 1990, the government spent only $171 million on the National Endowment for the Arts, less than it allocated to the Pentagon for military bands. This amounts to around 70 cents per capita spent on art and culture. In West Germany the per capita figure, over $70, is a hundred times greater. Even the British, after more than a decade of free-market government policy, spent nearly twenty times as much per capita.

Apart from minuscule grants to public broadcasting, the survival of radio and TV stations depends almost entirely on their ability to sell consumers (listeners or viewers) to advertisers. Moreover, broadcasters in the United States are required to do little in the way of public service. No regulations encourage quality, diversity, innovation, or educational value in programming. This means that the influence of advertising is twofold. Not only does it create a cultural climate that influences the form and style of programs that fill the spaces between commercials; it also commits television to the production of formulaic programming. Once television establishes cultural patterns, it is reluctant to deviate from them for fear of losing the ratings that bring in the station's revenue. [...]

In order to be successful and to stay on the air, *The Cosby Show* had to meet certain viewer expectations. This, as we have seen, meant seducing viewers with the vision of comfortable affluence that the Huxtables epitomize. Once television has succumbed to the discourse of the American dream, in which a positive image is a prosperous one, it cannot afford the drop in ratings that would likely accompany a redefinition of viewers' expectations. TV series that depart from conventional viewer expectations are necessarily short-lived. Series like *Frank's Place*, *Cop Rock*, *Twin Peaks*, or even *thirtysomething* all deviated from a norm; and, though watched by millions of viewers, they did not attain the mass audience required to keep them on the air. This puts us on a treadmill of cultural stagnation. Mainstream taste cannot significantly change or develop because it is rarely allowed to change or develop. Innovation, in a system that requires an immediate return on investment, is too great an economic risk. In such a system, it pays to meet viewers' expectations rather than upset them; the bland repetition of feelgood fantasies makes sound business sense. There are exceptions, of course, but they are infrequent. It could be argued that the only genuinely innovative show that has survived in the commercial sector of this cultural quagmire in recent years is *The Simpsons*.

In such a system, *The Cosby Show*'s survival depends upon meeting the demands of a formula that pleases as many people as possible. The series meets those demands with consummate success, pleasing blacks and whites, blue-collar workers and professionals, all in slightly different ways. It plays with an ambiguity that maximizes its audience. For *The Cosby Show* to challenge viewers' associations built up over the years of television that have preceded it, it would have to confront the culturally pervasive discourse of the American dream. This, in turn, would mean rethinking the way television is funded and regulated in the United States. The societal problems we have identified in the post-Cosby era, in other words, go far beyond the harmonious world inside the Huxtables' New York brownstone.

What we are suggesting is that we reconsider the whole notion of media stereotyping by examining the ideological and economic conditions that underpin it. If we do not, we place our culture on a never-ending treadmill of images and attitudes without ever giving ourselves, as a society, the time to think about the consequences of those images. Discussions about television's influence tend to be limited to the effect of its use of sex or violence. If our audience response study tells us anything, it is that we need to be more attentive to the attitudes cultivated by normal, everyday television. In the case of *The Cosby Show*, these attitudes can affect the way we think about issues like race and class and, in so doing, even influence the results of elections. [...] This is a call for diversity and variety and goes to the heart of how a democratic society works.

Our culture is much too important to be left to the lowest common denominator laws of the free market. We must begin to think qualitatively as well as quantitatively: choice should mean lots of different programs, not lots of different channels. Something is rotten in the state of television, and we should do something about it.

It is often said that a key characteristic of societies that claim to be democratic is their toleration and even support for messages that are not popular. The well-known argument goes something like this: 'I totally disagree with what you say, but I will defend to the death your right to say it.' A noble sentiment, it recognizes that democratic societies remain healthy and prosperous by encouraging debate and diversity. Yet in the United States we have permitted the television industry to be controlled by the notion of 'popularity', which is what determines profitability. In the quest for large numbers of viewers, program-makers cannot afford to confront viewers with challenging or unpopular messages. Lost viewers translate into loss of advertising revenue and ultimately to a show's cancellation.

For many reasons [...] Americans, whether black or white, do not want to see working-class black people play a part in television's stories or to see those stories deal with problems of crime, poverty, joblessness, broken families, or drug addiction. The only black people they will invite into their homes regularly are people like the Huxtables. Program-makers are not interested in the public good but in their private investment: if enough of the audience does not want something, then no part of the audience gets it. In such a context the prejudices of the audience have to be played to. To challenge and try to change those prejudices would result in financial failure within the present arrangements of American commercial television.

We suggest that what is needed is a television system that will air unpopular messages and in part, honestly confront the central problems of the day. If Bill Cosby can make large numbers of white Americans identify with a black middle-class family, perhaps someone else could do the same for a black working-class family if they were granted *the time*. The challenge for the people who control network television is to find the integrity and courage to allow socially unpopular or unconventional messages a presence in spite of the risks. Without such a commitment, television discourse will have more in common with authoritarianism than with democracy. We must admit to not being hopeful about the prospects.

References

Riggs, Marlon (1991) *Color Adjustment* (A film produced, directed, and written by Marlon Riggs), San Francisco, CA: California Newsreel.

Wilson, W. J. (1987) *The Truly Disadvantaged*, Chicago: University of Chicago Press.

6

Cultural Indicators: European reflections on a research paradigm

J. Mallory Wober

Overview

The 1970s were the heyday of an enterprise that some still term a 'cultural indicators' paradigm, though others generally refer to it by the phrase 'cultivation analysis'. It may not be unfair in retrospect to refer to the paradigm as one of philosophy and rhetoric as much as one of research. The *éminence grise* of the enterprise has unquestionably been Professor George Gerbner, for many years Dean of the Annenberg School at the University of Pennsylvania.

A recent chapter by his group emphasizes that the 'Cultural Indicators approach involves a three-pronged research strategy' (Gerbner *et al.*, 1994, p. 22); they call the first component 'institutional process analysis, designed to investigate the formation of policies directing the massive flow of media messages'; the second prong is message system analysis and the third, cultivation analysis. The full Cultural Indicators approach is too diverse to allow any one researcher or team to deal with its whole scope. There are probably no comprehensive studies anywhere designed upon the whole three-faceted theory as it has been set out, not even by Gerbner's group themselves.

Institutional process analysis uses the techniques of political science, social anthropology, or economics (e.g., Burns, 1977; Collins, 1990; Hansen, 1993; IIC, 1996). Few if any of such studies, however, fly the flag of 'institutional process analysis' explicitly under the broader banner of a Cultural Indicators approach. Anyone working on the latter two phases of a Cultural Indicators approach would do best to use their own specialized techniques, mostly in applied social psychology, and to adopt relevant findings from the specialists in institutional process analysis.

Breaking with the conventional over-preoccupation with imitative consequences of screen violence, Gerbner (1992a, p. 98) explains that 'violence is a demonstration of ... hierarchies of power – gender, racial, sexual, class and national power that the mass-cultural marketplace cultivates through its control of dramatic imagery –'; and (p. 106) 'bombarding viewers with violent images of a mean and dangerous world remains ... an instrument of intimidation and terror'; Gerbner also says (1992a, p. 102), 'major responsibility for the formative socializing process of story-telling has passed from parents and churches and schools to a small group of global conglomerates that have something to sell'. Then (1992a, p. 105) 'the cultural props for imperial policy are shifting from their anti-commu- nist rationalizations to a sharp and selective offensive against real and concocted terrorists ... An overkill of violent imagery helps to mobilize support for taking charge of the unruly at home and abroad'. Gerbner *et al.* (1994, p. 23) also write that 'institutional needs and objectives influence the creation and distribution of mass-produced messages that create ... and sustain the needs, values and ideologies of mass publics'. The theory is thus a conspiratorial one indicating that 'big business' wishes to domi- nate the political process, both domestically and internationally. Aside from this general analysis of the institutional process, Gerbner (1992b) has made a specific case, relating to the enterprise of the Gulf War in which he links the industrial with the military and the information networks to suggest that they promoted, waged and afterwards evaluated the war in their particular interests.

All this refers mostly to the system in the United States. Although the challenge has been made from Europe that the socially regulated televi- sion systems there deliver a different product (Wober and Gunter, 1988), the Gerbner group have not acknowledged this probe let alone discussed and answered it. A footnote in their 1994 chapter refers to 'cross-cultural extensions of this work' which have occurred in Japan, Finland, Hungary and the USSR, but nothing is then said about whether these extensions reinforced the American findings or not. Morgan (1990) has reported data from China, South Korea and Argentina that are said to support 'cultiva- tion effects' but their chapter contains little information on institutional or content analysis. In the same volume Reimer and Rosengren (1990) report on interactions between uses of all mass message systems, and personal value orientations, in Sweden; but they also say nothing about possible institutional motives or initiatives in trying to determine the culture.

Broadly, the Gerbnerist position was, and continues to be that (American, free-market, and through its sheer market strength, most systems world-wide) television provides a diet rich in images in which white, heterosexual, males have dominant positions while black, homosexual and female people tend to be dominated or even victims. This is essentially a Marxist view and it may be a reason why relatively little has been said both by the paradigm-leaders and other Americans who have worked in their wake, about institutional process analysis. Marxists are not well regarded in America; but Professor Gerbner has been very successful in projecting (the second and third parts of) his analysis – through appearances before Senate investigative committees and on television (see Gerbner, 1992a). Any study dealing mainly with content or 'cultivation' analysis should crucially focus back to an analysis of the institutional process, in order to qualify as a true 'cultural indicators' exercise.

The second 'leg' of the Cultural Indicators 'tripod' is *message system analysis*. On this front there has been much American and some European work. This kind of sociological and epidemiological study tends, in its drive to objectify matters, not to dwell so much on symbolic and ideological prob- lems; hence such studies neglect the institutional motives and processes that have produced the objects, the roles and the relationships that they count. Because of the effort involved in producing such studies, they tend not to tackle at the same time the third aspect of the three-fold theory.

Cultivation analysis is the third component of the overall theory. The chief procedure used to carry out cultivation analyses should be to correlate evidence of overall viewing of television, with some 'target' measure of perception, attitude or behaviour. If there is some parallel between increased viewing experience and greater evidence of the target measure (note: one should *not* call this a 'dependent measure' until it is unequivocally shown that a causal connection exists, and quite often a correlation between two attributes can be explained as adventitious by reference to some hidden third element), then there might be a process of 'cultivation' arising from this viewing experience. Many studies do not use a measure of overall television viewing, but focus more closely on viewing of particular genres. This is no doubt a more precise and justified procedure; correlations between watching particular genres and attitudes are the quarry of simple effects studies, which Gerbner says (Gerbner *et al.*, 1994, p. 23) 'our use of the term *cultivation* for television's contribution to conceptions of social reality is not just another word for "effects" ... television neither simply "creates" nor "reflects" images, opinions and beliefs. Rather, it is an integral aspect of a dynamic process.'

Some studies use measures of overall viewing as well as of particular genres. Results from such studies can be very telling in the effort to decide between the force of cultivation theory and that of simple learning effects. Where experience of advertising is being examined as a possible source of some effect, then it may be valid to use a measure of gross amount of television viewing in a situation where cultivation and more simple effects theories converge.

To detail European work that is relevant to the Cultural Indicators approach, one may discuss each of the 'phases' of the grand theory in turn, to examine ideas and evidence recently brought forward both in America (where this happens more often under the label of 'cultivation studies') and in Europe (where the term is less often used, though where some of the work may be relevant). Before that, however, it is relevant to summarize some of the theoretical points that have been made which modify, evolve or even challenge the simple three-stage model proposed by the Annenberg School.

Institutional process analysis

The social historian Raymond Williams (quoted by Granville Williams, 1994) noted in 1974 that 'television ... advertising ... and centralized ... data processing systems ... can be used to affect, to alter, and in some cases to control our whole social process'. Granville Williams indicates that the tide of technical innovation has flowed in an 'American' pattern. Multiplication of channels, smaller audiences for each one, cheaper programme-making, business mergers between hardware providers and those who make new and hold stocks of old programmes, erode societally controlled broadcasting systems. The notion that these changes amount to 'deregulation' is an illusion since new systems are governed by market forces which are harnessed by those who command its heights; the notion of deregulation is also a spell since it labels as free, and thus denotes as desirable something which might not be considered so if its true nature was more widely understood. These are the reasons why Gerbner insists that the true and full exercise of a Cultural Indicators approach must start with and include a meaningful element of institutional process analysis. As will be seen from other sections of this chapter, this reference point is all too often missing from what then become simple (though sometimes impressive enough) effects studies.

Message system analysis

The Annenberg group have argued the same case in 1994 as they published nearly two decades earlier, based on the notion that American television contents have remained essentially similar in their patterns. Greenberg and Levy (1996) analysed research in America on two social roles (gender and ethnic minority) and two kinds of behaviour (violence and sexual activity); they have considered the contents both of programmes (which are exported to Europe, both for relay on terrestrially broadcast and on cable and satellite channels) and of advertisements (which generally are not so exportable).

They report that 'television violence remains a domain primarily for males', while (hardly surprisingly?) 'television sex ... tends to use an equivalent number of participants from each gender'. Since these are the patterns reported by the Annenberg group in their 1970s' studies, it would appear that there has been little essential change in broadcast gender roles over the decades – the male is the voice of authority, boys and men are more aggressive than girls and women, and females are 'forever younger than their male counterparts'. The numbers of blacks have increased, though this representation has been concentrated in but a few programmes (making visible a 'ghetto') but Asians and Hispanics remain under-represented. Unless, therefore, European buyers are carefully selective, American material they import will continue to display the kinds of power relations between segments in society that were reported in the 1970s by the Annenberg scholars. Douglas and Olson (1996) looked at nine dramas spanning four decades, to examine intra-family relationships; they found that the experience of television children had deteriorated; modern families were more conflictual, less cohesive and less able to bring up their children effectively.

In Britain there have been fewer studies than in America about gender roles in programmes; however, there have been content counts concerning amounts of violence and of representation of ethnic minorities and of people with disabilities (Cumberbatch and Negrine, 1992). The Independent Television Commission (ITC) reported in its house journal *Spectrum* (June, 1996, p. 18) that 'there are more people from ethnic minorities appearing on our screens, they present major news and current affairs programmes and in our dramas they are just as likely to play the lawyer as the criminal'.

A monitoring exercise of two weeks also carried out for the ITC in 1994 (ITC, 1995)

> showed that the reduction in overall levels of programme violence which the ITC had called for in 1993 had not been achieved in the case of Channels 3 and 4. Nevertheless, the great majority of programmes before 9 pm on both channels contained, as before, no violence ... only about 7 per cent of programmes contained any strong ... violence".

What this means is that the overall amounts of violence in British terrestrial programming are not large, but have not reduced over time.

The studies of content, such as they are, can be taken as supporting Gerbner's contention that there has been no significant change over two decades. However, the levels of violence in Britain are clearly less than in America. Representation of black people is numerically fair, though not yet satisfying to black viewers; representation of people of Asian origin is uneven and also not entirely satisfying to Asian viewers; representation of women is not equitable in terms of numbers of those in roles of power and authority. Some explicitly gay shows appear from time to time, though the proportion they might be expected to represent is still debated, nor is it clear that, as reported by Gross and Gerbner in the United States, homosexuals are demeaned in their depiction.

Cultivation analysis: underlying assumptions

The drive of Cultural Indicators 'theory' is to infer or establish a top-down autocratic process. Two assumptions of homogeneity are crucial to this model. The first of these notions is of homogeneity of content (Gerbner, *et al.*, 1994, p. 19) say 'the most frequently recurring themes of television cut across all types of programming and are inescapable for the regular viewer; ... there is no evidence that proliferation of channels has led to substantially greater diversity of content'.

The other notion of homogeneity concerns patterns of viewing. Thus one assertion made in nearly every one of his pieces by Gerbner is that 'television is watched by the clock' (basically, undiscriminatingly, reducing the relevance of genre). Counter to this there is a great deal of evidence for the theory – and probably the fact – of 'the active viewer', one who selects and contributes to the meanings that are wrought from the array that are experienced. Much of the evidence in this area is from Europe. In this way, though European researchers do not specifically see themselves as working in the field of Cultural Indicators theory, many such studies can be seen as relevant to it.

Though there are occasional passing references in Gerbner's work to uses and gratifications theory, there is little recognition that viewing patterns are differentiated and that this matters. There is much evidence, however, that people view selectively. Using very large representative public samples of panellists filling in evaluation diaries Weimann *et al.* (1992) showed that patterns of viewing behaviour are certainly not homogeneous with regard to genre.

Crime programmes are a conspicuous site in which the Gerbnerian drama of inculcation of fear by the spectacle of violence is said to be performed. Yet many studies indicate that it is not just the violence but the other elements such as tension, plots, and retribution for wrongdoing that attract viewers to such material. Echoing an antique finding by Boyanowski *et al.* (1976), Reith (1996) reports evidence that social stress, indexed by high unemployment levels, is correlated with increased viewing of crime drama – in the USA and Canada, though not in Germany.

Intensive observational research, in which small numbers of researchers spend hours or days in people's homes paints a similar picture of the 'active' or the autonomous viewer. It was pointed out from a social psychological perspective (Wober, 1988) that perception is a crucial mediating stage in between message content and world view. Thus no matter how many role models or incidents 'objectively' depict white, male heterosexual power, if viewers for some reason perceive the screen population as containing a fair proportion of powerful and successful female role models, then the sequence of influence proposed by Gerbner is broken. Sparks *et al.* (1995) have shown that the personal attribute of vividness of imagery modifies responses to a potentially frightening screen text (a flying saucer drama). Wober (1986) also provided evidence that personality is a mediating construct which may influence perception; as personality structures are considerably genetically determined, research should take this into account, from the earliest age of screen experience, as a mediator of received meaning.

From a sociological perspective Morley (1992) and other small-group investigators such as Corner *et al.* (1990) noted that viewers' group memberships and situational experience also contribute to the meanings they derive from what they see. A major illustration of such phenomena is the O.J. Simpson trial outcome; in America it is known that, no matter what television programming people saw or did not see on this, white people very largely considered him guilty and black people (along with the largely black jury) felt he was innocent.

The chief group of scholars who currently explicitly explore difficulties with the theory of cultivation analysis are American. Evidently influenced by the teaching of Hawkins and Pingree at the University of Wisconsin at Madison, and by the Social Cognition Group at the University of Illinois at Urbana-Champaign, L. J. Shrum (1995) sets out a number of cognitive processes[1] (many also mentioned by Tapper, 1995) that might be responsible for producing the correlations that some describe as cultivation effects. These scholars have examined how meanings are compiled and stored in the first place, and then retrieved and reported when researchers ask for them. Other 'positivist' theorists have argued that the 'active viewer' has needs which determine uses of mass message system content that deliver gratifications and perceptions of television, and of reality; the consumer is therefore not a clean slate upon which meanings are written by an outside hand.

Advancing their own theoretical position to (partly) cope with early criticisms, the Annenberg group have introduced the notions of *mainstreaming* and of *resonance*. In mainstreaming, wherever there is some characteristic (say, age) which discriminates noticeably so that, for example, young people more readily accept a drug-using culture while older people oppose it, among light viewers these age-related differences will be marked but among heavy viewers such differences will be much less noticeable. Resonance refers to the situation in which, if the 'television message' (for example, that there is a lot of crime and the world is a dangerous place) coincides with real world circumstances (say, for the inhabitants of a high crime neighbourhood), then the alleged conse-quences of the television message are fortified.

Cultivation analysis: particular studies

Reporting from South Africa on a mailed self-completion survey on personal health care behaviour among over 1000 Americans, Marks and Calder (1989) observed that television shows a great deal of illness as well as precautionary measures, both in series fiction and in advertisements. Heavy viewing of television should then increase viewers intentions to 'perform healthcare behaviours' first because there would be an increased perception of vulnerability to becoming ill, and then because it will be seen to be useful to visit doctors and use medicines, as well as to manage one's own health positively through nutrition, exercise and avoiding health risks.

Using multiple regression analyses, the authors claim that 'television directly, as well as indirectly contributes to cultivating a passive, depen-dent orientation toward healthcare'; they say this because viewing was linked with the use of medicine but not with health building activities. This double finding is important as it escapes two kinds of processual explanations that have been put forward possibly to explain positive 'cultivation' findings without recourse to the cultivation theory itself. One such suggestion was offered by Wober (1978), that positive correlations might be an outcome of 'response set' – the television viewing questions were asked in such a way that high scores were given for heavier viewing, and attitude questions were all asked in a similar direction (greater fear of crime corresponded with a higher numerical score); thus people who were 'exaggerators' might tend to reply high on both measures, without there being any underlying causal connection between them.

In a simpler study in the Midwest of America, Ogles and Sparks (1993) measured perceived probability of experiencing each of 16 different crimes, and the degree of fear connected with each possibility. Only one of the probabilities, and five out of 16 fears were linked with amount of viewing. The authors interpret this as partial support for cultivation theory, but it is not easy to explain why, if people do not increase their expectation of being victimized, *pro rata* with increased television viewing, they should increase their fear in due proportion with viewing.

Olson (1994) measured total viewing and that of soap operas, and replies to eight statements concerning sexually-related behaviour. Using seven control measures (including 'perceived reality'), only two relation-ships between soap opera viewing and attitude items appeared. Heavier soap opera viewers made higher estimates of rates of pregnancy and of the need for contraception; they did not differ from light viewers in their attitudes towards premarital sex, adultery or the amount of contraceptive use by females. The discussion does little to disentangle the logic, if any, of these results but claims 'slight ... support for cultivation of sexual issues'. Learning effects, quite possibly; cultivation, in Gerbner's sense – no.

Shrum and O'Guinn (1993) studied accessibility as a possible mechanism for explaining what they persist in calling (before they are demonstrated, or even refuted) 'cultivation effects'. The authors measured subjects' reaction times as they replied to 'various types of cultivation questions'; they found that heavy viewers, who gave higher estimates on these questions also had quicker responses. However, when controlling for speed of response, the relationships between weight of viewing and social perceptions diminished or disappeared. They concluded that accessibility of information 'contributed to the cultivation effect'.

The Annenberg theorists imply that the cultivation effects they claim exist are deeply etched; that is, a couple of weeks' holiday without television, or some other hiatus would be unlikely to remove the impressions of a mean and scary world. Shrum and O'Guinn's foregrounding of the role of accessibility raises a question as to whether the connections they found might be relatively shallow and erasable without regular 'topping up'. There would be other sources of daily experience and other content would become more accessible. In short, the connections they undoubtedly did find might better be described as short-term (though consistently replenished) specific genre effects.

Shrum (1996) more recently examined individuals' estimates of the frequency of real-world crime, marital discord and of certain professionals (doctors and lawyers); all these were found to be over-represented in television in comparison to real life. Total viewing was not significantly related to social perceptions, but soap opera viewing was; the speed at which people replied was related with amount of soap opera viewing, and with social perceptions, but when the speed measure was partialled out (together with several other 'control variables' including grade point average, need for cognition, reading speed, family income and reports of television viewing style), there was still a significant connection between soap opera viewing and social perception. Shrum describes this as accessibility 'mediating the cultivation effect'; but again, what is invoked is not Gerbner's notion of cultivation.

It has begun to be clear in reading these American studies that what had hitherto been called learning effects are now referred to as cultivation ones. The distinction offered by Greenberg (1988) between 'drip' and 'drench' forms of learning is the real one that underlies what these studies are describing. Drip refers to a cumulative learning experience (which may be deep, or shallow, studies of long-term effects remain to be done). The other form of learning, 'drench' has less often been studied, one example being the class of events that are so striking (President Kennedy's death, Mrs Thatcher's resignation) that witnesses recall them vividly so that Greenberg has termed them 'flashbulb memories' (for an account of several such instances, see Wober, 1995).

Pfau *et al.* (1995) made content analyses of the representation of attorneys in network prime time programming, and ran a survey among attorneys themselves and another amongst ordinary viewers. Content-specific viewing was a more powerful predictor than total television viewing on perceptions of five items, but contrary to hypothesis total viewing was a more powerful predictor on one measure. Pfau *et al.* consider that 'those who view more aggregate television perceive attorneys as embodying less character and composure, the exact opposite of the way they are depicted in prime-time television'. This last finding runs counter to the 'purist' cultural indicators expectations, which should be that this essentially power-broking profession should work through television to awe the public.

The hegemonistic view of cultivation assumes that patterns of message content on the established American networks are much the same across genres and accepts as a corollary that patterns of viewing of one or another genre do not reveal anything in particular. It is now clear that this segment of viewing has fallen to 60 per cent in the United States (though it is still above 85 per cent in the UK), and the remainder is self-sought on cable stations or on VCR. Perse *et al.* (1994) tested whether greater use of such autonomy-conferring equipment (including remote control devices) would reduce 'cultivation' of fear and mistrust. They found that while interpersonal mistrust was linked to greater (viewing) of broadcast-type cable channels, both fear of crime and mistrust were lower among those who spent more time viewing more specialized cable channels; fear of crime was also less among VCR owners.

Most studies claiming to deal with cultivation and fear take it that heavier viewing increases personal trepidation; in one area, however, Shanahan (1993) points out that more viewing of 'orthodox' television content is likely to induce the opposite of fear, namely apathy. This area concerns the environment and the argument is that the powerful institutions of commerce are concerned with immediate profit at the price of long-term environmental health; so it is in their interest that television should inculcate confidence. Shanahan reported that among student samples on three occasions from 1988 to 1992 there was a tendency for heavier viewers overall, and also for heavier news viewers to score higher on a scale of environmental optimism; in a fourth sample however, this relationship was absent. Involving a measure of political activism, it emerged that the decrease in environmental concern, along with heavier viewing was steeper among politically active than less active respondents; this was considered evidence of Gerbner's concept of 'mainstreaming'.

Without mentioning cultivation a British study after the San Francisco earthquake (Wober, 1990) is relevant to the above two reports. Questions were asked about the anticipated likelihood of three future negative events (including another earthquake) and three positive ones (including the possibility that ozone lost in the upper atmosphere might be replaced as a result of 'effective international action'). Amount of viewing of television coverage of the recent earthquake correlated positively with apprehension of a new one, but not with two other calamities (increased AIDS, and a new Chernobyl-type accident), and had zero correlation with each of the three positive possibilities. This gives no support for the notion that, at least in Britain, there was 'cultivation' of a false confidence in what Shanahan termed the DSP (dominant social paradigm).

Shanahan *et al.* (1997) next showed that mainstream television messages were neutral or 'apathetic' on environmental matters; overall viewing levels were connected with less environmental knowledge and a greater degree of perceived threat from science and technology. The study can be considered close to a true Cultural Indicators project, as it is aware of the possible role of entrenched business in promoting a message climate that at least does not profess environmental danger; the path along these stages is, however, not wholly in support of the cultivationist view, since although message content was anodyne, it should have followed that perceptions were not correlated in relevant ways with total viewing. However, there was this robust relation between heavier viewing and a feeling that science and technology are bad for the environment. Shanahan and colleagues' discussion is open to the notion (see Wober, 1986) that a personality construct such as locus of control may covary both with heavier viewing and a pessimistic view of science, enough to explain the relation between the two as an artefact.

Summary and discussion

The Cultural Indicators 'project' launched at the Annenberg School of Communications by Professor Gerbner in the 1970s makes firm and important claims in three areas: institutions holding power in the society (business in the USA, possibly an established Church elsewhere, or a family as in some Third World countries – research remains to be done on these possibilities) determine what is the 'Dominant Social Paradigm' in mass message system content. In particular, underlying meanings of portrayals show who has power (men, whites, heterosexuals, middle-aged people) and who is subjugated (women, blacks, gays, old and the very young). Second, such meanings are present across all genres of television, which people watch 'by the clock' indiscriminately as regards choice of programmes or of genres. Third, the more that people watch the screen, the more they imbibe and will express this pattern of meanings.

Relatively few studies have done the institutional analysis needed to corroborate the CI theory. Systems of social regulation of broadcasting still exist in Europe as the century closes, distinguishing this continent from the United States and immediately suggesting that the CI theory is likely to work differently, if at all, in Europe. Not many studies of the contents of mass message systems have been done, either; American studies are relevant to Europe because much material is imported.

There are many studies of effects of mass message system content, and many that adopt the term 'cultivation analysis' as used by the Gerbner team. However, many of these self-termed cultivation studies do not use their own analyses of content patterns, and even fewer refer back to institutional analysis to suggest that the content is instrumental in procuring the effects on the mass public that suit the entrenched institutions. The reasons for this restriction of scope are clear enough; it is expensive enough to carry out an effects study so that few can afford to locate such an effort within the two other frames, of content and of institution analysis. Effects research calls on techniques of applied social psychology, while other skills of sociology and social anthropology are needed to examine the other areas.

Assailed by uses and gratifications, and by active audience theorists who say that people watch what they want and make sense of it in ways that spring from their own natures, so that the chance of hegemonistic effects is small or nullified, the Gerbner group advanced the idea of 'resonance'. This at least takes into account that if the environment transmits the same meanings as does the mass message system, then the chances of these meanings being learned are increased. The Gerbner group have not themselves studied exactly how the effects they claim to occur might come about. An offshoot group, influenced by Hawkins and Pingree at the University of Wisconsin have, however, explored the processes by which people may store, and then retrieve information and impressions which may influence attitudes and ultimately behaviour.

Possibly because they are protected by the umbrella of social regulation of broadcasting systems, Europeans have done localized effects studies but virtually none that can be classed as Cultural Indicators work, since this essentially claims that effects at the mass individual level have to be traced back to influences that entrenched and unregulated powers wish to produce. Nevertheless, uses and effects studies similar to the American cultivation analytic work suggest that people do determine their own viewing diets and meanings to a considerable extent. The one American study available on the consequences of new forms of diversity of hardware and of programming suggests that this may lessen any hegemonistic effects of the 'traditional' national networks. This might encourage those Europeans who welcome 'deregulation'; it might be wiser though to treat this with caution since it will mean an increase of cheap American imported material that may carry certain effects with it.

Note

1. These include frequency and recency viewing, and vividness and distinctiveness of presentations, which affect accessibility; personal characteristics – such as reading speed and grade point average (and though Shrum does refer to traits, he does not elaborate on personality structures – which have been examined in the literature, for example, locus of control, which may modify the formation of fear or aggression – and many other constructs such as extraversion, which have occasionally been woven into effects studies); demographic characteristics, priming of access to cognitions, which can arise from the way an order in which research questions are asked, expectations of or reservations about reality in the screen text, encoding strategies by viewers (who may for example perceive earthquakes as natural disasters and generalize these answers about floods and lightning strikes) and other processes. Curiously, Shrum omits to discuss response set induced by questions all 'in the same direction' and which might in some cases induce 'false' cultivation-style correlations.

References

Boyanowski, E. O., Newtson, D. and Walster, E. (1976) Film preferences following a murder. *Communication Research*, 1, 32–3.

Burns, T. (1977) *The BBC Public Institution and Private World*, London: Macmillan.

Collins, R. (1990) *Television Policy and Culture*, London: Unwin Hyman.

Corner, J., Richardson, K., and Fenton, N. (1990) *Nuclear Reactions: Form and Response in 'Public Issue' Television*, London: Routledge.

Cumberbatch, G. and Negrine, R. (1992) *Images of Disability on Television*, London: Routledge.

Douglas, W. and Olson, B.M. (1996) Subversion of the American family? An examination of children and parents in television families. *Communication Research*, 23(1), 73–99.

Gerbner, G. (1992a) Violence and terror in and by the media. In Raboy, M. and Dagenais, B. (eds) *Media, Crisis and Democracy: Mass Communication and the Disruption of Social Order*, London: Sage.

Gerbner, G. (1992b) Persian Gulf War: the movie. In Mowlana, H., Gerbner, G. and Schiller, H. I. (eds) *Triumph of the Image: The Media's War in the Persian Gulf. A Global Perspective*, Boulder, CO: Westview Press.

Gerbner, G. and Gross, L. (1976) Living with television: the violence profile. *Journal of Communication*, 26, 173–99.

Gerbner, G., Gross, L., Morgan, M. and Signorielli, N. (1994) Growing up with television: the cultivation perspective. In Bryant, J. and Zillman, D. (eds) *Media Effects: Advances in Theory and Research*, Hillsdale, NJ: Lawrence Erlbaum.

Greenberg, B. S.(1988) Some uncommon television images and the drench hypothesis. In Oskamp, S. (ed.) *Television as a Social Issue: Applied Social Psychology Annual*, 8, Newbury Park, CA: Sage, 88–102.

Greenberg, B. S. and Levy, M. R. (1996) Television in the changing communication environment: audience and content trends in U.S. television. *Studies in Broadcasting*, Tokyo: NHK.

Hansen, A. (ed.) (1993) *The Mass Media and Environmental Issues*, Leicester: Leicester University Press.

IIC (1996) *Media Ownership and Control in the Age of Convergence*. London: IIC (in particular, see Schiller, H., 249–64).

ITC (1995) *Independent Television Commission Annual Report and Accounts 1994*, London: ITC.

Jones, C. (1996) Representing reality. *Spectrum*, 21, Spring, 16–19.

Marks, A. M. and Calder, B. J. (1989) *Cultivation and Consumption: Television Exposure and Healthcare Intentions*, University of Cape Town, Graduate School of Business, Working Paper, 89–38.

Morgan, M. (1990) International cultivation analysis. In Signorielli, N. and Morgan, M. (eds) *Cultivation Analysis in Media Effects Research*, London: Sage.

Morley, D. (1992) *Television, Audiences and Cultural Studies*, London: Routledge.

Ogles, R. M. and Sparks, G. G. (1993) Question specificity and perceived probability of criminal victimization. *Mass Communication Review*, 20(1 and 2), 51–61.

Olson, B. (1994) Soaps, sex and cultivation. *Mass Communication Review*, 21(1), 106–13.

Perse, E. M., Ferguson, D. A. and McLeod, D. M. (1994) Cultivation in the newer media environment. *Communication Research*, 21(1), 79–104.

Pfau, M., Mullen, L. J., Diedrich, T. and Garrow, K. (1995) Television viewing and public perceptions of attorneys. *Human Communication Research*, 21(3), 307–30.

Reimer, B and Rosengren, K. E. (1990) Cultivated viewers and readers: a life-style perspective. In Signorielli, N. and Morgan, M. (eds) *Cultivation Analysis in Media Effects Research*, London: Sage.

Reith, M. (1996) The relationship between unemployment in society and the popularity of crime drama on TV. *Journal of Broadcasting & Electronic Media*, **40**, 258–64.

Shanahan, J. (1993) Television and the cultivation of environmental concern: 1988–1992. In Hansen, A. (ed.) *The Mass Media and Environmental Issues*, Leicester: Leicester University Press, 181–97.

Shanahan, J., Morgan, M. and Madson, M. N. (1997) Green or brown? Television and the cultivation of environmental concern. *Journal of Broadcasting and Electronic Media*, **41**(3), 305–23.

Shrum, L. J. (1995) Assessing the social influence of television: a social cognition perspective on cultivation effects. *Communication Research*, **22**(4), 402–29.

Shrum, L. J. (1996) Psychological processes underlying cultivation effects. *Human Communication Research*, **22**(4), 482–509.

Shrum, L. J and O'Guinn, T. C. (1993) Processes and effects in the construction of social reality. *Communication Research*, **20**(3), 436–71.

Sparks, G. G., Sparks, C. W. and Gray, K. (1995) Media impact on fright reactions and belief in UFOs: the potential role of mental imagery. *Communication Research*, **22**(1), 3–23.

Tapper, J. (1995) The ecology of cultivation: a conceptual model for cultivation research. *Communication Theory*, **5**(1), 36–57.

Weimann, G., Brosius, H.-B. and Wober, J. M. (1992) TV diets: towards a typology of TV viewership. *European Journal of Communication*, **7**, 491–515.

Williams, G. (1994) *Britain's Media – How They are Related: Media Ownership and Democracy*, London: Campaign for Press and Broadcasting Freedom.

Wober, J. M. (1978) Televised violence and paranoid perception: the view from Great Britain. *Public Opinion Quarterly* **42**, 315–21

Wober, J. M. (1986) The lens of television and the prism of personality. In Bryant, J. and Zillman, D. (eds) *Perspectives on Media Effects*, Hillsdale, NJ: Lawrence Erlbaum.

Wober, J. M. (1988) *The Use and Abuse of Television: A Social Psychology of the Changing Screen*, Hillsdale, NJ: Lawrence Erlbaum.

Wober, J. M. (1990) *Knowledge in Britain of the San Francisco Earthquake*, London: Independent Broadcasting Authority, Research Report.

Wober, J. M. (1995) The tottering of totems on TV. Some implications of the diffusion of news in Britain. *Communications*, **20**(1), 7–24.

Wober, J. M. and Gunter, B. (1988) *Television and Social Control*, Aldershot: Avebury Press.

7

Critique: meaning, the media and the market

Michael Tracey

One of the few questions really worth asking about the media and society is what the relationship is between the things they purvey and the meanings and understandings that we carry around with us as world views, mental pictures, ideologies, belief systems. How do we understand reality? To what extent do we define meanings for ourselves as against having meanings defined for us by others? And if there is an 'other' doing the defining, who is it, from whence does their influence flow, and what exactly is it that they are defining for us and why?

For some time now – historians of media studies will be more precise as and when, or if, they get around to chronicling this work – some notable authors in the field who have thought about this relationship between the message and the act of thinking got caught up within a delusional state, which imagined that the essential force within the making of meaning was that of the individual who, though washed over by countless messages, had a remarkable capacity to make their own meanings. The whole literature of American cultural studies is littered with this profound error. Stuart Hall decided that it was important to remind us that the members of the audience were not 'dupes', that they had capacities for self-definition and the creation of meaning which denied more determinist views of how mental worlds come into being. In that more recent tradition from within media and cultural studies we have seen the increasing shift away from attempts to understand thought as ideology, from any serious examination of the nature of power within the industrial societies and certainly from any concern with the possibility that while we may not, as audiences, be 'dupes', we are highly vulnerable to a basic social fact that a relatively small group of people are disproportionately able to articulate the ideas and values out of which public 'understandings' will inevitably be fashioned. From this perspective, and in their different ways, the readings in this book are a useful corrective.

There is certainly a proper concern within the work of Herb Schiller for the formation of 'consciousness,' though the term itself is never defined. What he seems to have in mind is the view that the things that people think, their understandings, world view, values, beliefs are to a profound extent fashioned by their experience of cultural messages. This is especially the case in the age of large multinational conglomerates: 'The capability of the private, resource-rich conglomerates to transmit or shift messages and images, capital, currency, production and data – almost at will – constitutes the true levers of contemporary power' (p. 4). There is clearly much here that is obviously true, when the issue is considered from the standpoint of the arrangement of material resources on a global basis. Given the fact that part of those resources involve cultural products, images represented in various forms, he concludes that the 'net effect of such total cultural packages on the human senses is impossible to assess but it would be folly to ignore' (p. 4). An important part of Schiller's thesis is that 'people everywhere are consumers of (mostly) American images, sounds, ideas, products and services' (p. 4). All of which he believes has a 'direct, though immeasurable, impact on human consciousness' (p. 5). It was almost inevitable that he would use the opening of the world's largest McDonald's restaurant in Moscow in 1991, and then later in Beijing as a metaphor for his thesis.

The image of Muscovites and Beijingers ingesting Big Macs was loaded with an obvious other meaning, that they were also taking in all the values of the culture out of which McDonald's had risen. The problem with this lies in the question of whether one can actually make that leap of theory. It is not being overly facetious to say that the fact that beginning in the 1960s Britain saw the opening of increasing numbers of Chinese and Indian restaurants somehow suggested a cultural and ideological transformation of Anglo culture. It may have meant that the total mix of British culture was being added to, but that is very different to a suggestion that the epicureal is a vector for ideological transformation.

There is also a problem with the basic belief that 'people everywhere' are consuming '(mostly) American images'. That is simply not the case. The implicit model which Professor Schiller is using also assumes a relative simplicity and immediacy of consequence, that the structural dynamics of trade will inevitably and necessarily have ideological effects. This is the significance of his statement that 'there is a least one critical difference in the media-informational sphere that distinguishes it from the rest of the for-profit industrial system. This is its direct, though immeasurable, impact on human consciousness' (p. 115). That phrase 'though immeasurable' is revealing because what it is in effect saying is that we are here engaged in an act of faith because one doesn't have to be some crazed positivist to demand some kind of rational and evidential basis to an analytical judgement.

The issue of taste, however, does provide some kind of conceptual basis on which to judge Schiller's arguments, because the problem that needs to be addressed is what is the nature of the demand for, say, American movies in France. The reason why the French political and cultural elite were concerned with American movies is that they were increasingly popular among young people. One might regret that as not in the interest of the integrity of French culture, but it does not mean that one can avoid the question of 'why?'. Was it a case of imposed taste, a pressganging of French youth or are the dynamics more complex and subtle? He points out that anxieties similar to those of the French are evident elsewhere, including the Middle East, without seeming to be too concerned that those objections more often than not emerge from clerical fascist regimes with a deeply repressive attitude to their own people and a deep, intuitive fear that Western imagery may well undermine their hegemonic role.

In this world view human consciousness is, to say the least, malleable. Where, however, Schiller's work is vitally important is in staying true to the notion that we must at least consider the idea of consciousness as something which may indeed be an act of creation towards a particular end. His analysis, however, tends perhaps to lend too much weight to the ability of global capital to completely determine the global mind. At one point he approvingly uses the term 'cultural bondage', forgetting perhaps that there are considerable movements around the planet which are altogether unimpressed by Hollywood. One thinks of, for example, the rise of Islam in the Arab world and the feudal nationalisms of southern Europe.

On first blush Aggrey Brown's idea of looking at how the evolution of the game of cricket as an expression of culture has been impacted by media technologies appears curiously parochial. On second blush, one realizes that it is a brilliant idea, grounding discussions that usually remain somewhat lost in the abstract. He does so by peering within an element of life of the Caribbean which is as important and evocative to its peoples as is, say, ice hockey to Canadians, baseball to Americans, rugby to South Africans, soccer to the English and hurley to the Irish.

Brown's argument is that no part of cricket remains untouched by what he refers to as 'infocom technologies': the game itself, its rules and procedures, its pace and presentation; the players in everything from what they wear, to how much they are paid, to how they are assessed; the spectators in the ground and at home; the administrators, who almost overnight found themselves governing a global game that was not just watched by many millions, but was suddenly big business and, sometimes, even bigger politics.

One of the interesting aspects of Professor Brown's piece is that having traced the various impacts of 'infocoms' on cricket, he does not – as one might have anticipated – utter tones of shock and horror. He celebrates what has happened. He notes, for example, 'Prior to the advent of radio broadcasting, there was no such thing as an audience for the game. There were spectators. With contemporary infocom technologies global audiences have become virtually the *raison d'être* of the game (p. 24).' He then adds, the 'bold use of innovative technologies ensures that TV audiences command a unique view of the game up close from a distance: a view rich in detail and nuance and otherwise quite inaccessible.' In that sense he seems, somewhat refreshingly, to be pointing to the positive benefits that can flow from new communication technologies.

His view is perhaps not unaffected by the fact that what we were witnessing up close from a distance was the almost two decades long dominance of world cricket by his beloved West Indies. Here was technology showing the whole world that the formerly colonized were now colonizing the sport invented and exported, as a powerful symbol of domination, by their former colonial masters. One can't help feeling that Professor Brown is expressing a feeling among his fellow West Indians of technology expressing sweet revenge.

There is, however, for him a beast in the bushes:

while it may be a unique and information-rich view, it is also an increasingly homogenized view. And ultimately that might be the most enduring effect of the media on the culture of cricket and cricket as an expression of culture – its transformation from parochial leisure activity to a form of commercially packaged global entertainment.

(p. 24)

Here is a very specific argument that flows through all such writings as those in this book that an essential effect of the creation of meaning by mediated communications – of whatever kind, old or new – is to create meaning which is not authentic, that is not true to the meanings of a time before.

There is much that is important in the agenda-setting studies, represented here by Professor McCombs, even though one is hardly surprised by the observation that the media have a capacity to lead the public to think about certain issues. Clearly the public mind ebbs and flows with the messages washing over it emanating from a mass media which needs new stories like an alcoholic craves another drink. Remember the great cold fusion debate in which the headlines of the planet were announcing a new, infinite source of energy. Visions of the nuclear winter haunted the popular imagination for a while, to be followed in short order by global warming, a story which shot to prominence when a publicity-minded scientist drew the analogy with a greenhouse and conjured up the image of low-lying locales such as Belgium and New York disappearing beneath waves as the icecaps melted, the seas rose and the land was consumed. Stories of ozone depletion then leapt forward prompting more and more people to use sun block or, in the fashion of Singapore, to sport umbrellas to protect them from the increased celestial radiation. Pit bulls had their moment in the limelight, a four-legged version of the football hooligan, that beer-bellied, tattooed, obscenity-mouthing figure that, for a time, also captivated and occupied acres of newsprint. Iraq's bellicosity and Clinton's alleged promiscuity also had their days of frenzy, in headlines that were flashy and splashy, simple and crude, all echoed in the gossip and chatter of ordinary folk.

In his essay McCombs notes that 'considerable evidence has accumulated that journalists play a key role in shaping our pictures of the world as they go about their daily task of selecting and reporting the news. Here may lie the most important effect of the mass media; their ability to structure and organize our world for us' (p. 27). He adds that through 'their routine structuring of social and political reality, the news media influence the agenda of public issues around which political campaigns and voter decisions are organized' (p. 27). Agenda-setting studies have been useful in pointing to the role the media play in leading us to think about certain things, and thus conversely not to think about other things. What it is less good at, indeed what it doesn't seem to concern itself with, is how people go about thinking of those issues. What, for example, is the relationship between the notion of thinking about this or that issue and the idea of 'consciousness' raised by Professor Schiller, and by which he really means ideology? Should we properly see these as operating at different levels, or does the larger idea of consciousness construct how we will understand the 'issue' once we have been led to think about it?

Innumerable examples come to mind: the Gulf War, or a Single European Currency or welfare or the balanced budget. Clearly many people are thinking about these issues, but in what ways are they thinking and how does that come to be? It is perhaps a larger canvass than only the media which is required if we are to begin to understand these kinds of questions.

The problem of the audience which all of these works address is always a question not of what it knows – which is anyhow usually bitty and picky – but what does it think about what it knows and why? If in terms of our own lives we function within a dependency culture, in which we are dependent on the media for information about the world around us, then what goes on inside, and emerges from, those institutions becomes crucial in understanding the question of what is going on inside the public mind. This is something we have long known but tended to forget in more recent times, particularly within the error that constitutes American cultural studies. It is obvious that if the audience is being provided with 'information' and 'understandings' by the media and that there are what we might call 'errors' within those messages that there will necessarily be errors within the public mind. This is these days not a popular way of looking at how the public thinks. McCombs's essay illustrates the problem. He refers to contingent conditions in which issues will be either obtrusive or unobtrusive, in the former being part of our experience of daily life and in the latter being outside of the parameters of our life. The understandings that we have of an obtrusive issue will therefore not be media dependent, whereas the understandings we have of an unobtrusive issue will to a considerable extent be dependent on the media, a point which was by the way made powerfully by Lippmann in 1922 and Berelson in 1949.

McCombs uses the example of unemployment, with the argument that for a university professor any understanding will tend to be drawn from the media, whereas for a car worker or a steelworker the understanding will flow from the experience of real life. In reality, what the worker knows about why he or she is unemployed may be highly dependent on interpretations offered by the media. If, for example, one looks at the whole discourse about trade unionism in the UK after 1979 it was essentially about creating a construction of 'the problem' of the British economy which had at its heart the problematic nature of the trade unions. That was a necessary part of the process, from the standpoint of capital, of persuading enormous numbers of workers that their unemployment was in the larger interest and indeed that they may have been culpable in their own demise. Thatcher's argument about there being no such thing as society was a necessary part of creating an 'understanding' among the public that would allow them 'to see' unions as dangerous and disruptive, a prerequisite for dismantling them as a source of countervailing power to the Tory government.

In similar vein, McCombs says of inflation and gasoline prices that because we experience them directly we are not dependent for our knowledge of their significance on the news media. What he doesn't consider is that our understanding of the nature of the rise in inflation or gas prices is heavily dependent on the interpretations offered to us through the news media, and those interpretations have proven to be politically highly potent in structuring the pattern of Western industrial politics in the past two decades.

Agenda-setting studies do, however, lead to the understanding that there are clearly some moments, what one might call primal moments, in which the public comes to 'know' something with remarkable speed and forcefulness. Let me offer, as a kind of sidebar, two examples of what I mean, drawn from two inquiries that I currently have underway. The first is about Aids, the second concerns a murder case in Boulder, Colorado.

In the months and years after 1981 the world, it was suggested, faced a fearful new disease, one that struck particularly at young gay men. The immune systems of this very specific population had, it appeared, been trashed by causes unknown. The word plague was increasingly heard. Then on 24 March 1984 Margaret Heckler, Ronald Reagan's Secretary of Health and Human Services convened a press conference in Washington. She announced, 'we have found the cause of Aids', a statement that was likely to get the serious attention of the scores of journalists gathered there to hear her statement. She then announced, pointing to a man who stood behind her, 'and here is Dr Robert Gallo, who found the cause of Aids through his discovery of the virus that is the culprit' and just for good measure she added, 'we are only two years away from producing a vaccine'. Inevitably and immediately the story went around the planet, and where on the 23 March there had been fearful ignorance, now there was 'understanding'. Everyone who cared to read a newspaper, listen to radio or watch television news now 'knew' what caused Aids and could therefore begin to take comfort from the fact that in the wake of defining the cause would follow a discovery of 'the cure'.

The slight problem was that each of the three statements by Heckler was, in effect, a lie: there was absolutely no evidence that the virus identified by Gallo 'caused' Aids or anything else; Gallo did not discover the virus; he stole it from Luc Mantagnier at the Pasteur Institute in Paris (as we know from the Congressional inquiry into Gallo's actions); and there was no sign of any vaccine being developed.

It is not difficult to begin to explain why there was such a readiness to believe Heckler and Gallo: no one present asked Gallo where the scientific evidence had been published – it hadn't; the argument of a viral cause suited those news values that spoke of plague, and was readily understood by a public whose consciousness carries within it an understanding of the devastation of plague that comes from millennia of human development; the realm of science journalism is an utterly dependent and therefore naïve professional culture; a viral cause suited the new gay establishment nicely since the only other serious argument that would explain why gay men were being targeted by the new bug related to the immune suppressant toxicities of recreational drugs that were a key feature of much gay sex, for example, amyl nitrates otherwise known as poppers; a viral cause opened up federal and industry coffers in search of a cure, and there is absolutely nothing quite like a research grant for persuading the men and women in white coats of the brilliance of an initial thesis.

The net result of this confluence of forces was to construct a way of 'seeing' Aids which had, then and some would argue now, absolutely no rational, evidential basis. It was a classic example of the vulnerability of the public mind, fed by an equally vulnerable and innocent mass media. The result, however, is also to inhibit the possibility of seeing in other ways. The reasonable and properly scientific thing to have done would have been to have seen the virus as a possible cause, but to leave open the possibility of there being other causes. That did not happen in 1984 and beyond, just as it did not in so many other instances. 'Knowing' almost always runs ahead of understanding, sometimes so far ahead that the latter can never catch up. The critical question becomes 'why?' but at least part of the answer is that the 'conclusions' of the few – in the case of Aids a crooked scientist, a Reaganite politician, a fearful gay establishment and a lip-smacking pharmaceutical industry – are told to the many. And the many have little choice but to become true believers.

There is another illustration of this point from a very different context. In the early hours of 26 December 1996 JonBenet Ramsey was murdered in her home in Boulder, Colorado. As the story developed it became clear that there was a widespread assumption in the community and beyond that her parents were guilty of the crime. That feeling has unquestionably been sustained among large numbers of people in spite of the clear fact that the evidence that is available in no way points in their direction. It is in this vein interesting to go back to the first moments. In January 1997 the Ramseys gave an emotional interview on CNN during the course of which of which Patsy Ramsey told the people of Boulder, 'keep your babies close by – there's someone out there'. The police chief, Tom Koby, refused to comment, saying that he wasn't going to respond 'to the comments of grieving parents'. The mayor Leslie Durgin, however, in a statement the following day, said that because there was no sign of a break-in at the Ramsey's home, parents should not be concerned that there is a murderer at large. 'It's not like there is someone walking around the streets of Boulder prepared to strangle young children.' She also suggested that the police were not looking for anyone outside of the family.

Her comments were immediately and inevitably taken to mean that the prime suspects were the parents. However, when asked later by one of the defence attorneys what hard evidence she had which would allow her to make the statement, she admitted that she had none and that she had merely wanted to calm the fears of the people of Boulder. Whatever her motives, her comments, picked up by the media and assumed to have a solid basis, almost immediately framed a story, that the parents had done it, which was very quickly embellished to include the notion that the murder had a sexual dimension – an interpretation which gripped and shaped public understanding.

As with the example of the impact of the 1984 Aids press conference, there are a number of reasons as to why the 'understanding' was accepted so powerfully and quickly: authority figures were telling the media, who were telling the public that this is the way it was; there were no available alternative sources of information and explanation that the public could tap into; there is a prevailing cultural disposition to believe that it is possible, even likely, that parents would murder their children as part of a pattern of sexual abuse.

The fact of the matter is, however, that in the primal moment of Durgin's statement a deep-seated 'understanding' of the crime was provided for both the public and the media that was to guide ways of seeing the crime in the ensuing months. As with the Aids press conference the net effect was to inhibit other possible ways of seeing what might have happened.

In his essay, Professor Kellner aligns himself with what he terms, reasonably, 'radicals' such as Chomsky and Herman, Althusser, Schiller and Parenti. He does so on the basis that 'only the radicals have attempted to provide even a rudimentary account of television's place in the system of institutions established in the United States and to analyze its sociopolitical functions and effects' (p. 40). Later in language that has more echoes of Parsons than Althusser he says that

> television has taken on the function of systems maintenance within the structure and dynamics of corporate capitalism and liberal democracy – that is within the dominant economic and political institutions that together constitute techno-capitalist societies in the present age. Accordingly, the development of a theory of television requires one to situate television within a theory of society.

> (p. 42)

What is a little unclear is whether or not Professor Kellner sees this as some conceptual breakthrough. The notion of locating the media industries theoretically within a larger context of social practice and other social institutions is familiar and of long standing. One might point out that the very Centre which is publishing this volume was established on the basis of that very argument. The real difficulty has been in moving to the level of demonstrable praxis, where the significance of the relationships suggested by the idea of context can be defined and explained.

In their analysis of *The Cosby Show*, Jhally and Lewis point to the paradoxical nature of the show's success. In becoming the most successful programme on American television in the 1980s and transforming an African American, Bill Cosby, into a national treasure, *The Cosby Show* was widely regarded as having been a powerful vehicle for legitimizing the presence of Black America within mainstream America: 'Bill Cosby's series, we were inclined to think, had pushed popular culture ever so gently in a positive direction' (p. 50). The authors therefore began their research into the programme with a quite extraordinary assumption that one successful programme could indeed impact and change a society. Their research suggests to them that the actual consequences of the programme rather than being benign and progressive, were, in fact regressive and negative:

> What we discovered, in essence, was that the social and cultural context that gives the show its meaning turns its good intentions upside down. The social success of black TV characters in the wake of *The Cosby Show* does not reflect a trend toward black prosperity in the big, wide world beyond television. On

the contrary, the Cosby era has witnessed a comparative decline in the fortunes of most African Americans in the United States.'

(p. 52)

What they are suggesting is that at the time when Bill Cosby seemed to suggest an upwardly mobile successful, even wealthy black experience, the reality for most black Americans was very different. The problem was that for most white Americans Cosby became held up as illustrating a belief that problems of race and class within American culture had been resolved: 'The Cosby–Huxtable persona [...] tells viewers that, as one respondent put it, "there really is room in the United States for minorities to get ahead without affirmative action"' (p. 53). Their study, they suggest, 'reveals that opposition to affirmative action among white respondents was overwhelming. What was particularly notable was that although most white people are prepared to acknowledge that such a policy was once necessary, the prevailing feeling was that this was no longer so' (p. 53). They then ask, 'why is affirmative action suddenly thought to be no longer necessary? Partly, we would suggest, because our popular culture tells us so.' It does so by creating the general impression that 'racial inequality is behind us; we now live in Bill Cosby's brave new world, where anyone can make it' (p. 54). Therefore, the logic continues, white folk conclude that if someone doesn't make it then it is their own fault rather than being a consequence of systemically generated disadvantage. On this basis, they argue, television 'has pushed our culture backward ... is partly responsible for this lurch backward ... What we end up with, in the apparently enlightened welcome that white viewers extend to the Huxtables, is a new, sophisticated form of racism' (pp. 54–5).

These are large claims, placing on such programmes as *The Cosby Show* considerable social and cultural force, a vehicle for a further potent rendering of the myth of an American Dream which 'is insidious, not innocent.' They continue, the 'ideological dominance of the American dream is sustained by its *massive presence* in popular culture. The TV and film industries churn out fable after fable, reducing us to spellbound passivity.' (p. 57, emphasis added). Here, in a description which is Schillerian in its nature, is the nub of the problem since it reduces the discourse about the articulation of ideology of American life to a rather simple, some might say simplistic, level.

There is a certain consistency, however, when their argument then moves on to suggest that if only there was more innovative and progressive programming on American television then 'mainstream taste' would change: 'mainstream taste cannot significantly change or develop because it is rarely allowed to change or develop' (p. 58). At one and the same time they ascribe enormous power to television and an inherently potential high level of fluidity to the stuff that constitutes taste – images maketh the society, rather than society the images. At the very least this begs the question of how to explain away those societies which historically have had the kind of television culture which the authors seem to have in mind and yet which themselves were mired in precisely the same kind of regressive and conservative thinking which is to them so anathema. Britain, for example, is widely recognized as having one of the more intelligent systems of television in the world. In the early 1980s it also had a new channel, C4, which was seen by many as a veritable laboratory of the radical and the innovative. Yet throughout the 1980s Britain was politically characterized by exactly the same kind of politics of the market and the shrinkage of government that were also characteristic of American political life.

Jhally and Lewis's fundamental argument is, as they put it, that 'our culture is much too important to be left to the lowest common denominator laws of the free market' (p. 59). The implicit logic is that those societies which have television systems which are not driven by the market but, say, by the principles of public service broadcasting, will somehow be 'better', more caring, less likely to believe in, for example, personal culpability for individual economic failure. One really does wonder what the evidence is for this not inconsiderable proposition. What one is left with in reading this account of the *The Cosby Show* is an exaggerated sense of the importance of television in defining the currents of political thought. This is not to suggest that their political analysis is incorrect, merely that their explanation of the aetiology of ideology is a mite underdeveloped.

Mallory Wober presents a detailed examination of the research evidence which may be said to support or refute George Gerbner's 'Cultural Indicators' thesis. A thesis which he summarizes as making

> firm and important claims in three areas: institutions holding power in the society . . . determine what is the 'Dominant Social Paradigm' in mass message system content. In particular, underlying meanings of portrayals show who has power (men, whites, heterosexuals, middle-aged people) and who is subjugated (women, blacks, gays, old and the very young). Second, such meanings are present across all genres of television, which people watch 'by the clock' indiscriminately as regards choice of programme or of genres. Third, the more that people watch the screen the more they imbibe and will express this pattern of meanings.
>
> (p. 70)

Wober is quick to conclude that what is absent from Gerbner's thesis is the detailed understanding of the ways in which institutions go about producing the messages-with-meaning which are so important to certain vested interests; and the detailed examination of the linked moments in which the meaning is transferred, takes on life and form in the mind of the audience member. He points out that in face of evidence that questioned the essential thesis – such as the fact that heavy viewers tend to be of lower socio-economic status and thus live in neighbourhoods which are disproportionately violent – Gerbner developed new ideas such as mainstreaming and resonance.

However, one is constantly left with the feeling – though Wober is too polite to say this – that Gerbner is so convinced of the relatively straightforward deterministic nature of the relationship between the message and the mind, that consideration of the subtleties and complexities of the process border on the boring. This has led Gerbner to avoid – much to the detriment of his work – examination of what one might call the sociology of power and, crucially, the sociology of the audience. At the very least, and to cite but one obvious problem, it is quite clear that there are discriminations in the viewing experience. It is being only slightly facetious to say that if I mapped my own viewing with that of my 10-year-old daughter there is an outside chance that there would be definable differences.

Conclusion

None of this is totally new. In his 1959 essay 'The Cultural Apparatus', published in *The Listener*, C. Wright Mills made a powerful case for the way in which the media and other instruments of culture come between us and 'reality':

> The first rule for understanding the human condition is that men live in second-hand worlds. They are aware of much more than they have person-ally experienced; and their own experience is always indirect. The quality of their lives is determined by meanings they have received from others. Everyone lives in a world of such meanings. No man stands alone directly confronting a world of solid fact. No such world is available. Their images of the world, and of themselves, are given to them by crowds of witnesses they have never met and never shall meet. Yet for every man these images – provided by strangers and dead men – are the very basis of his life as a human being ... Between consciousness and existence stand meanings and designs and communications which other men have passed on. They provide the clues to what men see, to how they respond to it, to how they feel about it, and to how they respond to these feelings ... For most of what men call solid fact, sound interpretation, suitable presentation, every man is increasingly dependent upon the observation posts, the interpretation centres, the presentation depots which in contemporary society are estab-lished by means of . . . the cultural apparatus.
>
> (Mills, 1959, p. 552)

This is not so distant from the way in which Gramsci understood the force of hegemony which proceeds from the assumption that a social group or class that is capable of forming its own particular knowledge and of trans-forming this into general and universally applicable conceptions of the world, becomes the group that exercises intellectual and moral leadership. For Gramsci, reality is perceived and knowledge acquired through moral, cultural and ideological prisms or filters by which the society finds its form and meaning.

The necessary characteristic of a society whose intellectual parameters are provided by the market is that all social action must be boundaryless consumption, and devoid of any countervailing moral structure, espe-cially where such structures might lead to a questioning of the act of consuming. The market cannot be governed by moral strictures, lest they inhibit an essential and continuous expansion that is always primarily in the interests of a relatively tiny elite, and which if it ceases will implode.

This is not a new observation, having been the central concern of the major nineteenth-century social theorists. When Marx said, 'All that is solid melts into air, all that is holy is profaned', what he was referring to was the savage assault on the fundamentals of humanity, the debasement of that which is good by the desiccation of the values by which that good is constructed. If we are reduced to objects of labour, a tiny component of someone else's scheme, then we will behave as objects devoid of the guiding principles of ethical behaviour and democratic impulse. In not dissimilar vein, when Max Weber wrote: 'Man is dominated by the making of money, by acquisition as the ultimate purpose of his life. Economic acquisition is no longer subordinated to man as the means for the satisfaction of his material needs', he was saying that we had confused a social practice, work, which should properly be used to help us be human, that is as means, with something that was an end in itself. That is economic activity became what it is to be human. And that other member of the trinity of great nineteenth-century social theorists, Emile Durkheim, added this thought: 'Industry, instead of being still regarded as a means to an end transcending itself, has become the supreme end of individuals and societies alike.' Elsewhere he noted:

> Precisely because the economic functions of society today concern the greatest number of citizens, there are a multitude of individuals whose lives are passed almost entirely in the industrial and commercial world. From this, it follows that as that world is only feebly ruled by morality, the greatest part of their existence takes place outside the moral sphere.

And where there is no moral system will breed the bacilli of self-absorption, disinterestedness in the well-being of others, no sense of the power of sacrifice, an absence of any discipline other than that provided by the calculativeness of the market:

> Money is concerned only with what is common to all: it asks for the exchange value, it reduces all quality and individuality to the question: How much? All intimate emotional relations between persons are found in their individuality, whereas in rational relations man is reckoned with like a number, like an element which is in itself indifferent.
>
> (Simmel)

In these writings is the clear indication that the nineteenth century was the kindergarten of the twentieth. We can look at their analysis and see a vast amount which just isn't relevant to our own age but which explains much of what we have become. The only difference between now and then is that today there is a kind of hyper-ness, an even greater expansion of the place of the market and economic calculativeness in all our todays. There is barely left a facet of life which is not so influenced, from the boardroom to the schoolroom, from the hospital operating theatre, where life is no longer precious though it does have a price, to the university where performance is arithmetically measured rather than properly judged, to the broadcasting organization where the language is less of art and more of accountancy procedures and unit costs. In very few places is the mantra not one of 'how much?'. The examples are endless. Add them all together and what one has is the utter triumph of the forces which were nevertheless readily observable within the nineteenth century. That triumph is both a function and a consequence of globalization, which is a code word for the emergence of 'stateless' multinational enterprises and the integration of international economic systems. The modern history of globalization begins in the 1950s, though its roots are traceable to the eighteenth century. The result is a world order in which it has been estimated, for example in a recent study of data in *Forbes* magazine, that of the world's 100 largest companies 50 are private.

The essential role which the forces of globalization play is to maintain the centrality of the market, naturalizing the idea that at the heart of human relationships lie principles of calculative exchange. The fact of the matter is that the global economy has moved from a long-standing trade between nations and morphed into a series of institutional forms, most notably multinationals, undergirded by politico-legal entities such as the GATT, the WTO, APEC, NAFTA, and the EU. The global economy, and its courtiers, were, however, created as a consequence of economic action and private interest, rather than as a consequence of political, and specifically democratic, practice. And yet the institutions that constitute or represent the global economy act and make decisions in ways and with consequences which are intrinsically political in nature.

The reason why heresy and heretics are so interesting is that they step outside of the language game, their imagination is not fashioned from within, and by the priesthood of, the orthodoxy. They are different precisely because they offer a different voice, which is also why they must be neutered, marginalized, ridiculed or worse. They speak uncomfortable thoughts and utter troubling ideas and all the while in doing so provide a litmus test of the strength of the orthodox. Where it is powerfully naturalized they can be dismissed with a smirk or wry amusement as would be a Leninist at Hyde Park Corner calling for the renationalization of the banking industry. Where, however, the orthodox is built of plywood not oak, the relationship with the heretical voice is very different, more likely to be brutal as with a bloodied square in China.

In their various ways the chapters in this book are properly struggling with the need to get back to an understanding of the way in which the media function in our lives which at least allows for the fact of differentiated power in human relations. In that sense they are engaged in the rediscovery of the force of ideology at the end of the twentieth century. For that we should be extremely grateful.

References

Berelson, B. (1949) What missing the newspaper means. In Lazarsfeld, P. F. and Stanton, F. (eds) *Communication Research 1948/49,* New York: Duel, Sloan & Pearce, 111–29.
Lippmann, W. (1922) *Public Opinion,* New York: Harcourt Brace.
Mills, C. W. (1959) The cultural apparatus. *The Listener* **61**(1565), 552–3, 556.

Section 2

Individuals, impacts and influences

8

Media violence: four research perspectives[1]

Cecilia von Feilitzen

Within the field of mass communication research considerable resources have been invested, particularly in the United States, in studies of the effects of entertainment violence on the individual. Researchers, like policy-makers and participants in the public debate, have concentrated on the manifest physical (and sometimes on the verbal) violence shown on television and in film. Studies of violence in other media are less common. Above all, researchers have focused on possible causal effects in the form of aggression and violent actions among children and adolescents.

Even if this traditional media violence research has given certain well-founded results (see below), it has been criticized as too limited by many researchers who also wanted to redefine the research problem to find more relevant answers. In this chapter international and Nordic examples of such redefinitions will be presented. The aim of the chapter is to show that, over time, the redefinitions have become frequent. Especially from the 1980s onwards it was no longer reasonable to talk about *one* perspective within media violence research. The research is not, however, always empirical but often explores ontological, epistemological, theoretical, and methodological outlooks and critical questions.

Here, four main perspectives will be put forward, according to the researcher's starting point on what, to oversimplify a little, is most determining for the importance of media violence: *media violence itself*, *culture*, *the audience*, or *the power relations in society*.

Perspective 1: the effects of media violence – the traditional model and its further development

Traditional research on media violence and aggression is based on theories which assume that aggression originally arises via cultural learning and/or frustration (but hardly ever on theories of human aggression as biologically innate or as a psychic internal instinct). It further assumes that media violence is the cultural learning factor. Traditional aggression studies carried out up to and including the 1970s arrived at the following results:

- Violent actions in the media can lead to imitation among younger children. In a similar vein but to a much lesser extent young people and adults can copy 'tips' on how to perform violence. But even if media contents often activate, in particular, younger children to say, do, or play something of what they have seen, these impulses are most often short term. And while imitation can be modelling, this does not mean that one has incorporated conceptions, norms, and values that lead to an intentional action.

- Media content seldom has a direct or sole influence on our actions. We get instead from the media mental impressions that are mixed with other conceptions, norms, values, feelings, and experience from our own practice, and from family, school, peer groups, and so on – impressions of much greater importance – that, taken together, increase or diminish the disposition to act. In this indirect and most often reinforcing way, in interplay with the more important factors, entertainment violence contributes in some measure to increased *aggression* in the short term for certain individuals under certain circumstances.

- Mass communication research has not been able to discern any corresponding causal relation between entertainment violence and violent crimes. Criminologists, also, find completely different factors from media essential (e.g., Hurwitz and Christiansen, 1983).

During the 1980s and 1990s considerable resources continued to be spent on analysing the influence of TV violence according to this traditional approach, but the perspective has also widened. Even though short-term effects are still studied, a characteristic trait of more recent investigations is that they are made up of longitudinal field studies (often initiated in the 1970s), in which the same individuals have been followed in order to analyse causal relations in the long term. Furthermore, several new theoretical assumptions have been developed about the mental processes that lie behind or facilitate aggression. Neither is media studied in isolation or in a vacuum as often as it used to be, but the role of family, school, and peers is increasingly observed.

What the long-term studies indicate, in sum, (e.g., Milavsky *et al.*, 1982; Huesmann and Eron, 1986; Viemerö, 1986; Sonesson, 1989) is that the viewing of entertainment violence seems to explain at the most 5–10 per cent of children's and young people's aggression over time (one to ten years or more), while at least 90–95 per cent of the aggression is dependent on other factors: the child's and adolescent's personality, capacities, and earlier aggression; conditions in family, school, and peer groups; sociocultural background and societal conditions (although the latter have not been empirically studied). Thus, the entertainment violence plays in the long (as in the short) run only a contributory role and emerges as a faint reinforcement of a syndrome caused by other far more important circumstances.

Moreover, certain longitudinal studies point to a reciprocal causal relation, a circular or spiral effect: the case is both that more aggressive children and adolescents seek entertainment violence, and that the entertainment violence reinforces the aggression. But, accordingly, in this interaction the latter causality appears somewhat stronger.

As well as the development towards longitudinal studies, and more

sophisticated and widened theories of aggression and socialization processes, other effects have been more studied within the traditional
approach, and many researchers underline that these are more relevant
than aggression.

Traditional violence research has, during recent years, also examined
new media, like horror, gore and splatter videos; violent music videos;
computer games based on aggression and the player's active participation; as well as violent representations on Internet. However, this research
is often similar to the earlier short-term TV and film research and is as yet
in its infancy.

Critical question: what is aggression?

'Aggression' means an attack. Attacking societal evils, defending oneself
against oppression, and applying aggression to meaningful activity are
examples of constructive aggressive acts; submission and inhibited
aggression would in such cases be something negative. In public debate
and in research, however, aggression has become a negatively loaded
concept. What is referred to is, in fact, destructive aggression – for
example, injuring without a conscious end or assaulting and oppressing
in order to maintain or strengthen a superior position. Similarly, there are
problems with the concept of 'violence'. Some violence, albeit not very
much, can have positive consequences (as when smashing crockery
relieves a person of her or his aggression).

The traditional studies of media violence would, then, be more fruitful
if they were to leave the composite notion of aggression and in exchange
were to differentiate between (a) constructive aggression, violence with
positive consequences, and aggression that is a defence or a struggle
against oppression; and (b) destructive aggression, negative consequences
of violence, and aggression that is really oppression.

Several studies are very vague on whether they concern aggression in
the form of feelings or actions. Likewise, research has emphasized physical aggression, with the consequence that the measured or found aggression often is higher among boys than girls, among working-class
children/adolescents than middle-class ones, or among adolescent gangs
compared to adults. But physical aggression may partly depend on
gender differences, and on class and generation conflicts in society; partly
it may be a way of expression that is more useful in boys'/working-
class/young people's intercourse and culture. At the same time this
aggression may be only apparently higher – girls, members of the middle
class, and adults, respectively, tend to express their aggression in other
ways, not least verbally (including being silent).

Critical question: can other media content contribute to aggression?

Traditional research can be criticized not only for its biased definition of
aggression, but also because only in exceptional cases has it dealt with
influences on entities other than the individual, for instance, on groups,
politics, industry, culture in a wide sense, societies, animals, and nature.

Furthermore, it has focused on manifest physical (sometimes verbal) entertainment violence. Thus, even if there are exceptions, the effects research is meagre regarding realistic, psychic, structural, and latent violence. Moreover, energy has been directed towards popular culture and not towards high culture in media output.

For a long time some researchers have wondered whether violence is really required in the programme or film for viewers to become more aggressive. The theory of emotional arousal, or the instigation theory, which is empirically supported by studies with adults, points to the possibility that any media content that is found exciting or inspires strong feelings, reinforces the viewer's mood prior to viewing (aggression, depression, erotic disposition, etc.). This leads in the short run to more intensive behaviour corresponding to that very mood (Tannenbaum, 1980).

Another assumption with empirical support is that sustained viewing of programmes where the tempo is very fast contributes to aggressive and uneasy behaviour, so-called hyperactivity, among young children (Singer and Singer, 1983).

A third hypothesis is that a great deal of the entertainment media output as a whole contributes to increased expectations in the viewer about a more glamorous life-style, expectations that cannot be fulfilled for all groups due to their relative deprivation in society. The result may be frustration, which in its turn can be a cause of aggression (e.g., Halloran *et al.*, 1970a). Such a possible influence of the media is reinforced by a societal development that is also built on steadily increasing expectations – societies that emphasize increased production, increased consumption, achievement, and individual competition, in spite of the fact that different groups have different economic, social, and cultural possibilities of realizing such goals (von Feilitzen, 1975).

The assumption that entertainment output in general might lead to frustration and aggression is, in fact, in the light of criminal statistics, more plausible than the assumption that media violence does so. For example, since the 1960s Sweden has had a relatively slight increase in the number of violent crimes. On the other hand, we have had a substantial increase in theft and other economic crimes (Svensson, 1985; Sarnecki, 1988).

Perspective 2: the power of culture

During the 1960s and 1970s, some researchers generally came to view media output as a cultural or symbolic environment, thus reflecting the values and/or myths of society. This cultural environment – which, according to Williams's definition (1974), is sometimes thought of as a flow – in turn has power over, nourishes, or exerts long-term influences over culture as a whole. That is, the cultural environment also means a lifelong contributory cultivation of individuals' common world views, ideas, norms, and values. This view is rooted in the critical theory of the Frankfurt school, Gramsci's theory of hegemony, and theories of structuralism, semiotics, linguistics, and anthropology, among others. It opposes the concentration of traditional research on specific effects of certain media contents on specific individuals.

Media contents generally may, for example, be regarded as a ritual, cultural narrative according to linguistic conventions and genres. The myths being told symbolize the collective discomforts and pleasures of human, subcultural, and national character (people's problems, conflicts, anguish, uneasiness, fear, fantasies, wishes, hopes, dreams, needs of identification).

More empirically based research is represented by Gerbner and his colleagues (e.g., Gerbner *et al.*, 1986; Signorielli and Morgan, 1990), who, through their Cultural Indicators approach and cultivation analyses, have performed continuous content analyses of the violence on US TV dramas and correlated them with studies on children's and adults' conceptions. The results indicate that the audience can get exaggerated ideas of the amount and kind of violence in society. Such erroneous conceptions can, in their turn, give rise to fear in the viewer of becoming a victim of violence her- or himself – when walking alone in parks, and the like – as well as to a pessimistic outlook that it is impossible to trust people and that the state of things in the world is just getting worse. This might, further, lead to more support for law and order and increased dependence on authorities.

In spite of the fact that the cultivation analyses, in particular, have been criticized methodologically, Gerbner-inspired research has been performed in many countries. These studies have sometimes yielded divergent results, perhaps partly due to national differences (e.g., Wober and Gunter, 1988). In Sweden, for example, the amount of TV or video viewing generally has not been linked to audience fear, but identification and parasocial interaction during TV viewing seem to reinforce exaggerated conceptions of violence in real life in young people (Hedinsson, 1981; Wall, 1987).

Cannot news violence, as well, influence conceptions of violence in real life? In Sweden many adolescents overestimate the number of real murders and manslaughters (while they underestimate the number of traffic accidents), and believe, too, that violence among young people has become more brutal – probably as a result of how the violence is presented in the news (Wall, 1987). Press and TV news often greatly exaggerates how violent the world is (e.g., Halloran *et al.*, 1970a). According to this perspective, then, culture defines for the people both the violent events that are important and how the events should be interpreted. Fictional and non-fictional violence appear to contribute to public opinion that reinforces the interests of the dominating strata of society and legitimizes their means of control.

Latently embedded in the violence-as-entertainment, however, there is another kind of victimization (Gerbner, 1980; Signorielli, 1986). In US TV programmes there is a pecking order that includes those who commit the violence and those who are subjected to it. At the top, among the assailants, there are white male adults; at the bottom, among the victims, are women, black people, members of the working class, poor people, elderly people, children, and adolescents. Thus, the dramatized commission of violence seems, as a matter of fact, to reflect the societal hierarchy of power. This, too, indicates that TV is a cultural control of society that has a function of maintaining social order.

Critical question: are the effects of media violence and the power of culture always something negative?

The dramatized and the true-to-life media violence, or the reflection of a hierarchy of power in a culture, ought to give the audience insight into the causes and consequences of violence/power in society and, in this way, contribute to *realistic conceptions, democratic norms* and *values*, and *constructive actions*. In all likelihood such cultural contents with positive influences exist, although traditional media violence research, as well as the research on the power of culture, have focused on negative consequences.

Another positive influence is *excitement*. Violence, hatred, and death – and power, fame, and money – are, like love, important phenomena for human beings and therefore exciting. They have a dramatic value in themselves, which agrees with the audience's preferences, needs, and identification. They are particularly exciting if they are portrayed dramatically – as conflicts or struggles with threats and obstacles – and if they mean testing where the limits are, for example defying something forbidden or showing what the characters are ultimately able to do, dare, and can endure.

It is, however, wrong to believe that entertainment violence as such always gives rise to feelings of excitement. The human being's (genuine) need for excitement is not the same as an (alleged) need for entertainment violence. Other TV programmes, apart from those with entertainment violence, are sometimes felt to be more exciting. This can be valid for, e.g., sports, other fiction, erotic programmes, quizzes, and news (Berg and von Feilitzen, 1979; Pearl *et al.*, 1982).

Excitement and fear are emotions along the same dimension, at least if one believes Spinoza's ([1678] 1959) analysis of the contents and mutual connections of different feelings. He would have called (positive) excitement hope with a little strain of fear. Negative excitement (fear), on the other hand, consists, according to Spinoza, of fear with a little strain of hope. It is also shown empirically that the kind of media contents that children and adolescents like because they are exciting, are often the same as those that are frightening. Children and young people want to be a *little* frightened – but cannot always foresee when the unwieldy fear gets out of control (von Feilitzen, 1989a).

The ability to be afraid is a biological gift, a condition of survival. Accordingly, more genuine fear, as well, can have positive consequences, for instance when it makes us guard ourselves against – and fight – real external dangers like accidents, assaults, and outrages of power. It is also conceivable that media fear is positive in another way – if the symbolic vicarious experience of fear relieves the individual of real inner agony, that is, raises unconscious and tabooed conflicts and problems to a more conscious level, which, then, the media content or the individual indirectly can work upon. Such hypotheses about catharsis (purification), which appear in the next part of this chapter, come from Aristotle's ideas on the Greek tragedy ([3rd century BC] 1994), from Bettelheim's (1975) view of folktales, and from psychoanalysis. Catharsis on a societal level may be imagined, too, if the media reproduction of myths of violence and power relations releases human fantasy, treats collectively experienced problems, and functions as ritual in an anthropological sense. There are no empirical data, however, that support the hypothesis of catharsis being the decisive influence.

Neither has the mass communication theory that posits cathartic effects for the individual when it comes to *aggression* – that the vicarious experience of viewing entertainment violence relieves the viewer from prior aggression so that she or he becomes *less* aggressive after viewing (Feshbach, 1955, 1961; Feshbach and Singer, 1971) – received much empirical support. However, perhaps much *smaller* cathartic effects can occur, even though they neither neutralize other influences nor are the most common influence of entertainment violence.

Quite another thing is the fact, mentioned above, that aggression as such (that is, *more* aggression) in certain cases can be something positive. Also, *imitation* of violent acts can sometimes be desirable, especially for small children. Imitation and play are fundamental factors in the socialization process, that both function as a working upon, and freeing oneself from, impressions, and as a learning of things. Thus, even if imitation sometimes means learning by modelling (negative impact), imitation is, from the view of treating impressions, now and then necessary (positive impact) for children after watching entertainment violence (von Feilitzen, 1989a).

Perspective 3: the active audience

Traditional media violence research and the perspective of the powerful culture have been criticized for looking upon media output as too homogeneous, media and cultural influences as too negative, and the receiving individual as too passive. A contributory cause, it is said, is that the studies seldom have been deep and qualitative with smaller groups for whom the media are of more or less importance. The media may have an agenda-setting function (McCombs and Shaw, 1972), defining for the audience what to think and talk about – but not *how* to think about it. A great deal of empirical research shows that individuals, both adults and children, are active in the process. Each person selects media contents according to her or his specific aims, pays attention to it, comprehends and remembers what is useful and has a meaning to her or him, and interprets it in her or his own special way. The individual is creative and partly construes her or his own media content according to gender, sociocultural background, experience, interests, expectations, and needs, as well as through stronger or weaker imagination, identification, and emotional engagement. Family, peer groups, preschool, school, work, and various interested parties are often more essential than the media, and also often the purpose for which media contents are used, what import is put into them, and which underlying meanings are perceived. The texts (media contents) are read (watched) on the basis of socially formed conventions and codes, but readers (viewers) of different subcultures may, thus, decode other meanings, in oppositional or negotiating ways, than those encoded (Hall, 1980).

The British audience, for example, interprets American and British media violence differently in several respects (Gunter and Wober, 1988). The fact that social class, membership of an ethnic group, as well as having been victim of violence oneself also greatly influence the significa-tion and experience of violent media representations is illustrated by a study with women (Schlesinger *et al.*, 1992). For instance, women who had been subjected to domestic violence found comparable scenes on televi-sion violent and disturbing, and had no sympathy with the perpetrators, whereas other women could understand the perpetrators' actions and gave more attention to other themes than violence in the programmes.

Due to different personal interpretations and cultural competencies among audiences, the media culture does not – from this perspective – appear so homogeneous, and is, consequently, not such a strong negative factor or such a powerful exerciser of cultural control.

Not least within the humanities, which earlier mostly paid attention to high culture or analysed the ideology of popular culture critically, popular culture has, during the 1980s and 1990s, been studied from the perspective of the active audience and their positive usage of it. The starting points include literary theory, reception theory, film theory, aesthetics, cultural history, anthropology, structuralism, linguistics, semi-otics, and psychoanalysis. A certain amount of this media violence research means drawing conclusions from textual analysis about the readers' use of the text and the needs it fulfils. Other research includes empirical qualitative (ethnographic, ethnomethodological) studies of readers' reception. But quantitative and/or social scientific studies are also at hand.

Among other things, researchers have tried to understand the fascina-tion of media violence. One hypothesis (among many) is that in the Age of Enlightenment and Reason, above all in our postmodern, rational society, we are allowed to give expression to our sadistic instincts, or aggressive impulses, less often than people were in earlier periods, for which reason the aggressive inclination now has increasingly been attached to media viewing (Hartwig, 1988; Gripsrud, 1989). This process can also be expressed in other words: civilization, that allows people to fight for one's own country against another one, demands that the individuals in everyday life discipline their dark sides – sides that nevertheless are there and therefore can be treated fictitiously in media form. At the same time, many violent pictures of today have their roots in historical myths, folk tales and classical drama.

Another assumption is that adolescents' viewing of film and video horror is a ritual of initiation, which on a deeper level means treatment of bodily and erotic crises of puberty, the feeling of isolation, psychic iden-tity seeking, powerlessness against parents and school, and feelings of hatred and revenge for the oppression exercised by adults and bullying peers (Sjögren, 1985).

Moreover, there is empirical support for the finding that TV viewers, children as well as adults, all within the frame of normality, often select programmes to regulate their emotional state. One reason for choosing action and exciting programmes is boredom. For instance, adults with monotonous and tedious work (more often working class) choose action on television to decrease their weariness, whereas those who return home stressed (more often middle class) select more restful programmes to reduce the overstimulation (Zillmann, 1980; Zillmann and Bryant, 1986). Psychological needs are involved here, too. Individuals who are attracted by horror films have higher than average needs for emotional and social stimulation in the form of, e.g., risk taking and internal sensation (Lawrence and Palmgreen, 1996).

A sub-cultural stream of the research on the active audience starts from the total life situation of children and young people. Media and media contents, popular culture and popular music especially, are included as important ingredients, symbols and signs of children's and adolescents' own everyday practices and learning processes – in play and identity work, cultural forms of expression, development of life-styles, and social acting. Also, the usage of media is related to sociocultural conditions, and the individual's cultural practices can sometimes signify protest and resistance that emancipatorily counteract dominant ideologies of media, family, school, and so on. This view is rooted in, e.g., West German socialization theory, British cultural studies, the uses-and-gratifications model, and a structural–cultural approach that combines traditional socio-economic differences with new hierarchic differences caused by the explosion of education and cultural capital.

Among other things, interviews with 15- and 16-year-olds have revealed that viewing of violent and horror videos may be a way of measuring toughness, a test of manliness in the circle of male peers, and also a countercultural manifestation of protest, as a consequence of low marks in and negative attitudes to school. The latter result is valid, as well, of special youth groups' adoption of less socially accepted forms of music – such music as adults or 'mainstream' adolescents find hard to understand (Roe, 1983, 1984; Holmberg, 1988). Male adolescents' interest in violent computer games has been interpreted in a similar way. Young boys live in a subordinated and powerless situation in society. Playing violent computer games means exercising resistance, giving expression to one's masculinity, and creating power and control – on a symbolic level (Jensen, 1993). Media violence can, thus, sometimes and in various manners, play a role in identity-seeking, in a feeling of group-belonging, opposition, and growing up.

It ought to be underlined that since this media violence research has directed its energy on sub- and countercultures, mainly male and not female cultures have been observed. Watching films with extreme violence on TV, video, and in the cinema, as well as playing computer games, are chiefly male occupations. The culture of violence is to a great extent built on male values.

Critical question: what happened to the overall view?

Research on the active audience has constructively criticized perspectives that are too one-sided. At the same time, however, it has a tendency – even if the causes of aggression and violence are mainly to be found outside the media and culture – to ignore the fact that media output and culture nevertheless have influences (sometimes negative) in the short and long term. In all likelihood, the individual is both active, selective, treating and creative *and* positively and negatively influenced by the environment (of which the media are a part). Moreover, even though the third research perspective underlines the fact that the sociocultural situation plays a role in the usage of media, it disregards the fact that the communicators, the institutions, and the economy behind the popular products impinge upon the spread and use of popular culture. Furthermore, it does not deal with the question of whether other economic and political forces in society exert an influence on media violence and culture.

Thus, the perspective of the active audience has a tendency to be too one-sided; it often places itself on a microlevel and overemphasizes individualism and freedom of human acting. In addition, in its most simplified form it starts solely from the viewer's subjective opinions and needs. According to Rönnberg (1989), for example, good culture is culture that the user likes and finds good use for; if children do not perceive the violence, then it is not violence. This populism too easily agrees with the selling argument of the entertainment industry: 'We give people what they want.'

Carey (1978) says that different theories and results may be valid for different periods and societal circumstances. The fact that many now stress the individual's activity might, accordingly, not only be a counter-reaction to other research perspectives, but also be a consequence of the individual's greater independence in today's changing and flexible society. It could also be, however, that the *view* in itself of the individual as active and creative is functional for societal development. A high-technology, changing society urgently needs independent, mobile individuals who can cope with choice among the contradictory pluralistic value systems. A theoretical view does not always tell what the whole is like. In other words, it *might* be that the researchers, due to the character of society, more or less unconsciously overemphasize the individual's activity.

Perspective 4: economy and power relations in society

Some researchers emphasize the economic, technological, political, and other material conditions in society, as well as the conditions of media production, direct culture and media contents; owning and power are thus, in their view, more fundamental and decisive factors in the communication process than specific media contents (e.g. media violence), culture, or single viewers' actions. Thus, research on media violence becomes distorted if it does not also ask questions about the policy-making process of the media and the political and economic institutions and control agencies that feed and sustain the media (Murdock, 1982).

Emphasis on economy and power relations as basic forces, means, among other things, research on media organizations in a social context. Such studies point, for example, to the fact that popular culture and entertainment violence turn over so many services and products that their primary function is to maintain the financial balance in the mass communication system, which is tightly integrated into the economy of the whole society (e.g., DeFleur, 1966). Other analyses show that the economic structure and technological development of the media industry are related to the military, space, computer and telecommunication industries, transnational enterprises, and the rest of world trade – an economic development that means that various big companies producing weapons, cars, electronics, foods, etc., are those which have the principal interest in disseminating entertainment violence in the industrialized and Third World countries (e.g., Schiller, 1976). An analysis of the reasons why the extensive research on media violence has not been able to make the media industry in the United States reduce entertainment violence, indicates that partly the violence is a question of cultural values rooted in the whole of American society, and partly the result of powerful economic factors that steer the industry (Rowland, 1983).

As entertainment violence is economically functional for society, it legitimizes the activity of the media. Media violence might be functional for society in other respects as well. Another research approach within this fourth perspective takes content analyses as a starting point, not for further studies about influences on the audience but for studies about media production or societal conditions. For instance, several studies of entertainment violence, and of media representations of non-fictional crimes, terrorism, wars, political violence, citizens' conflicts, racism, and other news violence, have led to conclusions about the policy and roles of media organizations, journalists and producers. One finding is that 'official' violence, that which is sanctioned and initiated by state and society, has direct parallels with the 'official' view of violence within the media institutions (e.g., Schlesinger et al., 1983; Gerbner, 1988).

Also, content analyses mentioned earlier in this chapter showed that media representations of violence at an overall level reflect the power hierarchy in society and in so doing appear to legitimize and reinforce it, stabilize economic structures, and are in line with the objectives of established groups and institutions.

Analyses of violence and power in the media and culture can be particularly fruitful if comparisons of media outputs and cultures are made between nations and in an historical perspective. Why is it, for instance, that in Japanese television entertainment, compared to that of the United States, the hero is more often subject to violence, and the suffering is shown more clearly and for a longer time? In US TV entertainment the subject of violence is more often the villain, and the consequences of violence are shown to a much lesser extent or not at all (Iwao et al., 1981). Why is the violence in American detective stories on TV committed between two or few individuals, and the motives for murder almost exclusively to get hold of money or things (Nordlund, 1977)? While American entertainment violence is individual and connected to personal success, achievement, and private property, the violence in ex-Soviet drama programmes during the 1970s was more often committed collectively and in order to support or destabilize society (Pietilä, 1976). Why are American programmes more violent than, for example, European and Nordic ones, and why is it that the entertainment programming exported over the globe emanates chiefly from the United States (Nordenstreng and Varis, 1974; Varis, 1985; UNESCO, 1989)? Why has entertainment and news violence on, for instance, Norwegian and Swedish public service TV increased between the 1970s and 1990s, at the same time as commercial channels show even more violence (Vaagland, 1979; Hellbom, 1982; Bøthun et al., 1991; Höijer, 1994; Cronström and Höijer, 1996)?

One explanation may be that the violence is produced, imported and presented in different cultural contexts, and that the function is to reinforce the norms and values of the society in question. However, cultural or symbolic violence does not only have different meanings in different nations and epochs, and different ways of glorifying and condemning violence are not only due to different cultural intentions – but also are due to economy, technology, politics, and powerful groups in society and the media (Golding and Middleton, 1982). Increasing news violence is, for example, also a consequence of the augmenting competition between TV channels, and of the fact that production and distribution techniques are easier to handle nowadays (Berg, 1994; Liblik, 1994).

An economic, political, and cultural elite dominates media institutions as well as media output – both through its presence and its ideology – *because* it has a stronger economic position in society, greater political power, and more extensive cultural influence. With another economy and other power relations, culture would, consequently, be different. In the interplay between media violence, culture, the individual, as well as the economy and power relations in the society, the latter are, after all, the motor of the changes – those who divide, among other things, the manifestations, functions, and influences of media violence and media power (von Feilitzen, 1989b).

Concluding remarks

The fourth perspective can, naturally, be questioned. Is it reasonable to lay so much stress on materialistic conditions in society and so little on the violent media representations in themselves, on power or hegemony of culture, and on the needs, intentions, tastes and life situations of various audiences? A consequence of this perspective is that direct action against media violence – for instance, information to the audience, policy-makers, producers, and other interest groups; media education in the school and in the home; ethical and practical regulation of the media (whether legal or self-determined); and production of alternative media contents without violence – cannot bring about any radical changes but only minor ripples on the surface. If one really wants to address the problem, one must, instead, intervene against economy, ownership, and other power factors prevailing in media organizations and society.

But this discussion will not be developed further, since in a way we have returned to the beginning. Media violence research has been criticized for not asking the right questions. However, this chapter has shown that during recent decades researchers have found more than one way of asking about and looking upon the meanings, functions, and influences of media violence.

Research findings on media violence often seem to be contradictory. However, the fact is that various studies have different questions and perspectives as starting points – and therefore elucidate different parts of reality. Often the perspectives and the findings complement each other in an interesting way, like pieces in a jigsaw puzzle. The pieces imply, too, that we all get impressions from or are influenced by media violence – but in various ways. The research perspectives dealt with in this chapter further indicate that if research of the 2000s is to better comprehend the import of media violence and achieve more practical results, it must be directed by an overall view, that is, it must theoretically embrace media violence as well as the power of culture, the active audience, and the economy, power relations, and media technology in society. It must, therefore, combine teleological understanding and causal explanations, and quantitative and qualitative methodology. It must also leave the simplified notion of 'entertainment violence' aside and realize that the borderlines between fictional and non-fictional media violence are often blurred and sometimes non-existent, and that all kinds of media violence are cultural or symbolic constructions. In particular, future research must regard the question of media violence as a process that varies in time and space. International, comparative, and diachronous studies between different countries and periods ought to be carried out, and the results would be clearer if the analyses are performed in parts of the world where great changes are occurring.

Notes

1. This is a revised and updated version of Feilitzen, C. von (1994) Media violence: research perspectives in the 1980s. In Hamelink, C. J. and Linné, O. (eds) *Mass Communication Research: On Problems and Policies*, Norwood, NJ: Ablex.

References

Aristotle ([3rd century BC] 1994) (*Peri Poietikes*, chapter 6) *Aristoteles – om diktkonsten. Översättning av Jan Stolpe*, Göteborg: Anamma böcker.

Berg, H. (1994) *Tror du inte att bilderna är sanna, eller? En studie av hur journalister på TV4:s Nyheterna resonerar kring våldsskildringar i nyhetprogram*, Stockholm: Department of Journalism, Media and Communication.

Berg, U. and Feilitzen, C. von (1979) *Metodstudie om spännande program*, Stockholm: Sveriges Radio, Publik- och programforskningsavdelningen, no. 19.

Bettelheim, B. (1975) *The Uses of Enchantment: The Meaning and Importance of Fairy Tales*, London: Thames & Hudson.

Björkqvist, K. (1985) *Violent Films, Anxiety and Aggression: Experimental Studies of* the Effect of Violent Films on the Level of Anxiety and Aggression in Children, Helsinki: Commentationes Scientiarum Socialium, no. 30.

Bøthun, B., Finsrud, E., Hesjedal, O. and Isrenn, K. (1991) *TV-vold på 6 skandinaviske kanaler*, Bergen: Universitetet i Bergen, Institutt for massekommunikasjon.

Carey, J. (1978) The ambiguity of policy research. *Journal of Communication* **28**(2), pp. 114–19.

Cronström, J. and Höijer, B. (1996) *40 timmar i veckan – en studie av våld i sex svenska TV-kanaler*, Stockholm: Våldsskildringsrådet, no .14.

DeFleur, M. (1966) *Theories of Mass Communication*, New York: David McKay.

Feshbach, S. (1955) The drive-reducing function of fantasy behavior. *Journal of Abnormal and Social Psychology*, **50**(1), 3–11.

Feilitzen, C. von (1975) *Children and Television in the Socialization Process*, Stockholm: Swedish Broadcasting Corporation, Audience and Programme Research Department, No. 28.

Feilitzen, C. von (1989a) Spänning, rädsla, aggression och våld. In von Feilitzen, C., Filipson, L., Rydin, I. and Schyller, I. *Barn och unga i medieåldern: fakta i ord och siffror*, Stockholm: Rabén & Sjögren, 188–208.

Feilitzen, C. von (1989b) Ungdomar som problem, ideal och identitetssökare. Synen på ungdomar i mediekulturen. In Wulff, H. (ed.) *Ungdom och medier: klass, kommersialism och kreativitet*, University of Stockholm, Centrum för masskommunikationsforskning, MASS 17, 87–110.

Feshbach, S. (1961) The stimulating versus cathartic effects of a vicarious aggressive activity. *Journal of Abnormal and Social Psychology*, **63**(2), 381–385.

Feshbach, S. and Singer, R. D. (1971) *Television and Aggression: An Experimental Field Study*, San Francisco: Jossey Bass.

Gerbner, G. (1980) Children and power on television: the other side of the picture. In Gerbner, G., Ross, C. J. and Zigler, E. (eds) *Child Abuse: An Analysis and Agenda for Action*, New York: Oxford University Press, 239–48.

Gerbner, G. (1988) *Violence and Terror in the Mass Media*, Paris: UNESCO, Reports and Papers on Mass Communication, No. 102.

Gerbner, G., Gross, L., Morgan, M. and Signorielli, N. (1986) Living with television. The dynamics of the cultivation process. In Bryant, J. and Zillman, D. (eds) *Perspectives on Media Effects*, Hillsdale, NJ: Lawrence Erlbaum, 17–40.

Golding, P. and Middleton, S. (1982) *Images of Welfare: Press and Public Attitudes*, Oxford: Martin Robertson.

Gripsrud, J. (1989) De fryktinngytende bildene. Z. *Filmtidskrift*, **3**, 10–17, and **4**, 16–23.

Gunter, B. and Wober, M. (1988) *Violence on Television: What the Viewers Think*, London: John Libbey and Independent Broadcasting Authority.

Hall, S. (1980) Encoding/decoding. In Hall, S., Hobson, D., Lowe, A. and Willis, P. (eds) *Culture, Media, Language*, London: Hutchinson, 128–38.

Halloran, J. D., Brown, R. L. and Chaney, D. C. (1970a) *Television and Delinquency*, Leicester: Leicester University Press.

Halloran, J. D., Elliott, P. and Murdock, G. (1970b) *Demonstrations and Communication: A Case Study*, Harmondsworth: Penguin Books.

Hartwig, H. (1988) *Grymhetens bilder, bildernas grymhet: skräck och fascination i gamla och nya media*, Göteborg: Daidalos.

Hedinsson, E. (1981) *TV, Family and Society: The Social Origins and Effects of Adolescents' TV Use*, Stockholm: Almqvist & Wiksell International.

Hellbom, B. (1982) *TV-våld. En innehållsanalys*, Stockholm: University of Stockholm, Pedagogiska institutionen.

Holmberg, O. (1988) *Videovåld och undervisning*, Stockholm/Lund: Symposion.

Höijer, B. (1994) *Våldsskildringar i TV-nyheter. Produktion, utbud, publik*, Stockholm: Våldsskildringsrådet, no. 9.

Huesmann, L. R. and Eron, L. D. (eds) (1986) *Television and the Aggressive Child: A Cross-national Comparison*, Hillsdale, NJ: Lawrence Erlbaum.
Hurwitz, S. and Christiansen, K. O. (1983) *Criminology*. London: Allen & Unwin.
Iwao, S., de Sola Pool, I. and Hagiwara, S. (1981) Japanese and US media: some cross-cultural insights into TV violence. *Journal of Communication*, **31**(2), 28–36.
Jensen, J. F. (1993) Powerplay – maskulinitet, makt och våld i datorspel. In von Feilitzen, C., Forsman, M. and Roe, K. (eds) *Våld från alla håll. Forskningsperspektiv på våld i rörliga bilder*, Stockholm/Stehag: Symposion, 151–73.
Lawrence, P. A. and Palmgreen, P. C. (1996) A uses and gratifications analysis of horror film preference. In Weaver, III, J. B. and Tamborini, R. (eds) *Horror Films. Current Research on Audience Preferences and Reactions*, Mahwah, NJ: Lawrence Erlbaum, 161–78.
Liblik, M. (1994) *Eurovision News och våldsrapporteringen i svenska nyheter. En studie av EVNs internationella nyhetsutbyte och dess betydelse för våldsrapporteringen i Aktuellt och Rapport*, Stockholm: University of Stockholm, Institutionen för journalistik, medier och kommunikation.
McCombs, M. E. and Shaw, D. (1972) The agenda-setting function of the press. *Public Opinion Quarterly*, **36**, 176–87.
Milavsky, J. R., Kessler, R. C., Stipp, H. H. and Rubens, W. S. (1982) *Television and Aggression: A Panel Study*, New York: Academic Press.
Murdock, G. (1982) Mass communication and social violence: a critical review of recent research trends. In Marsh, P. and Campbell, A. (eds) *Aggression and Violence*, Oxford: Basil Blackwell, 62–90.
Nordenstreng, K. and Varis, T. (1974) *Television Traffic – A One-way Street? A Survey and Analysis of the International Flow of Television Programme Material*, Paris: UNESCO, Reports and Papers on Mass Communication, No. 70.
Nordlund, R. (1977) *PM angående underhållningsvåld*. Stockholm: Radionämnden.
Pearl, D., Bouthilet, L. and Lazar, J. (eds) (1982) *Television and Behavior: Ten Years of Scientific Progress and Implications for the Eighties*, Washington DC: Department of Health and Human Services.
Pietilä, V. (1976) Notes on violence in the mass media. *Instant Research on Peace and Violence*, **VI**(4), 195–7.
Roe, K. (1983) *The Influence of Video Technology in Adolescence*, Lund: Lunds University, Sociologiska institutionen, Mediapanel, No. 27.
Roe, K. (1984) *Youth and Music in Sweden: Results from a Longitudinal Study of Teenagers' Media Use*, Lund: Lunds University, Sociologiska institutionen, Mediapanel, No. 32.
Rowland, W. (1983) *The Politics of TV Violence: Policy Uses of Communication Research*, Beverly Hills, CA: Sage.
Rönnberg, M. (1989) *Skitkul! Om s k skräpkultur*, Uppsala: Filmförlaget.
Sarnecki, J. (1988) *Föredrag om våldet i samhället*, Folkpartiets Kvinnoförbund, Studieförbundet Vuxenskolan, 12 March.
Schiller, H. (1976) *Communication and Cultural Domination*, New York: International Arts and Sciences Press.
Schlesinger, P., Dobash, R. E., Dobash, R. P. and Weaver, C. K. (1992) *Women Viewing Violence*, London: British Film Institute.
Schlesinger, P., Murdock, G. and Elliott, P. (1983) *Televising Terrorism: Political Violence in Popular Culture*, London: Comedia Publishing Group.
Signorielli, N. (1986) Television's mean and dangerous world: a continuation of the cultural indicators perspective. In Signorielli, N. and Morgan, M. (eds) *Cultivation Analysis: New Directions in Media Effects Research*, Newbury Park, CA: Sage, 85–106.

Signorielli, N. and Morgan, M. (eds) (1990) *Cultivation Analysis: New Directions in Media Effects Research,* Newbury Park, CA: Sage.

Singer, J. L. and Singer, D. G. (1983) Implications of childhood television viewing for cognition, imagination and emotion. In Bryant, J. and Anderson, D. R. (eds) *Children's Understanding of Television,* London: Academic Press.

Sjögren, O. (1985) Den förbannade tröskeln. Skräckfilm som modern övergångsrit. In Forselius, T. M. and Luoma-Keturi, S. (eds) *Våldet mot ögat. Filmforskare om film- och videoskräck,* Stockholm: Författarförlaget, 13–58.

Sonneson, I. (1989) *Vem Fostrar våra barn – videon eller vi? TV video och emotionell och social anpassning,* Stockholm: Esselte studium.

Spinoza, B. ([1678] 1959) *Ethics,* London: J. M. Dent.

Svensson, B. (1985) Välfärd och kriminalitet i Sverige. *BRÅ Apropå* 11(1), 25–32.

Tannenbaum, P. H. (1980) Entertainment as vicarious emotional experience. In Tannenbaum, P. H. (ed) *The Entertainment Functions of Television,* Hillsdale, NJ: Lawrence Erlbaum, 107–31.

UNESCO (1989) *World Communication Report,* Paris: UNESCO.

Vaagland, O. (1979) *Fjernsyn og vold,* Bergen: Bergen University, Senter for mediaforskning.

Varis, T. (1985) *International Flow of Television Programs,* Paris: UNESCO, Reports and Papers on Mass Communication, No. 100.

Viemerö, V. (1986) *Relationships Between Filmed Violence and Aggression,* Åbo: Åbo Akademi, Department of Psychology.

Wall, J. (1987) Enkätundersökning – rapport. Hur använder ungdomar video? In Eklundh, C., *Videovåld. En rapport från våldsskildringsutredningen,* Stockholm: Utbildningsdepartementet, DsU 1987: 8, 89–114.

Williams, R. (1974) *Television: Technology and Cultural Form,* Glasgow: Collins.

Wober, M. and Gunter, B. (1988) *Television and Social Control,* Avebury: Gower.

Zillmann, D. (1980) Anatomy of suspense. In Tannenbaum, P. H. (ed.) *The Entertainment Functions of Television,* Hillsdale, NJ: Lawrence Erlbaum, 33–163.

Zillmann, D. and Bryant, J. (1986) Exploring the entertainment experience. In Bryant, J. and Zillmann, D. (eds) *Perspectives on Media Effects,* Hillsdale, NJ: Lawrence Erlbaum, 303–24.

9

Research about violence in the media: different traditions and changing paradigms

Olga Linné and Ellen Wartella

This chapter analyses the changing face of the research, if not necessarily the debate, about media violence and, in so doing, will describe some 40 years of research. We have chosen to examine research about violence on the screen from the three areas of the globe where research on this topic has been high on the agenda, namely the USA, the UK and the Scandinavian countries (Denmark, Norway and Sweden).

In a recent survey of academics engaged in research on children and the media in the 15 EU countries, Linné (1996) demonstrated that the majority of respondents, out of 107 universities sampled, felt that research and teaching about mass media and children had been most developed in the countries of North-Western Europe, including the UK. On the question of how the researchers would evaluate the development of research in their own country, Italy, Spain, Austria, Greece, Luxembourg and Portugal all reported that the state of affairs regarding research was relatively poor. The voices from the UK and the North-Western part of Europe were much more positive. Linné argues that this has less to do with demographic factors such as size of populations, than a combination of social and historical forces.

We have chosen to concentrate on the three regions – UK, USA and Scandinavia – as a result of the work just mentioned. Linné questioned European Community social scientists on their attitudes to media research on violence and asked them if they applied research evidence from other countries to explain effects of mediated violence in their own. Some 49 per cent of the academics said they did. Most of the answers came from the countries which had not been able to carry out research in their own environment, mostly the Mediterranean countries.

Linné further asked which countries, in the academics' view, had produced useful research on children and mediated violence. The 15 European Community countries were listed as well as USA, Canada and Australia. The majority, 67 per cent of the European scholars pointed to the fact that relevant research had been carried out in the UK, a country where most scholars persistently have argued against the direct/causal effects of screened violence (e.g. Halloran, 1968 and 1978; Murdock and McCron, 1979; Howitt and Cumberbatch, 1975; Buckingham, 1993; Gauntlett, 1995; Barker and Petley, 1997). However, almost the same number of scholars (65 per cent) mentioned American research which has often linked screened violence with violent behaviour (Bandura, 1977; Berkowitz,1984; Eron,1982; De Fleur and Ball-Rokeach, 1982; Huesmann, 1986; Comstock, 1990; Gerbner, 1994). Surprisingly, given its relatively small population, the third most frequently mentioned country was Sweden (43 per cent). Denmark and Finland received 20 per cent and 18 per cent, respectively, as producing useful research evidence on children and media violence.

Although questions about images of violence in the media have been on the research agenda in many countries for over four decades, the evidence about the impact of violence on the screen varies, not only from researcher to researcher, but also between the research communities in the three geographical areas. In all three the research questions have been differently phrased and the emphasis and interpretations of the results have led to different arguments.

We will examine to what extent the research traditions have changed, to what extent coincided, or still, 40 years later, kept their distinctive character in pinpointing the effects of watching media violence. The main focus here is the necessity to interpret research results not only in relation to the sometimes idiosyncratic analyses and recommendations of a single researcher, but to widen one's interpretation to the community of which the researcher is a member.

It seems that the debate about the possible effects of violence on the media will always be with us. In this chapter we argue that this is rightly so, but it is important to remember that this is deeply rooted in the society into which the academics are socialized. We would agree with Richard Hoggart, that 'the cultural air we breathe, the whole ideological atmosphere of our society' is of utmost importance when analysing the research evidence (Hoggart, 1976: x).

In the constellation of factors that influence the social behaviour of adolescents – personality, peers, family, school, social background – in popular theorizing about the problems of youth, the mass media seem to occupy a central role. Concerns about the effects of mass media on youth have been part of the social commentaries accompanying the introduction of each new technology of this century – film, radio, television and video (Wartella and Reeves, 1985) and this agenda of public concern has regularly given rise to social science research on the topic of media effects on children and youth.

The Scandinavian case

In this case study we will analyse how research traditions have changed in Scandinavia from the 1960s to the 1990s. It is significant that the most prominent research theories were developed in the USA: the Catharsis Hypothesis, the Aggressive Cue model, the Observational Learning Theory, the Reinforcement Model and the Cultivation Model (De Fleur and Ball-Rokeach, 1982). Four out of these approaches assume that mediated violence can influence aggressive behaviour, the Catharsis Hypothesis being the exception.

These theories have had a significant impact on European research in general, and have perhaps been particularly influential in Scandinavia. Researchers in Scandinavia in the 1960s favoured theoretical models which assumed a causal relationship between violence in the media and the behaviour of young people. This might appear rather surprising when one considers the difference in media proliferation between the Scandinavian countries and the USA at that time. Denmark had from 1951 to 1986 only one television channel, DR, and three radio channels, all following the public service broadcasting model and financed by the licence fee (Nordahl Svendsen, 1989). Television in Sweden was similarly introduced as a public service medium in 1955, when SR was granted a monopoly of broadcasting. A second television channel, also without advertising, was opened in 1969 within the same corporation. In Norway only one public institution existed with one radio channel and one television channel broadcasting until 1981 (Oestbye, 1992).

Times have changed. In Denmark, Nordahl Svendsen (1989) reports that, apart from the new channel TV2, which is financed through advertising (3/4) and a licence fee (1/4), Danes can now receive nine local television channels. Satellite television can be received by 61 per cent (1994) and 53 per cent of Danes (1994) can choose to watch Swedish television channels and 48 per cent German television channels. Currently there are two terrestrial channels, three satellite channels and two satellite/pay channels.

In Norway, a second television channel was established in 1992. In a country where the population was used to receiving only one television channel (apart from roughly a quarter of the Norwegians who in earlier days could also receive Swedish television), its citizens could suddenly choose between two domestic channels, and in addition, five satellite channels from Britain, France, Germany and the rest of Scandinavia and two satellite/pay-TV channels.

In Sweden developments were similar. In 1985, the first Swedish households were connected to cable on a commercial basis. In 1994, 60 per cent of the population had access to satellite television, and in the late 1980s satellite channels specially intended for Swedish audiences – TV 3, TV 4, TV 5 Nordic, SF-Succe and Film-Net – became available to cabled households (Cronholm, 1993). In 1995 there were three terrestrial channels, five satellite channels and four satellite/pay-TV channels.

It is important to describe the changing media systems in Scandinavia. Research is never free-floating, but must be seen in the context of the society in which it is located, as the media systems are a highly significant part of that society. This must be of special importance when discussing the discourses of research on violence on television, because one valid argument appears to be that the discourses would vary with the amount of television a society offers its citizens, and that the quantity of television, theoretically, if not actually, might influence the availability of violent images.

Public concern about media violence and its alleged effects was evident in Scandinavia from the introduction of television. In Sweden, for example, the Swedish branch of the Save the Children Fund ran two campaigns against violence on television during the 1970s, and actions against violent television content have been taken by parent associations and groups concerned with children. However, writing in 1977, von Feilitzen and her colleagues noted: 'the Scandinavian countries, particularly perhaps Sweden and Norway, have the least television violence in the world' (p. 61). This appears paradoxical. Given that the media systems at the time were so restricted, and that the output of violent programmes was rather small, why did researchers, the Save the Children Fund, other organizations, parents and general debaters worry so much? The answer comes promptly in von Feilitzen and her colleagues' argument: 'Even if Swedish television is on an average less "hard" (violent) than in many other countries, such series have also been broadcast which are high on the American violence ratings, such as *Kojak, Baretta*, and the *Rockford Files*' (von Feilitzen *et al.*, 1977: 62). One can question how violent the above-mentioned programmes actually were compared with the satellite programmes and video nasties of later decades, but it is essential to realize that this argument was considered to be an urgent one then, as it also appears to be today in both Western and Eastern Europe.

Most of the early Scandinavian research reports are summaries of foreign studies, above all American ones. The media systems in the USA and Scandinavia were, of course, very different from each other in those days. This did not appear to bother Bruun Pedersen from Denmark (1984), who concluded:

> It is unthinkable that something would appear which changed the main research evidence we have referred to earlier: violence on television has harmful effects on children and young people. It is about time that we proceed from this conclusion and establish controls on this, because in a very few years the violence influence from television will have a scope much larger than today. We should be prepared for when that time comes.
>
> (Bruun Pedersen, 1984 : 77)

On the whole, Scandinavian researchers at the time were not afraid to apply foreign research evidence to the Scandinavian setting. The main arguments were that foreign programmes with violent images were part of the Scandinavian output and that the few Scandinavian studies undertaken agreed with international research.

The other classical discourse was over the question of whether researchers had agreed on the results from the research or not. This is obviously connected to the debate about how applicable research from other countries is. As we have just seen, Bruun Pedersen (1984) was convinced of the relevance of the research for Denmark. However, Vaagland already in 1977 was critical of the methodology of such studies because he pointed out that politicians and other moral entrepreneurs had accepted the conclusions from foreign studies without asking questions about the methods used. For example, he was especially critical of laboratory experiments with young children that tested levels of aggression in children's behaviour after viewing violence.

Vaagland's position thus is similar to the critical position of some British scholars working in this field at the time. Halloran (1978) pointed out that much of the research on violence had been carried out in the USA and that cross-cultural generalizations were not really valid because the USA, media-wise and otherwise, historically and at the present time, differed from what was prevalent in many other countries. As there were so few Scandinavian studies carried out, most of the public debates in the early years were not only influenced, but based on American models and paradigms. The more critical British tradition, at the time, here illustrated by Halloran's work, was much less influential on this specific issue.

The first Scandinavian studies demonstrated the importance of both parental influence and the child's background in their negotiation of media texts and they also pointed to the relatively limited number of violent incidents on television (Linné, 1969; Vaagland, 1977), These studies were less alarmist than many results of studies from the USA, but nevertheless the debates continued.

In the 1990s the climate of opinion has been reversed, because now only occasionally we hear arguments agreeing that findings from the USA could be imported to the Nordic context. The main reason for this is that today there exists much more Scandinavian-based research in comparison with some 30 years ago. Contemporary research on the whole has demonstrated much less spectacular effects than was previously assumed (Linné, 1995). At the same time there is a growing awareness among social scientists of the necessity of studying the media in its social context, rather than in isolation.

The most intriguing and rather unexpected trend is that the causal effects of television on violent behaviour are not high on the agenda in the literature from the 1990s. There are still a group of researchers who treat television violence as a possible contributory factor in real-life violence, but even these researchers never (or hardly ever) see it as the sole cause. There are also voices from Scandinavia denying any harmful effects whatsoever of watching violence on television.

Thus when the Scandinavian countries had only one public broadcasting channel each (or two in Sweden), and also very restrictive policies about the importation of television programmes with violent content, the 'moral panic' among the researchers seems to have been much more evident. This trend is very clear when one analyses studies concerning programmes portraying 'extreme violence', such as video nasties, horror films, violent images in music videos, pornographic violent images and violent computer games. The researchers studying these areas and themes have not been interested in questions about effects, but rather they have studied content, images and how different sub-groups use the media material and negotiated the texts. Contemporary media research has focused upon active audiences and their reading of texts rather than the effects of the media on them – an audience-centred rather than a media-centred approach.

Have the researchers in Scandinavia changed their attitudes or have new paradigms come into being? It is important here to remember that most researchers during the early years were trained as social scientists and that in Scandinavia at the time, the social sciences were very influenced by the American behaviourist tradition. Most of the voices from

Scandinavia in the 1990s, working in the effects tradition, proceed much more carefully than their early colleagues. Undoubtedly this is also due to the fact that the contemporary research community actually knows more about the media than their counterparts did in the 1970s. The other part of the answer is that there are now many more researchers in the 1990s who have been trained in disciplines other than the social sciences. Having a different background has steered their research interests in other directions.

The Scandinavian scholars still frequently refer to 'moral panics' surrounding the media. The paradox is that in the very early years the scholars participated and argued for more censorship, but in the 1990s most of the researchers are opposed to more censorship, even though they are discussing 'extreme violence' and not the '*Kojak*-type' violence.

In the 1990s the 'moral entrepreneurs' no longer seem to be the researchers, but politicians, journalists, parents and generally concerned public debaters. In Scandinavia there also seems to exist a growing hesitation in the research community to give just one cause as an explanation for complicated social issues. This might be another reason for most media scholars in the 1990s in these countries to study constructions and narratives of media images and how the media are used and negotiated by different sub-cultures, rather than to continue to concentrate on the elusive effects of violent media.

The case of the United Kingdom

The first large-scale British study to address violence on the screen was Himmelweit *et al.*'s 1958 study of the introduction of television into British society. In one sense, their study set the tone for much of the subsequent research and academic debate on media violence in the UK. Their analysis emphasized the importance of the family and they were careful not to study the children in isolation. Their conclusion was that television on the whole 'proves to be far less colourful and dramatic than popular opinion is inclined to suppose' (Himmelweit *et al.* 1958: 41).

One well-known British field study of violence and adolescents is Belson's survey of more than 1500 12- to 17-year-old adolescents in London (Belson, 1978). This was a carefully constructed survey, with great care taken in drawing the sample and designing the systems of measurement. Belson measured 13 different types of violence (for example, violence that is 'in a good cause' as against violence that is 'horrific', as well as criminal actions of the real world such as attacking someone with a tyre lever); he also developed detailed measures of the adolescent viewing of different kinds of television (for example, sport, news, comedies, cartoons), and exposure to violent content in other media such as newspapers, film and comic books. Further, he matched respondents in his sample when comparing heavy and light violence viewers on various dependent measures. He found, for instance, that heavy violence viewers committed more acts of serious antisocial behaviour (7.48 acts in previous six months) compared to light viewers of television violence (5.02 acts), but even less serious acts of antisocial behaviour showed statistically significant differences between heavy and light television violence viewers. Furthermore, Belson found that this pattern of correlation between exposure to violent fare and antisocial behaviour held when other media were examined as well (film and comics).

Interestingly Comstock and Paik (1991), writing from a distinctly American perspective, considered Belson's study to be of great importance, as, according to them, he had found a relationship between viewing media violence and serious, real world criminal behaviour on the part of adolescent boys. However, when first published the study was heavily criticized in Britain, by among others, Murdock and McCron (1979). They called attention to the fact that Belson's respondents were asked to recollect programmes they had watched which had been broadcast between 1959 and 1971 (the study was carried out in 1972 and 1973), which meant that some of the boys would have been 'only a few years old' at the time. (Murdock and McCron, 1979: 57).

Another weakness of the Belson study was that, because it was cross-sectional, it could not demonstrate a causal relationship between exposure to media violence and violent behaviour, nor could it show the direction of the causation. Belson assumed that exposure to media violence caused the boys to behave violently, but it is possible that boys inclined to violence sought out violent television programmes to watch. Wober (1988) indicated this as a possibility. He examined the characteristics of children who were drawn to items that contained violence and also examined consistency of use of certain types of programmes by age. He found that there were substantial and significant correlations indicating that people who watched a great deal of a particular programme type in one week also watched that type more heavily in another week than did light consumers of the programme type. Even at younger ages certain individuals showed a consistent tendency to watch adventure action programmes.

Of interest to this chapter one can note that some British researchers evidently felt the need to carry out very large-scale field studies quite early on, rather than accepting unproblematically the American evidence. Of even more interest are the early critical arguments about violence on the screen. As early as 1968, Halloran argued that people do not appear to bemoan:

> with references to news reels, rocket trials, the explosion of hydrogen bombs, historical documentaries or war films. Yet it is possible that for some people these may, in the long run, produce more injurious reactions than Westerns and detective thrillers.

> (Halloran, 1968: 149)

In the same article Halloran argues that violence on television cannot be studied in isolation:

> We need to look at the whole social and economic structure and examine the portrayal of television and the concern and disquiet which this brings about in this wider setting. No state of mind, no perceptual patterns, no needs, no reactions, no effects, no criticisms and no condemnations can be fully under-

stood unless these factors are related to those forces in society which both produce and require the violence.

(Halloran, 1968: 151)

This is, as one can see, a completely opposite view to the one expressed in Scandinavia at around this time and, as we will see, in the USA.

During the 1970s and 1980s more and more critical accounts about contemporary research about violence were published in Britain. There was the article, just cited, by Murdock and McCron emerging from a critical sociological point of view; there were criticisms mainly against the methodology used in the American studies launched by Howitt and Cumberbatch (1975), and there were only a few attempts to defend the laboratory studies, Eysenck and Nias's (1978) defence from a psychological perspective probably being the most well known.

In 1994, however, when the British tradition of regarding the debate about screen violence as a matter of class and unequal opportunities seemed to be very well established, the Newson Report appeared (Newson, 1994). Written by a psychologist, Professor Elisabeth Newson, and called 'Video Violence and the Protection of Children', it immediately made headlines in all the media in Britain. Here is Martin Barker's reaction from the introduction to the book *Ill Effects* (Barker and Petley, 1997):

> The end of March 1994. I opened my newspaper to read that, apparently, twenty-five of my colleagues – all leading experts in my field – had changed their minds on the vital question of 'media violence and the young'. A new report had been published whose conclusions were so damning that they had no choice but [to] abandon their traditional 'liberal' stance, and call for further restrictions on 'violent' videos.

(Barker and Petley, 1997 :1)

Barker then claims that this report was worse than he could have imagined, because 'It had not a single fact to its name, good or bad. It was a thin tissue of claims whose only virtue was that they were what every politician and newspaper wanted' (Barker and Petley, 1997: 1). The book he and Petley edited came out as a reaction to the Newson Report. Needless to say, it has so far not been in the headlines, or referred to by the newspapers. So while there remains a great deal of public concern in the UK about violence and the media and this is reflected in the Newson Report and the public and media reaction to it, the research community continues to be sceptical.

The basis of British academic criticism today is not very different from Halloran's original 1960s' view and is also quite similar to the present Scandinavian stance. The main arguments are that scholars in the past have asked 'the wrong questions', that there are misconceptions about 'effects' and 'violence' (Halloran 1978; Gauntlett, 1995; this volume, Chapter 10); that the research ignores children's own perspectives, and the complex ways in which they make sense of what they watch; and that television viewing is not a mindless activity but has a positive influence on some aspects of social development (Buckingham, 1993 and this volume, Chapter 11). Jones summarizes these arguments when she says that children today: 'engage with media texts according to their subjective experience, cultural knowledge and social characteristics' (Jones, 1997: 21).

Thus similarly to those in Scandinavia, most scholars in Britain today want to open new perspectives, study subgroups and reception and try to find answers to 'the right questions' (although these are as yet not very well defined). Corresponding to the Scandinavian scenario, many scholars in the field have a linguistic, humanist background, but Britain has also had a strong and well-developed tradition of critical research and these scholars were, as noted here, among the first to be seriously critical of the violence research traditions. With a few exceptions, the British tradition seems to be sceptical of the alleged effects of causal or even contributory effects of the media to violent behaviour in society. This brings us to the third case study.

The case of the United States

The brief description of American research which follows summarizes the evidence on the impact of media on adolescent problem behaviours, including violent behaviour. It considers the major theoretical accounts of the links between media exposure and problem behaviours, the empirical evidence for such links, and the questions that remain to be addressed in this field.

Critics in the USA are concerned that young people spend too much time with media products that are too violent, commercialized, and of inappropriate morality (Huston *et al.*, 1992). Content analysis of violence on television has been carried out predominantly in the United States. For over two decades American researchers have devised and applied measures of violent 'content' of programmes. One of the best known of these is George Gerbner's Violence Profile which came out of his 1968 'Cultural Indicators' project (Gerbner, 1969; 1972). A problem of this type of work is that the measurements of violence are necessarily subjective. The overall rates of violence found by the Cultural Indicators team in the USA have remained 'remarkably constant' over the years. 'An average of 5 or 6 acts of overt physical violence per hour menace over half of all major characters' on prime time television. (Gerbner *et al.*, 1980. For an examination of this work, see Wober, Chapter 6, this volume).

A second measure of violence is the proportion of broadcast programmes containing violence. The figures for the USA (80 per cent) are far higher than those for the UK (56 per cent), (Cumberbatch *et al.*, 1987). Cumberbatch *et al.* pointed out that the low rate for Britain must be seen in the context of a relatively small proportion of broadcast television being devoted to dramatic fiction. This genre, in particular 'action adventure series', contains (along with film) more violence than does soap opera or situation comedy (Wober, 1988). Some 19 per cent of the 2 078 programmes analysed by Cumberbatch *et al.* (1987) fell into the category of dramatic fiction. This proportion of their sample contributed over three-quarters (81 per cent) of all violence coded. The proportion of television output that is of US origin varies between European countries.

Cumberbatch *et al.* (1988) reported that the primary difference between US and UK programmes shown on British television was in the quantity of violence they contained. American programmes made up only 15 per cent of the output they analysed.

As Comstock and Paik (1991) have noted, from a North American perspective, a variety of meta-analytic studies of violence research (for example Andison, 1977) have demonstrated that the effects of exposure to television violence on aggressive behaviour of adolescents and young adults is *best* illustrated in experimental research. However, as a plethora of critics, mostly from Europe, have noted, laboratory studies are fraught with serious challenges to external validity: most importantly, the experimental setting, the lack of definition of violence and the measures of violent behaviour used are simply too far removed from the real interpersonal setting of young peoples' lives. The moderating forces of real social situations, the presence of adults and authority figures, for example, are simply left out of account.

The American scholars argue that more convincing evidence of causal relationships can be provided by longitudinal studies. Eron and colleagues' longitudinal study of adolescents in the United States found a relationship between viewing television violence and real-world aggressive behaviour. For instance, boys' viewing of television violence at age 8 predicted these boys' aggressive behaviour at age 18, and more importantly, predicted serious criminal behaviour at age 30 (Eron, 1982; Eron *et al.*, 1972; Huesmann *et al.*, 1984a).

Importantly, the American social science scholars claim that this same research team has carried out similar longitudinal studies in four other countries (Australia, Finland, Poland and Israel) which parallel the US study (see Huesmann and Eron, 1986). Again, the data *across nations* support the conclusion that viewing televised violence leads to aggressive behaviour and not *vice versa*. However, it should be noted that the overall levels of violence viewing varied considerably between the countries studied. The one US longitudinal study (Milavsky *et al.*, 1982) that did not support the assertion that television violence viewing causes later aggressive behaviour has been vigorously criticized by American researchers on methodological grounds, and the data themselves have been reinterpreted to support a causal explanation (Comstock and Paik, 1991).

Two major American theories have been proposed to support the notion that the screening of violence can lead to violent behaviour in society. First, there is the social learning theory originally proposed in the 1960s by Bandura (1977), who focused on the imitative effects of television; a variation on the theory was developed by Berkowitz (Berkowitz and Rawlings, 1963) which stressed the disinhibitory effects of television violence. This idea that viewing can be a disinhibition mechanism – that viewing television violence can reduce constraints on viewers' pent-up aggressive behaviour, has been perhaps the mostly widely explored and cited theoretical explanation for violence effects.

A second theoretical explanation is proposed by Zillmann's (1982) arousal and Drabman and Thomas's (1974) desensitization hypotheses. Both these hypotheses propose that television violence is an arousing stimulus which when viewed in heavy amounts over time can actually desensitize heavy viewers such that each subsequent exposure to violence on television becomes less arousing. Eventually, it has been argued, such desensitization leads to more callous attitudes toward real-world violence (Donnerstein *et al.*, 1987).

It is quite likely that these are not competing theories of television violence effects, indeed some evidence from the US suggests that both may be operative. Indeed, since the 1960s and 1970s when the earliest research on Bandura's social learning theory was conducted, increasingly elaborate theories of television violence have been offered. For instance, from Berkowitz's early theorizing about the disinhibitory effects of media violence, he (Berkowitz, 1984) has now developed an elaborated view of how media portrayals of violence stimulate associative networks or cognitive scripts or thoughts. When primed by a real world situation, a media-related script sparks an acting out of an aggressive behaviour. This theoretical reformulation, then, tries to account for instances when real-world aggressive behaviour does not imitate media portrayals of aggression, but may none the less be stimulated by the media portrayal. In this formulation, media portrayals of violence are important in initially implanting ideas about aggression. That is, violence from television is 'encoded' in the cognitive map of viewers, and subsequent viewing of television violence helps to maintain these aggressive thoughts, ideas and behaviours. Over time such continuing attention to television violence thus can influence people's attitudes towards violence and their maintenance and elaboration of aggressive scripts. Finally, the arousing aspect of viewing media violence can stimulate the actual production of violent behaviour on the part of viewers.

In this theory, it is not television violence alone that causes violent action. Rather, media violence is one environmental factor that may contribute to the maintenance of a stable pattern of aggressive behaviour in children and adults. Other environmental factors that may frustrate and victimize the child also reinforce aggressive behaviour. Here, Huesmann's (1986: 138-9) account is relevant. His research shows that aggressive scripts for behaviour are acquired from observation of media violence and aggressive behaviour itself stimulates the observation of media violence. In both childhood and adulthood, certain cues in the media may trigger the activation of aggressive scripts acquired in any manner and thus variables may mitigate or exacerbate these reciprocal effects. However, if undampened, this cumulative learning process can build enduring schemes for aggressive behaviour that persist into adulthood. Thus, early childhood television habits are correlated with adult criminality independently of other likely causal factors.

The view of media violence effects just presented is a distinctly American one, but even though the Americans have their own critics, such as Freedman (1984), the strongest criticisms come from Europe. European academic critics have helped to identify many of the concerns regarding the American media violence research but in their defence, American scholars have made three main points. First, compared to more than a thousand American studies of media violence effects, much fewer

European studies have examined television and media violence effects over the past 30 or so years of television. Second, European media, particularly the public broadcasting systems that dominated European television until recently, were never as violent as American television. The prior European lack of concern with violent images in the media may well change when their media become saturated with similar amounts of violence. Third, European insistence that the conclusions from laboratory studies may be dismissed as externally invalid does not address the overall consistency of the survey and field experimental research which, with a few exceptions (notably the disputed Milavsky *et al.* study, 1982), are supportive of a causal link between television violence viewing and aggressive behaviour.

Overall, say the American researchers, their critics do not undermine the substantial body of convincing evidence to show that television violence is among the causes of real-world violence. However, they are persuasive in arguing that the magnitude of the effects of television violence in comparison with other causes is not well understood, and may be small, and both American and European researchers now broadly share the view that it is difficult to see how more research on the short-term effects of television violence can be beneficial. Continuation of the longitudinal studies, cross-nationally, such as those by Eron and his colleagues, however, could further increase the understanding of the role of media violence in the aggressive behaviour of adolescents.

In short, the American view is that the question that remains is not whether media violence has an effect, but rather how important that effect has been, in comparison with other factors, in bringing about major societal changes such as the post-war rise in crime. Future research will aim to establish who precisely is most susceptible to media violence, and what sorts of intervention may help to diminish its influence.

Conclusion

It is important to remember that all categorizations are based on *interpretations* by scholars. There are exceptions to all analyses. As we have seen, the Newson Report was one such case in Britain. The report claimed that violence on video had direct effects on viewers and its author demanded more censorship. The report was published in a country with long traditions of scepticism of the alleged effects of screen violence on behaviour and there have been similar 'exceptional' statements published in Scandinavia during the 1990s, stressing the causal effects of watching violence on the screen. There are also examples from American research which demonstrate opposite results from the mainstream arguments. Our interest was, however, to examine the trends, rather than the exceptions, evident in the three geographical areas chosen.

In all three cases, there has been an increase in the number of television channels broadcast by satellite and cable organizations, the most dramatic increase being in the Scandinavian countries. The early Scandinavian argument was that only when a proliferation of stations broadcasting American programmes (often assuming that they were filled with violent incidents), would policy-makers act upon the research evidence. The American researchers still believe that when the Europeans become over-whelmed by an increase of TV channels, that they will take the American research much more seriously (Wartella, 1996). However, this has not happened and the focus of research on media violence has changed. The Scandinavian researchers seem, if anything, more at ease with the media situation in the 1990s than they appeared to be in the 1960s. The British researchers have become increasingly more critical of the mainstream research about violence, because of its psychological approach and its neglect of social context. By contrast, members of the American research community have demonstrated how many violent images on television still exist in their country, and they have taken this for their rationale to carry out more effects research. Why haven't the research traditions in the different countries merged?

There is no doubt that technological changes in broadcasting are offering more images on the screen. However, we would argue that it is more important to examine the scholars' theoretical considerations. The Scandinavian researchers' 'view of society' changed when they started to study their own society, but also when critical research from Europe became of more interest and appeared to have more relevance than that from the more pluralistic, American tradition.

British media research, with its strong political economist or critical tradition, has from the very beginning been more interested in theories of power and class than in psychological or individualistic explanations of human behaviour. American research has been dominated by a more positivist empirical, often psychological theoretical framework. There are still arguments that European scholars have a tendency to concentrate on the construction of theories, while American scholars are intent on the collection of empirical data. There is little doubt that the American scholars have carried out a lot of empirical research, and that this research has been leaning on psychological, rather than sociological traditions. While the concept of power and who exercises power, have been of almost marginal interest in the USA, it has been a central focus in Europe.

What this overview of research has shown is that research traditions change in some societies and merge with some other traditions over time. The analysis has also demonstrated that the theorizing and research about the alleged effects of media violence are different in Europe and the USA. Quite a few Scandinavian researchers have changed their attitudes, and now agree with the British researchers that the power structure of a society is of greater analytical importance in explaining society's ills than the messages and the images that most people receive from the television set. However, the majority of American researchers still believe that one day they will be able to confirm that television, after all, is a cause of a disrupted and violent society.

We believe that it is not enough for media researchers to demonstrate the flaws of laboratory experiments. We would argue that now is the time to seriously consider the various research paradigms and to explore the extent to which they apply to one's own country. At the beginning of this chapter we demonstrated that most researchers in Southern Europe stated that they used the research findings from all three geographical areas examined here. Given the results of this investigation, we would recommend them to lobby for more research to be carried out in their own countries, in their own social and cultural environments.

References

Andison, F. S. (1977) TV violence and viewer aggressiveness: a cumulation of study results. *Public Opinion Quarterly,* **41**, 314–31.

Bandura, A. (1977) *Social Learning Theory*, Englewood Cliffs, NJ: Prentice Hall.

Barker, M. and Petley, J. (eds) (1997) *Ill Effects: The Media/Violence Debate*, London: Routledge.

Belson, W. (1978) *Television and the Adolescent Boy*, Farnborough: Saxon House.

Berkowitz, L. (1984) Some thoughts on anti- and prosocial influence of media events: a cognitive-menoassociation analysis. *Psychological Bulletin,* **95**, 410–27.

Berkowitz, L. and Rawlings, F. (1963) Effects of film violence on inhibitions against subsequent aggression. *Journal of Abnormal and Social Psychology,* **661**, 405–12.

Bruun Pedersen, J. (1984) *Violence on the Screen*, Copenhagen: Gyldendals Pedagogic Library.

Buckingham, D. (1993) *Children Talking Television*, London: The Falmer Press.

Comstock, G. (1990) Deceptive appearances: television violence and aggressive behaviour. *Journal of Adolescent Health Care,* **11**, 31–44.

Comstock, G. and Paik, H. (1991) *Television and the American Child*, New York: Academic Press.

Cronholm, M. (1993). *SR/PUB 1969–1993. 25 Years of Broadcasting Research in the Audience and Programme Research Development of Sveriges Radio*, Stockholm: Swedish Broadcasting Corporation.

Cumberbatch, G. and Brown, N. (1989) Violence to television: effects research in context. *British Journal of Social Psychology,* **31**, 147–64.

Cumberbatch, G, Jones, I. and Lee, M. (1988) Measuring violence on television. *Current Psychology: Research and Reviews,* **7**, 10–25.

Cumberbatch, G., Lee, M., Hardy, G. and Jones, I. (1987) *The Portrayal of Violence on British Television*, London: British Broadcasting Corporation.

De Fleur, M. L. and Ball-Rokeach, S. (1982) *Theories of Mass Communication*, 4th edition, New York: Longman.

Donnerstein, E., Lintz, D. and Penrod, S. (1987) *The Question of Pornography: Research Findings and Policy Implications*, New York: The Free Press.

Drabman, R. S. and Thomas, M. H. (1974) Does media violence increase children's toleration of real-life aggression? *Developmental Psychology,* **10**, 418–21.

Eron, L. D. (1982) Parent child interaction, television violence and aggression of children. *American Psychologist,* **27**, 197–211.

Eron, L. D., Lefkowitz, M. N., Huesmann, L. R. and Walder, L. O. (1972) Does television violence cause aggression? *American Psychologist,* **27**, 253–63.

Eysenck, H. and Nias D. K. (1978) *Sex Violence and the Media*, London: Maurice Temple Smith.

Feilitzen, C. von., Filipson, L. and Schyller, I. (1977) *Open Your Eyes to Children's Viewing*, Stockholm: Swedish Broadcasting Corporation.

Freedman, J. L. (1984) Effect of television violence on aggressiveness. *Psychological Bulletin,* **96**, 227–46.

Gauntlett, D. (1995) *Moving Experiences: Understanding Television's Influences and Effects*, London: John Libbey.

Gerbner, G. (1969) Dimensions of violence in television drama. In Baker, R. K. and

Ball, S. J. (eds) *Mass Media and Violence*, Washington, DC: US Government Printing Office.

Gerbner, G. (1972) Violence in television drama: trends and symbolic functions. In Comstock, G.A. and Rubinstein, E.A. (eds) *Television and social behavior, Vol. 1: Content and Control*, Washington, DC: US Government Printing Office.

Gerbner, G. (1994) The politics of media violence: some reflections. In Hamelink, C. and Linné, O. (eds) *Mass Communication Research: On Problems and Policies*, Norwood, NJ: Ablex Publishing, 147–70.

Gerbner, G., Gross, L., Morgan, M. and Signorielli, N. (1980) The mainstreaming of America: violence profile No. 11. *Journal of Communications*, **30**, 10–29.

Halloran, J. D. (1968) Television and violence. In Larsen, O. (ed.) *Violence and the Mass Media*, New York: Harper & Row.

Halloran, J. D. (1978) Mass communication: symbol or cause of violence? *International Social Science Journal*, **30**(4), 816–34.

Himmelweit, H. T., Oppenheim, A. N. and Vince, P. (1958) *Television and the Child: An Empirical Study of the Effects of Television on the Young*, London: Oxford University Press.

Hoggart, R. (1976) Introduction: that was the world that was. In Glasgow University Media Group (eds) *Bad news*, London: Routledge & Kegan Paul.

Howitt, D. and Cumberbatch, G. (1975) *Mass Media, Violence and Society*, London: Paul Elek.

Huesmann, L. R. (1986) Psychological processes promoting the relation between exposure to media violence and aggressive behaviour in the viewer. *Journal of Social Issues*, **42**, 125–39.

Huesmann, L. R. and Eron, L. D. (1986) *Television and the Aggressive Child: A Crossnational Comparison*, Hillsdale, NJ: Lawrence Erlbaum.

Huesmann, L. R., Eron, L. D., Lefkowitz, M. H. and Walder, L. O. (1984a) The stability of aggression over time and generations. *Developmental Psychology*, **20**, 1120–34.

Huesmann, L. R., Lagerspetz, K. and Eron, L. (1984b) Intervening variables in the television violence–viewing–aggression relation: evidence from two countries. *Developmental Psychology*, **20**, 746–75.

Huston, A., Donnerstein, E., Fairchild, H., Feshback, W. D., Katz, P. A., Murray, J P., Rubinstein, E. A., Wilcox, B. and Zuckerman, D. (1992) *Big World, Small Screen: The Role of Television in American Society*, Lincoln: University of Nebraska Press.

Jones, M. (1997) Insights: media violence and children revised. Return to the killing screens? *Sociology Review*, **7**(1), September 1997.

Linné, O. (1969) *Children's Reactions to Violence on Television*, Stockholm: Swedish Broadcasting Corporation.

Linné, O. (1995) Media violence research in Scandinavia. *The Nordicom Review*, **2**, 1–16.

Linné, O. (1996) *Children and the Media: An Inventory of the State of the Art of European Research and Teaching*, Leicester: Centre for Mass Communication Research, University of Leicester.

Milavsky, J. R., Kessler, R., Stipp, H. H. and Rubens, W. S. (1982) *Television and Aggression: A Panel Study*, New York: Academic Press.

Murdock, G. and McCron, R. (1979) The television and delinquency debate, *Screen Education*, **30**, 55–68.

Newson, E. (1994) *Video Violence and the Protection of Children*. Report of the Home Affairs Committee, 29 June, 45–9.

Nordahl Svendsen, E. (1989) The media research in Danish radio. *Nordicom Information*, **3**, 3–10.

Oestbye, H. (1992) Norwegian media in the 1980s: structural changes, stable consumption. *Nordicom Information*, 1, 3–18.

Vaagland, O. (1977) *Violence on Television and Aggressive Behaviour*. Report No 2, Bergen: Centre for Media Research, University of Bergen.

Wartella, E. (1996) Media and problem behaviour in young people. In Rutter, M. and Smith, D. (eds) *Psychosocial Disorders in Young People: Time Trends and Their Origins*, Chichester: Wiley.

Wartella, E. and Reeves, B. (1985) Historical trends in research on children and the media: 1900–1960. *Journal of Communication*, 15, 118–33.

Wober, M. (1988) The extent to which viewers watch violence-containing programmes. *Current Psychology: Research and Reviews*, 7, 43–57.

Zillmann, D. (1982) Television and arousal. In Pearl, D., Bouthilet, L. and Lazar, J. (eds) *Television and Behaviour: Ten Years of Scientific Progress and Implications for the Eighties*, Washington, DC: US Government Printing Office, 53–76.

10

Ten things wrong with the 'effects model'[1]

David Gauntlett

It has become something of a cliché to observe that despite many decades of research and hundreds of studies, the connections between people's consumption of the mass media and their subsequent behaviour have remained persistently elusive. Indeed, researchers have enjoyed an unusual degree of patience from both their scholarly and more public audiences. But the time comes when we must take a step back from this murky lack of consensus and ask – why? Why are there no clear answers on media effects?

There is, as I see it, a choice of two conclusions which can be drawn from any detailed analysis of the research. The first is that if, after over sixty years of a considerable amount of research effort, direct effects of media upon behaviour have not been clearly identified, then we should conclude that they are simply *not there to be found*. Since I have argued this case, broadly speaking, elsewhere (Gauntlett, 1995a), I will here explore the second possibility: that the media effects research has quite consistently taken the *wrong approach* to the mass media, its audiences, and society in general. This misdirection has taken a number of forms; for the purposes of this chapter, I will impose an unwarranted coherence upon the claims of all those who argue or purport to have found that the mass media will commonly have direct and reasonably predictable effects upon the behaviour of their fellow human beings, calling this body of thought, simply, the 'effects model'. Rather than taking apart each study individually, I will consider the mountain of studies – and the associated claims about media effects made by commentators – as a whole, and outline ten fundamental flaws in their approach.

1. The effects model tackles social problems 'backwards'

To explain the problem of violence in society, researchers should begin with that social violence and seek to explain it with reference, quite obviously, to those who engage in it: their identity, background, character, and so on. The 'media effects' approach, in this sense, comes at the problem *backwards*, by starting with the media and then trying to lasso connections from there on to social beings, rather than the other way around.

This is an important distinction. Criminologists, in their professional attempts to explain crime and violence, consistently turn for explanations not to the mass media but to social factors such as poverty, unemployment, housing, and the behaviour of family and peers. In a study which *did* start at what I would recognize as the correct end – by interviewing 78 violent teenage offenders and then tracing their behaviour back towards media usage, in comparison with a group of over 500 'ordinary' school pupils of the same age – Hagell and Newburn (1994) found only that the young offenders watched *less* television and video than their counterparts, had less access to the technology in the first place, had no particular interest in specifically violent programmes, and either enjoyed the same material as non-offending teenagers or were simply *uninterested*. This point was demonstrated very clearly when the offenders were asked, 'If you had the chance to be someone who appears on television, who would you choose to be?':

> The offenders felt particularly uncomfortable with this question and appeared to have difficulty in understanding why one might want to be such a person . . . In several interviews, the offenders had already stated that they watched little television, could not remember their favourite programmes and, consequently, could not think of anyone to be. In these cases, their obvious failure to identify with any television characters seemed to be part of a general lack of engagement with television.
>
> (p. 30)

Thus we can see that studies which take the perpetrators of actual violence as their first point of reference, rather than the media, come to rather different conclusions (and there is certainly a need for more such research). The point that effects studies take the media as their starting point, however, should not be taken to suggest that they involve sensitive examinations of the mass media. As will be noted below, the studies have typically taken a stereotyped, almost parodic view of media content.

In more general terms, the 'backwards' approach involves the mistake of looking at individuals, rather than society, in relation to the mass media. The narrowly individualistic approach of some psychologists leads them to argue that, because of their belief that particular individuals at certain times in specific circumstances may be negatively affected by one bit of media, the removal of such media from society would be a positive step. This approach is rather like arguing that the solution to the number of road traffic accidents in Britain would be to lock away one famously poor driver from Cornwall; that is, a blinkered approach which tackles a real problem from the wrong end, involves cosmetic rather than relevant changes, and fails to look in any way at the 'bigger picture'.

2. The effects model treats children as inadequate

The individualism of the psychological discipline has also had a significant impact on the way in which children are regarded in effects research. Whilst sociology in recent decades has typically regarded childhood as a social construction, demarcated by attitudes, traditions and rituals which vary between different societies and different time periods (Ariés, 1962; Jenks, 1982, 1996), the psychology of childhood – developmental psychology – has remained more tied to the idea of a universal individual who must develop through particular stages before reaching adult maturity, as established by Piaget (e.g. 1926, 1929). The developmental stages are arranged as a hierarchy, from incompetent childhood through to rational, logical adulthood, and progression through these stages is characterized by an 'achievement ethic' (Jenks, 1996, p. 24).

In psychology, then, children are often considered not so much in terms of what they *can* do, as what they (apparently) cannot. Negatively defined as non-adults, the research subjects are regarded as the 'other', a strange breed whose failure to match generally middle-class adult norms must be charted and discussed. Most laboratory studies of children and the media presume, for example, that their findings apply only to children, but fail to run parallel studies with adult groups to confirm this. We might speculate that this is because if adults were found to respond to laboratory pressures in the same way as children, the 'common sense' validity of the experiments would be undermined.

In her valuable examination of the way in which academic studies have constructed and maintained a particular perspective on childhood, Christine Griffin (1993) has recorded the ways in which studies produced by psychologists, in particular, have tended to 'blame the victim', to represent social problems as the consequence of the deficiencies or inadequacies of young people, and to 'psychologize inequalities, obscuring structural relations of domination behind a focus on individual "deficient" working-class young people and/or young people of colour, their families or cultural backgrounds' (p. 199). Problems such as unemployment and the failure of education systems are thereby traced to individual psychology traits. The same kinds of approach are readily observed in media effects studies, the production of which has undoubtedly been dominated by psychologically-oriented researchers, who – whilst, one imagines, having nothing other than benevolent intentions – have carefully exposed the full range of ways in which young media users can be seen as the inept victims of products which, whilst obviously puerile and transparent to adults, can trick children into all kinds of ill-advised behaviour.

This situation is clearly exposed by research which seeks to establish what children can and do understand about and from the mass media. Such projects have shown that children can talk intelligently and indeed cynically about the mass media (Buckingham, 1993, 1996), and that children as young as seven can make thoughtful, critical and 'media literate' video productions themselves (Gauntlett, 1997).

3. Assumptions within the effects model are characterized by barely concealed conservative ideology

The systematic derision of children's resistant capacities can be seen as part of a broader conservative project to position the more contemporary and challenging aspects of the mass media, rather than other social factors, as the major threat to social stability today. American effects studies, in particular, tend to assume a level of television violence which – as Barrie Gunter shows in this volume – is simply not applicable in other countries such as Britain. George Gerbner's view, for example, that 'We are awash in a tide of violent representations unlike any the world has ever seen . . . drenching every home with graphic scenes of expertly chore-ographed brutality' (1994, p. 133), both reflects his hyperbolic view of the media in America and the extent to which findings cannot be simplisti-cally transferred across the Atlantic. Whilst it is certainly possible that gratuitous depictions of violence might reach a level in American screen media which could be seen as unpleasant and unnecessary, it cannot always be assumed that violence is shown for 'bad' reasons or in an uncritical light. Even the most obviously 'gratuitous' acts of violence, such as those committed by Beavis and Butt-Head in their eponymous MTV series, can be interpreted as rationally resistant reactions to an oppressive world which has little to offer them (see Gauntlett, 1997).

The condemnation of generalized screen 'violence' by conservative critics, supported by the 'findings' of the effects studies – if we disregard their precarious foundations – can often be traced to concerns such as 'disrespect for authority' and 'anti-patriotic sentiments' (most conspicu-ously in Michael Medved's well-received *Hollywood vs. America: Popular Culture and the War on Traditional Values* (1992)). Programmes which do not necessarily contain any greater *quantity* of violent, sexual or other controversial depictions than others, can be seen to be objected to because they take a more challenging socio-political stance (Barker, 1984, 1989, 1993). This was illustrated by a study of over 2 200 complaints about British TV and radio which were sent to the Broadcasting Standards Council over an 18-month period from July 1993 to December 1994 (Gauntlett, 1995c). This showed that a relatively narrow range of most complained-of programmes were taken by complainants to characterize a much broader decline in the morals of both broadcasting in particular and the nation in general.

This view of a section of the public is clearly reflected in a large number of the effects studies which presume that 'antisocial' behaviour is an objective category which can be observed in numerous programmes and which will negatively affect those children who see it portrayed. This dark view is constructed with the support of content analysis studies which appear almost designed to incriminate the media. Even today, expensive and avowedly 'scientific' content analyses such as the well-publicized US National Television Violence Study (Mediascope, 1996; run by the Universities of California, North Carolina, Texas and Wisconsin), for example, include odd tests such as whether violent acts are punished *within* the same scene – a strange requirement for dramas – making it easier to support views such as that 'there are substantial risks of harmful effects from viewing violence throughout the television environment' (p. ix)'.[2] This study also reflects the continuing willingness of researchers to impute *effects* from a count-up of content.

4. The effects model inadequately defines its own objects of study

The flaws numbered four to six in this list are more straightforward methodological, although they are connected to the previous and subsequent points. The first of these is that effects studies have generally taken for granted the definitions of media material, such as 'antisocial' and 'prosocial' programming, as well as characterizations of behaviour in the real world, such as 'antisocial' and 'prosocial' action. The point has already been made that these can be ideological value judgements; throwing down a book in disgust, smashing a nuclear missile, or – to use a *Beavis and Butt-Head* example – sabotaging activities at one's burger bar workplace, will always be interpreted in effects studies as 'antisocial', not 'prosocial'.

Furthermore, actions such as verbal aggression or hitting an inanimate object are recorded as acts of violence, just as TV murders are, leading to terrifically (and irretrievably) murky data. It is usually impossible to discern whether very minor or extremely serious acts of 'violence' depicted in the media are being said to have led to quite severe or merely trivial acts in the real world. More significant, perhaps, is the fact that this is rarely seen as a problem: in the media effects field, dodgy 'findings' are accepted with an uncommon hospitality.

5. The effects model is often based on artificial studies

Since careful sociological studies of media effects require amounts of time and money which limit their abundance, they are heavily outnumbered by simpler studies which are usually characterized by elements of artificiality. Such studies typically take place in a laboratory, or in a 'natural' setting such as a classroom but where a researcher has conspicuously shown up and instigated activities, neither of which are typical environments. Instead of a full and naturally-viewed television diet, research subjects are likely to be shown selected or specially-recorded clips which lack the narrative meaning inherent in everyday TV productions. They may then be observed in simulations of real life presented to them as a game, in relation to inanimate objects such as Bandura's famous 'bobo' doll, or as they respond to questionnaires, all of which are unlike interpersonal interaction, cannot be equated with it, and are likely to be associated with the previous viewing experience in the mind of the subject, rendering the study invalid.

Such studies also rely on the idea that subjects will not alter their behaviour or stated attitudes as a response to being observed or questioned. This naïve belief has been shown to be false by researchers such as Borden (1975) who have demonstrated that the presence, appearance and gender of an observer can radically affect children's behaviour.

6. The effects model is often based on studies with misapplied methodology

Many of the studies which do not rely on an experimental method, and so may evade the flaws mentioned in the previous section, fall down instead by applying a methodological procedure wrongly, or by drawing inappropriate conclusions from particular methods. The widely cited longitudinal panel study[3] by Huesmann, Eron and colleagues (Lefkowitz, *et al.*,

1972, 1977), for example, has been less famously slated for failing to keep to the procedures, such as assessing aggressivity or TV viewing with the same measures at different points in time, which are necessary for their statistical findings to have any validity (Chaffee, 1972; Kenny, 1972). The same researchers have also failed to adequately account for why the findings of this study and those of another of their own studies (Huesmann *et al.*, 1984) absolutely contradict each other, with the former concluding that the media has a marginal effect on boys but no effect on girls, and the latter arguing the exact opposite (no effect on boys, but a small effect for girls). They also seem to ignore that fact that their own follow-up of their original set of subjects 22 years later suggested that a number of biological, developmental and environmental factors contributed to levels of aggression, whilst the mass media was not even given a mention (Huesmann *et al.*, 1984). These astounding inconsistencies, unapologetically presented by perhaps the best-known researchers in this area, must be cause for considerable unease about the effects model. More *careful* use of the same methods, such as in the three-year panel study involving over 3000 young people conducted by Milavsky, Kessler, Stipp and Rubens (1982a, 1982b), has only indicated that significant media effects are not to be found.

Another misuse of method occurs when studies which are simply unable to show that one thing causes another are treated as if they have done so. Correlation studies are typically used for this purpose. Their finding that a particular personality type is also the kind of person who enjoys a certain kind of media, is quite unable to show that the latter *causes* the former, although psychologists such as Van Evra (1990) have casually assumed that this is probably the case. There is a logical coherence to the idea that children whose behaviour is antisocial and disruptional will also have a greater interest in the more violent and noisy television programmes, whereas the idea that the behaviour is a product of these programmes lacks both this rational consistency, and the support of the studies.

7. The effects model is selective in its criticisms of media depictions of violence

In addition to the point that 'antisocial' acts are ideologically defined in effects studies (as noted in section three above), we can also note that the media depictions of 'violence' which the effects model typically condemns are limited to fictional productions. The acts of violence which appear on a daily basis on news and serious factual programmes are seen as somehow exempt. The point here is not that depictions of violence in the news should necessarily be condemned in just the same, blinkered way, but rather to draw attention to another philosophical inconsistency which the model cannot account for. If the antisocial acts shown in drama series and films are expected to have an effect on the behaviour of viewers, even though such acts are almost always ultimately punished or have other negative consequences for the perpetrator, there is no obvious reason why the antisocial activities which are always in the news, and which frequently do *not* have such apparent consequences for their agents, should not have similar effects.

8. The effects model assumes superiority to the masses

Surveys typically show that whilst a certain proportion of the public feel that the media may cause other people to engage in antisocial behaviour, almost no-one ever says that they have been affected in that way themselves. This view is taken to extremes by researchers and campaigners whose work brings them into regular contact with the supposedly corrupting material, but who are unconcerned for their own well-being as they implicitly 'know' that the effects will only be on 'other people'. Insofar as these others are defined as children or 'unstable' individuals, their approach may seem not unreasonable; it is fair enough that such questions should be explored. None the less, the idea that it is unruly 'others' who will be affected – the uneducated? the working class? – remains at the heart of the effects paradigm, and is reflected in its texts (as well, presumably, as in the researchers' overenthusiastic interpretation of weak or flawed data, as discussed above).

George Gerbner and his colleagues, for example, write about 'heavy' television viewers as if this media consumption has necessarily had the opposite effect on the weightiness of their brains. Such people are assumed to have no selectivity or critical skills, and their habits are explicitly contrasted with preferred activities: 'Most viewers watch by the clock and either do not know what they will watch when they turn on the set, or follow established routines rather than choose each program as they would choose a book, a movie or an article' (Gerbner *et al.*, 1986, p. 19). This view, which knowingly makes inappropriate comparisons by ignoring the serial nature of many TV programmes, and which is unable to account for the widespread use of TV guides and VCRs with which audiences plan and arrange their viewing, reveals the kind of elitism and snobbishness which often seem to underpin such research. The point here is not that the content of the mass media must not be criticized, but rather that the mass audience themselves are not well served by studies which are willing to treat them as potential savages or actual fools.

9. The effects model makes no attempt to understand meanings of the media

A further fundamental flaw, hinted at in points three and four above, is that the effects model *necessarily* rests on a base of reductive assumptions and unjustified stereotypes regarding media content. To assert that, say, 'media violence' will bring negative consequences is not only to presume that depictions of violence in the media will always be promoting antisocial behaviour, and that such a category exists and makes sense, as noted above, but also assumes that the medium holds a singular message which will be carried unproblematically to the audience. The effects model therefore performs the double deception of presuming (a) that the media presents a singular and clear-cut 'message', and (b) that the proponents of the effects model are in a position to identify what that message is.

The meanings of media content are ignored in the simple sense that assumptions are made based on the appearance of elements removed from their context (for example, woman hitting man equals violence equals bad), and in the more sophisticated sense that even *in* context the meanings may be different for different viewers (woman hitting man equals an unpleasant act of aggression, or appropriate self-defence, *or a* triumphant act of revenge, *or* a refreshing change, or is simply uninteresting, *or* any of many further alternative readings). In-depth qualitative studies have unsurprisingly given support to the view that media audiences routinely arrive at their own, often heterogeneous, interpretations of everyday media texts (e.g. Buckingham, 1993, 1996; Hill, 1997; Schlesinger *et al.*, 1992; Gray, 1992; Palmer, 1986). Since the effects model rides roughshod over both the meanings that actions have for characters in dramas *and* the meanings which those depicted acts may have for the audience members, it can retain little credibility with those who consider popular entertainment to be more than just a set of very basic propaganda messages flashed at the audience in the simplest possible terms.

10. The effects model is not grounded in theory

Finally, and underlying many of the points made above, is the fundamental problem that the entire argument of the 'effects model' is substantiated with no theoretical reasoning beyond the bald assertions that particular kinds of effects *will* be produced by the media. The basic question of *why* the media should induce people to imitate its content has never been adequately tackled, beyond the simple idea that particular actions are 'glamorized'. (Obviously, *antisocial* actions are shown really *positively* so infrequently that this is an inadequate explanation.) Similarly, the question of how merely seeing an activity in the media would be translated into an actual *motive* which would prompt an individual to behave in a particular way is just as unresolved. The lack of firm theory has led to the effects model being based in the variety of assumptions outlined above – that the media (rather than people) is the unproblematic starting-point for research; that children will be unable to 'cope' with the media; that the categories of 'violence' or 'anti-social behaviour' are clear and self-evident; that the model's predictions can be verified by scientific research; that screen fictions are of concern, whilst news pictures are not; that researchers have the unique capacity to observe and classify social behaviour and its meanings, but that those researchers need not attend to the various possible meanings which media content may have for the audience. Each of these very substantial problems has its roots in the failure of media effects commentators to found their model in any coherent theory.

So what future for research on media influences?

The effects model, we have seen, has remarkably little going for it as an explanation of human behaviour, or of the media in society. Whilst any challenging or apparently illogical theory or model reserves the right to demonstrate its validity through empirical data, the effects model has failed also in that respect. Its continued survival is indefensible and unfortunate. However, the failure of this particular *model* does not mean that the impact of the mass media can no longer be considered or investigated.

The studies by Greg Philo and Glasgow University Media Group colleagues, for example, have used often imaginative methods to explore the influence of media presentations upon perceptions and interpretations of factual matters (e.g. Philo, 1990; Philo, 1996). I have realized rather late that my own study (Gauntlett, 1997) in which children made videos about the environment, which were used as a way of understanding the discourses and perspectives on environmentalism which the children had acquired from the media, can be seen as falling broadly within this tradition. The strength of this work is that it operates on a terrain different from that occupied by the effects model; even at the most obvious level, it is about *influences* and *perceptions*, rather than *effects* and *behaviour*. However, whilst such studies may provide valuable reflections on the relationship between mass media and audiences, they cannot – for the same reason – directly challenge claims made from within the 'effects model' paradigm (as Miller and Philo (1996) have misguidedly supposed). This is not a weakness of these studies, of course; the effects paradigm should be left to bury itself whilst prudent media researchers move on to explore these other areas.

Any paradigm which is able to avoid the flaws and assumptions which have inevitably and quite rightly ruined the effects model is likely to have some advantages. With the rise of qualitative studies which actually listen to media audiences, we are seeing the advancement of a more forward-thinking, sensible and compassionate view of those who enjoy the mass media. After decades of stunted and rather irresponsible talk about media 'effects', the emphasis is hopefully changing towards a more sensitive but rational approach to media scholarship.

Notes

1. This is a different version of an article which first appeared as 'Introduction: Why no clear answers on media effects?', in Tony Charlton and Kenneth David, eds (1997) *Elusive Links: Television, Video Games, Cinema and Children's Behaviour*, London: Park Published Papers.
2. Examination of programmes in full, sensibly also included in this study, found that 'punishments occur by the end of the program (62 per cent) more often than not for bad characters', however (Mediascope, 1996: 15). Despite this finding, and the likelihood that a number of the remaining 38 per cent would be punished in subsequent programmes, much is made of the finding that 'violence goes unpunished (73 per cent) in almost three out of four *scenes*' (point repeated on pp. x, 15, 25; my emphasis).
3. A longitudinal panel study is one in which the same group of people (the panel) are surveyed and/or observed at a number of points over a period of time.

References

Ariès, P. (1962) *Centuries of Childhood*, translated by Robert Baldick, London: Jonathan Cape.

Barker, M. (ed.) (1984) *The Video Nasties: Freedom and Censorship in the Media*, London: Pluto.

Barker, M. (1989) *Comics: Ideology, Power and the Critics*, Manchester: Manchester University Press.

Barker, M. (1993) Sex violence and videotape. *Sight and Sound*, 3(5) (new series; May), 10–12.

Borden, R. J. (1975) Witnessed aggression: influence of an observer's sex and values on aggressive responding. *Journal of Personality and Social Psychology*, 31(3), 567–73.

Buckingham, D. (1993) *Children Talking Television: The Making of Television Literacy*, London: The Falmer Press.

Buckingham, D. (1996) *Moving Images: Understanding Children's Emotional Responses to Television*, Manchester: Manchester University Press.

Chaffee, S. H. (1972) Television and adolescent aggressiveness (overview). In Comstock, G.A. and Rubinstein, E.A. (eds) *Television and Social Behavior: Reports and Papers, Vol. III: Television and Adolescent Aggressiveness*, Maryland: National Institute for Mental Health.

Gauntlett, D. (1995a) *Moving Experiences: Understanding Television's Influences and Effects*, London: John Libbey.

Gauntlett, D. (1995b) 'Full of very different people all mixed up together': Understanding community and environment through the classroom video project. *Primary Teaching Studies*, 9(1), 8–13.

Gauntlett, D. (1995c) *A Profile of Complainants and their Complaints*, BSC Research Working Paper No. 10, London: Broadcasting Standards Council.

Gauntlett, D. (1997) *Video Critical: Children, the Environment and Media Power*, Luton: John Libbey.

Gerbner, G. (1994) The politics of media violence: some reflections. In Linné, O. and Hamelink, C. J. (eds) *Mass Communication Research: On Problems and Policies: The Art of Asking the Right Questions*, Norwood, NJ: Ablex Publishing.

Gerbner, G., Gross, L., Morgan, M. and Signorielli, N. (1986) Living with television: the dynamics of the cultivation process. In Bryant, J., and Zillmann, D. (eds) *Perspectives on Media Effects*, Hillsdale, NJ: Lawrence Erlbaum Associates.

Gray, A. (1992) *Video Playtime: The Gendering of a Leisure Technology*, London: Routledge.

Griffin, C. (1993) *Representations of Youth: The Study of Youth and Adolescence in Britain and America*, Cambridge: Polity Press.

Hagell, A., and Newburn, T. (1994) *Young Offenders and the Media: Viewing Habits and Preferences*, London: Policy Studies Institute.

Hill, A. (1997) *Shocking Entertainment: Viewer Response to Violent Movies*, Luton: John Libbey.

Huesmann, L., Rowell, E., Leonard D., Lefkowitz, M. M. and Walder, L. O. (1984) Stability of aggression over time and generations. *Developmental Psychology*, 20(6), 1120–34.

Huesmann, L. R., Lagerspetz, K. and Eron, L., P. (1984) Intervening variables in the TV violence–aggression relation: evidence from two countries. *Developmental Psychology*, 20(5), 746–75.

Jenks, C. (1982) Introduction: constituting the child. In Jenks, C., (ed.) *The Sociology of Childhood*, London: Batsford.

Jenks, C. (1996) *Childhood*, London, Routledge.

Kenny, D. A. (1972) Two comments on cross-lagged correlation: threats to the internal validity of cross-lagged panel inference as related to 'Television violence and child aggression: a follow-up study'. In Comstock, G. A. and Rubinstein, E. A. (eds) *Television and Social Behavior: Reports and Papers*, Maryland: National Institute for Mental Health.

Lefkowitz, M. M., Eron, L. D., Walder, L. O. and Huesmann, L. R. (1972) Television violence and child aggression: a followup study. In Comstock, G. A. and Rubinstein, E. A. (eds) *Television and Social Behavior: Reports and Papers, Volume III: Television and Adolescent Aggressiveness*, Maryland: National Institute for Mental Health.

Lefkowitz, M. M., Eron, L. D., Walder, L. O. and Huesmann, L. R. (1977) *Growing Up To Be Violent: A Longitudinal Study of the Development of Aggression*, New York: Pergamon Press.

Mediascope, Inc. (1996) *National Television Violence Study Executive Summary 1994–95*, California: Mediascope.

Medved, M. (1992) *Hollywood vs. America: Popular Culture and the War on Traditional Values*, London: HarperCollins.

Milavsky, J. R., Kessler, R. C., Stipp, H. H., and Rubens, W. S. (1982a) *Television and Aggression: A Panel Study*, Academic Press, New York.

Milavsky, J. R., Kessler, R., Stipp, H., and Rubens, W. S. (1982b) Television and aggression: results of a panel study. In Pearl, D., Bouthilet, L. and Lazar, J. (eds) *Television and Behavior: Ten Years of Scientific Progress and Implications for the Eighties, Volume 2: Technical Reviews*, Maryland: National Institute for Mental Health.

Miller, D. and Philo, G. (1996) The media do influence us. In *Sight and Sound*, 6(12), (December 1996), 18–20.

Palmer, P. (1986) *The Lively Audience: A Study of Children Around the TV Set*, Sydney: Allen & Unwin.

Philo, G. (1990) *Seeing and Believing: The Influence of Television*, London, Routledge.

Philo, Greg (ed.) (1996) *Media and Mental Distress*, London: Longman.

Piaget, J. (1926) *The Language and Thought of the Child*, New York: Harcourt Brace.

Piaget, J. (1929) *The Child's Conception of the World*, London: Routledge.

Schlesinger, P., Dobash, R. E., Dobash, R. P. and Weaver, C. K. (1992) *Women Viewing Violence*, London: British Film Institute Publishing.

Van Evra, J. (1990) *Television and Child Development*, Hillsdale, NJ: Lawrence Erlbaum Associates.

11

Children and television: a critical overview of the research

David Buckingham

One of the most immediately striking things about research into children and television is the sheer quantity of it. At a conservative estimate, there have probably been over seven thousand accounts of research in the field published since the introduction of television in the 1950s, ranging from brief reports of one-off experiments to extensive and lavishly funded surveys. So why has the relationship between children and television been such a major focus of research? Why have children been singled out for attention, and considered separately from adults? Why has television been chosen from among the myriad of other factors in children's lives? And why has so much of the research concentrated on the potential harm which television might cause them?

There are no easy answers to these questions. On one level, the research might be seen simply as a response to the relative importance of television. Thus, it is frequently pointed out that children today spend more time watching television than they do in school, or indeed on any other activity apart from sleeping – although elderly people are in fact the heaviest viewers, while teenagers watch the least of all. Yet the identification of children as a 'special audience' for television is not simply a matter of viewing figures. On the contrary, it invokes all sorts of moral and ideological assumptions about what we believe children – and, by extension, adults – to be.

Defining 'the child'

As histories of childhood have shown, the definition and separation of children as a distinct social category are a relatively recent development, which has taken on a particular form in Western industrialized societies (Ariès, 1962; James, 1993). This process has been accompanied by a veritable explosion of discourses, both *about* childhood and directed *at* children themselves. The emergence of developmental psychology, and its popularization in advice literature for parents, for example, indicates some of the ways in which norms about what is 'suitable' or 'natural' behaviour for children have been enforced. Likewise, the production of children's literature and children's toys – and eventually of children's television – has invoked all sorts of assumptions about what it means to be a child.

As these examples imply, this construction of 'the child' is both a negative and a positive enterprise: it involves attempts to restrict children's access to knowledge about aspects of adult life (most obviously sex and violence), and yet it also entails a kind of pedagogy – an attempt to 'do them good' as well as protect them from harm. The constitution of children as a media audience, and as objects of research and debate, has been marked by a complex balance between these positive and negative motivations. In the early days of television, for example, one of the primary advertising appeals made by the equipment manufacturers was on the grounds of the medium's educational potential for the young (Melody, 1973); and while some have argued that this pedagogical motivation has increasingly been sacrificed to commercialism, it remains a central tenet of public service provision for children. Likewise, early debates about the role of television in the family, both in the UK and in the US, were characterized by genuine ambivalence about its potential, as either an attack on family life or as a means of bringing about domestic harmony (Spigel, 1992; Oswell, 1995).

This definition of what it means to be a child is an ongoing process, which is subject to a considerable amount of social and historical variation. Policies on the regulation of children's programming (Anderson *et al.*, 1982), for example, often reflect much more fundamental assumptions about the nature of childhood. Likewise, the struggle between parents and children over what is 'appropriate' for children to watch and to know is part of a continuing struggle over the rights and responsibilities of children; and yet the definition of what is 'childish' or 'adult' is also a central preoccupation among children themselves, not least in their discussions of television (Buckingham, 1994).

Public debates

While there is certainly a considerable amount of diversity in the actual uses of television, the dominant assumption in public debates is that children's relationship with the medium is a fundamentally negative and damaging element in their lives. In this respect, it is important to locate the concern about television historically, in the context both of evolving definitions of childhood and of recurrent responses to the advent of new cultural forms and communications technologies. Concern about the negative impact of the media on young people has a very long history (Lusted, 1985; Buckingham, 1993a). Over 2000 years ago, the Greek philosopher Plato proposed to ban dramatic poets from his ideal Republic, for fear that their stories about the immoral antics of the gods would influence impressionable young minds. In more recent times, popular literature, music hall, the cinema and children's comics have all provoked 'moral panics' which have typically led to greater censorship designed to protect children from their allegedly harmful effects. In this respect, more recent controversies such as the 'video nasties' scare of the 1980s or the debates about screen violence that followed the killing of James Bulger in 1993 can be seen as merely heirs to a much longer tradition (Barker, 1984; Buckingham, 1996).

These different areas of concern share a fundamental belief in the enormous power of television, and in the inherent vulnerability of children. Television has, it would seem, an irresistible ability to 'brainwash' and 'narcotize' children, drawing them away from other, more worthwhile activities and influences. From this perspective, children are at once innocent and potentially monstrous: the veneer of civilization is only skin deep, and can easily be penetrated by the essentially irrational appeals of the visual media (Barker, 1984). Such arguments often partake of the fantasy of a 'golden age' before television, in which adults were able to 'keep secrets' from children, and in which innocence and harmony reigned. By virtue of the ways in which it gives children access to the hidden, and sometimes negative, aspects of adult life, television is accused of having caused the 'disappearance of childhood' itself (Postman, 1983).

To a large extent, what appears to be occurring here is a process of displacement. Genuine, often deep-seated anxieties about what are perceived as undesirable moral or social changes lead to a search for a single causal explanation. Blaming television may thus serve to deflect attention away from other possible causes – causes which may well be 'closer to home' or simply much too complicated to understand (Connell, 1985). The symbolic values that are attached to the notion of childhood, and the negative associations of an 'unnatural' technology such as television, make this a particularly potent combination for social commentators of all persuasions. Yet they also make it extremely difficult to arrive at a more balanced and less sensationalist estimation of the role of television in children's lives.

All research is based on epistemological and theoretical assumptions, even if these are not always made explicit. Not least because of the intense emotions that often surround the issue of children's relationship with television, and because of the quantity and diversity of the work itself, it is thus extremely difficult to produce definitive statements about what 'research has shown'. The review which follows, therefore, is organized in terms of the different research paradigms – that is, the broad theoretical orientations – which have guided and informed specific research projects. As I shall indicate, there are several fundamental incompatibilities between them, not only in what they take to be valid knowledge, but also in terms of the questions they have chosen to address in the first place.

The search for negative effects

Research into the effects of television violence on children has remained the most prominent preoccupation in this field. Yet the search for negative effects has also encompassed other areas, some of which I go on to consider here. Broadly speaking, this research regards the relationship between television and children as one of cause and effect: the 'messages' contained within the medium are assessed in terms of their quantifiable impact on viewers' attitudes or behaviour. Nevertheless, research has gradually moved away from the cruder form of behaviourism (the so-called 'magic bullet theory') which was apparent in some of the early research on children's responses to television violence. While the influence is still seen to flow in one direction, the emphasis now is on the range of 'intervening variables' which mediate between the stimulus and the response. In the process, effects researchers have tended to adopt rather more cautious estimates of the influence of the medium. Brief accounts of research in two areas will serve to illustrate some of these developments.

Advertising

Advertising is perhaps a 'special case' in communications research, in that its intention is clearly and explicitly to persuade, and hence to produce specific behavioural effects – namely, purchasing. Of course, advertising may have broader effects, for example in terms of encouraging more generalized forms of 'consumerism' or 'materialism', or in terms of ideology: advertising is often accused of promoting 'false needs' and irrational fantasies, or reinforcing exaggerated gender stereotypes. Nevertheless, it is often children who are seen to be particularly at risk here, precisely because of their apparent inability to recognize the persuasive intentions of advertising. Even researchers who reject more exaggerated notions of advertising as 'manipulation', and of audiences as simply 'malleable consumers', have made a special case when it comes to children: unlike adults, children are seen here as lacking in 'the level of conceptual and experiential maturity needed to evaluate commercial messages rationally' (Leiss *et al.*, 1990: 365), and hence as especially vulnerable to influence.

In fact, research has largely failed to substantiate many of the more exaggerated claims about the effects of advertising on children. As with the violence research, this is partly because of methodological limitations (Goldberg and Gorn, 1983). For example, most children are likely to respond positively to a question like 'would you like to have most of the things they show on TV commercials?' (Atkin, 1980), but this can hardly be said to prove the advertising stimulates these desires, or that they are necessarily 'false' – or indeed, that such responses can be taken as evidence of a more general set of 'materialistic' values (Greenberg and Brand, 1993). Similarly, while it might be proven that 'heavy viewers' are likely to eat more Hershey bars or to use more mouthwash or acne cream than 'light viewers' (Atkin, 1980), this does not necessarily prove anything about the *causal* role of advertising.

As such, much of the evidence here remains equivocal. For example, researchers have tended to conclude that advertising has a relatively weak influence on nutritional knowledge, and that parental attitudes and socioeconomic status are more important (Young, 1990). While advertising may influence preference for individual brands, there is less evidence that it causes children to consume more of any given *type* of product (Goldberg and Gorn, 1983). Indeed, research would suggest that television is a less significant source of product information than other sources, such as visits to the shops (Wartella, 1980).

Despite these qualifications, the dominant view which informs the research here is one that has been aptly characterized by Brian Young (1986) as 'child-as-innocent and advertiser-as-seducer'. Children tend to be defined here as passive victims of persuasion, as essentially trusting and uncritical viewers. In fact, there is a good deal of research which points to children's growing cynicism about the claims of advertising. While estimates vary, it seems that children become aware of the persuasive intentions of advertising at an early age (Gaines and Esserman, 1981; Dorr, 1986), and that by the time they reach middle childhood an intense scepticism becomes the order of the day (Young, 1990; Buckingham, 1993b). From a psychological perspective, these 'cognitive defences' are seen as intervening variables which moderate the impact of advertising – although the fact that children possess such defences does not necessarily mean that they will be used (Brucks *et al.*, 1988). Here again, the significance that is attributed to such defences is heavily dependent upon the methods used to measure them: performance data should not be confused with competence data (Young, 1990).

Young (1990) reformulates this issue in terms of the notion of 'advertising literacy', arguing that children's growing awareness of the functions of advertising, and their increasing scepticism about it, can be seen as part of a more general development in 'metacommunicative' abilities. In middle childhood, he suggests, children become much more capable of standing back from language and other forms of communication, and reflecting upon how they work. For example, they increasingly recognize that utterances may not be intended literally, that they may be inconsistent or indeed deliberately ambiguous; and they become much more sensitive to metaphor, irony, humour and other non-literal uses of language – precisely those which are so central to advertising. Young's argument here usefully moves beyond the behaviourist assumptions of effects research, and towards a 'constructivist' position (to be considered in more detail below); although in common with that research, it tends to neglect the social and interpersonal dynamics that surround the viewing process (and indeed the purchasing process), and to leave aside the considerable pleasures which are involved (Buckingham, 1993b).

Stereotyping and 'social learning'

Similar assumptions would seem to inform research on children's social learning from television – that is, its contribution to forming their attitudes and beliefs about society. Television is routinely cited as a powerful influence on children's political socialization (Chaffee and Yang, 1990), and on their beliefs about social institutions such as the family (Dorr *et al.*, 1990), the police (Murray, 1993) and government (Conway *et al.*, 1981). While there is a limited amount of research on the 'pro-social' or educational effects of television, much of the work in this field has concentrated on the influence of negative 'stereotyping' of particular social groups. Thus, many studies have concluded that television is a powerful source of children's beliefs about gender roles (Morgan, 1987; Signorielli, 1993), about other ethnic groups (Graves, 1993) and about the elderly (Kovaric, 1993); and in each case, it is suggested that television causes them to adopt beliefs which are inaccurate, intolerant or otherwise negative.

Here again, however, there are significant methodological problems, which are perhaps more acute than in the other areas discussed so far. One tendency here – which is also characteristic of a great deal of public debates in this field – is to assume that effects can simply be 'read off' from the analysis of content. Statistical studies of the representation of particular social groups on television, for example, are often implicitly taken as evidence of its influence on children's beliefs about those groups (Berry and Asamen, 1993). Such analyses frequently seem to take the form of a simplistic 'head count', or a reductive (and sometimes very impressionistic) analysis of characters' attributes (Palmer *et al.*, 1993). In-depth analysis of television, and particularly of children's television, is conspicuous by its absence here.

Of course, it is much more difficult to gather evidence about attitudes or beliefs than about aggressive behaviour or purchasing decisions; and establishing proof of the *causal* role of television in such longer-term processes is bound to be fraught with problems. 'Before-and-after' studies which attempt to quantify the effects of exposure to a 'stereotypical' stimulus (e.g. Tan, 1979) are perhaps particularly inappropriate in this respect. Yet even much more elaborate forms of 'cultivation analysis' which have attempted to correlate attitudes with levels of television exposure have encountered considerable difficulties in establishing evidence of causality (Wober and Gunter, 1988). For example, dividing people into 'light viewers' and 'heavy viewers', which is characteristic of this approach, implicitly assumes that television is all the same, and neglects the diversity of material to which viewers might be exposed. For example, 'heavy viewers' may be more likely to encounter 'counter-stereotypical' representations; and since these are exceptions to the norm, they may well have more impact upon some viewers.

Kevin Durkin (1985) provides a valuable critique of this approach, which focuses particularly on television's contribution to children's learning of 'sex roles'. While he agrees that television tends to provide 'stereotyped' representations of male and female roles, he rejects the view that these are somehow 'burned' into the viewer's unconscious, or that they necessarily have a cumulative effect. Durkin argues that the 'direct effects' approach tends to neglect the relationship between television and other factors which contribute to sex role socialization; and that it ignores developmental changes in children's understanding and use of the medium as they mature. While he does not go so far as to question the more fundamental assumptions which are at stake here – notions such as 'stereotyping' and 'sex role', for example, have been heavily contested elsewhere (e.g. Barker, 1989; Davies, 1990) – Durkin does point to the need to locate children's responses to television within their social context, and to acknowledge the ways in which they actively make sense of what they watch. This emphasis is one which will be pursued later in this chapter.

Active audiences?

While advocates of the 'magic bullet' theory are still to be found, the development of effects research has largely been in the direction of emphasizing the role of 'intervening variables' which mediate between television and its audience. Far from seeing the audience as a mass of undifferentiated individuals, the focus has increasingly been on 'individual differences' which lead viewers to respond in different ways to the same messages. Over the past two decades, this tradition has been joined by newer perspectives, which have defined children as 'active viewers'. The notion of 'activity' here is partly a rhetorical one, and it is often used in rather imprecise ways. Yet what unites this work is a view of children, not as passive recipients of television messages, but as active interpreters and processors of meaning. The meaning of television, from this perspective, is not delivered *to* the audience, but constructed by it.

Uses and gratifications

Two distinct traditions of research can be identified here. The first is that of 'uses and gratifications'. In practice, uses and gratifications research has tended to focus largely on adults, although there are some important studies which focus on children and young people. Rosengren and Windahl (1989), for example, paint a complex picture of the very heterogeneous uses of television among Swedish adolescents, and its interaction with other media such as popular music. In the process, they challenge many general assertions about media effects, for example in relation to violence and displacement, arguing that the socializing influence of television will depend upon its relationship with other influences, and upon the diverse and variable meanings which its users attach to it. Thus, for example, television viewing or popular music will have a different significance depending upon the child's orientation towards the school, the family and the peer group. As they indicate, the influence of variables such as age, gender and social class means that different children can effectively occupy different 'media worlds' – an argument which clearly undermines any easy generalizations about 'children' as an homogeneous social group.

Constructivist perspectives

Uses and gratifications research also has a great deal in common with the 'constructivist' or cognitive approach, which is the second major perspective I shall discuss here. This tradition is both extensive and diverse, yet the shared emphasis here is on the psychological processes whereby viewers construct meaning from television. Rather than simply responding to stimuli, viewers are seen here as consciously processing, interpreting and evaluating information. In making sense of what they watch, viewers use 'schemas' or 'scripts', sets of plans and expectations which they have built up from their previous experience both of television and of the world in general (for a review, see Dorr, 1986). In studying children's understanding of television, cognitive psychologists have tended to concentrate on the 'micro' rather than the 'macro' aspects – on detailed aspects of mental processing, rather than on questions about television's role in forming attitudes or beliefs. The following sections offer brief 'snapshots' of some of the principal concerns.

Attention and comprehension

The work of Daniel Anderson and his colleagues (e.g. Anderson and Lorch, 1983) illustrates the ways in which research in this area has increasingly come to regard children's relationship with television as an active, rather than merely a reactive, process. Anderson refutes the idea that attention is a kind of conditioned reflex which will be produced automatically by certain stimuli, such as rapid movement or loud sound effects. On the contrary, he argues that children actively choose to pay attention to television, and that the choices they make depend upon their efforts to understand what they watch, and on the other activities which are available in the viewing environment. According to Anderson, comprehension does not follow automatically from attention: rather, children's attention is partly determined by their comprehension processes.

Anderson's focus is primarily on visual attention, and he tends to neglect the role of auditory or linguistic factors – not least because auditory attention is far more difficult to identify simply by observation. Nevertheless, the argument that children actively choose the amount of mental effort they invest in television has been strongly supported by the influential work of Gavriel Salomon (e.g. 1983). Significantly, Salomon argues that these choices may be affected by children's preconceptions about the medium as a whole, which may themselves be culturally specific: his comparative research with Israeli and North American children indicated that the latter's view of television as a 'less demanding' medium led them to invest less mental effort, and hence to learn less (Salomon, 1984).

Children's understanding of narrative

While studies of attention and comprehension have tended to focus on a fairly limited range of 'formal features' (Meyer, 1983), there has been some cognitive research into broader aspects of television, such as narrative. W. Andrew Collins (e.g. 1981) and his colleagues have looked at the ways in which children's understanding of narrative varies according to the 'world knowledge' which they bring to it, and also according to their past experience of television itself (their 'television literacy'). As they develop, children acquire an increasingly flexible knowledge of 'common event sequences' which enable them to predict and interpret narrative.

One problem with this approach – and indeed with most studies of comprehension – is that it implicitly assumes the existence of an 'objective' meaning within a given text. Thus, Collins evaluates children's ability to distinguish between 'central content' and 'peripheral content', or between 'essential' and 'non-essential' features, although the distinctions between them are made by the researchers (or by other adult subjects) rather than by children themselves. Likewise, his judgement of children's ability to make inferences, for example about characters' motivations and feelings, depends upon a comparison with the 'correct' inferences which are made by the researchers (see Buckingham, 1993b). In common with much cognitive research, there appears to be an implicit view here of the child as a 'deficit system': children at certain ages are seen to be unable to accomplish the 'logical' sequencing of visual images, to recall the 'essential' features of a narrative, or to 'correctly' distinguish between positive and negative characters – which of course implies that adults' responses to such things are taken as the norm (Anderson, 1981).

Developmental studies

One of the major concerns of the constructivist approach is with the ways in which children's understanding of television changes along with their general intellectual development. Much of the research in this area has been heavily informed by the work of Piaget, which is perhaps surprising given the extensive critiques to which it has been subjected in other areas of psychology (e.g. Donaldson, 1978; Walkerdine, 1984). Grant Noble (1975), for example, is one of many researchers who seeks to provide an account of the televiewing styles of children at each of Piaget's developmental stages, which represents a steady progression towards 'the sophistication which will take final shape at the University film club' – an approach which may seem to neglect those who only get as far as the local video shop.

One particular concern here is with the development of children's ability to distinguish between reality and fantasy on television. According to Hawkins (1977), children's judgements of television depend both on their knowledge of the constructed nature of the medium (which he terms 'magic window' knowledge) , and on their knowledge or 'social expectations' about the world in general. As Dorr (1983) indicates, such judgements depend both on children's general cognitive development and on their experience of the medium: children use formal or generic 'cues', and build up a growing body of knowledge about the processes of television production. 'Judging reality' is a complex and multi-faceted process, which involves the application of a wide range of different (and sometimes conflicting) criteria.

Some qualifications

While the theoretical basis of this research is outwardly very different from that of the more behaviourist effects studies, several limitations can be identified. Indeed, in some respects, the 'cognitive revolution' which was so apparent in other areas of psychology has remained incomplete here. Cognitive researchers have often continued to rely on behaviourist hypotheses and methods, for example about the negative effects of television viewing on mental processes. Cognitive processing is often seen merely as an 'intervening variable'; and meaning continues to be seen as something which is inherent in the text, which can be objectively identified and quantified.

As in many other areas of psychology, cognitive researchers have focused almost exclusively on the intellectual aspects of children's relationship with television. This focus on the individual's internal mental processes has made it difficult to assess the role of social and cultural factors in the formation of consciousness and understanding. While some cognitive researchers do acknowledge these factors in theory, much of the research itself appears to function with a notion of 'the child' which is abstracted from any social or historical context. Factors such as gender, 'race' and social class tend to be bracketed off, or regarded as influences which only come into play when the already-formed individual enters the social world.

Both within effects research, and in the constructivist approach, the relationship between children and television has thus predominantly been conceived in *psychological* terms, as a matter of the isolated individual's encounter with the screen. The central questions are about what television does to the child's mind – or, more recently, about what the child's mind does with television. In the process, television itself, and the social processes through which its meaning is established and defined, have often been neglected. These are central issues in the third research paradigm I shall consider here.

Cultural Studies: an emergent paradigm?

Studies of children's relationship with television have been a relatively marginal concern in Media and Cultural Studies. To some extent, this may reflect a wider division of academic labour, whereby the study of children is still largely seen as the proper domain of psychology. At the same time, the study of audiences in general has been a relatively recent development in Cultural Studies; and while there is now a growing body of debate about the issue, there are still very few substantial empirical studies. While it is not necessarily incompatible with many of the concerns and theoretical perspectives discussed above, the Cultural Studies approach would appear to go beyond many of the limitations both of effects research and of 'active audience' theories.

Cultural Studies is itself a rather broad area, whose boundaries are far from well defined. Yet it has often been conceptualized in terms of an interaction between *institutions, texts* and *audiences* (e.g. Johnson, 1985/6); and it is under these three headings that I will offer a brief review of its potential contribution to the study of children's relationship with television.

Institutions

Accounts of children's television written from within the industry have perhaps inevitably tended towards public relations (e.g. Home, 1993; Laybourne, 1993). Yet the study of the institutional context of children's television production has been a relatively marginal concern within communications research generally. Early studies such as Melody (1973) and Turow (1981) adopted a broad 'political economy' approach, focusing on questions of ownership, marketing and regulation. With the exception of Palmer (1987), there has been very little analysis of producers' assumptions and expectations about their child audience; and while there has been some historical work on the evolution of regulatory policy on children's television (e.g. Anderson *et al.*, 1982; Kunkel and Watkins, 1988), this also has remained under-researched.

More recently, however, the increasing 'commercialization' of children's television and the apparent retreat from the public service tradition have generated a growing body of academic research and debate (e.g. Engelhardt, 1986; Blumler, 1992; Kline, 1993; Seiter, 1993; Buckingham, 1995a). On the one hand, there has been concern about the decline in factual programming for children, and the extent to which production is increasingly tied in with merchandising; yet there have also been calls for a more positive (or at least less Puritanical) account of 'consumption', and a more thoroughgoing discussion of what is meant by 'quality'. The highly 'gendered' nature of a great deal of children's television has been a particular focus of analysis here; although such studies implicitly raise some very challenging questions about the 'taste cultures' of children, and the ways in which their specific needs as an audience are to be defined.

Texts

As I have implied, the study of television texts within the mainstream communications research tradition has been dominated by statistical content analysis. Television is typically seen to contain fixed 'messages' which can be objectively identified and quantified. This is most obvious in the case of effects research, for example in the 'head counts' which have characterized research into social learning from television. Yet despite the much more sophisticated approach to 'mental processing' within the constructivist tradition, cognitive psychologists' analysis of television texts frequently appears to neglect the complexity of even the most simple programmes (Livingstone, 1990). Ambiguity, 'openness' and contradiction, which many analyses of popular television have shown to be fundamental to its success (e.g. Fiske, 1987), have effectively been ignored.

By contrast, researchers in Media and Cultural Studies have tended to adopt much more complex forms of *textual* analysis, which are variously informed by semiotics, structuralism, psychoanalysis and post-structuralist theory. Until recently, there has been very little attempt to extend this approach to the study of children's television, although in many respects this would seem to provide an important testing ground for wider arguments about television's role in 'positioning' the viewer (Buckingham, 1987a, b). Thus, analysis has focused on the ways in which children's television provides opportunities for 'para-social interaction' (Noble, 1975), how it handles the relationship between 'information' and 'entertainment' (Buckingham, 1995b), and how it addresses the child viewer (Davies, 1995). As in children's literature, the position of television as a 'parent' or 'teacher' and the process of attempting to 'draw in' the child is fraught with uncertainties (cf. Rose, 1984).

Audiences

As I have indicated, Cultural Studies offers a perspective on the audience which is significantly more 'social' than that of the research discussed above. At least in principle, viewers are seen here not as unique and coherent individuals, but as sites of conflict, 'points of intersection' between a variety of potentially conflicting discourses, which in turn derive from different social locations and experiences (for example, in terms of social class, gender and ethnicity) Different discourses will be mobilized in different ways by different viewers in different contexts; and the production of meaning is therefore seen as a complex process of social negotiation (for a review, see Moores, 1993).

Hodge and Tripp (1986) apply a social semiotic perspective, both to the analysis of children's programming, and to audience data. The central focus here is on the social processes through which meaning is constructed, and the power-relationships which inevitably characterize them. This approach has been pursued in my own work, where there is a central emphasis on the ways in which children define and construct their social identities through talk about television (Buckingham, 1993b, 1996).

In parallel with this work, it is possible to identify a more strictly 'ethnographic' approach to studying children's viewing, both within the context of the home (e.g. Palmer, 1986; Lindlof, 1987; Richards, 1993) and in the context of the peer group (Willis, 1990; Wood, 1993). Marie Gillespie's (1995) study of the use of television among a South Asian community in London, for example, integrates an analysis of the role of television within the dynamics of the family and the peer group with an account of children's responses to specific genres such as news and soap opera. Television is used here partly as a heuristic means of gaining insight into 'other' cultures, although (as with the work discussed above), there is a self-reflexive emphasis on the role of the researcher, and on the power-relationships between researchers and their child subjects, which is typically absent from mainstream research.

The work discussed here is both new and comparatively tentative in its claims, and it would be false to claim that it has resolved the problems it has set itself. In particular, the challenge of *integrating* the different areas of concern – with institutions, texts and audiences – remains a central priority in future work, and indeed in media research more broadly. This is not, I would argue, simply a matter of balancing the equation, and thereby finding a happy medium between the 'power of the text' and the 'power of the audience'. Nor is it something that can be achieved in the abstract, through the application of theory. Like many other areas considered in this book, the relationship between children and television can only be fully understood in the context of a wider analysis of the ways in which both are constructed and defined.

References

Anderson, D. R. and Lorch, E. P. (1983) Looking at television: action or reaction? In Bryant, J. and Anderson, D. R. (eds) *Children's Understanding of Television*, New York: Academic Press.

Anderson, J. A. (1981) Research on children and television: a critique. *Journal of Broadcasting,* 25(4), 395–400.

Anderson, J. A., Meyer, T. and Hexamer, A. (1982) An examination of the assumptions underlying telecommunications social policies treating children as a specialized audience. In Burgoon, M. (ed.) *Communication Yearbook 5*, New Brunswick: Transaction Books.

Ariès, P. (1973) *Centuries of Childhood*, Harmondsworth: Penguin.

Atkin, C.K. (1980) Effects of television advertising on children. In Palmer, E. L. and Dorr, A. (eds) *Children and the Faces of Television: Teaching, Violence, Selling*, New York: Academic Press.

Barker, M. (ed.) (1984) *The Video Nasties*, London: Pluto.

Barker, M. (1989) *Comics: Ideology, Power and the Critics*, Manchester: Manchester University Press.

Berry, G. L. and Asamen, J. K. (1993) *Children and Television: Images in a Changing Sociocultural World*, London: Sage.

Blumler, J. (1992) *The Future of Children's Television in Britain: An Enquiry for the Broadcasting Standards Council*, London: Broadcasting Standards Council.

Brucks, M., Armstrong, G. M. and Goldberg, M. E. (1988) Children's use of cognitive defences against advertising: a cognitive response approach, *Journal of Consumer Research*, **14**, 471–82.

Buckingham, D. (1987a) The construction of subjectivity in educational television. Part one: towards a new agenda. *Journal of Educational Television*, **13**(2), 137–46.

Buckingham, D. (1987b) The construction of subjectivity in educational television. Part two: You and Me – a case study. *Journal of Educational Television*, **13**(3), 187–200.

Buckingham, D. (1993a) Introduction: young people and the media. In Buckingham, D. (ed.) *Reading Audiences: Young People and the Media*, Manchester: Manchester University Press.

Buckingham, D. (1993b) *Children Talking Television: The Making of Television Literacy*, London: Falmer Press.

Buckingham, D. (1994) Television and the definition of childhood. In Mayall, B. (ed.) *Children's Childhoods Observed and Experienced*, London: Falmer Press.

Buckingham, D. (1995a) The commercialisation of childhood? The place of the market in children's media culture, *Changing English*, **2**(2), 17–41.

Buckingham, D. (1995b) On the impossibility of children's television. In Bazalgette, C. and Buckingham, D. (eds) *In Front of the Children*, London: British Film Institute.

Buckingham, D. (1996) *Moving Images: Understanding Children's Emotional Responses to Television*, Manchester: Manchester University Press.

Chaffee, S. H. and Yang, S-M. (1990) Communication and political socialization. In Ichilov, O. (ed.) *Political Socialization, Citizenship Education and Democracy*, New York: Teachers College Press.

Collins, W. A. (1981) Schemata for understanding television. In Kelly, H. and Gardner, H. (eds) *Viewing Children Through Television*, San Francisco: Jossey-Bass.

Connell, I. (1985) Fabulous powers: blaming the media. In Masterman, L. (ed.) *Television Mythologies*, London: Comedia/MK Media Press.

Conway, M. M., Wyckoff, M. L., Feldbaum, E. and Ahern, D. (1981) The news media in children's political socialization. *Public Opinion Quarterly*, **45**(2), 164–78.

Davies, B. (1990) *Frogs and Snails and Feminist Tales*, Sydney: Allen & Unwin.

Davies, M. M. (1995) Babes 'n' the hood: pre-school television and its audiences in the United States and Britain. In Bazalgette, C. and Buckingham, D. (eds) *In Front of the Children*, London: British Film Institute.

Donaldson, M. (1978) *Children's Minds*, London: Fontana.

Dorr, A. (1983) No shortcuts to judging reality. In Bryant, J. and Anderson, D. R. (eds) *Children's Understanding of Television*, New York: Academic Press.

Dorr, A. (1986) *Television and Children: A Special Medium for a Special Audience*, Beverly Hills: Sage.

Dorr, A., Kovaric, P. and Doubleday, C. (1990) Age and content influences on children's perceptions of the realism of television families. *Journal of Broadcasting*, 34(4), 377–97.

Durkin, K. (1985) *Television, Sex Roles and Children*, Milton Keynes: Open University Press.

Engelhardt, T. (1986) The strawberry shortcake strategy. In T. Gitlin (ed.) *Watching Television*, New York: Pantheon.

Fiske, J. (1987) *Television Culture*, London: Methuen.

Gaines, L. and Esserman, J. F. (1981) A quantitative study of young children's comprehension of television programs and commercials. In Esserman, J. F. (ed.) *Television Advertising and Children*, New York: Child Research Service.

Gillespie, M. (1995) *Television, Ethnicity and Cultural Change*, London: Routledge.

Goldberg, M. E. and Gorn, G. J. (1983) Researching the effects of television advertising on children: a methodological critique. In Howe, M. J. A. (ed.) *Learning from Television: Psychological and Educational Research*, London: Academic Press.

Graves, S. B. (1993) Television, the portrayal of African Americans, and the development of children's attitudes. In Berry, G. L. and Asamen, J. K. (eds) *Children and Television*, London: Sage.

Greenberg, B. S. and Brand, J. E. (1993) Television news and advertising in schools: the 'Channel One' controversy. *Journal of Communication*, 43(1), 143–51.

Hawkins, R. P. (1977) The dimensional structure of children's perceptions of television reality. *Communication Research*, 4(3), 299–320.

Hodge, B. and Tripp, D. (1986) *Children and Television: A Semiotic Approach*, Cambridge: Polity Press.

Home, A. (1993) *Into the Box of Delights: A History of Children's Television*, London: BBC Books.

James, A. (1993) *Childhood Identities*, Edinburgh: Edinburgh University Press.

Johnson, R. (1985/6) What is Cultural Studies anyway? *Social Text*, 16, 38–80.

Kline, S. (1993) *Out of the Garden: Toys and Children's Culture in the Age of TV Marketing*, London: Verso.

Kovaric, P. (1993) Television, the portrayal of the elderly, and children's attitudes. In Berry, G. L. and Asamen, J. K. (eds) *Children and Television*, London: Sage.

Kunkel, D. and Watkins, B. (1987) Evolution of children's television regulatory policy. *Journal of Broadcasting and Electronic Media*, 31(4), 367–89.

Laybourne, G. (1993) The Nickelodeon experience. In Berry, G. L. and Asamen, J. K. (eds) *Children and Television*, London: Sage.

Leiss, W., Kline, S. and Jhally, S. (1990) *Social Communication in Advertising*, London: Routledge.

Lindlof, T. (ed.) (1987) *Natural Audiences*, Newbury Park, CA: Sage.

Livingstone, S. (1990) *Making Sense of Television*, Oxford: Pergamon.

Lusted, D. (1985) A history of suspicion: educational attitudes to television. In Lusted, D. and Drummond, P. (eds) *TV and Schooling*, London: British Film Institute.

Melody, W. (1973) *Children's Television: The Economics of Exploitation*, New Haven: Yale University Press.

Meyer, M. (ed.) (1983) *Children and the Formal Features of Television*, Munich: Saur.

Moores, S. (1993) *Interpreting Audiences*, London: Sage.

Morgan, M. (1987) Television, sex-role attitudes and sex-role behavior. *Journal of Early Adolescence*, 7(3), 269–82.

Murray, J. P. (1993) The developing child in a multimedia society. In Berry, G. L. and Asamen, J. K. (eds) *Children and Television*, London: Sage.

Noble, G. (1975) *Children in Front of the Small Screen*, London: Constable.

Oswell, D. (1995) Watching with mother. In Bazalgette, C. and Buckingham, D. (eds) *In Front of the Children*, London: British Film Institute.

Palmer, E. (1987) *Children in the Cradle of Television*, Lexington, Mass: Lexington Books.

Palmer, E., Smith, K. T. and Strawser, K. S. (1993) Rubik's tube: developing a child's television worldview. In Berry, G. L. and Asamen, J. K. (eds) *Children and Television*, London: Sage.

Palmer, P. (1986) *The Lively Audience*, Sydney: Allen & Unwin.

Postman, N. (1983) *The Disappearance of Childhood*, London: W. H. Allen.

Richards, C. (1993) Taking sides? What young girls do with television. In Buckingham, D. (ed.) *Reading Audiences: Young People and the Media*, Manchester: Manchester University Press.

Rose, J. (1984) *The Case of Peter Pan: Or the Impossibility of Children's Fiction*, London: Macmillan.

Rosengren, K. E. and Windahl, S. (1989) *Media Matter: TV Use in Childhood and Adolescence*, Norwood, New Jersey: Ablex.

Salomon, G. (1983) Beyond the formats of television: the effects of students' preconceptions on the experience of televiewing. In Meyer, M. (ed.) *Children and the Formal Features of Television*, Munich: Saur.

Salomon, G. (1984) Television is 'easy' and print is 'tough': the differential invest- ment of mental effort as a function of perceptions and attributions. *Journal of Educational Psychology*, **76**, 647–58.

Seiter, E. (1993) *Sold Separately: Parents and Children in Consumer Culture*, New Brunswick: Rutgers University Press.

Signorielli, N. (1993) Television, the portrayal of women, and children's attitudes. In Berry, G. L. and Asamen, J. K. (eds) *Children and Television*, London: Sage.

Spigel, L. (1992) *Make Room for TV: Television and the Family Ideal in Postwar America*, Chicago: University of Chicago Press.

Tan, A. S. (1979) TV beauty ads and role expectations of adolescent female viewers. *Journalism Quarterly*, **56**, 283–8.

Turow, J. (1981) *Entertainment, Education and the Hard Sell*, New York: Praeger.

Walkerdine, V. (1984) Developmental psychology and the child-centred peda- gogy. In Henriques, J. *et al.* (eds) *Changing the Subject*, London: Methuen.

Wartella, E. (1980) Individual differences in children's responses to television advertising. In Palmer, E. L. and Dorr, A. (eds) *Children and the Faces of Television: Teaching, Violence, Selling*, New York: Academic Press.

Willis, P. (1990) *Common Culture: Symbolic Work at Play in the Everyday Cultures of the Young*, Milton Keynes: Open University Press.

Wober, M. and Gunter, B. (1988) *Television and Social Control*, Aldershot: Avebury.

Wood, J. (1993) Repeatable pleasures: notes on young people's use of video. In Buckingham, D. (ed.) *Reading Audiences: Young People and the Media*, Manchester: Manchester University Press.

Young, B. M. (1986) New approaches to old problems: the growth of advertising literacy. In Ward, S., Robertson, T. and Brown, R. (eds) *Commercial Television and European Children*, Aldershot: Gower.

Young, B. (1990) *Children and Television Advertising Oxford*, Oxford University Press.

12

Ten theses on children and television

Bob Hodge and David Tripp

From Hodge, B. and Tripp, D. (1986) *Children and Television: A Semiotic Approach*. Cambridge: Polity Press, pp. 213–18.

Our project was not set up to prove a single point or a set of closed conclusions. Rather, it was designed in an open-ended way to explore and perhaps explicate some aspects of the interlocking set of structures and processes that together constitute the field of study of children and television. We have looked at children's developing powers of mind, and their strategies for making sense as they interact with the complex levels and structures of the television message, in potentially determining social contexts and sets of relationships. We have assessed how this whole complex has been interpreted and used in an institutionalization of knowledge that is a powerful force in shaping public beliefs and public policy. This is our sense of our brief, in this book. We hope we have done some justice to it. At various stages, however, people have quite rightly pressed us to say what follows, for certain practical purposes, from our study. 'Practice', of course, is not a single simple outcome: what a parent will want to know and do will be different from the interests of say, a teacher or a producer of children's television. So to meet this kind of request we will conclude this book with a set of ten propositions, ten theses about children and television, the plausibility of which we believe our study has helped to establish. In the process we will address in an informal way some major implications these theses may have for various people concerned with children and television: parents, educators, concerned citizens, government agencies, media professionals, researchers and students.

1. Children typically have the capacity to be active and powerful decoders of television, and programmes watched by them are potentially rich in meaning and cultural value; though not all programmes and ways of viewing are of equal benefit for all children.

Children's semiotic powers, and the complexity of the meanings they construct and consume make up the central premise of our whole argument. This premise is not a blanket excuse for anything on television that children watch. It is not the end of discrimination in this area, but the rational basis for a beginning. We do not see all children as equally active and adequate 'readers' under all circumstances; nor do we see all programmes as equally dense in meaning or culturally valuable. Media professionals should not underrate children's ability to handle great complexity, nor should they under-provide for that need of children for relevant complexity. Lobbyists are very important in maintaining high production standards. Children's television is notoriously given the smallest budgets and least attention, and economic reasons are too often justified by reductive assumptions about children's semiotic abilities. It seems better to give them good programmes made for adults than cheap, insubstantial programmes whose main claim to be tailored to children's needs appears to be the fact that adults would not watch them with enjoyment. Educationalists, parents and researchers alike should take this generally despised area of children's lives and development more seriously and with greater respect for its actual and potential value. However, there can be too much television watching by children. Though television is functionally redundant up to a point, there will be a decreasing return from heavy viewing as more of the same kind of viewing displaces other important activities. So it is generally more important for adults to limit the total time spent viewing than to select the programmes viewed.

2. Children's cognitive and semiotic systems develop at least up till the age of 12, so that they not only prefer different kinds of programmes from adults, they also respond differently: but from the age of 9 they are capable of their own kind of understanding of most mainstream television.

It is impossible to capture in a few short sentences the nature, scope and implications of children's growing powers of interpreting and understanding television. For media producers the concept of multilevel 'family' programming, capable of being 'read' in different but appropriate ways by different age levels, is a valid one, better we would suggest than an attempt to match specific levels of development with programming targeted to very specific age ranges. In general children enjoy and can learn much from some programmes that are regarded by many adults as 'too old' for them, though they will be responding in their own distinctively 'childlike' way. We believe that there is a parallel in children's developing ability to handle complex television messages, with the idea of young children not being imperfectly socialized miniature adults, but well adjusted to a social system which is different from that of adults, not necessarily inferior (Mackay, 1974). As with the development of language, it seems that children's systems increasingly approximate to adult systems as they are exposed to, and allowed to operate in, adult systems. This means that educationalists and parents need not be too concerned at children watching the most popular adult shows.

3. Children's television typically carries dominant ideological forms, but also a range of oppositional meanings.

This mixed content of children's television (and other television and other media) and the typical contradictions of response to which it gives rise, is, we believe, the crucial content issue for children's television. Media producers should be, and mostly are, well aware that an excessive overbalance of the dominant ideology makes for dull and unprofitable children's television: though producers sell programmes to advertisers and networks, rather than to children, and these corporate bodies tend to have a different attitude towards the dominant ideology. Different programmes give different amounts of space to oppositional readings, and recuperate the dominant ideology with different degrees of effectiveness. However, since these components are so subtly intermixed, and since different ways of reading and conditions of reception can so readily alter the thrust of a programme, any attempt to use legislation to specify and control the ideological content of television programming is likely to be futile – and any such attempt would itself have to take sides on ideological issues. However, although tight legislative control of television content would prove ineffective, or else would remove much of the entertainment and stimulus value of children's television, there are other more constructive responses to the mixed ideological content of children's television. Parents and educators can recognize and use the contradictions of specific programmes to help to clarify some fundamental social issues, for children and for themselves. They should do this, not only by relying on children's active processing of the message, but also by making children more conscious and aware of what they are processing and how.

4. It has long been known that the reality factor – television's perceived relation to the real world – is variable, depending on age, experience and social conditions. Indeed, it is a decisive factor determining the nature of media responses and media effects. But the ability to make subtle and adequate reality judgements about television is a major developmental outcome that can only be acquired from a child's experience of television.

Differences in modality judgements account for most of the reactions by children that most surprise and trouble parents: their apparent over-reaction, their impressionability. Parents are right to protect their children from over-stimulation when they are young, but they should not worry unduly about occasional 'modality mistakes' or over-reactions to specific programmes. These are indicative that learning is taking place, as children try to make things fit their scheme of the world by experimenting. Nor should parents be over-anxious at older children's seeming callousness, as if it were 'narcotization', when it is simply an accurate perception of the unreality of television.

The process of refining modality judgements – about television messages and other message systems – should be a major concern to educators, since it is of such obvious importance in equipping them to cope with the barrage of messages they will be confronted with as citizens in a mass-communications society. The processes of media production, as part of the necessary knowledge for a media modality system, should be part of everyone's school knowledge.

The pathological modality problems which do exist, for some children, should be seen as part of a more general social problem, and it is principally that problem, not merely its associated television symptoms, which should be the focus of attention by government agencies and other concerned bodies. Using television as a scapegoat is too often an excuse for inaction with regard to deeper causes.

5. All children need some fantasy programmes, such as cartoons for younger children. All children, particularly older ones, also need some programmes which touch more closely their reality.

Young children's liking for cartoons, so frequently a target for lobbyists and concern for parents, is a natural and healthy developmental phenomenon. Older children need programmes with the greater impact that comes from higher modality. Successful children's programmes utilize this, though they do not always seem to be explicitly and consistently aware of it. But people of all ages prefer a mix of modality types, to give the range of media effects, from relaxation to excitement. It is only by providing programmes with range of modality values that children will experience a sufficiently rich modality environment to enable them to learn to distinguish one kind from another.

6. Media violence is qualitatively different from real violence: it is a natural signifier of conflict and differences, and without representations of conflict, art of the past and present would be seriously impoverished.

The issue of violent content cannot be considered apart from the modality value of media representations of violence. The strong move by lobbyists, especially overt in the USA but also effective in Britain and Australia, to limit the depictions of violence on television is therefore based on a radical misconception of how the media work. This said, it remains true that high-modality violence is likely to be disturbing to young children, who will neither enjoy nor learn well from such programmes. Furthermore the ideological meaning of some kinds of violence – as in some kinds of pornography or racism – must be sufficiently offensive to be banned on those grounds: not because of violence as such but because of the world-view they are proclaiming and legitimating.

7. Meanings gained from television are renegotiated and altered in the process of discourse, and in that form have social status and effect.

The activity of children in response to television does not stop with watching programmes, but continues with all sorts of other acts of meaning-making. Anyone concerned with the effects of television must follow up the sometimes tortuous course of this redefinition and appropriation. This is especially true for parents and teachers, if they want to engage constructively and directly with the real meanings at issue. That is, adults in their contact with children should taken an active part in helping to mediate children's interaction with an ideas about television. Significant adults should be wary of blanket rejection of programmes which are avidly viewed by children, or which provoke strongly positive responses. They should also acknowledge the role of peer interaction, as vital for a child's normal development.

8. General ideological forms have an overall determining effect on interpretations of television.

Ideological forms in television can only confirm and replicate what is widely promulgated by other means. Television is often unjustly blamed for the breakdown of other ideological apparatuses by the Right, or attributed with the combined effectivity of all the rest by the Left. But television has too diffused and contradictory a content to have a single effect one way or another on its own: it has a social role to play, but only in conjunction with other forces and structures, and can never be singly and aberrantly determining.

9. The family remains a powerful agent of socialization in contemporary society. There are determinations of the family itself in a class society and parental authority is contested by other sites of power, including school and peer groups. Whereas parents may feel powerless, or seek to exercise power by limiting their children's viewing, a more open and equal relationship over television could be an educative and bonding factor. Families need to think about and act upon the way in which they interact with their televisions, not simply try to control the quantity or kind of programmes viewed when and by whom. Such control will typically produce friction and struggle, as it usually combines arbitrary routines with *ad hoc* exceptions.

10. The school is a site where television should be thoroughly understood, and drawn into the curriculum in a variety of positive ways.

The suspicion of television by educators, the barriers that are set up between television and schooling, are, we feel, unjustified and wasteful of a potentially valuable resource. The common argument is that one should keep television out of the school because 'children spend too much time in mindless television viewing anyway'. This is in fact as good a reason for bringing television into the school curriculum as it is for excluding it. The less one knows and understands about the medium, the less one engages with it in a discriminating fashion. Television literacy and appreciation are obvious school subjects which seem to be making too little progress. Overall, television is a factor which modern education cannot simply deplore or ignore, but should come to terms with as part of its primary function of equipping students to be adequate citizens in the society in which they live.

References

Mackay, R. W. (1974) Conceptions of children and models of socialisation. In Dreitzel, H. P. (ed.) *Recent Sociology*, **5**, London: Macmillan. Revised in R. Turner, *Ethnomethodology*, Harmondsworth: Penguin.

13

With the benefit of hindsight: reflections on uses and gratifications research

Denis McQuail

From *Critical Studies in Mass Communication* **1**(2) (1984), Annandale, VA: Speech Communication Association, pp. 177–93.

Historical perspective

The uses and gratification tradition of research has been the object of a good deal of a denigration as well as advocacy. It started life in the early 1940s, as a fairly simple and straightforward attempt to learn more about the basis of appeal of popular radio programs and about the connection between the attraction to certain kinds of media content and other features of personality and social circumstances. Happily without the name with which it is now irrevocably saddled, it was one of several lines of advance in the new branch of social science concerned with mass communication. Its origins and underpinnings included: a simple wish to know more about the audience; an awareness of the importance of individual differences in accounting for the audience experience; a still fresh wonderment at the power of popular media to hold and involve their audiences; and an attachment to the case study as an appropriate tool and an aid to psychological modes of explanation.

There was enough work accomplished by the time that Klapper (1960) put together his review of research to allow an overview which still bears reading. There had also been some development of theory and method, as the exploratory case study gave way to the more systematic collection of numerical data and to the testing of hypotheses by statistical methods. The early research was quite diverse, although as it developed, there was some bias towards television and towards the child audience. This may simply reflect the circumstances of the time, when television was becoming established on both sides of the Atlantic and was being perceived as the new threat or promise in the socializing of young children. An additional factor, however, is probably a view of television as a continuous and undifferentiated use of time by children which was more amicable to analysis according to broad categories of type of content than was either book or film. Both film-going and reading had also largely ceded their 'social problem' character to the new medium and were looked at almost benignly. By the time television came to be investigated in any large-scale way during the 1950s and early 1960s (e.g., Himmelweit *et al.*, 1958; Schramm *et al.*, 1961), the method of 'uses and gratifications' research was sufficiently developed for it to be used as an instrument for investigating this large, undifferentiated, allocation of time by children. The appeal of the approach was its potential for differentiating, within an otherwise seemingly featureless field of media behavior and providing variables of attention to television, beyond that of sheer amount, which could be related to possible causes of 'addiction' or to the consequences of over-indulgence.

It is interesting to recall how broadly defined and diverse this field of research was at least until the early 1960s. It covered: enquiries into the allocation of time to different media; relations between media use and other uses of time; relations between media use and indicators of social adjustment and relationships; perceptions of the functions of different media or content types; and reasons for attending to media. It would be hard to distinguish much that is now placed within the 'tradition' from other kinds of media research. The common strand was, nevertheless, a concern with the 'function' of media, in its several senses, but especially the question of the kind and the strength of motive for media use and the links between such motives and the rest of experience.

1960 as a turning point

The decade of the 1960s has been treated as a watershed in respect of more than one feature of mass communication research and, however exaggerated this picture or distorted by hindsight, there are some reasons for so regarding it. Firstly, it was time when communication research appeared to 'take off' once more, certainly in Europe, as the social sciences became better established and discovered post-war energy and direction. Even in the United States, there seemed to occur a new beginning after the golden age of communication research whose passing was mourned by Berelson (1959). Secondly, there was a coming to terms with the accumulating evidence about media effect or the lack of it. Thirdly, there was the fact of television as a new medium of seemingly immense appeal, if not effect. Fourthly, although later in the decade of the 1960s, there was a growing tendency in the social sciences to react against 'positivist' methods and concepts and against functionalism in its several variants. The favored modes of thinking were more 'social-critical' interpretative, anti-scientistic, ethnographic, phenomenologistic. The particular turning point for uses and gratifications research seemed to follow the (rather obscure) publication of an important article by Elihu Katz in 1959, which provided a manifesto of a kind and a number of key slogans and terms. Thus:

> less attention [should be paid] to what media do to people and more to what people do with the media. Such an approach assumes that even the most patient of mass media content cannot ordinarily influence an individual who has no 'use' for it in the social and psychological context in which he lives. The 'uses' approach assumes that people's values, their interests, their associations, their social roles, are pre-potent and that people selectively 'fashion' what they see and hear to these interests.
>
> (Katz, 1959, p. 2)

While the thoughts expressed in this vein, belonging more generally to the 'rediscovery of people', were very important for the blossoming of more research on media use (especially in connection with the re-assessment of media effects), the development was running counter to the stream of critical theory and research of the later 1960s.

Revival and redefinition of the 'uses' tradition

While early conceptions of the process of media effect had a place for a notion of audience response as a type of independent effect (Klapper had considered media gratifications almost exclusively in this light), researchers now turned to the possibility of using a motive or a satisfaction as an intervening variable in its own right. This was guided in part by the early use of indicators of interest as a relevant way of categorizing an audience (Lazarsfeld *et al.*, 1944), and by the accumulation of evidence that audience choice and reaction were always selective in systematic ways. Thus, one of the innovations in the search for better concepts and methods of inquiry in relation to media effect was in take more account of the kind and strength of motivation of the relevant public. The guiding thought was that effects would be more likely to occur where a corresponding or relevant motive existed on the part of the receiver (e.g. Blumler and McQuail, 1968). In turn, this had a place in the development of theory and research concerning the active or 'obstinate' audience (Bauer, 1964) and of interactive, in place of one-way, models of media influence. The rise of television has increased the demand for research into audiences that would go beyond head-counting and reach some more qualitative accounting of the audience and help relate program provision to various audience demands by ways other than pure market forces (Emmett, 1968/69). More 'qualitative' audience research could be seen as a 'half-way house' between the collection of 'ratings' and the ultimate delivery of evidence about the longer-term social effects of the new medium, allowing some provisional evaluation of what might be going on.

The advance and then retreat of positivism and functionalism concerned uses and gratifications research especially during the late 1960s and the early 1970s for a number of reasons. Firstly, most of the research involved was inescapably cast in the functionalist mold. The theory and research described by Klapper (1960) already presupposed a distinct functionalist framework in which media use is likely to be interpreted as a means of adjustment to, or reaction in, a system of connected personal relations or a wider social context. Moreover, the concepts and methods typical of the research were essentially individualist, psychologistic and had a strong, leaning towards the 'variable analysis' which had been an early target for more holistically-minded sociologists (e.g., Blumer, 1956) and historically-minded media theorists (e.g., Smythe, 1954). What came to be viewed, by the early 1970s, as typical of the tradition was a) functionalist in conception; b) individualist in method of data collection; and c) lending itself to multivariate statistical analysis. It embodied the methodological advances of the period with the demonic characteristics which became, increasingly, an object of disdain by the 'critically' minded; that is, positivism, scientism, determinism, value-neutrality, and conservatism [...]

Uses and gratifications and the study of popular culture

[...] The substance of the post-1960s renascence of uses and gratifications research, which still continues, can only be summarily characterized by a few key references. The account given here cannot pretend to be either full or unbiased, given the participation of the present writer in some of the work. However, an essential aspect of the tradition is its diversity and lack of coordination or of a common program. The wide currency and convenience of the shorthand label 'uses and gratifications', the targeting of fairly coherent critiques by single authors, the use of the term 'functionalist' as a blanket description, have all tended to exaggerate the degree to which the approach shares an identity and common philosophical and scientific basis. What we now see as evidence is a series of projects, which can be classified under a few broad headings. Firstly, there have been many studies of children and media, especially: Schramm *et al.* (1961); Riley and Riley (1951); Maccoby (1954); Himmelweit, Oppenheim and Vince (1958); Furu (1971); Noble (1975); Greenberg (1974); various, mainly European, researches collected by Brown (1976); ongoing work in Sweden (e.g., Hedinsson, 1981; Johnsson-Smaragdi, 1983). Secondly, there has been a good deal of attention to political communication and media gratifications. This is well-reviewed by McLeod and Becker (1981) and may be thought to begin with the work of Blumler and McQuail (1968). Thirdly, there have been numerous studies of particular forms and the basis of their appeal, including: McQuail *et al.* (1972); Mendelsohn (1964); Levy (1978); Tannenbaum (1980); and many others. Fourthly, there have been studies of media and wide social integration, the most significant being that of Katz *et al.* (1973). Fifthly, there have been studies of information-seeking and of the more cognitive aspects of media use: Atkin (1972); Kline *et al.* (1974); and Kippax and Murray (1980). Finally, we can distinguish a set of contributions to the development of theory and the formation of models. Some of these are to be found in Blumler and Katz (1974), and more recent examples include Blumler (1979) and Windahl (1981).

Criticism

The diversity mentioned earlier refers to theory, methods, aims and the kinds of media content studied. No common model, set of procedures or purposes informs the tradition, despite the attempts of Katz, Blumler and Gurevitch (1974) to give some shape to the assumptions that have guided 'users' research and to assess the state of the art. Ten years after that rendering of account there is probably no greater unity and there is some reason to look back on the direction taken by the revived tradition. Criticism of the approach has been lucidly and not infrequently expressed, notably by Chaney (1972), Elliott (1974), Carey and Kreiling

(1974) and Swanson (1977). There have been three main lines of attack or sources of dislike: one relating to its theoretical underpinnings and associated method; another to its social and political implications; a third to its model of man and its way of handling cultural phenomena. The main theoretical charge is that it is essentially lacking in theory and such theory that it has is inadequate and confused. The common element of many studies seems to be a certain way of devising lists of verbal statements about media or media content which are labelled, variously, as 'use', 'gratification', 'motivation', 'satisfaction', 'need', etc., implying distinctions and a conceptual status which cannot be validated. If there is a theory, according to critics, it is pure tautology moving from measured satisfaction back to an imputed need or forwards from a need to a use and gratification, with no independent way of measuring need, or even any coherent theory of needs, and certainly no way of determining the direction of influence between measured 'need' and media use. The lack of theory is said to lead to a misuse of empirical method, to the extent that verbal statements or aggregate statistics derived from responses to verbal statements are reified to become new constructs supposed to stand for the gratifications offered by media content. At times these new constructs are seen merely as reflections of social class or other background variables and when used instead of the latter, they are likely to be mystifying, and distorting.

The social and political objections advanced from a perspective of critical theory rest mainly on the view that the incurable functionalism of the method ties the researcher to a conservative model of a social system in which all adjustment is for the best and which ends up portraying all kinds of media content as helping individuals to adjust. The method, as typically practiced, can only increase the chances of manipulation, since it adduces psychological and social reasons why people like what they get which can easily be turned to support the view that people get what they like, thus blunting any possible critical edge in the application of new knowledge which comes from the research.

The 'cultural' objection has several grounds but, most centrally, exception is taken to the utilitarianism and behaviorism of the whole underlying model, in which cultural 'behavior' is treated as both determined and instrumental and rarely as 'consummatory' or an end in itself. The version of the meaning of cultural consumption as derived from statements ore recognitions of statements by individuals is regarded as a poor substitute for an overall view in which the ritual nature of culture is recognized along with its great diversity of meanings. There is also a wide reluctance to accept a value-free and mathematical treatment of matters which should be seen as evaluative and qualitative and not amendable to sociological categorization. From a cultural point of view there seems to be no recognition, or use, of any kind of aesthetic theory. [...]

The central point of the tradition

The point of summarizing criticism is not to offer a new defense and assessment, but to consider the possibilities for future work, taking account of objections which deserve to be taken seriously. [...]

It is worth being reminded of some of the relative success of the research tradition as it has been practiced, partly to redress the balance, partly to account for the appeal of the line of work. One apparent success has been to express, in differentiated verbal formulas, which are widely recognizable and available for consistent use, key elements of the image or dominant associations of specific media cultural products and kinds of media experience. The verbal expressions show some stability across cultures and over time an yet the methods used are sensitive enough to record differences in the perception of similar kinds of material. Information of this kind is often open to interpretation in terms of differences of plot, style or format and it does seem that cultural analysis and audience analysis can be mutually enriching. The research has also identified and given names and definitions to a set of 'functions' of media-cultural experience which help to make sense of the innumerable details of audience reaction. These possibilities lend themselves, further, to making comparisons between media and between different audience groups which would otherwise be impossible.

We have, thus, the basic terms for discourse about media content and experience which have been discovered, drawn together and ordered by empirical procedures, rather than invented or put forward as concepts. This means that some form of three-way exchange is possible between the makers of culture, the audience and social scientists. This may be more a potential than an actuality, but the existence of something like a common terminology has been demonstrated (Himmelweit *et al.*, 1980) and it is a necessary precondition for talking sensibly about the audience experience. Without this accomplishment, it would be difficult to approach the central issue of whether content 'producers particular values and patterns of behavior amongst its devotees or do its devotees become devotees because of the values and behavioral tendencies they already possess' (Klapper, 1960, p. 190).

While the achievement in respect of explanation and interrelation of different kinds of evidence about people and their media use has been modest, it is not wholly lacking. There are too many, albeit scattered, indications of clarifying or meaningful associations between expectations form, and ideas about, media and other relevant indications of choice to doubt that approaches to media, as expressed in the terms developed by this tradition (and there is really no alternative source except introspection and invention) are not independently influential. In other words, on some occasions at least, prior experience, behaviour, tendencies and values shape attention and response, and it would be untenable to claim otherwise and unreasonable to claim total agnosticism. [...]

The problem, of course, lies not with this claim itself (although it is not uncontested), but with what to do if one accepts it, since it is almost impossible to find an acceptable name for this *thing*. There are too many names for it and the choice of any one presupposes a theoretical schema which can take the researcher into deep waters. Users and gratifications researchers have found something by empirical investigation, they know some of its properties and users, but they do no really know what it is. If this *is* the case, it gives some support to criticism of the approach as the poorer for its lack of theoretical foundation.

A readjustment of view

[...] There are those who would not accept that serious problems have been encountered, beyond what is the normal result of academic competition, fundamental theoretical divergence and the inevitably slow growth of scientific knowledge. To the present writer, however, it seems that there are grounds for disappointment in the history of the tradition to date and that the research in the main direction being currently taken is not very likely to deliver all of its early promise. This refers especially to the understanding of cultural experience and to the explanation of variations which might be of relevance for social-cultural policy. Thus, one of the original aims of the research was to shed light on both 'cultural-gaps' and 'knowledge-gaps' in society and suggest ways of reducing them. Thus may no longer seem a very urgent goal in an era of media abundance, media deregulation and cultural relativism, but the facts of communication inequality are barely changed and the theoretical interest of the associated questions remains high. By contrast, although the fruits may still lie just beyond our grasp, the work that continues to be done does seem to have a potential for clarifying the process of media effect.

The tradition of uses and gratifications research has thus seemed to reveal an inescapable bias: despite its diversity it tends towards what can most conveniently be called a 'dominant paradigm', however overworked and tendentious that phrase has become. This paradigm or model is no secret and is to be read from the 'state of the art' assessment by Katz *et al.* (1974). It involves: a view of media consumption as a logical and sequential process of need-satisfaction and tension-reduction, relating the social-psychological environment to media use; a set of assumptions about the audience (notably its activity, rationality, resistance to influence, capacity for reporting about itself); and a recommendation to value-relativism on the part of the investigator. This basic paradigm has organized much work and continues to lend itself to further elaboration and application in research. [...] It is in fact more flexible than it sounds and can provide a powerful framework for looking at media in a wide social and cultural context. Yet it is also, not inconsistently, imperialistic, perhaps too powerful and tending to develop Moloch-like characteristics in the sacrifices which it demands from its devotees. These sacrifices are mostly in the form of a narrowing of vision and a submission to the ever-growing machine of data-collection and elaborate statistical analysis of numbers formed from much less substantial qualities.

While admitting an element of exaggeration in this picture, it does not seem very useful now to worry about the main component parts of the paradigm, although each merits critical attention, but better to consider whether there is really any alternative. [...] The suggestion which follows, although it involves a radical departure from the dominant model, would not, if adopted, render all work until now and all current debate redundant. It would, however, introduce some new concepts and change the balance of discussion. It would also move the model- (or road-) building to a new site.

An alternative by-way

If there is a broad highway in the development of uses and gratifications research, it can be characterized by an elaboration of models, by its statistical methods and its theory for relating social and cultural experience 'forward' to media use and its later consequences and back again to experience. I worked on some sections of the road and travelled some way along it, by adapting a 'uses' approach to the study of political campaign effects and by trying to establish connections between social background and media use (McQuail *et al.*, 1972). The suggestion which follows is for a return to the bridge-building between the social sciences and the humanities, urged by Katz, but never really achieved. Broadly, it may be described as involving a 'cultural-empirical' approach, using some of the concepts and advances of 'main-road' work, but with some new concepts added and all within a new framework or model. A good many of the new elements are untried and the proposal has, consequently, a very tentative character.

The users and gratifications 'main road' approach has tended towards utilitarianism and determinism, treating 'consumption' of media content of all kinds as having a place or purpose in larger schemes of individual need-gratification. A cultural approach would be much more likely to consider 'consumption' of culture as an end in itself (the 'consummatory' view urged by Carey and Kreiling, 1974) and, in any case, requiring an understanding in its own right and not only as a stage in some behavioral process of adjustment. Attention should thus be concentrated on the making of choices and on the meaningful encounter with cultural products. Towards this end, a distinction will have to be made between the more 'cultural' kinds of content and the more informational kinds – between affectual/imaginative and cognitive spheres. This kind of distinction is often made for practical reasons, but most user and gratifications theory adopts fundamentally the same model for all kinds of imputed need and media use, partly because different kinds of content can serve the same function, partly because the underlying process is held to be the same.

The first model suggested is intended to deal with the 'non-cognitive' area, with audience use of fiction, amusement, drama or spectacle, which appeals to the imagination or seeks to provide various kinds of pleasure the time of use, and has no consciously intended application afterwards in the rest of life. It seems advisable to take some account of the built-in purpose of media content, as well as the purpose formed by the audience member, although this practice has seemed to fall victim to an exclusive policy of 'taking the audience point of view'. Moreover, if cultural experience is to be considered according to its functionality or utility in a more or less behavioural model, it is reasonable to suppose that some kinds of media fare will be less amenable to this kind of treatment than some others. Indeed, it may be necessary to treat some media experiences not only neutrally in this respect, but as if according to a counter-behavioral stance. This is an important feature of the alternative conceptual framework sketched below.

The key proposition (it is no more) on which the following rests is that cultural experience (what happens at the time of attention to media) be treated as a generalized process of involvement, arousal or 'capture'. To the observer there is little to see except varying degrees of rapt attention and to the participant, the most salient aspect of the experience is an awareness of 'being lost' in something, 'involved', 'carried away', 'caught up', 'taken out of oneself', or simply 'existed' or 'thrilled'. There are conventional variations of expression for this according to the kind of content – whether comedy, tragedy, adventure, romance, etc. – but there seems to be an underlying similarity of what is meant by these kinds of expression and what is experienced in terms of mental and physiological reaction. [...]

To go beyond the fact of this sense experience and relate it with its typical content, we can propose that the essence of this general sensation is to *free* the spectator/reader/listener mentally from the immediate constraints and/or dullness of daily life and enable him or her to *enter into* new experiences (vicariously) which would not otherwise be available (except by use of the imagination). The media-cultural experience is thus potentially a powerful aid to, or substitute for, the imagination, enabling, a person to enjoy a variety of emotional experiences and mental states – involving joy, anger, sexual excitement, sadness, curiosity, etc. We can identify with people and share the illusion of living in interesting situations or observe it all, with inside knowledge, from a privileged position and one of physical and emotional security. [...] Consequently, there is likely to be a positive *dissociation* from social circumstances and future consequences. This is often part of the conscious purpose and pleasure of 'experience' to cultural experience – we do want to be somewhere or someone else, with no thought for the future. Insofar as this is true, it does undermine a major premise of the mainstream uses and gratifications model, which holds that media use is often a direct reflection of pre-media experience and in some underlying way is structured as to its amount and kind by the rest of experience. The implication of what has just been written is that, if there is a relation, it may well be of a contradictory or quite unpredictable kind. In the view advanced here, the essence of audience 'activity' is a process of self-liberation, however temporary, from everyday self and surroundings. Consequently, there is no obvious way to make causal connections between media experience and behavior.

There are some important practical consequences of all this for a revision of the dominant model of the process of mass media use. First of all, as noted above, we should treat affective/imaginative content separately from cognitive content, since the arousal-involvement factor is either less relevant or of a different kind. In Himmelweit's (1980) study of audience judgement, the most 'highly rated' of the television programs assessed was 'The News' and 'absorbing' was one of the terms applied to it 'very much', but it was only one of five 'stylistic attributes' applied, rather than a single main criterion, as it was for other popular fictional programs. Secondly, the generalized 'arousal' factor should not be included in the lists of gratifications or satisfactions and should be treated on another level, as a prior condition of attention or for what it is, as a general factor, which finds several more specific forms of expression, according to the individual or the content concerned.

Further elaboration is needed in order to cope with these 'second order' concepts. In a 'culturalist' model it is appropriate to use the concept of culture itself and it can be used in two senses. Firstly, 'culture' in the collective sense as the body of objects and practices which pertains to, or is available to, a given group or public, or subset of society. It is in this sense, for instance, that the term 'taste culture' (Lewis, 1980) has been used – to indicate a more or less structured set of preferences. A member of the media public can only choose from, or have ideas about, what is available physically or is accessible and familiar by reason of a collective situation and provision. Cultural differentiation is an important element in the model of media use because it is a directing or constraining factor in choice. It may have much to do with class and social position, but more generally it has to do with closeness and familiarity, more so probably than with individual competence, skill, or any 'need' for culture.

The second relevant sense of culture is that of individual 'taste'. […] Cultural taste provides the key to selection amongst what is offered by the (collective) culture and is essentially arbitrary and unaccountable. If it were accountable it would explain the differences of preference for genres, themes and authors. It is evidently not entirely random, but the regularities that do appear, such as gender differences in choice as between, for example, 'adventure' and 'romance' are really an aspect of collective cultural distribution which makes the former less accessible to girls from an early age and steers them towards 'romance'. While 'taste' relates to choice of content and habits of use, it is usual and perhaps only possible to describe it in terms of content. Media content (and most cultural production) is constructed according to a knowledge of tastes and likely preferences, and has some built-in appeal to a sector of the potential public.

There is one further element in the scheme of things which provides a bridge to the dominant behavioral model described above, helping to characterize and differentiate the vicarious experience and emotion offered by culture more finely and objectively than does the concept of taste. This element is *content*. Thus, affective media content can be differentiated according to the specific experience offered and gained. In practice, such gratifications, assuming the experience to be wanted, are hard to identify except by general types of content – much as in taste specification of basic themes, plots and genres. A given genre or type of content normally promises and gives a set of experiences of a predictable kind, which might have to do with curiosity about human situations, or laughter, or sex, or tension and release, or mystery, or wonder and so on. These (and others) are the satisfactions which people claim to expect or receive from the media and which are to be found both in descriptions of cultural (media) content and in lists and typologies of media gratifications. There is a necessary place in a culturalist model for the reflection on (and anticipation of) emotions, thoughts and sensations evoked by the cultural experience. There remains, nevertheless, a difficulty, familiar to uses and gratifications researchers, of distinguishing between the general and the particular, and between expectation and satisfaction.

Two models

Little more need be said before setting out the main terms and their sequence of a model of cultural (affective) experience (Figure 13.1). One may point out that 'general expectation of involvement', 'taste' and 'satisfaction' can easily be associated with different things and thus be used as orientations towards, or descriptions of, several different things: a theme; a genre or type; a medium or channel; and actual media experience (specific film, television viewing, reading a particular book); an author or performer; a particular work. The situation in this respect is not very different from the case of conventional uses and gratifications research, where 'gratifications', etc., are used to differentiate media and types of content. In both the cultural and the 'uses' model, we can also use the same terms to characterize people. This should not lead to confusion, since quite different statements are involved. For example, it is quite different to say that someone has a taste for thrillers than to say that someone's 'need for escape' is met by thrillers. In general, the lexicon of terms in a developed cultural model would depend on and say more about the specific content than about people and circumstances. Finally, the model, as drawn in Figure 13.1, is also sequential, since the general information to seek cultural experience precedes actual involvement, as does the pattern of taste. Actual media experience does lead to some awareness and reflection on what has happened, with some consequences for future cultural choice, and other more immediate consequences, depending on the specific content and the degree of satisfaction obtained.

It is neither possible, nor really necessary, to give a full account of what an equivalent cognitive model (Figure 13.2) would look like. [...] However, there are important differences of conceptualization from the

I MOTIVATION		II CULTURE (i)		III CULTURE (ii)	IV SATISFACTION
General expectation of involvement	differentiated according to:	Individual taste	leading to choice from and attention to:	Accesible media content	for Imaginative experience of: – excitement – arousal – sadness – empathy – value resonance – wonder
			(change or reinforcement of taste)		– etc.

Figure 13.1 A cultural model

I MOTIVATION		II INTERESTS		III INFORMATION		IV SATISFACTION
General interest/ curiosity	differentiated according to:	Individual preference	leading to choice from and attention to:	Accesible media content	for	Experience of benefit or use such as: – guidance – surveillance – application – social exchange – orientation
			(change or reinforcement of interest)			– etc.

Figure 13.2 A cognitive model

cultural model. Firstly, the arousal/involvement factor would be replaced by a general factor of interest/curiosity. In turn, this would divide according to a set of interests, which are equivalent to cultural tastes and, in a similar way, a mixture of the arbitrary and the socially or culturally given in a particular environment. Thus some people are interested in football for reasons which are mysterious to some others, yet these are regularities in the aggregate distribution of interest in football, which show it to go with some other characteristics. As with 'culture', information is variably available or accessible according to social position. Finally, there are specific gains or satisfactions which can be accounted for, much as in the uses and gratifications tradition, as uses and benefits, such as: helping in decisions and choices; opinion formation; providing subjects for conversation, etc. On the whole, one would expect more certainty of relationship between prior experience, information choices and satisfactions obtained. The key difference from the previous model (and at the same time, the factor which links this model to the dominant paradigm) is the absence of that *disconnection* between ordinary life and the moment of cultural experience. The motivating factor is one of connection and extension rather than disconnection.

Conclusion

It is early to assess the prospects for such an approach, or its implications for the research tradition as a whole. It needs itself to be tried out empirically, either in the collection of new data, or in reworking existing data, since there could be a considerable overlap between the kind of work generated by such a cultural model and what has been done already. At some points it clearly challenges the established tradition, at others it might be supportive or supplementary. The most fundamental challenge is to the notion of a direct causal connection between background circumstances, cultural choice and the 'effects' of cultural experience. In effect, this model resurrects the motion of 'escape' as a dominant motive for media use and emphasizes discontinuities, although the 'escape' may well be subjectively perceived in a positive light – thus as escape into a better world (of the imagination). [...]

On the positive side, the framework suggested here may, by reviving the notion of 'taste' and the value judgements which go with that concept, add to the refinement and accuracy of description of content and improve our understanding of individual differences. It can also help to increase sensitivity to essentially 'cultural' attributes. The notion of 'taste' (and, on the cognitive side, 'interests') may also help to clarify the nature of the central concept of the tradition (use, gratification, motive, etc.) which has proved virtually impossible to pin down. On the one hand, it offers one other possible meaning, perhaps only compounding the problem by so doing. On the other hand, the separation of a generalized 'drive' or 'set', as motivational factor, from its specific manifestations in taste, choice and satisfaction may open the way to a more consistent treatment (or multiple treatment) of the second order concept.

In the end, one has to make a rather important choice as to whether one really wants to know most about *culture* (its origin, production, meaning, and use), or about *people* in audiences (their identity, attributes, reasons for being there), or about individual *behavior* (kind, frequency), causes, consequences, interconnections), or about *society* and the working of the media within it. It is unlikely that any one paradigm or model can serve all four purposes and the one sketched here has most relevance for the first. The main thrust of the uses and gratifications tradition has been towards the construction of a major highway which serves to link all four purposes in one investigative enterprise. Real highways do facilitate very long, fast, journeys by large vehicles (research teams), but they also change the landscape they traverse, have restricted views and stimulate travel for its own sake or that of the vehicle. By comparison, the byway mapped out for reaching one rather limited goal of knowledge might be slow and winding, but should enable one to see more on the way and keep one generally in closer contact with nature.

References

Atkin, C. K. (1972) Anticipated communication and mass-mediated information seeking. *Public Opinion Quarterly*, **36**, 188–99.

Bauer, R. A. (1964) The obstinate audience. *American Psychologist*, **19**, 319–28.

Berelson, B. (1959) The state of communication research. *Public Opinion Quarterly*, **23**, 1–6.

Blumer, H. (1956) Sociological analysis and the 'variable'. *American Sociological Review*, **21**, 683–90.

Blumler, J. G. (1979) The role of theory in users and gratifications studies. *Communication Research*, **6**, 9–36.

Blumler, J. G. and Katz, E. (eds) (1974) *The Uses of Mass Communication*, London and Beverly Hills: Sage.

Blumler, J. G. and McQuail, D. (1968) *Television in Politics*, London: Faber.

Brown, J. R. (ed.) (1976) *Children and Television*, London: Collier Macmillan.

Carey, J. W. and Kreiling, A. L. (1974) Popular culture and uses and gratifications. In Blumler, J. G. and Katz, E. (eds) *The Uses of Mass Communication* London and Beverly Hills: Sage, 225–48.

Chaney, D. (1972) *Processes of Mass Communication*. London: Macmillan.

Elliott, P. (1974) Uses and gratifications research: A critique and a sociological alternative. In Blumler, J. G. and Katz, E. (eds) *The Uses of Mass Communication*, London and Beverly Hills: Sage, 249–68.

Emmett, B. (1968/69) A new role for research in broadcasting. *Public Opinion Quarterly*, **32**, 654–65.
Furu, T. (1971) *The Functions of Television for Children and Adolescents*. Tokyo: Sophia University.
Greenberg, B. G. (1976) Gratifications of television viewing and their correlates for British children. In Blumler, J. G. and Katz, E. (eds) *The Uses of Mass Communication*, London and Beverly Hills: Sage, 71–92.
Hedinsson, E. (1981) *Television, Family and Society*, Stockholm: Almquist & Wiksel.
Himmelweit, H. T., Oppenheim, A. N. and Vince, P. (1958) *Television and the Child*, London: Oxford University Press.
Himmelweit, H. T., Swift, B. and Jaeger, M. F. (1980) The audience as critic: a conceptual analysis of television entertainment. In Tannenbaum, P. H. (ed.) *The Entertainment Functions of Television*, Hillside, NJ: LEA, 67–97.
Johnsson-Smaragdi, U. (1983) *TV Use and Social Interaction in Adolescence*, Stockholm: Almquist & Wiksel.
Katz, E. (1959) Mass communication research and the study of culture. *Studies in Public Communication*, **2**, 1–6.
Katz, E., Blumler, J. G. and Gurevitch, M. (1974) Utilization of mass communication by the individual. In Blumler, J. G. and Katz, E. (eds), *The Uses of Mass Communication*, London and Beverly Hills: Sage, 19–32.
Katz, E., Gurevitch, M., and Haas, H. (1973) On the use of mass media for important things. *American Sociological Review*, **38**, 164–81.
Kippax, S. and Murray, J. P. (1980) Using the mass media: need gratification and perceived utility. *Communication Research*, **7**, 335–60.
Klapper, J. T. (1960) *The Effects of Mass Communication*, Glencoe, IL: Free Press.
Kline, G., Miller, P. V. and Morrison, A. J. (1974) Adolescents and family planning information. In Blumler, J. G. and Katz, E. (eds) *The Uses of Mass Communication*, London and Beverly Hills: Sage, 113–36.
Lazarsfeld, P. F., Berelson, B. and Gaudet, H. (1944) *The People's Choice*, New York: Duell, Sloan & Pearce.
Levy, M. R. (1978) The audience experience with television news. *Journalism Monographs*, **55**.
Lewis, G. H. (1980) Taste cultures and their composition. In Katz, E. and Szescko, T. (eds) *Mass Media and Social Change*, Beverly Hills and London: Sage, 201–7.
McLeod, J. and Becker, L. B. (1981) The uses and gratifications approach. In Nimmo, D. and Saunders, R. R. (eds) *Handbook of Political Communication*, Beverly Hills and London: Sage, 67–100.
McQuail, D., Blumler, J. G. and Brown, J. R. (1972) The television audience: a revised perspective. In McQuail, D. (ed.) *Sociology of Mass Communications*, Harmondsworth: Penguin, 135–65.
Maccoby, E. (1954) Why do children watch television? *Public Opinion Quarterly*, **18**, 239–44.
Mendelsohn, H. (1964) Listening to radio. In Dexter, L. A. and White, D. M. (eds) *People, Society and Mass Communications*, Glencoe, IL: Free Press, 239–69.
Noble, G. (1975) *Children in Front of the Small Screen*, London: Constable.
Rosenberg, B. and White, D. M. (eds) (1957) *Mass Culture*, Glencoe, IL: Free Press.
Riley, M. W. and Riley, J. W. (1951) A sociological approach to communications research. *Public Opinion Quarterly*, **15**, 444–60.
Schramm, W., Lyle, J. and Parker, E. B. (1961) *Television in the Lives of Our Children*, Stanford: Stanford University Press.

Smythe, D. W. (1954) Some observations on communication theory. *Authorized Communication Review*, **12**, 24–37.

Swanson, D. L. (1977) The uses and misuses of uses and gratifications. *Human Communication Research*, **3**, 214–21.

Tannenbaum, P. H. (1980) *The Entertainment Functions of Television*, Hillsdale, NJ: LEA.

Windahl, S. (1981) Users and gratifications at the crossroads. In Wilhoit, G. C. and de Bock, H. (eds) *Mass Communication Review Yearbook*, Beverly Hills: Sage, 174–85.

14

Social psychological perspectives in reception analysis

Birgitta Höijer

A viewer interprets a fiction scene on television.

> The mother looks a little afraid and very hesitant. Apparently her husband wouldn't like her to be there. I got a feeling that she feels very uneasy because of the father to her daughter's baby. But at the same time she wants to be there, and she likes it. But she is a little afraid.

The concept of reception in audience studies signals an interest in audiences' interpretations, decodings, readings, meaning productions, perceptions or comprehension of media texts. The terminology varies as a result of the researcher's academic and theoretical anchoring. Reception research has developed into an area which crosses the traditional borderlines between social science and humanistic approaches.

We find such research with cultural studies perspectives (e.g. Ang, 1985; Fiske, 1987; Morley, 1980; 1992), semiotic perspectives (e.g., Jensen, 1986; 1995; Lewis, 1985; Schrøder, 1988), and socio-psychological perspectives (e.g., Höijer, 1989; 1992a and b; Livingstone, 1990). There are many other studies with mixed perspectives as well (e.g. Hagen, 1994; Liebes and Katz, 1993; Silj *et al.*, 1988). Another closely connected trend is the so-called ethnographic approach. The interest in this approach is on audiences' uses of media rather than on interpretations and reactions to specific texts and genres (e.g., Alasuutari, 1995; Ang, 1996; Hagen, 1996; Lull, 1990; Morley, 1986). I will not take up this tradition, but focus on text cum audience which has been proposed as the core of reception analysis (Jensen & Rosengren, 1990).

This chapter outlines social psychological perspectives relevant for our understanding of how audiences create meaning in what they read, hear and see. According to Fiske and Taylor (1991: 9-10) 'social psychology has always been cognitive', by which they briefly mean a focus on people's perceptions of their worlds. Cognitive theory will thus be brought up. Since human interpretation also involves psycho-dynamic processes, I will further discuss theories that deal with cultural and personal tensions within the individual. I will illustrate my arguments with examples taken from a corpus of reception interviews which I have conducted over several years.

I will start, however, with a historical review of early reception studies. Although the word reception was not used until the 1980s, reception studies have always been conducted in mass communication research. In a critical review of what unjustly has been called the 'new' audience research, Curran (1990) points out the superficial critique of other traditions, and a total lack of awareness of earlier audience studies: 'Effects researchers argued long ago that the predispositions that people bring to texts crucially influence their understanding of these texts, and that different predispositions generate different understandings' (p. 147). In summarizing thirty years of media research, Klapper (1960), concluded that a persistent theme is that audiences interpret and recall information in ways congruent with their existing beliefs and values.

One reason for the ahistorical accounts might be the unwillingness of many researchers with a humanistic background to seriously consider social science audience research. Therefore, we see that many writers with cultural studies perspectives do not refer to audience research other than that within their own paradigm. This certainly is a kind of academic chauvinism which in the long run is very unhelpful.

Historical reception research

In the early days of audience studies psychological theories played an important role. Many classic media researchers, such as Klapper, Schramm and Tannenbaum had an academic background in psychology. Even if the dominant research focus for audience research then was on attitudes and opinions, there also was some interest in how audiences give meaning to mediated messages. In fact, in the 1920s and 1930s studies were already being conducted which showed how individual characteristics and socio-cultural factors affected the way audiences perceive and give meaning to media texts (Freeman, 1924; Cressey, 1938). Later on we find, for example, the studies by Herzog (1944) on the meaning of listening to daytime radio soap operas, Hovland and his colleagues' studies of soldiers' receptions of a documentary series by Frank Capra about the Second World War (see Lowery and DeFleur, 1988, chapter 3), Schramm's (1949) studies of news reading, and Cantril's (1947) studies of the reception of the radio play 'The Invasion from Mars' dramatised by Orson Welles. These studies are still worth reading and they are impressive not least methodologically. In many cases, qualitative and quantitative studies were combined, and huge numbers of informants were involved. Modern reception research here has much to learn.

These classic studies are also interesting theoretically. Schramm (1949), for instance, outlines a theory about an interplay between pleasure rewards and reality rewards in news reading. He was of course inspired by Freud's notion of the Pleasure principle and the Reality principle. This also holds for Stephenson (1964) and his play theory of news reading, which like the modern reception research, he based on empirical audience studies. Therefore, not even psychoanalytic perspectives on audience's meeting with media texts are new. Pleasure and play have been discussed before, and interestingly, not only in relation to fiction, but in relation to informative media genres.

The genres and texts themselves, however, received little attention. Instead, psychological needs were focused quite isolated from texts and social contexts when this audience research tradition then developed within the uses and gratifications paradigm. Although there are important intersections between reception research and uses and gratifications research (cf. Curran, 1990; Jensen and Rosengren, 1990; Livingstone, 1990; Swanson, 1992), I will concentrate on those aspects that concern the production of meaning that occurs in the meeting between a given type of text and audiences.

Before I turn to the social psychology of interpretation, I would like to mention another important but neglected predecessor to reception analysis, namely, the research that since the 1950s has been carried out on comprehension of radio and television programmes. The focus of this empirical audience research tradition rests squarely on the meeting between text and reader. Several studies have related comprehension to both psychological and social characteristics of the individual and to numerous characteristics of the form and content of the text (Vernon, 1950; Belson, 1967; Trenaman, 1967; Findahl and Höijer, 1976, 1985; Gunter, 1987; Höijer and Findahl, 1984; Linné and Marosi, 1976; Poulsen, 1988). These studies stress the complexity of the interplay between programme and listener/viewer, yet some consistent patterns of a general nature do emerge. Widely documented are the social factors (e.g., occupation and education) that affect comprehension, most important of which is the audience's previous knowledge or 'knowledge reserve', which 'reflects not only individual and private interests, but social group affiliation and life situation, as well', (Höijer and Findahl, 1984: 178). Somewhat strangely, British scholars within the cultural studies tradition do not even mention their British predecessors and colleagues within the comprehension studies tradition.[1]

A few years ago Berger (1989: 75) remarked:

> It is ironic that communication researchers have expended so little energy studying the processes involved in the understanding of spoken discourse and written text. ... This oversight is difficult to understand given that comprehension is such a basic part of the communication process. ... Not only is message comprehension a kind of message effect, it is perhaps the primary effect that message exchanges produce.

Also Corner (1991: 274) has pointed out that 'Reception research as a whole could benefit from a firmer engagement with the kind of issues raised in recent text comprehension literature'.

I will later elaborate the concept of comprehension, but I also will consider other psychological concepts relevant for reception theory.

Psychology and mind

I would argue for a mental perspective but not for mentalism which is the belief that the ultimate reality is mental. On the contrary, we need a mental perspective based on theories about how culture is turned into conceptualizations, ideas, memories, knowledge, and images, in our heads. There is a bias in reception theory towards seeing external behaviour and external circumstances as the very centre for reception. The concrete viewing situation is, for instance, emphasized in terms of family interaction patterns, social talk, sideline activities in front of the television set, zapping behaviour, and so forth. I interpret this as a behaviourist tendency probably based on a fear of mentalism. Of course such factors do have an influence on interpretation, but they cannot compete with the more basic influences of our collected social knowledge and experiences which we carry within ourselves. Mind is, therefore, a central concept which we need to address.

Mind

Culture is a component of mind. Cultural models can be mental as well as material. In a recently published book anthropologist Bradd Shore (1996) even argues that 'culture is best conceived as a very large and hetero-geneous collection of models or what psychologists sometimes call schema' (p. 44).

The interplay between culture and cognition touches many dimensions and it takes place at several levels. Mind or cognitive structures are built up in the intersection between three contexts: (1) socio-historical processes, (2) socio-cultural interaction with the world, and (3) inner psychic processes.

Socio-historical processes shape our cognitions. If our minds were developed only on hereditary dispositions and our own direct experiences as the basis for knowledge of the world, we certainly would not reach far beyond the level of Neanderthal man. Instead we meet and assimilate culturally experiences formed by generations after generations and inherit language, behaviour, ways of life, social institutions, and so forth. We are included in history and culture by a multitude of social connections.

All human experience has two faces: one side faces external life and social activity, and the other faces our inner mental life and cognitive activity. It is in the interaction between these activities that meaning construction – a socio-cognitive phenomenon – is generated. Experience is incorporated in our minds and transformed into some inner psychic reality. Mental activity does not simply reflect social reality, it continuously interprets and reconstructs it. In this process, social reality turns into internal mental models or cognitive schemas. We are also capable of creating new inner experiences in the form of thoughts, dreams and fantasies without some direct external stimuli or social interaction. We are constantly in an inner dialogue with ourselves.

Given these arguments, in the following sections I focus on cognitive and psycho-dynamic processes in relation to audience reception.

Cultural and individual identities

Shore (1996:46) makes an important statement when he says, 'The human ability to create mental models as ways of dealing with reality has two distinct dimensions: personal and cultural'. *Cultural experiences* connect to all those experiences which are products of a specific society, culture or subculture within a society. We are socialized into norms, habits, knowledge and images typical for the society we live in, the gender and social class to which we belong, the schools we attend, our occupations, and so on. Elsewhere (Höijer, 1992a) I have also argued for *universal experiences* as those humans experience by virtue of being human beings. Examples are experiences of daily cycle of sleeping, wakefulness, feeding, or of the life cycle, that is, of life and death, birth, childhood, ageing, and of health and illness. We might also include some universal emotions, like pain, fear, love and hate. Without a universal dimension to our experiences global success of narratives and genres would probably not be possible.

Personal experiences are those which are unique to the individual. No two individuals' experiences are completely the same, not even if they have grown up in the same family. Further, we are also to some extent born with different abilities and personalities, and not even a very homogeneous culture is capably of casting its members in the same mould (Daun, 1989).

On one hand, it is quite unproblematic that we do not share all our experiences, ideas, attitudes, and values with others. Life would be quite boring if cultures and individuals were homogeneous. On the other hand, we easily come into conflict because of different opinions, and deep within ourselves, in the very core of our identities, the gap between the private and the cultural is problematic, and we struggle with the dilemma to unite our personal and cultural identities. The tension between culture and individual identities is an existential dilemma which we all carry within us.

This is also apparent in our roles as audience. Regarding reception, this is especially evident in relation to the interpretation of violent news. Audiencehood takes a turn for the worse when we see documentary pictures of innocent victims of war or other violent events. Exposure of such pictures have increased considerably in television news (Cronström, 1994; Gleich, 1994), and the meeting between the private and social lives of the viewers and the reports about inconceivable violence give rise to many dilemmas with conflicting feelings and thoughts.

The dilemmas of watching violent news

Sitting in our warm and cosy living rooms and watching television news, we often witness brutal events in the world outside, the violent death and suffering of others. We only need to think of pictures we all have seen of the swollen dead bodies in the rivers of Rwanda, Burundi or Zaire, or of burned corpses, mutilated people and blood pools in Bosnia or Tjetjenia. Since news viewing is an ordinary and socially desirable practice (Hagen, 1992; Höijer, 1995), we must as viewers handle evidence about evil as part of this social practice. This is problematic, and as audiences we develop different interpretation strategies to cope with the situation. The quotations below are from interviews with viewers reported in Höijer (1994).

To be able to watch the news at all the viewer must protect themselves by, for instance, fending off the violence: 'If you react to all the violence that's shown on the television news you couldn't stand watching the news.' Not watching the news, which is a potential way of avoiding shocking violence, is regarded as an undesirable act. Another social dilemma implies a conflict between being upset by the violence in the news programmes and performing other social duties of daily life: 'I feel sick and start crying when I watch the violence. But it is my responsibility to care for my children when I come home since I work long hours. I can't sit on the couch and feel suffering for the shape the world is in.'

Such a dilemma may also imply contradictory feelings between the wish to avoid viewing violence and the wish to acquaint oneself with the violence in order to be informed about what is going on: 'You don't want to watch it but then you have to. Many times I tell myself not to watch it. I know it's only going to be about something violent. You're ambivalent but you do watch it after all. It's your duty to know about matters.' This comment illustrates how deeply the culturally shaped ideology of the Enlightenment is rooted in audience's mind, and how it may conflict with personal wishes.

To witness the depiction of documentary violence in the news may further imply deeper psychological dilemmas within the individual. Violence is traumatic for everybody since it deals with suffering and death. This is the universal side of the experience. Hearing about and watching violence may fill us with agony because it awakens mortal fears within ourselves or painful memories of the deaths of our relatives. Among immigrants from Latin America, alarming memories of violence against themselves or other people in their homelands were brought to the fore in their minds when they watched violent news (Pereira-Norrman, 1994). However, still they watched the news containing violence because they want to be informed citizens fulfilling their social roles.

Cognitive schemas

Schemas are complex types of cognitive structures representing generic experiences and cultural knowledge. They contain the common and characteristic features of similar phenomena, for example, similar objects, events, situations, and discourses. Emotions and attitudes are included in the schemas. As our experience is emotionally loaded, so is our inner representation of experience. Schemas are subjective in the sense that they are the result of an interpretation act. At the same time schemas are cultural products. They are constructed by the individual in relation to a social environment and a stock of shared social experiences (Shore, 1996). Schemas structure past experience and are used as frames of references when interpreting whatever we might encounter in a given moment.

Cognitive schemas vary from highly abstract structures to very specific and concrete ones, and may thus be conceptualized at different levels as well as in relation to different spheres of lives or domains of experiences.

Mode schemas

At an overall level we can imagine two types of organizing schemas, *narrative schemas* and *paradigmatic (or argumentative) schemas*, or modes of thinking according to Bruner (1986). Narration is based on stories and deals with sequences of events, characters or actors, mental states, happenings, and so forth. It has dramatic qualities, and some moral point. 'To tell a story is inescapably to take a moral stance, even if it is a moral stance against moral stances' (Bruner, 1990: 51). The narrative mode is developed very early in childhood (Stern, 1985) and used in our everyday interaction with the world. It is the basic form in which we structure and tell others the stories of our own lives and things we experience.

The paradigmatic (or argumentative mode) is based on a more 'scientific' way of thinking in which logical reasoning and concept formation play important roles. It is based on arguments, propositions, facts and figures, and causality. Piaget (1926/1955) and Vygotsky (1934/1986) describe the development of this kind of thinking in young people.

In my own reception studies I have found a large difference between fiction and news genres when it comes to how well texts are understood. News reception is often quite brief and sketchy, sometimes fragmentary, and not at all as coherent and elaborated as the reception of fiction (Höijer, 1995). One reason may be that fiction is easier to interpret, because it is close to the basic narrative mode used in our everyday interpretation of the world. News, on the other hand, follows the more difficult paradigmatic mode. Although there is a tendency for news to become fictionalized (Dahlgren, 1995), news usually also relates facts and figures, and all kinds of propositions and arguments. This is not, however, the only reason for the sketchy reception of news (see Findahl and Höijer, 1982; 1984; Gunter, 1987; Lewis, 1991).

Perspectivising schemas

One way to anyway find meaning in news is to interpret news in concise or metaphoric form: 'He was such a rolling stone. Cream of the cream' (Höijer, 1995). Jensen (1998) shows how news viewers in different cultures use different perspectivizing schemas or superthemes, as he prefers to call them. Perspectivizing schemas correspond to *foundational schemas* in Shore's (1996) theoretical outline of culture, mind and meaning. They are highly abstract and global in the sense that they help us understand a wide range of social experiences.

At this level we find general cultural schemas in the form of overall perspectives, for example, ideological ones such as class and gender perspectives, or moral and religious perspectives, or general textual perspectives focusing on genre conventions. The example below shows how a female viewer uses a gender perspective on society to find meaning in a countryside lunch scene from a fiction series about the late 1940s (Höijer, 1995):

Typical men of that time. I am sure it was like that then. Men had lunch and it had to be cultured and they should talk about business and serious matters. Men talk to men. Trying to butter them up with a good lunch and the like.

Concretizing content schemas

There is also a level at which various types of more concrete social schemas have been suggested. These include *person schemas* which focus on personality traits, *role schemas* which focus on behaviours in particular social situations, *self-schemas* which represent generic self-knowledge, *event schemas* including generalized knowledge about what will happen in a given situation (sequences of events), *scene schemas* representing places, the rooms and streets and buildings in which our daily routines take place, and *story schemas* consisting of sets of expectations about the way in which different kinds of stories proceed (Fiske and Taylor, 1991; Mandler, 1984).

Different types of schemas overlap and we simultaneously use many schemas in the interpretation process. Bartlett (1967/1932) argues that the past operates as an active organized totality, that schemas are vivid, developing and dynamic, that we can mix material emanating from different schemas, and that emotions and motives are part of the schemas.

Reception studies show that viewers use a mix of cognitive schemas from various experience spheres when interpreting television genres (Höijer, 1992b).

When interpreting a television programme or other texts, the 'reader' spontaneously (usually unconsciously) uses a whole set of cognitive schemas to serve as interpretative frames of references. The mix of schemas which may be activated depends partly on central conceptions in the readers mind, partly on the text. There are differences between genres with regard to how dominant various experience spheres are used as frames of reference for the interpretation. For example, schemas emanating from the private sphere are quite rare in the interpretation of glamorous soap operas. Instead, intertextuality dominates, that is schemas emanating from genre knowledge. In relation to social-realistic fiction, however, private sphere experiences play a prominent role (Höijer, 1995; 1996a).

Social schema theory is important for our understanding of the reception process, yet it is not sufficient. Schema theory emphasizes the preconscious constructivistic aspects of audience interpretations. But what happens when viewers do not find a frame of reference for the interpretation? And what about hidden unconscious influences? Here we need to address questions of comprehension processes and of psycho-dynamic processes involved in the reception process.

Comprehension processes

Comprehension is the act of grasping what a text is all about. In the comprehension process we try to find out the story line in fiction, understand the protagonists, their motives, and so forth, and in factual genres we try to understand the verbal and visual content, the arguments, and the propositions. It is important to analytically distinguish comprehension and different types of reactions to texts, for example, positive and negative feelings. Together they constitute what we may call reception. The preferred, negotiated and oppositional decodings as they are defined in Morley's (1980) study are, for instance, not very much related to comprehension. His decoding positions focus on audience's degrees of agreement with the views and the perspectives presented in the programme. Ways in which the different audience groups comprehend and interpret the statements and reasoning in the programme are not discussed. In his critical postscript to the 'Nationwide' study Morley (1981:5) also concluded: 'Minimally, the model as it stands would seem to blur together the axis of comprehension/incomprehension of signs with that of agreement/disagreement with forms of propositional meaning generated from these signs'. Later Corner (1991) distinguished between comprehension and a more general level, in which audience's evaluation of a text is in focus. Neither he, nor Morley, however, make any attempt to recognize comprehension studies conducted in Great Britain, Germany or the Nordic countries. We very well may react to a text without having understood it, so it is important to theoretically distinguish between comprehension and reception. Reception is a broader concept subsuming comprehension as well as, for example, critical evaluations, and positive and negative responses. The relations between different types of subsuming processes vary depending on the context. This is the reason why we need to theoretically separate different processes.

The comprehension process is quite well theorized in psychology. I will here only briefly present the theory of Alexander Luria (1976). His theory mainly focuses on language discourses, but, according to Luria (1973), visual comprehension is mentally organized in accordance with the same principles as verbal comprehension, that is, analysis of visual components, creating of synthesis, and holistic perspectives.

Comprehension is thus a complex process at several interrelated levels. According to Luria (1976) there are three main levels, each connected to a specific area in the brain, and together making a functional unit:

1. The first level concerns the analysis of single components – the words – in the language. (Located in the temporal zones of the left hemisphere.)
2. At the second level the word components are analysed in larger units as sentences. It is a question of making a synthesis of the components. Central at this level is the cognitive process in which social schemas are activated for how the components might be related (see event schemas, and so forth above). These processes take place in the parieto-occipital zones of the left hemisphere.
3. The third level concerns the text as a whole. It is an analysis in which the meaning is interpreted within a holistic perspective. According to Luria, we must deal with quite other psychological structures than for the other levels. The interpreter must create hypotheses about some general meaning and make a 'departure outside the limits of the

external text to look for hidden meanings' (Luria, 1976: 170). To take an example from Luria, who liked to let people listen to fables, it could be a question of finding some moral sense in a text. (The frontal lobes are central in this process.) Here we use perspectivising schemas, for example moral or ideological.

The three levels form a functional unit, and they co-operate in very flexible and dynamic ways. Luria emphasizes that the analysis is not sequential but simultaneously goes on at the different levels, and there is a complex interaction between all levels. Different levels can dominate depending on the circumstances. It is possible, for instance, to construct a general idea about a theme in a text without analysing it fully at level one and two. This is what might happen in reception of informative discourse when it is hard to grasp the content in detail (see above).

Psycho-dynamic processes

As Brewin (1988) has noted, cognitive processes are hidden in psychoanalytic theories, for instance, when certain reactions are explained by the presence of traumatic memories that have been repressed and made inaccessible to conscious awareness.

However, we need not go so far as to dwell on traumatic memories. There are *symbolic traumas* in the form of cultural ideas which are hard to accept or myths hidden in discourses. Such hidden ideas are also assimilated into our cognitive structures. They have an influence on our interpretations and reactions, and they may touch us deep in our identities. As an example I would like to discuss violent news and myths of manliness. It is documented that female viewers react much more to documentary pictures of violence. Men are more inclined to steel themselves so that they do not react to what they see. They more frequently say that they have grown accustomed to seeing acts of cruelty in the world via the news. 'Seeing a dead body doesn't affect me particularly. I guess I've become blasé' is a much more typical reaction among men than among women (Höijer, 1994; 1996b).

This gender difference may partly be explained by differences in socialization and social roles between the sexes. But at a deeper level other processes may also be involved. Men may steel themselves to protect themselves against the myth of violence as a specific male characteristic, i.e., against their fear of becoming a perpetrator of violence, themselves.

Rollo May (1991: 20) defines myths as 'self-interpretations of our inner selves in relation to the outside world'. Myths are narratives about the self and society. Television news about acts of violence tells us that men are aggressive and violent, and that men commit most acts of violence in the world around us. They tell us that violent behaviour is part of masculine culture; it is part of the male sphere. When men hear and see documentary depictions of violence they meet a story about themselves through the myth of violence and manliness. This is an unacceptable idea, a painful experience, and the violence-imbued self-conception is something one tries to keep at arm's length. This is achieved by not allowing oneself to react very strongly to images of violence, death and suffering. Men shield and defend themselves by looking at the pictures without showing any outer signs of emotion.

Women are not threatened in their identities at all in the same way when confronted with documentary depictions of violence. On the contrary, women may be even be confirmed in their more positive self-conception, assured that violence is not part of feminine culture. Since women do not experience any threat to their self-conception, they can afford to remain more open to the depictions of violence and have greater leeway for emotional reactions. They do not have the same need as men to dull their sensibilities, but can surrender to feelings of sorrow and pain.

Psycho-dynamic processes may thus be embedded in cultural discourses. They certainly take place within the individual, but the tensions are not only the result of very personal traumas but also of cultural ideologies and myths. Psycho-dynamic processes also include the mental room in which the never-ending task to build bridges between our cultural and individual identities takes place. According to Winnicott (1953; 1971), some activities are especially well suited to this. Already the baby creates what Winnicott calls an *intermediate area of experiencing* where cognitions about the outer reality and the inner conditions can meet. When the baby finds relief and solace from a comforter, a blanket, a piece of rag, a doll, or a teddy bear (transitional objects according to Winnicott), it creates the intermediate area of experiencing in which one can comfort oneself and reduce the tension between outer and inner worlds. Later in childhood children's play has this function, and also a variety of other activities such as lying on top of the bed, listening to music, drawing, reading, and watching television (Leffler, 1985). As adults, we still need an intermediate area of experiencing since 'no human being is free from the strain of relating inner and outer reality' (Winnicott, 1953: 399). Winnicott stresses the cultural field of arts and religion. Fiction narration on television may, however, play an even more profound role in post-modern societies.

Fiction viewing is mostly perceived as very relaxing, compared with news viewing which is perceived as more demanding (Alasuutari, 1991; Höijer, 1995). Viewers have often told me that a nice thing with watching fiction is that you can 'relax the brain'. It is something you can 'watch with a smile', or 'just sit idle'. This non-demanding quality of the activity is something which, according to Winnicott (1953:90), characterizes the intermediate area of experiences:

> It is an area which is not challenged, because no claim is made on its behalf except that it shall exist as a resting-place for the individual in the perpetual human task of keeping inner and outer reality separate yet interrelated.

The balance between illusion and disillusionment is another important dimension of the intermediate area of experiences (Winnicott, 1953). In narration we become cognitively-emotionally involved in an illusion of reality yet we know it is only a story. The character of the involvement differs, however, between fiction genres. Viewers' receptions show diverse involvement patterns between glamorous popular fiction and social realistic fiction (Höijer, 1996a; Livingstone, 1988). The viewers' quotations below are from my own genre studies (Höijer, 1991; 1995), and they illustrate the main differences.

Stories within the glamorous popular fiction[2] genre are interpreted as fabrications which bear very little relation to reality. The plots, the events, and the protagonists are given meaning in light of what the audience knows from earlier episodes or ideas about genre conventions, that is, how they perceive that things used to be within this narrative tradition:

> After all she is disgusting, spoiled. But that's the part she has had all the time. Her thing is to be disgusting. After all, in this series all women are supposed to be very female and all men very male.

It is rare that viewers' own experiences are used as frames of reference for the interpretations, and viewers also rarely draw conclusions or generalize about social or human phenomena from the programmes. The narration does not give very much room for an illusion of reality and for bridging gaps between outer and inner reality. Instead, intertextuality is the basis for the interpretations and the viewers devote themselves to the actions and events in the story: 'I never thought they would win those $25 000. I thought something would happen. I also thought they might replace her or that he would report that Harry was cheating.'

The involvement with the social–realistic genre[3] is quite different. The protagonists are perceived as socio-culturally believable and they are interpreted in the light of everyday knowledge about human beings: 'He was an unkind farmer, just like my grandfather', or 'That terrible stubbornness. I started to think of a person I know'. Similarly, the social setting, the events and the plot are interpreted with reference to life itself and the audience also generalize from the programme back to reality: 'I recognize parts of the way they showed family relations. You can bring parts of it with you in real life.' An illusion of reality is clearly experienced although the viewer is aware that it is a fiction story. 'It is fabricated but it could have been taken from any northern community.' The audience gets involved in the narration in many ways, through identification and recognition, through reading the persons and the social settings in depth, and through activation of oneself in the form of personal memories. Outer and inner reality meet. In this way, the narrative may mediate between the individual and the cultural identity of the viewer, and work in the personal dilemma of these contradictory identities:

> This is my childhood. It's pieces of it. The whole 1950s when I was a kid. The cars and the motor bikes and the cycles and the clothes. And the women's hairdos. They were my aunts and my mother and father. They were those people. I remember the machines in the bakery. We lived next to a bakery. We kids ran around the bakery and they gave us bread crumbs and cookies and biscuits. I could feel the smell when I watched those scenes from the bakery.

Conclusions

This chapter has presented a theoretical outline for social psychological perspectives in reception research. Meaning construction or interpretation has been seen as the core of the reception process.

'Social psychological' has been understood cognitively, in line with Fiske and Taylor's (1991) claim that social psychology always has been cognitive, that is, put an emphasis on the 'thinking' organism (in contrast to narrow behaviourism), an emphasis on processes of the human mind. 'It concerns both how people think about the social world and how they think they think about the social world' (p. 19). Social schema theory and comprehension theory have been suggested as relevant theoretical frames for reception research. Schema theory focuses on social and cultural experiences and the constructivistic aspects of interpretations. Comprehension theory focuses on the textual decoding process (language and pictures), the fact that there is a text to be understood.

The theoretical perspective has been broadened to include psycho-dynamic processes, that is, processes that cope with cultural and personal tensions within an individual. Such processes also influence reception.

Cognitive and psycho-dynamic processes are by no means separated. On the contrary. Cognitive dimensions are part of psycho-dynamic processes and vice versa. They have, however, been treated within totally different theoretical schools. Traditionally, psycho-dynamic theories have focused on the most problematic and tension-filled sides of life, often traumatic, while cognitive theory has focused on quite unproblematic and trivial everyday situations and activities, like visits to restaurants or understanding short stories. However, as Shore (1996:48) notes, 'not infrequently, individuals have conflicting personal and conventional models for a given domain of experience'. In fact, our everyday thinking may be filled with all kinds of social dilemmas (Billig, *et al.*, 1988).

We obviously need a synthesis between the cognitive and the psycho-dynamic, between the ordinary and the conflict-filled. As human beings we both smoothly interpret and deal with a stream of everyday situations, and experience dilemmas and conflicts. In media reception we, for instance, quickly identify genres, position ourselves as audience, orient ourselves in a story line, and so forth. At the same time dilemmas may appear such as those I have described in relation to violent news. Other types of dilemmas in news viewing have been described by Hagen (1994) and by Alasuutari (1991) in relation to fiction viewing.

Festinger's (1957) solution to the problem of conflicts or inconsistency within the individual, the theory of cognitive dissonance, is to regard inconsistencies as something uncomfortable which the individual tries to avoid or repair in different ways. The ultimate goal for the individual is harmony and consistency in thinking patterns and value systems. This may, for instance, be achieved by selective perception, that is, by only paying attention to information or discourses that will decrease the dissonance. Avoiding further problematic discourses is an expected behaviour. This is certainly what will happen in some cases.

But we probably live our lives with many more contradictory thoughts and dilemmas which we never solve or even try to solve. News viewers may find it very hard to watch pictures of victims of brutal violence, but they continue to watch such news items, and they continue to experience the dilemma between wanting to avoid everything that is brutal and a wish to follow what is going on in the world (Höijer, 1994).

Dilemmas may be seen as very natural parts of our understanding of our selves and the world. According to Billig *et al.*, (1988) dilemmas may be enabling, rather than restricting. Dilemmas may help people to reflect upon themselves and the world. I have suggested psycho-dynamic theories as a relevant theoretical frame of reference for understanding basic dilemmatic aspects of audience reception, and for understanding the different functions that different genres have for the audience.

No single theory can account for the complexity of audience reception. Even working with several theories omits aspects and dimensions of relevance. When considering social psychological perspectives you can easily pass over macro levels. Society becomes subordinate in your analysis. Concepts, such as dominant ideologies, hegemony structures, cultural reproduction or power relations are hardly part of psychological theories. They point at societal structures and sociological theories. Interestingly, however, Hall (1986: 29), in his struggle with the concept of ideology, redefines it from an emphasis on abstract systems of ideas and ideals to

> the mental frameworks – the languages, the concepts, categories, imagery of thought and the systems of representation – which different classes and social groups deploy in order to make sense of, define, and figure out and render intelligible the way society works.

A cognitive perspective certainly is implied here. Shore (1996) shows that schema theory can be developed to include social institutions and public forms. He suggests 'instituted models' as a concept covering the public and institutionalized life of culture. There seems to be a promising possibility of building a theoretical bridge between cognition, on one hand, and society and public culture, on the other. In this bridge building we need to take into consideration that neither human thinking, nor societies, are coherent and ideologically consistent structures. Rather, they are emotionally loaded, partly irrational and filled with social dilemmas. And so, too, are audiences.

Notes

1. In the early 1950s several British studies were conducted on how informative radio and television programmes were understood by listeners and viewers. The studies were initiated by the BBC (Vernon, 1950; Belson 1967; Trenaman 1967).

   Theoretically, these studies were not sophisticated. They were founded in pragmatic concerns about information problems of broadcast media. Comprehension was defined in behaviouristic mode by operational definitions, that is, what the comprehension test measured. They also relied heavily on quantitative data and statistical correlation analysis which is based on the assumption of linearity (one unit-sized change in one variable is associated with one unit-sized change in the other). This excludes other more complex types of relationships, for example, based on levels and critical thresholds (Findahl and Höijer, 1984).
2. Programmes included in the studies have been an episode of *Falcon Crest* and the television film *Against All Odds*. (A survey study also included *Dallas*.)
3. Programmes included in the studies have been an episode from *Three Loves* and the television film *Ängslans boningar*, both Swedish productions. (A survey study included other series as well.)

References

Alasuutari, P. (1991) The value hierarchy of TV programs: an analysis of discourses on viewing habits. In Alasuutari, P., Armstrong, K. and Kytömäki, J. (eds) *Reality and Fiction in Finnish TV Viewing*, Helsinki: Oy. Ylesradio Ab, Research Report No 3.

Alasuutari, P. (1995) *Researching Culture: Qualitative Method and Cultural Studies*, London: Sage.

Ang, I. (1985) *Watching Dallas: Soap Opera and the Melodramatic Imagination*, London: Methuen.

Ang, I. (1996) *Living Room Wars. Rethinking Media Audiences for a Postmodern World*, London: Routledge.

Bartlett, F. C. (1932/1967) *Remembering: A Study in Experimental and Social Psychology*, London: Cambridge University Press.

Belson, W. A. (1967) *The Impact of Television: Methods and Findings in Programme Research*, London: Crosby Lockwood.

Berger, C. R (1989). Goals, plans and discourse comprehension. In Bradac, J. J. (ed.) *Message Effects in Communication Science*, Newbury Park, CA: Sage.

Billig, M. *et al.* (1988) *Ideological Dilemmas: A Social Psychology of Everyday Thinking*, London: Sage.

Brewin, C. R. (1988) *Cognitive Foundations of Clinical Psychology*, Hillsdale, NJ: Lawrence Erlbaum.

Bruner, J. (1986) *Actual Minds, Possible Worlds*, Cambridge, MA: Harvard University Press

Bruner, J. (1990) *Acts of Meaning*, Cambridge, MA: Harvard University Press.

Cantril, H. (1947) *The Invasion from Mars: A Study in the Psychology of Panic*, Princeton, NJ: Princeton University Press.

Corner, J. (1991) Meaning, genre and context: the problematics of 'public knowledge' in the new audience studies. In Curran, J. and Gurevitch, M. (eds) *Mass Media and Society*, London: Arnold.

Cressey, P. G. (1938) The motion picture experience as modified by social background and personality, *American Sociological Review*, 3(5), 16–25.

Cronström, J. (1994) The depiction of violence and victims of violence in Swedish television newscasts: a content analysis of the evening news on public service and private channels. Paper presented at the International Conference on Violence in the Media, New York, 3 and 4 October

Curran, J. (1990) The new revisionism in mass communication research: a reappraisal. *European Journal of Communication*, 5(2-3), 135–64.

Dahlgren, P. (1995) *Television and the Public Sphere. Citizenship, Democracy and the Media*, London: Sage.

Daun, Å. (1989) *Svensk Mentalitet* (Swedish Mentality), Kristianstad: Rabén and Sjögren.

Festinger, L. A. (1957) *A Theory of Cognitive Dissonance*, New York: Row Peterson.

Findahl, O. and Höijer, B. (1976) *Fragments of Reality. An Experiment with News and TV-visuals*, Stockholm: Swedish Broadcasting Corporation, Audience and Programme Research Department (Rep. No. 53).

Findahl, O. and Höijer, B. (1982) The problem of comprehension and recall of broadcast news. In Le Ny, J. F. and Kintsch, W. (eds) *Language and Comprehension*, Amsterdam: North-Holland.

Findahl, O. and Höijer, B. (1984) *Begriplighetsanalys* (Comprehension Analysis), Lund: Studentlitteratur.

Findahl, O. and Höijer, B. (1985) Some characteristics of news memory and comprehension, *Journal of Broadcasting and Electronic Media*, 29(4), 379–96.

Fiske, J. (1987) *Television Culture*, London: Methuen.

Fiske, S. T. and S. E. Taylor (1991) *Social Cognition*, New York: McGraw-Hill.
Freeman, N. (1924) *Visual Education*, Chicago: Chicago University Press.
Gleich, U. (1994) Gewalt in den Nachrichten: Zugeschüttet mit 'starken' Bildern. *Medien Concret*, January, 22–64.
Gunter, B. (1987) *Poor Reception: Misunderstanding and Forgetting Broadcast News*. Hillsdale, NJ: LEA.
Hagen, I. (1992) *News Viewing Ideals and Everyday Practices: The Ambivalences of Watching Dagsrevyen*, University of Bergen: Department of Mass Communication (Rep. No. 15).
Hagen, I. (1994) The ambivalence of TV news viewing: between ideals and everyday practices, *European Journal of Communication*, **9**, 193–220.
Hagen, I. (1996) Modern dilemmas: TV audiences' time use and moral evaluation. Paper presented at the IAMCR Conference in Sydney, Australia, 18–22 August. (Forthcoming in Hagen, I. and Wasko, J. (eds) *Consuming Audiences? Production and Reception in Media Research*.)
Hall, S. (1986) The problem of ideology: Marxism without guarantees, *Journal of Communication Inquiry*, **10**(2), 28–43.
Herzog, H. (1944) What do we really know about day-time serial listeners? In Lazarsfeld, P. L. and Stanton, F. N. (eds) *Radio Research 1942-1943*. New York: Duell, Sloan & Pearce.
Höijer, B. (1989) Television-evoked thoughts and their relation to comprehension, *Communication Research*, **16**(2), 179–203.
Höijer, B. (1991) *Lustfylld glömska, kreativ illusion och realitetsprövning. Om publikens tankeprocesser vid tittandet på fiktion och fakta* (Pleasurable forgetfulness, creative illusion and reality-testing. About viewers' thought processes in relation to different genres), Stockholm: Swedish Broadcasting Corporation, Audience and Programme Research Department (Rep. No. 15).
Höijer, B. (1992a) Socio-cognitive structures and television reception, *Media, Culture and Society*, **14**, 583–603.
Höijer, B. (1992b) Reception of television narration as a socio-cognitive process: a schema-theoretical outline, *Poetics*, **21**, 283–304.
Höijer, B. (1994) *Våldsskildringar i TV-nyheter (Depictions of violence on television news)*, Stockholm: University of Stockholm, Department of Journalism, Media and Communication (Rep. No. 5).
Höijer, B. (1995) *Genreföreställningar och Tolkningar av Berättande i TV (Genre Expectations and Interpretations of Television Narration)*, Stockholm: University of Stockholm, Department of Journalism, Media and Communication (Rep. No. 1).
Höijer, B. (1996a) Audiences' expectations on and interpretations of different television genres: a socio-cognitive approach. Paper presented at the IAMCR Conference in Sydney, Australia, 18–22 August. (Forthcoming in Hagen, I. and Wasko, J. (eds) *Consuming Audiences? Production and Reception in Media Research*.)
Höijer, B. (1996b) The dilemmas of documentary violence in television, *The Nordicom Review*, **1** (Special Issue), 53–61.
Höijer, B. and Findahl. O. (1984) *Nyheter, förståelse och minne* (News, comprehension and memory), Lund: Studentlitteratur.
Jensen, K. B. (1986) *Making Sense of the News*, Aarhus: Aarhus University Press.
Jensen, K. B. (1995) *The Social Semiotics of Mass Communication*, London: Sage
Jensen, K. B. (1998) The world in the head: world cultures look at television news. In Jensen, K.B., *News of the World: Audience Uses of Television News in World Cultures*, London: Routledge.
Jensen, K. B. and Rosengren, K. E. (1990) Five traditions in search of the audience, *European Journal of Communication*, **5**, 207–238.
Klapper, J. T. (1960) *The Effects of Mass Communication*, Glencoe, IL: Free Press.

Leffler, B. J. (1985) Transitional relatedness through the eyes of school-aged children: a qualitative study of children of divorce and intact families. In Horton, P. C., Gewirtz, H. and Kreutter, K. J. (eds) *The Solace Paradigm*, Madison, CT: International University Press.

Lewis, J. (1985) Decoding television news. In Drummond, P. and Paterson, R. (eds) *Television in Transition*, London: British Film Institute.

Lewis, J. (1991) *The Ideological Octopus: An Exploration of Television and Its Audience*, London: Routledge.

Liebes, T. and Katz, E. (1993) *The Export of Meaning. Cross-Cultural Readings of 'Dallas'*. Cambridge, UK: Polity Press.

Linné, O. and Marosi, K. (1976) *At opleve og forstå fjernsyn. En studie omkring en dokumentarfilm* (To experience and understand television: a study of a documentary programme), Copenhagen: Danish Broadcasting Corporation (Rep. No 4B/76).

Livingstone, S. M. (1988) Why people watch soap opera: an analysis of the explanations of British viewers, *European Journal of Communication*, 3(1), 55–80.

Livingstone, S. M. (1990) *Making Sense of Television. The Psychology of Audience Interpretation*, Oxford: Pergamon Press.

Lowery, S. A. and DeFleur, M. L. (1988) *Milestones in Mass Communication Research*, New York: Longman.

Lull, J. (1990) *Inside Family Viewing: Ethnographic Research on Television Audiences*, London: Routledge.

Luria, A. R. (1973) *The Working Brain: An Introduction to Neuropsychology*, London: Penguin Books.

Luria, A. R. (1976) *Basic Problems of Neurolinguistics*, The Hague: Mouton.

Mandler, J. M. (1984) *Stories, Scripts and Scenes: Aspects of Schema Theory*, Hillsdale, NJ: Lawrence Erlbaum.

May, R. (1991) *The Cry for Myth*, New York: Norton.

Morley, D. (1980) The 'Nationwide' audience: structure and decoding. BFI Television Monograph, No. 11, London: British Film Institute.

Morley, D. (1981) The 'Nationwide' audience: a critical postscript. *Screen Education*, 39, 3–14.

Morley, D. (1986) *Family Television: Cultural Power and Domestic Leisure*, London: Comedia.

Morley, D. (1992) *Television, Audiences and Cultural Studies*. London: Routledge.

Pereira-Norrman, L. (1994) Jag vill stoppa våldet. En publikstudie av latinamerikaner i Sverige (How immigrants from Latin America conceive of violence in the news) Stockholm: University of Stockholm, Department of Journalism, Media and Communication. (Paper).

Piaget, J. (1926/1955) *The Language and Thought of the Child*, Cleveland: Meridian Books.

Poulsen, I. (1988) *Radioavisens forståelighed* (Comprehension of Radio News), Copenhagen: the Danish Broadcasting Corporation.

Schramm, W. (1949) The nature of news, *Journalism Quarterly*, 26, 259–69.

Schrøder, K. C. (1988) Dynasty in Denmark: towards a social semiotic of the media audience. *Nordicom Review*, 1, 6–13.

Shore, B. (1996) *Culture in Mind. Cognition, Culture and the Problem of Meaning*, New York: Oxford University Press.

Silj, A. *et al.* (1988) *East of Dallas. The European Challenge to American Television*, London: British Film Institute.

Stephenson, W. (1964) The ludenic theory of newsreading, *Journalism Quarterly*, 41, 367–74.

Stern, D. N. (1985) *The Interpersonal World of the Infant. A View from Psychoanalysis and Developmental Psychology*, New York: Basic Books.

Swanson, D. L. (1992) Understanding audiences: continuing contributions of gratifications research, *Poetics*, **21**, 305–28.

Trenaman, J. M. (1967) *Communication and Comprehension*, London: Longmans.

Vernon, P. E. (1950) Intelligibility of broadcast talks, *BBC Quarterly*, **5**, 206–12.

Vygotsky, L. (1934/1986) *Thought and Language*, Cambridge, MA: The MIT Press.

Winnicott, D. W. (1953) Transitional objects and transitional phenomena, *The International Journal of Psycho-Analysis*, **34**, 89–97.

Winnicott, D. W. (1971) *Playing and Reality*, London and New York: Tavistock/Basic Books.

15

Critique: audiences 'Я' us[1]

Martin Barker

A conversation. Four of us are out for a walk, two married couples in late spring, on the Mendips. Good friends for a long time, we're catching up on things we've each been doing. In the flow of exchanges, a film comes up: *Breaking The Waves* (1996). Our friends had been to see it, mainly at Simon's behest – Maureen had been pretty unsure about seeing it, bearing in mind what she had heard about it on 'Barry Norman' (as most British people, of course, affectionately call 'Film-whatever-year-it-is').[2]

The film, they told me (I still haven't seen it), is set in Puritan Scotland, and concerns a woman, outsider to her own community, who marries a foreigner. After he becomes disabled, his only source of sexual gratification is to get his wife to have sex with other men, and then tell him about it. Unwillingly she agrees to this, and the film follows what happens to them and to their relationship as a result. I don't even know if this is an adequate description of the film,[3] and as I recall the conversation, I am aware that I am probably filling bits in to make it make sense for what I am going to use it to illustrate – but then that's what people do.

As I hadn't seen the film, I could only listen, and ask, while they re-swapped their very different reactions to it. Simon was enormously fascinated by it, and had particularly enjoyed the complexity of the interactions he felt it portrayed. Maureen was very uncomfortable. It was a 'good film', she granted, but she'd been really uneasy about the role the woman had taken on herself. She felt that the film had a 'message' she didn't like – something she couldn't quite articulate, but having to do with 'what a woman is expected to do for a man'.

Here was classic ordinary talk: people discussing in the way that people do, at many points in their lives, what they felt about a media experience – and in the very act of talking, working out what something meant to them. Here also were tangible 'media effects': complex and rich pleasures, unease provoking arguments about meanings, self-justifications, reinforcement of relationships via sharing experiences. Even (beloved of Hollywood) 'scuttlebutt', the everyday word-of-mouth publicity on which films heavily depend, and therefore much sought after. And it worked, because I shall now make a point of seeing the film. But here, also, were two very individuated responses, which I, as friend *and* analyst, can't help seeing as clothed and nuanced by all kinds of social processes. For example, the very evident gender-dimension to the difference: there's little point in denying that men are more likely than women to get an erotic charge out of this narrative, and that is one dimension of pleasure –

but it would be cheap and easy to say that Simon 'put himself in the place of the men' in the film.

Harder to diagnose is Maureen's notion of a 'message' that she tried to hunt out, by talking out loud about the film. It's self-evident that the message that disturbed her didn't in fact 'reach' *her*. If it had, either she would be able to articulate it, or she wouldn't be able to see it *as a message* – it would just *be* the point of the film, and she would be agreeing. (In other words: Maureen, it seems to me, is working with a non-academic version of the encoding/decoding model of media power, and the implications of that bear thinking about ...) But then, what does it mean to say that there *is* a message? For whom? What if it only 'exists' as a message for those who reject it? If it has to be 'hunted for', what does it mean to call it a message? The implications roll on, and importantly, for such reasoning (not in Maureen, but in many public arenas) readily participates in arguments for banning films with 'dangerous messages': *Kids*, recently, and *Crash*.[4]

A real conversation with real individuals, showing real media processes and effects ... as people indeed do. But these are not the kinds of 'individual', nor the kind of 'effect', that get much talked about in audience theory and research. Not because our friends are both teachers, and might be seen therefore to be 'protected' by having available to them some relatively self-conscious 'languages' for discussing their experiences. Rather, because when audience theory and research talks about 'the individual', it is not *actual* individuals, but an *idea* of an individual which is being debated. And the languages for description of this 'individual', the processes and problems attributed to this 'individual', are hardly recognisable for the *actual* individuals that I, for one, ever get to meet and talk with.

In principle, there is nothing wrong with that. Scientific theories do deal in concepts and terms which won't necessarily be recognized by those whom they seek to describe and explain – even, yes, when what are being examined are people's thoughts, experiences, responses, preferences, uses and needs. But there *is* a problem, I want to argue, when our scientific languages are so antithetical to those experiences, etc., that they undermine the possible authority of the people being investigated. Then, issues become indissolubly scientific *and* political, with a vengeance.

Take a couple of the terms unreflectively used in some of the essays in this section: 'exposure', and 'consumption'. People are assessed for their 'exposure' to television, or for how much television they have 'consumed'. Our normal use of the term 'exposure' has to do with processes over which we have no control (may not have known about, were hit by unexpectedly), but want to control. If I am exposed to radiation, or to pesticides, the term 'exposure' sums up my attitude towards something *I* don't like. It refers to something I will try to avoid in future. Maureen could well have used the term to mark her reaction to some of the sex scenes in *Breaking The Waves* – she didn't know it was going to come at her like that, and she felt uneasy at best; *in extremis* she might have closed her eyes, or left.

But in our 'scientific' parlance, to say that someone has been 'exposed' to television or film is not to describe them – it is to impute vulnerability to them, and to measure the degree of likely 'harm' done, on an analogy with the impact of radiation or pesticides. And they are vulnerable precisely to the degree that they aren't able to recognize what is happening to them. The issue is in real senses prejudged. But this means that the normal uses of 'exposure' by actual audiences are the precise opposite of the 'scientific' uses applied to them: normally, audiences are 'hit' by something they don't want, and try to get away. I am 'exposed' to something that makes me squeamish, and don't like it (my worst are embarrassing situations in sitcoms). You don't like to be 'exposed', without warning, to horrific scenes in the news. Whatever. The point is the wholesale conflict between the directions of the two languages.

Or take 'consumption': not immediately such a negative term, but ultimately having some of the same force, rather like 'heavy viewing' vs. 'light viewing'. In the 'scientific' discourses, such terms suggest a rising intake of media calories, a digestive stuffing of the senses and mind. Yet again, these terms *are* in use among us ordinary folks. Whenever I go abroad, I take with me some novels, bought as cheaply as possible second-hand (so I can leave them behind) because I fear boredom. The novels all have one characteristic – they are fat enough (I buy by the inch thickness) and narratively driven enough, that I can 'consume' them at great and undemanding speed.

Every holiday I do this, and every year I have a problem – the manner of my consumption is such that I can't even remember their titles. I am in real danger of rebuying the same books – though it would hardly matter since I probably could re-read most of the book and not recall even that I had read it before, let alone how it went. To 'consume' in this sense is to retain as little as possible – again, the exact opposite of the implications behind talk of 'audience consumption' and 'heavy' media use. The whole *point* of my books is that being heavyweight in size means they can be lightweight in demand! Whereas in the 'scientific' discourse the 'heavy viewer' who 'consumes' all the time is understood to be accumulating deposits of message-fat ...

'Exposure' and 'consumption' are of course the languages of residual behaviourism, for which media 'effects' are presumed to be cumulative. Our ordinary languages presume almost exactly the opposite – that which has the least impact is the expected, the ritually returned to, the repeat experience. That which has the most impact is the unexpected, the startling, the first-time encounter. But it isn't only behaviourism which offends, in my view. Take, just as much, the concept of 'activity': central concept of the 'new audience research'. 'Activity' poses as the concept which distinguishes the new research, which sees audiences as responsive and as constructing meanings, from the old research which sees them/us as passive, malleable. My problems with this are hardly different.

When Simon and Maureen argued over *Breaking The Waves*, one of their prime disagreements was over a scene in which the woman masturbates a man she sits next to on a bus. Apparently most people in the cinema, Simon included, burst out laughing at the scene. Maureen was appalled – to her, to laugh was to join in the woman's denigration. She stayed silent, 'inactive'. Simon argued that the *way* the film presented the scene, was *meant* to be funny – and he laughed.

Which was the 'active' response? Simon was *influenced* by the film to laugh, actively. Maureen *resisted* the film, and therefore *refused* the proposed activity of laughing. Of course I accept that in other (mental) senses Maureen was active – indeed, angrily reactive – at that point. But I use the example to show the extraordinary looseness and imprecision of the notion of 'activity'. In other research I have been doing recently, I have talked with film audiences for whom the very point of going to the cinema is to achieve a state of planned passivity. Choosing a warm cinema with good seats into which one can slump, in which surround-sound will engulf, close enough to the screen to get maximum whomping impact from special effects: these are sought-after pleasures. Exactly: activity (choice of cinema, of film, knowledge of genre, following the 'hype') leads to welcome passivity (hit my senses hard with those special effects). 'Audience activity' is another concept requiring a deal of critical scrutiny, far more than I am giving in these gestural remarks.

These are just a few among the many terms which populate these essays on 'the media and the individual'. Among the others deserving equivalent attention, in my view, are the following:

- 'arousal' (used as an indicator of readiness to 'behave') as though it is a 'state' from which our conscious selves are disconnected. Yet anyone who goes to see a film advertised as 'erotic' is surely taking part in *planned excitement*, hardly consonant with that image of disengagement of the brain;
- 'gratification' (used as a term to indicate the natural end of a process of seeking solutions to 'needs') when, from both personal experience and from research, I perceive the much larger problem of *dis*satisfaction. People visiting films which have been 'hyped' more often than not come away asking 'was it worth it?'. What does that tell us about the nature of those 'needs' and what, indeed, are the consequences of 'failure to satisfy' them? We wholly lack, as I see it, a theory of 'disgratification';
- 'desensitization' (used as a term to indicate a process of loss of affective response) I honestly report on a paradox. If I am watching something that for any reason I find uncomfortable, I can resolve the discomfort *by adopting an analytic mode of viewing*. In other words, for me, and I suspect for other individuals (as opposed to 'individuals'), desensitization is a strategic response, which goes along with decreasing power of the media to influence us – the exact reverse of the claimed process;
- 'meaning' (used as a term for something which audiences are supposed to produce as a result of their encounters with texts) in fact often our references to 'meaning' arise in two contexts: either when we are plain puzzled by a lack of narrative logic or evident point in a film ('what on earth does it mean when ...?'); or when, as Maureen illustrates, we wish to impute possible persuasive influences to *other people* by virtue of *our* seeing implications in a film which we don't like;
- 'watch': even this is a problem, as far as I am concerned. Not just because sometimes, with television especially, we don't pay attention in the ways the critics believe and the advertisers hope. Rather, because

if you talk with people you find that media experiences are almost always multi-sensual. Film involves hearing as much as seeing (contra Gaze theory's strange optical obsessions). It also involves virtual (even actual) conversations – with characters, with other members of the audience. In fact arguably we can do many other things with our eyes than 'watch'; Hodge and Tripp in a wonderful chapter title cite a child saying of a cartoon that 'you sort of hear with your eyes'.[5] This is surely the indissolubility of perception and imagination.

These are my next choices for further conceptual investigation. What are anyone else's?

Where might we go with the 'individual'?

This section of the book rightly contains a range of kinds of work, because that is where we currently are. Our academic world of audience research contains this uneasy mix of kinds of work. It is certainly a healthy sign that at least some of the traditions represented here have begun to acknowledge what might in principle be learnt by opening disciplinary boundaries. The growing recognition, for instance, in sociological approaches to audiences that there is something to be learnt from an encounter with sophisticated textual work; the sometimes grudging acknowledgement in cultural studies' audience work that there was intelligent life before 1980; the development within psychology of approaches based on rhetorical and discursive understandings of respondents, challenging the notion of fixed 'attitudes' and opening up psychology towards sociological understandings; and the healthier caution in textual studies towards eliding the differences between implied, ideal or other such textually produced 'audiences' and live performers of audience roles who will need to be researched by other means: all these constitute welcome reachings-out to each others' disciplines.

But it would be naïve and dangerous to suppose that some kind of easy 'merger' of approaches could take place. This is not so much because a residual *amour propre* prompts each discipline to protect and celebrate its own contributions. It is more because of the presence within each discipline, with more or less strength, of philosophical and methodological presumptions and resultant political and policy orientations which make research across disciplines not just incommensurable, but mutually incomprehensible.

When psychologists working within the effects tradition talk of 'violence' and of 'stimuli' and of 'identification', they are participating in a theoretical and policy universe which has almost nothing in common with that of the uses and gratifications theorists, who talk instead of 'needs' and their 'gratifications', of 'modes of use' and their outcomes. When reception theorists plan an investigation of 'frames of meaning' and 'interpretive repertoires', they can probably converse with rhetorical psychologists, but they will have real trouble even sharing a dictionary with either the effects or the gratification researchers. Yet all are working with and on notions of the 'individual'. It is just that their ideas of the 'individual' are incommensurate, and their methodologies for researching him/her each presume exactly what the others 'know' to be false. And the difficulty perhaps is that, more than we all like to admit, our conceptions of the 'individual', and of the ways in which the media bear down on 'individuals', have been fashioned at quite a distance from actual research, and are hardly ever altered in the foundations by subsequent research – and that is because, by and large, none of us ever choose to do that kind of research.

Most of the time, researchers conduct their studies in response to other work within their own established field. That is inevitable, because we teach in our fields, we send our articles to our own journals, we sell our books to colleagues and their students, we meet at conferences, and so on. It is largely only when we need polemically to challenge each other, that we speak across the walls of our disciplines. Crudely, we cross boundaries to cross swords. It is the rare study which does seek to incorporate critically the gains of other fields. Each person is likely to have their own preferences here. Mine would be for Janet Staiger's *Interpreting Films,*[6] which honestly explores the connections between theorizations of the individual in the course of proposing a historical account of audiences.

But this babel-science isn't a situation that we need just accept. If we had the will, there are ways to transcend our present situation. I do not in truth think it will happen, but it could. To break for real the boundaries of methodological isolation, it would be necessary to mount a programme of research of a very particular kind. We would need some sharp-nosed research designed to test and compare the validity of the very theoretical assumptions which underpin each approach. The way to do this would be to home in on some key concepts, to elaborate their implicit claims, and then to develop tests of their coherence, consistency, reliability, and validity. All of us would then really be at risk.

For instance, is it (as I believe) a problem for 'violence-effects' research if, for instance, audiences deny that cartoons are violent in the first place (as van Voort, for instance, found)?[7] If not, what *would* test the applicability of researchers' conceptions of what constitutes 'violence' in the media? What exactly are the processes believed to encapsulated in the claim that audiences 'identify' with characters, or indeed with filmic presentation – and what could test whether any of these occur at all? Cumberbatch and Howitt believed that one was that 'identifiers' should show evidence of greater acceptance of a character's value judgements – and then found that they did not seem to.[8] If that is not a valid test, what might be? What possibilities are there for 'decoding' encoded messages, without altogether giving up the notion that some version is 'preferred'? David Morley classically tested the claim, derived from Frank Parkin, that there might be three determinate positions with specific characteristics – and found, to his own surprise, that his hypothesis largely failed.[9] Why, then, have researchers not abandoned the language of 'encoding' and 'decoding', of polysemy, and perhaps the very metaphors of 'reading' and 'meaning' (though the reception theorists might want to reclaim some of those – provided of course they are prepared to elaborate them, and see them tested)? If uses and gratifications research is created around postulates of 'needs' which different media function to meet, what consequences are there when (as seems so often to happen) what audiences actually report is failure to satisfy? If it doesn't matter, then what kinds of needs are these – can they be exported to the hungry, please, as an instant solution to food shortages? And so on.

There is an irony buried in here for me. I am personally particularly hostile to the claims of 'effects' theorizing, as is probably well known. Yet as I have argued before, quantitative 'effects' psychology has one virtue within its fold that I am not sure any of the other approaches can claim – it has tough procedures for checking the strength and validity of research internal to its own discipline. That is far less true in other fields of audience research. The research I am suggesting would precisely have to show that it was meeting tough criteria – because everyone would look at it like hawks.

I am not so naïve as to think that such tests, even if developed and even if (as I would expect) provoking difficult questions to all audience researchers, would result in atheistic rejection of challenged theoretical models – let alone conversion to others that stand up better. But at least those which did badly would then have to elaborate their defences. A quality of debate might emerge which is largely lacking at the moment, as the traditions represented here speak past and behind each other. And in the course of that, perhaps there might be some gain for the *individuals* whose 'individuality' has so often been publicly defined against them.

I return to my friends, Simon and Maureen. I have yet to meet any individual whose responses to the media are articulated in ways that seem to fit the kinds of account theorists give of 'media impacts'. That is not a plea for rank subjectivism, that the only accounts worth having are participants' own – apart from anything else, Simon and Maureen know very well that they *struggle to articulate their own accounts*, and one thing they turn to is how others hear them, talk back to them, argue with them. My plea is for two things.

First, among the measures we use for assessing the utility of academics' accounts of the 'individual's' relations to the media should be their ability to throw light on what real, concrete audiences do and say with their media. At present, media theory and research is largely used to initiate searches for *possible* audiences – be they 'vulnerable children' or 'preferred decoders' or 'gratified users' or 'implied/ideal/competent etc. readers'. Only a small amount is used to study *actual* audiences in lived environments.

Second, yet in inverse proportion to this, media-audience research tends to achieve public hearing. The research that most contradicts and steals people's languages for their *own* media responses is that which most informs political and policy debates. That in itself deserves considerable attention, as an topic for research – what, concretely, are the impacts on individuals' self-understandings of the ways they get defined by *us*? Recently, I heard David Buckingham argue cogently that media studies has as a central responsibility to encourage and contribute to democratic understanding of the media's role in society. That is surely right – but then our own claims may have a particular cogency.

Media researchers ought to acknowledge a responsibility not primarily to opinion-makers, moral progenitors and ... but to the individuals whose experiences and responses might benefit from our work – ourselves, our friends, neighbours, colleagues, all the people walking the aisles of that greatest of media emporia: AUDIENCES ' Я' US.

Notes

1. I have chosen this title deliberately, in the hope that readers will catch the reference to the very down-market Anglo-American toy firm which is decidedly cheap and cheerful. My point in choosing this title is to suggest that while, of course, many recent commentators on audiences have indeed stressed their own cultural involvements, these regularly turn out to be markedly learned if not high-cultural.
2. Barry Norman has long hosted a weekly film review programme on British television, entitled *Film 97* or whatever the year happens to be.
3. I cheated. My memory was at first at fault – I recalled being told that the husband was present when she was having sex. Spotting the book of the filmscript in a book shop, I stopped to check. But that is actually what people do – the element of accident in people's memories and uses of films is greater than most theories can allow.
4. *Kids* (1994) is a study of the sexual involvements yet naïvety of a group of American city young teenagers. Its authentic picture of their self-destructive life-style caused a scandal, with many standard cries that it was dangerous. Curiously, it also provoked a counter-reaction, even among some customary moralists, that this should be shown to young people to 'scare' them. *Crash* (1996), David Cronenberg's film of a J. G. Ballard novel, has generated – in Britain almost alone of all countries – the most bizarre and exaggerated sets of claims as to its nature and likely effects.
5. Hodge, R. and Tripp, D. (1988) *Children and Television: a Semiotic Approach*, Cambridge: Polity Press.
6. Janet Staiger (1992) *Interpreting Films: Sudies in the Historical Reception of American Cinema*, Princeton NJ: Princeton University Press.
7. See T.H. van der Voort (1986) *Television Violence: A Child's Eye View*, Amsterdam: Elsevier.
8. Cumberbatch, G. and Howitt, D. (1972) Affective feeling for a film character and evaluation of an anti-social act, *British Journal of Clinical & Social Psychology*, 102–8; see also their 'Identification with aggressive television characters and children's moral judgements', in Hartup, W. W. and de Wit, J. (1974) *Determinants and Origins of Aggressive Behaviour*, The Hague: Mouton. Cumberbatch and Howitt are rare in being psychologists who have sought to design and conduct experiments which might test the validity of some of the steps implicit in claims about 'identification'.
9. Morley, D. (1980) *The 'Nationwide' Audience*, London: BF; see also his 'The 'Nationwide' audience: a critical postscript', *Screen Education*, 1981. Morley was testing a proposition which had been taken from the work of sociologist Frank Parkin, that ideologies might typically provoke three kinds of response: a 'dominant' response, in which people accept the framework of ideas, and because they do so, see them as 'natural'; a 'negotiated' response, in which people accept the *general* validity of a set of ideas, but seek to except their application to themselves; and a 'resistant' response, in which the dominant ideas are identified as in some sense 'foreign' and imposed, and therefore not neutral serving others' interests.

Section 3

Cultures, communities and families

16

Television: polysemy and popularity

John Fiske

From *Critical Studies in Mass Communication*, **3**(4)(1986), Annandale, VA: Speech Communication Association, pp. 391–408.

The polysemic necessity

The failure of ideological criticisms to account for the polysemy of the television text is paralleled by its failure to account for the diversity of Western capitalist societies. Despite generations of life under the hegemony of capitalism there is still a wide range of social groups and subcultures with different senses of their own identity, of their relations to each other and to the centers of power. This diversity shows no signs of being homogenized into the unthinking mass so feared by members of the Frankfurt School, and, in a different way, by the ideological critics of the late 1970s. Rather, divergent and resistant subcultures are alive, well and kicking, and exerting various forms of pressure and criticism upon the dominant ideology of Western capitalist societies.

The main argument of this essay is this: In order to be popular, television must reach a wide diversity of audiences, and, to be chosen by them, must be an open text (Eco, 1979) that allows the various subcultures to generate meanings from it that meet the needs of their own subcultural identities. It must therefore be polysemic. But the television text is not anarchically open so that any meaning can be derived from it. The diverse subcultures in a society are defined only by their relations (possibly oppositional) to the centers of domination, so, too, the multiple meanings of a text that is popular in that society can be defined only by their relationships (possibly oppositional) to the dominant ideology as it is structured into that text. The structure of meanings in a text is a miniaturization of the structure of subcultures in society – both exist in a network of power relations, and the textual struggle for meaning is the precise equivalent of the social struggle for power.

Central to this theory is the notion that all television texts must, in order to be popular, contain within them unresolved contradictions that the viewer can exploit in order to find within them structural similarities to his or her own social relations and identity. [...]

I argue that the polysemy of television lies not just in the heteroglossia from which it is necessarily constructed, but in the ways that different socially located viewers will activate its meaning potential differently. Thus, any one utterance can be a member of a number of different 'languages': so when a character says, in an assumed southern accent, 'Oh, that's the cutest thing you've ever said to me, sugar' (see p. 196) this can be read as part of a traditional chauvinist discourse of gender, or as a more modern, liberated one. We may not be able to predict the actual reading that any one empirical viewer may make, but we can identify the textual characteristics that make polysemic readings possible, and we can theorize the relation between textual structure and social structure that make such polysemic readings necessary. One illustrative aspect of this structural relationship can be understood in terms of authority, and here I wish to exploit the semantic link between author and authority. By using the term I do not intend to extend the fallacy that the notion of an individual, creative author can help us to understand television, but rather to use the notion of the author-in-the-text which works through the form to prefer certain readings and to attempt to impose these upon the reader.[1] This implies a power relationship between text and reader that parallels the relationship between the dominant and subordinate classes in society. In both instances authority attempts to impose itself, but is met with a variety of variously successful strategies of resistance or modification that change, subvert or reject the authoritatively proposed meanings.[2] Grossberg (1984) has identified the strategy of *excorporation* (the opposite of the Frankfurt School's *incorporation*), by which members of subordinate classes can take the cultural products of dominance, turn them against the cultural producers and excorporate them into resisting discourses. My theoretical position. [...] stresses that heteroglossia and dialogue can only be understood in terms of power relationships and not just in terms of the social diversity of liberal pluralism. [...]

Meaning is as much a site of struggle as is economics or party politics, and television attempts (but fails) to control its meaning in the same way that social authority attempts (but fails) to stifle voices and strategies of opposition. It is the polysemy of television that makes the struggle for meaning possible, and its popularity in class structured societies that makes it necessary.

Demonstration of ideological criticism

I propose to take a typical piece of prime time television as my example for analysis. It is a segment of *Hart to Hart* consisting of two short scenes in the first of which the husband and wife detective team, the Harts, discuss ways in which a jewel robbery may have been committed on a cruise liner, and plan to set a trap for the thieves. In the second the villain and villainess plan their next 'hit'.

An ideological analysis would have no difficulty in showing how the various codes of television are working to construct the Harts as embodiments of the dominant ideology, and to swing our affective allegiance towards them, so that hegemonically we are led to accept the point of view that they stand for as the common sense one even if we are not members of the same class, race, age groups as they. Technical codes such as lighting, setting, music and camera work all function to make the Harts more attractive than the villain and villainess. Their cabin is lit in a softer, warmer light and is softened and humanized by flowers and drapes. The

Transcript

SCENE ONE

HERO: He knew what he was doing to get into this safe.

HEROINE: Did you try the numbers that Granville gave you?

HERO: Yeh. I tried those earlier. They worked perfectly.

HEROINE: Well you said it was an inside job, maybe they had the combination all the time.

HERO: Just trying to eliminate all the possibilities. Can you check this out for me. (He gestures to his bow tie)

HEROINE: Mm. Yes I can. (He hugs her) Mm. Light fingers. Oh, Jonathon.

HERO: Just trying to keep my touch in shape.

HEROINE: What about the keys to the door?

HERO: Those numbers can't be duplicated because of the code numbers. You have to have the right machines.

HEROINE: Well, that leaves the window.

HERO: The porthole.

HEROINE: Oh yes. The porthole. I know they are supposed to be charming, but they always remind me of a laundromat.

HERO: I took a peek out of there a while ago. It's about all you can do. It's thirty feet up to the deck port-hole. You'd have to be the thin man to squeeze through.

HEROINE: What do you think? (She shows her jewelry) Enough honey to attract the bees?

HERO: Who knows? They may not be able to see the honey for the flowers.

HEROINE: Oh, that's the cutest thing you've ever said to me, Sugar. Well, shall we? (Gestures towards the door).

SCENE TWO

VILLAIN: I suppose you noticed some of the icing on Chamberlain's cupcake. I didn't have my jeweler's glass, but that bracelet's got to be worth at least fifty thousand. Wholesale.

VILLAINESS: Patrick, if you're thinking what I know you're thinking, forget it. We've made our quota one hit on each ship. We said we weren't going to get greedy, remember.

VILLAIN: But darling, it's you I'm thinking of. And I don't like you taking all those chances. But if we could get enough maybe we wouldn't have to go back to the Riviera circuit for years.

VILLAINESS: That's what you said when we were there.

VILLAIN: Well maybe a few good investments and we can pitch the whole bloody business. But we are going to need a bit more for our retirement fund.

background music is in a major key when the Harts are on screen, but shifts to a minor for the jewel thieves. The camera treats them with the normal, respectful close-up, rather than the extreme close-up used for the villain and villainess. I have shown elsewhere (Fiske, 1985) that extreme close-ups (ECUs) are conventionally used to construct either villainy or intimacy, depending on the other codes working in their context. Here they are used to connote villainy by bringing us close to the villain so that we can see through his words and expression to the 'truth' that lies behind them, not in them. Similarly the dialogue allows the Harts an 'attractive' joke and metaphor (of which more later) and their actions and words show them as a couple cooperating together. The villain and villainess, on the other hand have their dialogue restricted to their criminal plans and are shown disagreeing and physically pulling apart from each other. All these codes are working hegemonically to attract the viewer to adopt the social position whose ideology is embodied by the Harts as the one from which to make sense of the events, and to reward the adoption of this position with the twin pleasures of recognition and of familiarity with the dominant ideological practice.

The dominant ideology, so this argument runs, informs this text largely through the differences and similarities between hero/ine and villain/ess. As Gerbner (1970) demonstrates, heroes are distinguished from villains largely through their greater attractiveness and greater efficiency: in other characteristics they are remarkably similar.[3] Here the attractiveness of the hero and heroine's mode of representation is supported by the casting. The language and accent of the villain identify him as non-American, probably British (though some viewers have read his swarthy appearance to place him as Hispanic). The villainess, however, is blonde, white American and thus is less 'villainous' than he (indeed, she finally repents and helps the Harts to catch the villain). The Harts are, of course, embodiments of American bourgeois appearance, morality and behavior.

The similarities between the hero/ine and the villain/ess are equally, if not more, significant, for they provide not the conflict that is to be resolved in the narrative, but the ideological common ground upon which that narrative is played out, and which is therefore not called into question, but remains at the level of common sense. Thus both sides take for granted that the getting and keeping of wealth is an unquestionable motive for action. Similarly, it is not called into question that in both cabins the men are planning, while the women are prettying themselves. [...]

A critical practice that goes no further than this is one hide-bound by the limits of the Frankfurt School or of the 1970s ideological criticism, both of which model the viewer as powerless, in the one case in the face of the manipulations of the producers in the culture industry, and in the other in the face of the authority of the text to construct a reading position for its subjects. The implication of this position is that texts such as this propagate American patriarchal capitalism internally and internationally and exert the irresistible hegemonic force of the dominant culture.

An inherent weakness of this model is its inability to accommodate either the possibility of social change or a theory of popularity that is capable of conceptualizing 'the people' as anything other than 'cultural dupes' (Hall, 1981) who are helpless before the power of the industry or of the text. The aim of this sort of ideological criticism, then, is limited to the not insignificant, but finally negative, one of increasing the viewer's ability to resist the imposition of cultural meanings that may not fit one's own social identity, and in so doing to resist the homogenization of culture. But we need to develop a more positive critical practice than this, and the strategy for achieving this posture is the topic of the next section.

Polysemy, popularity and the politics of reading

A more reader-centered critical theory leads us to investigate the extent to which the textual discourses may, or may not, correspond to the discursive practices of the wide variety of audiences that will have viewed this program over a large part of the Western and Third World. As these audiences have different material sociocultural positions, so their discursive practices and ideology frames must also differ. [...]

But the different audiences worldwide are only a larger and more dramatic sign of the different audiences within a nation, and if any program is to be popular it must allow for the different discursive practices and ideological frames of different subcultures to be used in the reception and decoding of the text.

A theoretical strategy that might account for both social change and a notion of popularity that allows 'the people' some say in the matter is one derived from deconstruction theory. The differences between this and the 'preferred reading' school are not great, in fact, they are often ones of emphasis and methodology. One such difference is that deconstruction asserts the instability of all meaning, and thus denies the possibility of meanings being structured into the text with any degree of clarity at all. If there is any stability of meaning, it can only derive from the ideology of the reader, never from the structure of the text. Another is that the preferred reading school derives the variety of textual readings from the varied social experiences of the readers; whereas deconstruction derives it from the inherent instability of language itself. It is this that finally invalidates deconstruction, for social struggle is always inscribed in language (Volosinov, 1973), and a preferred meaning is always structured into the mass media message [...]

The dominated classes [...] *do* have the power to make their own culture out of the products of the culture industry, which means that such excorporated culture cannot be defined in terms of its own essence, but only in terms of its (resisting) relationship to the dominant. The main enterprise of deconstruction is to deconstruct texts to reveal their instability, their gaps, their internal contradictions and their arbitrary textuality, and thus their potential for readings that are produced by the audiences, not by the culture industry or by the author-in-the-text. Thus when the villain says, 'Well maybe a few good investments and we can pitch the whole bloody business. But we are going to need a bit more for our retirement fund,' his words are treated by the text in a specific way. The ECU of his face, the heavy irony in his English accent, and the fact that the pretty American villainess has just characterized his attitude as greed combine to lead the viewer into a negative orientation towards him. Or do they? Is it not rather our own ideology or our capitulation to the dominant ideology-in-the-text that produces the reading? Can a subordinate non-white or non-American, whether in the US or the rest of the world, read this to be a subversive use of the discourse and ethics of capitalism which turns the system back on itself? Could not this conjuncture of the discourses of race and capitalist economics also mean that the only way in which members of the subordinate race/class can participate in the validated activities of capitalism (looking after one's female and preparing for old age) is by what the dominant class calls crime? If so, the definition and motivation of crime would be shifted from the realm of the (evil) individual and placed firmly in the domain of the social system, and the semiotic needs of an oppositional subculture would be catered for. Excorporation will have worked. Irony, as a rhetorical device, is fertile ground for deconstructive criticism because it necessarily works by simultaneously opposing meanings against each other. Screen theory, like the preferred reading one, would place these meanings in a hierarchical relationship with each other. That is, we 'know' that the moral one (this man is evil) takes precedence over, and is used to explain, the manifest 'meaning' of the words (he is behaving responsibly). In this case irony prefers one meaning over the other, and is seen to work in the same way as the perfect camera viewpoint does. It gives the reader/spectator privileged knowledge; we understand the villain's words better than he does, we have a privileged insight into him, and our understanding is complete and adequate. Irony is, in this reading, also part of MacCabe's (1981) 'hierarchy of discourses' that construct for the reader this position of 'dominant specularity'. But how do we *know*, the deconstructionist would ask, which meaning takes precedence? If 'this-man-is-behaving-responsibly' does, then the moral condemnation is shifted away from the individual towards the social system, and the politics of the meaning is reversed. Recovering such meanings from the margins of the text is the strategy of deconstruction. Using such meanings to make the text make self-interested sense may be the reading strategy of one or more of the audiences. [...]

This analysis has concentrated at the micro-level on identifying and investigating the fissures opened up by the relative freedom that associative structures offer the reader, but it can be argued that this is typical of television on a macro-level as well. In contrasting television with film, Ellis (1982) argues that a defining characteristic of television is the segmentation of its text. By this he means that its generic mode of presentation is by short, self-contained segments linked by association rather than by logic. [...]

Segmentation, with its associative structure, is more likely to produce an open text (Eco, 1979) that offers more readily a range of semiotic potential than a text like a film that relies more on narrative sequence and cause and effect for its structuring principles, for these are agents of semiotic closure.

In order to explore how the relative openness of the television text might allow for ideologically contradictory readings we need to investigate the notion of semiotic excess. This has some affinities with both the 'preferred reading' and the deconstructionist schools. It shares with the former the belief that dominant ideological values are structured into the text by the use of dominant codes and thus of dominant encodings of social experience. It shares with the latter the belief that the dominant reading does not exhaust the semiotic potential of the text. In a popular work of art these codes and their formal relationship must conform to the conventions of encoding and decoding that the dominant ideology has established as its natural signifying practice, because without them reader expectations would be defeated and popularity would be at risk. And here I am referring to that dimension of popularity that refers to a text's ability to give pleasure to as wide a range of audiences as possible. The text can appeal to this variety of audiences only if there is a common ideological frame that all recognize and can use, even if many are opposed to it. The preferred reading of a popular text in mass culture must necessarily, then, attempt a hegemonic function in favor of the culturally dominant. The reader, who statistically is almost certain to be one of the culturally subordinate, is invited to cooperate with the text, to decode it according to codes that fit easily with those of the dominant ideology, and if one accepts the invitation, is rewarded with pleasure. The pleasure is the pleasure of recognition, of privileged knowledge and of dominant specularity, and it produces a subject position that fits into the dominant cultural system with a minimum of strain.

Identifying and revealing this ideological work of the text is a vital part of critical practice, but when we have achieved this we are far from having exhausted the text's potential. The theory of semiotic excess proposes that once the ideological, hegemonic work has been performed, there is still excess meaning that escapes the control of the dominant and is thus available for the culturally subordinate to use for their own cultural-political interests. The motivation to use the semiotic excess for particular, possibly oppositional subculture purposes, derives from the differences between the sociocultural experiences of the producers and readers. Hodge and Tripp (1986) are in no doubt about what happens when the meanings that TV seems to prefer are in conflict with those used to organize the reader's perception of the world: 'non-television meanings are powerful enough to swamp television meanings'. This brings us to the fuller definition of 'popularity', its sense of being 'of the people, serving the grass roots interests of the subordinate' – a meaning that is closer to folk art than mass art (O'Sullivan, Hartley, Saunders and Fiske, 1983, pp. 174–6).

Bennett's (1987) work on James Bond has demonstrated the instability of the meanings of popular texts, and has shown that varying readings need not work by rejecting the dominant ideology, but rather by articulating their opposition in relation to it. The dominant and the oppositional are simultaneously present in both the text and its readings. The dominant is found in the preferred reading, the oppositional in the semiotic excess that the preferred reading attempts to marginalize, but that can never be finally or totally controlled by the dominant. It is this semiotic excess that a socially motivated deconstructionist reading recovers and attempts to mobilize in the interests of the subordinate; what is crucial here is the variety of readings that the variety of social experiences of subordination can produce. Hodge and Tripp (1986) argue that their work constitutes:

> a compelling argument for the primacy of general social relations in developing a reading of television, rather than the other way about, for it seems likely that the ideological meanings inscribed in general social relationships will have a powerful effect upon the total meanings of the television experience.

The subordinate reading may displace the dominant, or they may occur after and over the preferred ones; in this case they are necessarily mutually contradictory. [...]

A black fighting with a white on television will presumably lose, and the Aboriginal child who identifies with that black will not allow this defeat to deny the characteristics that led him or her to make the identification in the first place, rather it will be seen as another example of white power within which black values must struggle for expression. The ideological progress of the narrative will not be effective in swinging this child's moral and affective affiliation onto the official hero. Identifying with the loser in a television narrative may be an important way of making meanings that are useful in the social experience of the subordinate. One of the aims of criticism must be to demonstrate that the narrative defeat of the subordinate is part of the same system that produces the social subordination; the characteristics and actions of heroes and villains must be read as social and not personal.

Conclusion

If the text is able to contain simultaneously contradictory readings, then my argument is that the reading subject must be able to cope with them, and use them, for meanings occur only in the encounter between texts and subjects. These contradictions in subjectivities are accounted for in the theory of the divided subject. According to Lacan (1968), our subjectivity is formed as we enter the symbolic, the language or meaning system that is always already awaiting us, and that has always already mapped out the subject position for us to occupy. But our material social experience may well contradict our given subjectivity, may demand meanings of experience that this given subjectivity cannot provide. So we develop a split subjectivity in which more recently acquired and less deeply rooted subject positions can and do conflict with the original, given one. This conflict frequently occurs within consciousness, whereas an uncontested subject position remains largely in the unconscious, its labor in the sense-making process that we call culture unrecognized and uninspected.

So a given bourgeois subjectivity can acquire a contradictory radical one, a patriarchal subjectivity can acquire a feminist one, and a white subjectivity can acquire a black one. Contradictions in society reproduce themselves in subjectivities. As texts can never be totally controlled by the dominant, so subjectivities can never be produced by the dominant ideology alone – otherwise social change would be impossible. The correspondence between text and subjectivity as theoretical constructs is close. Both are makers of sense and consciousness, both bear similar relations to the dominant ideology and both are capable of working contradictorily, and it is this potential to activate contradictions that provides for their ability to be oppositional and subversive. Hodge and Tripp's (1986) work accounts for the co-existence of the subversive meaning with the dominant – they suggest that not only is the subversive meaning necessary, but that, for the child viewer, it becomes the preferred one: 'Of the two kinds of meaning, ideological (Parent) and subversive (Child) meanings, the emotional charge and attraction of the programme is invested in the subversive (Child) meanings.' In this they are developing Eco's (1980) argument that aberrant decodings are the norm for mass media messages.

Ideological control of both the text and the reading subject attempts to work through the denial of any contradictions which might disrupt the seamless homogeneity of bourgeois ideology. A socially responsible critical practice must recover these contradictions, and must concern itself with that central one between the hegemony of the text and the social needs of the subordinate.

Stuart Hall (1981) uses different rhetoric to make a similar point when he writes:

> The people versus the power-bloc: this, rather than 'class-against-class', is the central line of contradiction around which the terrain of culture is polarized. Popular culture, especially, is organized around the contradiction: the popular forces versus the power-bloc.
>
> (p. 238)

Critics need to develop strategies of textual analysis that are equally sensitive to the needs of the subordinate as to those of the controlling authority. We must first identify the semiotic excesses of the text, those potential meanings that escape the control of the producers of the dominant culture. This will enable us to identify where and how members of subordinate subcultures can use these semiotic opportunities to generate meanings for *them*, meanings that relate to their own cultural experience and position, meanings that serve their interests, and not those of cultural domination.

As a semiotician, I believe that meanings are the most important part of our social structure, and are potentially the main origin of any impetus to change it, for, as Hall (1984) has said, 'a set of social relations obviously requires meanings and frameworks which underpin them and hold them in place' (p. 10). If we are to resist the centralization of meaning, if we are to preserve the subcultures and alternative cultures that serve the interests of the people and whose differences form the only possible source of social change, then a socially motivated deconstructive critical and teaching practice is essential. It is this practice that can explain and legitimate the ability of the subordinate to take the signifying practices and products of the dominant, to use them for different social purposes, and to return them from where they came, stripped of their hegemonic powers. A critical theory and practice of this type offers us a way of understanding how television can be dialogically popular, that is, how it can serve the interests of the dominant and of the subordinate at one and the same time.

Notes

1. See Newcomb and Alley (1983) and Marc (1984) for accounts of the role of the creative individual in the production process that challenge my assertion.
2. See Fiske (1986) for a fuller account of empirical work by Hobson (1982) and Hodge and Tripp (1986) that demonstrates how effectively subordinate classes of viewers (in Hobson's case, women and in Hodge and Tripp's, children) can construct *their* meanings, *their* culture, out of the products of the television

industry. Radway (1984) gives a similar insight into the power of women readers of romance to produce a feminine culture from it.

3. Fiske and Hartley (1978) and Fiske (1982) discuss the implications of Gerbner's work for a cultural theory of heroes and villains in a society structured along axes of class, race, gender, nationality and age-group.

References

Bennett, T. and Woollacott, J. (1987) *Bond and Beyond: Fiction, The Political Career of a Popular Hero*, London: Macmillan.

Bennett, T., Boyd-Bowman, S., Mercer, C. and Woollacott, J. (eds) (1981) *Popular Television and Film*, London: BFI/OU.

Davis, H. and Walton, P. (eds) (1983) *Language, Image, Media*, London: Blackwell.

Eco, U. (1979) *The Role of the Reader: Explorations in the Semiotics of Texts*, Bloomington: University of Indiana Press.

Eco, U. (1980) Towards a semiotic inquiry into TV messages. In Corner, J. and Hawthorn, J. (eds) *Communication Studies: An Introductory Reader*, London: Arnold, 131–49.

Ellis, J. (1982) *Visible Fictions*, London: Routledge & Kegan Paul.

Fiske, J. (1982) *Introduction to Communication Studies*, London: Methuen.

Fiske, J. (1985) Television: A multilevel classroom resource, *Australian Journal of Screen Theory*, **17/18**, 106–24.

Fiske, J. (1986) Television and popular culture: Reflections for British and Australian critical practice, *Critical Studies in Mass Communication*, **2**, 200–16.

Fiske, J. and Hartley, J. (1978) *Reading Television*, London: Methuen.

Gerbner, G. (1970) Cultural indicators: The case of violence in television drama, *Annals of the American Association of Political and Social Science*, **338**, 69–71.

Gitlin, T. (1982) Prime time ideology: The hegemonic process in television entertainment. In Newcomb, H. (ed.) *Television: The Critical Review*, New York: Oxford University Press, 3rd edn, 426–54.

Greenfield, P. (1984) *Mind and Media*, London: Collins.

Grossberg, L. (1984) Another boring day in paradise: Rock and roll and the empowerment of everyday life, *Popular Music*, **4**, 225–57.

Hall, S. (1981) Notes on deconstructing the popular. In Samuel, R. (ed.) *People's History and Socialist Theory*, London: Routledge & Kegan Paul, 227–39.

Hall, S. (1984) The narrative construction of reality, *Southern Review*, **17**(1), 3–17.

Hall, S., Hobson, D., Lowe, A. and Willis, P. (eds) (1980) *Culture, Media, Language*, London: Hutchinson.

Hartley, J. (1982) *Understanding News*, London: Methuen.

Hartley, J. (1984) Encouraging signs: television and the power of dirt, speech and scandalous categories. In Rowland, W. and Watkins, B. (eds) *Interpreting Television: Current Research Perspectives*, Beverly Hills: Sage, 199–41.

Hobson, D. (1982) *Crossroads: The Drama of a Soap Opera*, London: Methuen.

Hodge, R. and Tripp, D. (1986). *Children and Television: A Semiotic Approach*, Cambridge: Polity Press.

Lacan, J. (1968). *The Language of the Self*, New York: Delta.

MacCabe, C. (1981) Realism and the cinema: notes on some Brechtian theses. In Bennett, T., Boyd-Bowman, S., Mercer, C. and Woollacott, J. (eds) *Popular Television and Film*, London: British Film Institute/Open University, 216–35.

Marc, D. (1984) *Demographic Vistas: Television in American Culture*, Philadelphia: University of Pennsylvania Press.

Morley, D. (1983) Cultural transformations: The politics of resistance. In Davis, H. and Walton, P. (eds) *Language, Image, Media*, Oxford: Blackwell, 104–17.

Newcomb, H. (ed.) (1982) *Television: The Critical View*, New York: Oxford University Press.

Newcomb, H. and Alley, R. (1983) *The Producer's Medium: Conversations with America's Leading Television Producers*, New York: Oxford University Press.

Newcomb, H. and Hirsch, P. (1984) Television as a cultural forum: Implications for research. In Rowland, W. and Watkins, B. (eds) *Interpreting Television: Current Research Perspectives*, Beverly Hills: Sage, 165–98.

O'Sullivan, T., Hartley, J., Saunders, D. and Fiske, J. (1983) *Key Concepts in Communication*, London: Methuen.

Radway, J. (1984) *Reading the Romance: Feminism and the Representation of Women in Popular Culture*, Chapel Hill: University of North Carolina Press.

Rowland, W. and Watkins, B. (eds) (1984) *Interpreting Television: Current Research Perspectives*, Beverly Hills: Sage.

Samuel, R. (ed.) (1981) *People's History and Socialist Theory*, London: Routledge & Kegan Paul.

Volosinov, V. (1973) *Marxism and the Philosophy of Language*, New York: Seminar Press.

17

Mass communication and the construction of meaning

Graham Murdock

From Armistead, N. (ed.) (1974) *Reconstructing Social Psychology*, Harmondsworth: Penguin, pp. 205–20.

The making and taking of meanings in everyday life

Traditionally social psychology has concerned itself with the forms rather than the contents of social action, and has concentrated on the observable behaviour to the neglect of subjective meanings. What mattered was how people's actions looked to the psychologist and not what they meant to the people themselves. In addition, by detaching people from their on-going everyday relationships and encapsulating them within controlled experimental settings, the prevailing methodology effectively isolated the study of action from its appropriate social context. The attempt to redress these imbalances constitutes one of the main departure points for a growing body of recent work both in social psychology, and increasingly in sociology as well. This work attempts firstly to map out the categories and make sense of their situation; and secondly, to explore the ways in which meanings are constructed, sustained and modified in the course of everyday social interaction.

To the extent that this shift of emphasis opens up a neglected and fruitful field of study it is to be welcomed. At the same time, however, an overemphasis on subjective meanings and on the immediate situation of interaction can lead to a drastically reduced consideration of the overall social context of action. The authors of one recent text, for example, have argued that 'social structure cannot refer to anything more than members' everyday sense of social structure since it has no identity which is inde-pendent of the sense' (Filmer *et al.*, 1972, p. 54). This sort of foreshortened focus by-passes any consideration of the fact that the various settings within which everyday interactions take place are themselves embedded in a wider system of social and symbolic relations erected on the basis of systematic inequalities in the distribution of property and wealth – in short, a social class structure. The dynamics underlying a general economic process such as inflation are immensely complex, and conse-quently it is scarcely surprising that they 'will frequently be opaque to actors in their everyday lives' (Goldthorpe, 1973, p. 457). However, the fact that people may have an understanding of 'inflation' which is muddled, incomplete, or just plain wrong, does not prevent them from experiencing its consequences very directly in the form of rising prices. Similarly, it is true that when asked many people will tend to deny or devalue the importance of class inequalities. But the fact that 'class' does not seem to be a salient category through which these people make sense of their situation does not mean that class inequalities do not exist or that they do not impinge on their everyday life. On the contrary, whether they acknowledge it or not, a person's class situation as mediated through the kind of job they do and the sort of house and neighbourhood they live in intervenes decisively to determine not only their basic standard of living, but also to circumscribe the nature and range of their social relationships, and their access to systems of meaning. It is this last point particularly which I want to explore in this present paper.

The essential starting point is the recognition that those groups in society which occupy positions of the greatest power and privilege will also tend to have the greatest access to the means of communication, with the result that their particular definitions and explanations of the social and political situation will 'tend to become objectified and enshrined in the major institutional orders' (Parkin, 1972, p. 83). Given the pervasiveness of these dominant meanings and their insistent institutional backing, it is scarcely surprising that they should provide at least some of the frameworks and categories through which those on the receiving end of class inequalities make sense of their situation. However, it is one thing to assert that the meaning system of the dominant group provides the dominant meaning system for the society as a whole, but it is quite another to show how this process actually works out in concrete practice. It is at this juncture that a consideration of the role of the mass media in relaying dominant meanings becomes crucial.

The mass media permeate everyday life in two very important ways. Firstly, contact with the various media provides the majority of the population with their dominant leisure activity. Secondly, for most people this contact constitutes their main source of information about, and explanations of, social and political processes, and also a major fund of images and suggestions concerning modes of self-presentation and general life styles. The mass media therefore represent a key repository of available meanings which people can draw upon in their continuing attempts to make sense of their situation and find ways of acting within or against it. At the same time, however, the operation of the media organizations is circumscribed by the general economic and political contexts within which they are embedded, with the result that the range of information, imagery and interpretive frameworks they relay tends to be restricted, repetitive and ultimately consonant with the interests of dominant groups (Murdock and Golding, 1974). The mass media are therefore, simultaneously, both a key resource for the everyday construction of meanings, and a significant constraint on the range and direction of such constructions. This present paper sets out to explore varying levels of this relationship between everyday constructions and contextual constraints, drawing on concrete illustrations from the two main areas of mass-media output: news and entertainment.

There is a considerable body of evidence now accumulating showing that the majority of people get most of their information about general social and political processes from media news coverage. This situation raises two important questions. Firstly, what are the mechanisms through which newsmen come to select certain happenings in the everyday world for processing and presentation as news, and how far do the resulting accounts coincide with, and support, the interests of dominant groups? Secondly, how far does the audience simply take these news accounts as given, and to what extent do individuals and groups differentially situated in the social structure remake these media-related meanings, deleting, highlighting and modifying elements in line with localized meaning systems erected on the basis of specific social experiences? These two questions are considered in the next section. The crucial relationship between situated and media-relayed meaning systems is then taken up again in the third section, and explored with reference to recent studies in the field of leisure.

Defining the situation: the reproduction of dominant meanings

So far, I have talked about the dominant meaning system as though it was more or less monolithic. Clearly, this is too simplistic and glosses over the undoubted differences in outlook between the various sectors of the dominant class. Despite these variations, however, dominant groups tend to share a common view of the social and political structure which legitimates their own privileged position and solicits the consent of the less privileged. Essentially, this view entails the denial of permanently structured inequalities in the distribution of wealth and power and the assertion of a 'national' interest as having greater reality than sectional interests; the denial of fundamental conflicts over ends and the assertion that residual disputes over means can be accommodated within the existing machinery of representation; and the labelling of any radical challenge to these assumptions as numerically insignificant, illegitimate, or ephemeral. The mass media in general, and the news media in particular, constitute the major means through which these consensual notions which form the core of the dominant meaning system are reproduced and relayed for public consumption. Of course, it is possible to offer an explanation of this situation in terms of direct manipulation. But this ignores both the relative political autonomy of news organizations and also the fact that the news presentations are the outcome of cumulative process of independent selection and meaning construction on the part of newsmen. Even so, news accounts do tend overall to support the consensual notions underpinning the dominant meaning system. In order to explain this coincidence, however, it is necessary to trace the operation of oblique rather than direct constraints, and more particularly to examine the ways in which the routine practices of news production and the professional assumptions which support them are circumscribed by the general economic and political context within which news organizations are embedded.

Newspapers and news bulletins are inextricably tied to time. They have to reproduce themselves once every twenty-fours hours. This means that situations which can be conveniently covered and processed within this time-span are much more likely to become news than situations which take longer to unfold. Thus a strike will probably become news whereas the steady deterioration of working conditions which preceded it will not. This immediacy of news coverage necessarily concentrates attention on the form of events, on what happened and who was involved, to the neglect of the underlying content and causes. As a consequence, radical challenges to consensual assumptions are emptied of their political content and appear as sudden and ephemeral happenings, rather than as manifestations of structured inequalities in the distribution of wealth and power (Murdock, 1973a). In this way news accounts reinforce one of the key consensual notions underpinning the dominant meaning system.

Having selected an event for presentation as news, newsmen face the problem of placing it within a context that will render it meaningful to the majority of their audience. Necessarily, therefore, news presentations must work with meanings and imagery which are both widely available and generally understood. The authors of a recent study of the press coverage of race relations in Britain, for example, have pointed to the frequent evocations of the colonial context. By way of illustration they cite a *Daily Express* story about a group of illegal Indian immigrants discovered hiding in a Bradford cellar, which was headed 'Police Find Forty Indians in "Black Hole"', an immediately recognizable allusion to the 'Black Hole of Calcutta' (Hartmann and Husband, 1971). Once selected, a framework will structure the subsequent coverage. That is, events which are consonant with the basic image are likely to be given prominence whereas contradictory developments will tend to be played down or excluded altogether. A study of the news coverage of a large demonstration against the Vietnam War provides an interesting instance of this process in practice (Halloran *et al.*, 1970). The dominant image of the event was set in an initial story printed some weeks before the demonstration. The story drew an explicit parallel between the expected situation in London and the widely publicized confrontations between police and student demonstrators in Paris and Chicago earlier that year, and predicted widespread street fighting. Subsequent coverage elaborated this basic image of the event. On the day, however, the demonstrations were predominantly peaceful. Nevertheless, the news coverage continued to structure its presentation around the original image, highlighting incidents of confrontation and depicting the police as representatives of the consensus successfully coping with the challenge of militant outsiders.

This habitual presentation of news within frameworks which are already familiar has two important consequences. Firstly, it recharges and extends the definitions and images in question and keeps them circulating as part of the common stock of taken-for-granted knowledge. This, in turn, further increases their chances of selection as frameworks for future stories. Secondly, 'it conveys an impression of eternal recurrence, of society as a social order which is made up of movement but no innovation' (Rock, 1973). Here, again, by stressing the continuity and stability of the social structure, and by asserting the existence of a commonly shared set of assumptions, the definitions of the situation provided in news accounts coincide with and reinforce essential consensual notions. This last coincidence has been further cemented by the recent intensification of the economic pressures acting on news organizations.

In recent years, newspapers, particularly the 'populars', have found themselves competing for a declining readership against a background of spiralling costs. Nor have television companies been immune from economic pressures. Steadily rising costs, coupled with the fact that the audience has now reached its numerical ceiling, have intensified the competition for viewers and made news bulletins important counters in the ratings game. In their ensuing attempts to encapsulate the widest possible audience, news presentations have tended to define the situation in terms of a basic set of generally shared concerns and values, a 'National Interest', which transcends and takes precedence over the interests of specific class groupings. In the case of television news organizations, this fundamentally consensual definition is underscored by their statutory obligation to remain impartial, which means in practice locating the prob-able truth and the reasonable solution somewhere in the space between the two accredited sides of the case (Hall, 1972). However, as one promi-nent commercial television executive has noted, 'impartiality does not require putting the case for things which have already earned the disap-proval of the majority consensus'.

The incessant pressures of time and the consequent problems of resource allocation and work scheduling in news organizations can be reduced or alleviated by covering 'pre-scheduled' events; that is, events that have been announced in advance by their convenors (Tuchman, 1973). However, one of the consequences of adopting this solution to scheduling problems is to increase the extent of newsmen's dependence on news sources, willing and able to pre-schedule their activities. In effect, this means an increased reliance on élite sources such as official announce-ments, political speeches and diplomatic exchanges. Thus a symbiotic relationship arises between newsmen and the élites, particularly the polit-ical élite, through which readily processable information is exchanged for publicity. This concentration on parliamentary events and political speeches is further reinforced by newsmen's conception of themselves as a 'Fourth Estate', acting as an indispensable channel through which the decisions and doings of the political élites, including their mistakes and miscalculations, are made known to the people at large. By making the debates between legitimated power holders a major category of everyday coverage, however, news presentation serves not only to publicize domi-nant definitions of the situation, but also to reinforce the key consensual notion that such conflicts as do exist can be adequately accommodated within the existing representative machinery without altering the basic distribution of wealth and power.

The cumulative outcome of the factors outlined here for the definitions of the situation conveyed by news presentations is well illustrated by a recent study of the press coverage given to race relations in four national daily newspapers (*The Times, Guardian, Mirror* and *Express*) during the period from 1963 to 1970 (Hartmann and Husband, 1974). This elongated time-span enables the authors to trace the cumulative build-up of definitions. Throughout the period one of the predominant themes of the coverage was the question of coloured immigration into Britain. The numbers coming in, the legislation introduced to regulate entry, and Enoch Powell's anti-immigration views all figured prominently as categories of news, and served to define coloured people as a problem. This basic problem-definition of the situation was amplified by the coverage of black–white relations within Britain. During the period examined in the study, coverage of coloured people's relationship to the major social resources of jobs, housing and education (which constitute the major structural bases of white hostility) became overshadowed by the increasing concentration on specific manifestations of prejudice and conflict and on the legislation introduced to regulate these matters. These findings provide an interesting illustration of the way in which news accounts tend to concentrate on the immediate forms of situations rather than their underlying causes in structured inequalities, and to underscore the ability of existing channels of representation to regulate conflict. Taking the coverage as a whole, the authors conclude that it defined the situation as one in which coloured people presented a problem to be coped with and accommodated within a basically white society. Finally, they argue that by presenting race and racial conflict as significant dimensions of social structure and social process, and by reiterating the communality of interests involved in 'the British Way of Life', the coverage effectively served to deflect attention away from the continuing centrality of class inequalities.

Having outlined the basic framework of meanings underlying the news presentation of race, the authors go on to examine how far this framework underpins the definition of the situation which people actually hold, and how far the meanings relayed by the media are subject to re-negotiation on the basis of situational experience and individual attitude. The information in this part of the study was gathered principally through detailed personal interviews with 415 white, mainly working-class adolescents, aged between eleven and fifteen. To maximize the difference in respondents' personal experience of racial situations, half the sample was drawn from areas of high immigration in the Midlands and West Yorkshire, and the remainder from areas of low immigration in Teesside and Glasgow. Respondents' general definitions of the situation were elicited through a series of open-ended questions, while their personal attitudes towards coloured people were assessed by means of a specially constructed Likert-type scale.

As might be expected, both individual attitude and personal experience did act as mediating influences, leading respondents to emphasize different aspects of the situation. Thus, respondents with a generally hostile attitude towards coloured people tended to stress the fact that they caused or occasioned problems for whites. However, while those in areas of low immigration tended to reiterate this point in very general terms, those living in areas of high immigration were more likely to mention concrete instances such as that blacks were threatening housing opportunities for whites. Similarly, the less hostile respondents were more likely to be aware of the problem faced by coloured people themselves; but whereas those in areas of low immigration framed this situation in general terms, those in areas of high immigration tended to cite specific situational instances of prejudice and discrimination. Individual attitudes and situational experiences did therefore have some mediating influence on respondents' definitions of the racial situation. But, at the same time, and this is the crucial point, the authors argue that their evidence tends to indicate that these mediations operate *within* the general framework of meanings relayed by the news coverage. That is, despite the differences of selection and emphasis, all the respondents shared a common overall definition of coloured immigrants as constituting a 'problem', tended to feel that there were 'too many coming in', and anticipated 'trouble' as a likely consequence.

Over and above the intrinsic interest of the specific findings, this study raises two very important points. Firstly, it underlines the importance of exploring people's overall definitions of the situation, and indicates that no matter how competently done, the conventional kind of attitude scales that form many social psychologists' stock-in-trade cannot adequately tap this key dimension of meaning. Secondly, it points to the centrality of media-relayed frameworks in providing pervasive and authoritative definitions of general social situations, and suggests that the meanings derived from situational experience are more likely to work within rather than against these definitions, modifying and negotiating rather than challenging and rejecting them.

In view of the limitations stemming from the relatively restricted subject matter and the reliance on one-off interviews as a means of mapping respondents' meaning systems, this study should be regarded as suggestive rather than conclusive. Nevertheless, despite these limitations, by highlighting the cental role of media-relayed meaning systems in framing people's accounts of general features of social structure and social process, this study marks a decisive advance on previous research, and opens up a key topic for future investigation. In the meantime, however, we can gain some further insight into the relationships between situated and media-relayed meaning systems by examining another key area of media output: entertainment.

Living in leisure

Historically, studies of the media audience have been dominated by the question 'What are the media doing to people?' Consequently, research has mainly concentrated on tracing the effectiveness of particular messages in inducing behavioural responses. Most typically, this has involved investigating the impact of advertising on subsequent purchasing behaviour and assessing the 'effects' of exposure to portrayals of aggression and violence on the later behaviour of children and adolescents. From the 1940s onward, however, a significant counter-tendency has developed, based on a reversal of the standard assumptions. Instead of starting from the message content and tracing the effects of this stimulus on audience responses, these researchers started from the disposition with which individuals approached the media. The emphasis therefore shifted from reaction to interaction, and the key question became not 'What are the media doing to people?' but 'What are people getting out of the material they choose to consume?' To the extent that this approach views people's involvement with specific media materials as the result of an active process of selection and meaning construction, it represents a significant and welcome advance over the simplistic stimulus–response models underlying 'effects' studies. However, by focusing on the individual, it effectively abstracts this process from its overall social context, and thereby produces a foreshortened analysis. This 'uses-and-gratifications' approach to the media–audience relationship has recently stimulated a good deal of discussion and research (Katz *et al.*, 1973), and consequently it is necessary to consider it a little more fully.

The leading British exponents of 'uses-and-gratifications' research base their work on the premise that: 'social experience gives rise to certain needs, some of which are directed to the mass media of communication for satisfaction' (McQuail *et al.*, 1972, p. 144). Unfortunately, however, by formulating the problem in this way they create several problems for themselves. The first problem is that the basic 'needs' which supposedly underlie particular patterns of gratifications can only be inferred from an individual's statements about these gratifications themselves. So that if a person claims to like quiz programmes because he finds the close finishes exciting, it is inferred that he has a need for excitement, and that this 'need' leads him to search for excitement in quiz programmes. Clearly this is a circular argument. Secondly, although they explicitly state that individual 'needs' are a product of specific social experiences, in the absence of a sufficient analysis of this experience or of the individual's overall response to it, they are unable to provide a systematic explanation of the considerable variations in media uses indicated by their own findings. In order to provide anything like a satisfactory account of the relationship between people's mass-media involvements and their overall social situation and meaning system, it is necessary to start from the social setting rather than from the individual; to replace the idea of personal 'needs' with the notion of structural contradiction; and to introduce the concept of subculture.

A situation can be viewed as contradictory when elements in it are simultaneously affirmed and denied. Typically, contradictions take the form of gaps between what is supposed to be happening and what is actually happening; between what has been promised and what is actually being delivered. Subcultures are the meaning systems and modes of expression developed by groups in particular parts of the social structure in the course of their collective attempt to come to terms with the contradictions in their shared social situation. More particularly, subcultures represent the accumulated meanings and means of expression through which groups in subordinate structural positions have attempted to negotiate or oppose the dominant meaning system. They therefore provide a pool of available symbolic resources which particular individuals or groups can draw on in their attempt to make sense of their own specific situation and construct a viable identity.

Historically, class situations have provided the primary social bases for the generation of subcultures, and locality the main mediation. 'Cockney culture', for example, can be seen as one localized variant of the more general subculture of the urban industrial working class. Over the last fifteen years or so, however, age groupings have assumed an increasing importance as social bases for subcultural styles, and a considerable amount of work has focused on the notion of 'youth culture'. This notion rests on two interlinked assertions. Firstly, that generational membership has displaced social-class situation as the key determinant of social experience and social consciousness; and secondly, that the generational consciousness of adolescents is sustained and expressed through the mass entertainments aimed at the youth market, and more particularly through pop music. By ignoring the continuing and decisive importance of class inequalities, these assertions simplify and distort the process of post-war social change. More particularly, they gloss over the increasingly complex interplay between the youth-oriented symbols and styles relayed by the entertainment media and the situational meaning systems and subcultures of particular class groupings. Rather than displacing class factions, age groups have become an increasingly important mediating context through which contradictions in class situations are experienced and resolved (Murdock, 1973b). It is exactly this complexity which makes youth subcultures particularly relevant to the present argument.

The fullest illustration of the approach advocated here is provided by P. Cohen's (1972) exploratory analysis of youth subcultures among the 'respectable' working class in the East End of London. He points out that whereas previously a boy leaving school could expect to follow his father or uncle into a trade, the decline in the traditional craft industries of the area has reduced the number of openings in skilled jobs. Hence, lacking the necessary academic qualifications for entry into the newer industries, increasing numbers of school leavers have been relegated to routine manual jobs. Their work situation therefore makes it impossible to uphold the notion of 'pride in the job' which formed the cornerstone of the traditional work ethic, and which constituted an important component in the male self-definition. Faced with a dull and boring work situation offering little or no intrinsic satisfaction, and lacking the means to change it, leisure time assumes a decisive importance as the key area within which they can construct a meaningful life-style and a viable self-identity.

From the beginning of the 'rock-and-roll' era, the styles of teenage leisure sponsored by the mass entertainment industries provided the most glamorous and widely publicized manifestation of the 'affluence' theme announced by Harold Macmillan in his celebrated 'Never had it so good' speech. However, as Cohen points out, these new media-relayed symbols and styles were laid over the top of pre-existing class subcultures and over specific structural contradictions, both of which 'framed' the direction of the selections actually made. He then goes on to suggest that the successive East End youth subcultures such as the mods and the skinheads can be considered as 'variations on a central theme – the contradiction at an ideological level between traditional working-class puritanism, and the new hedonism of consumption; at the economic level between a future as part of the new socially mobile élite, or as part of the new *lumpen*' (Cohen, 1972, p. 23). Each subculture therefore represents a way of working through, within the sphere of leisure, the possible resolutions to contradictions in the situation of the skilled working class. The mod lifestyle represented an attempt to explore the option of upward mobility into the white-collar class, while the skinhead style explained the *lumpen* option of downward mobility into the unskilled manual strata. At the same time, however, these explorations took place within the context of the overall meaning system provided by the pre-existing class subculture. Typically, therefore, youth subcultures combined elements drawn from the mass entertainment media with elements derived from situational subcultures. For example, whereas the music and dress styles incorporated into the mod style were drawn from the media-relayed milieux of the West End boutiques and discotheques, the characteristic styles of language and gesture were rooted in the class-based meaning system which permeated everyday life in the family and locality.

Another illustration of the relation between media-relayed elements and class-based meanings is provided by the results of a pilot study of pop music preferences among middle-class adolescents (Murdock and McCron, 1973). Theoretically, these pupils are 'free' to involve themselves with the whole range of current pop music. In actuality, however, the great majority chose to involve themselves most closely with those particular styles which they classified as 'progressive'. This term was typically applied to performers who were perceived to be breaking with, or 'progressing beyond', the standard pop formulas, through such devices as personalized lyrics, individual improvisation and experimental instrumentation. In order to explain the direction and meaning of this preference, however, it is necessary to explore the ways in which their choices are circumscribed by class-based meaning systems.

Everyday life within the family and local neighbourhood is permeated and underpinned by the patterns of meaning through which previous generations have negotiated their shared experience of common class situation. Through the process of socialization, particularly within the family, these class-based meaning systems are reproduced within the rising generation and come to constitute the basic framework of assumptions with which they approach their social experience. Consequently we can suggest that one of the factors framing adolescents' media involvements and subcultural identifications will be the extent to which the available symbols and styles are capable of containing and resonating with these previously assimilated patterns of meaning. Hence the 'successful' pupils' high valuation of 'progressive' performers who 'do their own thing' can be seen as a logical extension of the middle-class emphasis on self-development and individual achievement. Similarly, Davis has suggested that the consistent preference and valuation of LSD as against Methedrine among the middle-class 'hippies' of Haight-Ashbury can be viewed as a negotiated version of the basic values of self-exploration and self-improvement among the American middle class (Davis and Muroz, 1970).

It would, however, be a great mistake to see youth subcultures as explicable entirely in terms of their class context. On the contrary, once formed, they assume a degree of autonomy and the relations of opposition and antagonism between them become important in determining the media-relayed elements they will incorporate. For example, in addition to relating the heavy-duty denims, braces and industrial boots worn by the skinheads to the basic situational values of masculinity and toughness, it is also necessary to see them as representing a decisive rejection of the sexually ambiguous dress styles which characterize the middle-class 'hippie' subculture. To a considerable extent, therefore, 'the demarcations and oppositions between different youth subcultures may be seen as versions of the divisions and conflicts within the wider class structure, transposed into the specific context of youth' (Murdock, 1973b). The situation is not quite as simple as this, however, as oppositions occur not only between, but also within, class groupings.

An interesting instance of intra-class opposition is provided by Monod's study of youth subcultures in a working-class suburb of north Paris during the mid 1960s (Monod, 1967). He concentrated on two groups: a younger group of fourteen-year-olds and an older group aged eighteen and upwards. The older group had adopted the 'snob' style in which the dress and hair length of the Rolling Stones constituted key elements. Incorporating this explicit reference to contemporary pop music served several functions. Firstly, it marked them off from the local homosexuals whom they otherwise resembled in their general appearance and mannerisms. Secondly, and more importantly, it separated them from the younger group who based their *voyou* style on the black leather jackets and slicked-back hair of the early rock-and-roll era. In addition to symbolizing the separation of age groupings within the contemporary situation, the opposition between the two styles also served to confirm the older group's repudiation of their own support for the *voyou* style when they were themselves fourteen. By counterposing the contemporary elements of the 'snob' style against the *dépassé* elements of the *voyou* style, therefore, the older group symbolically encapsulated their own biographies.

The oppositions between different youth subcultures are not necessarily entirely conditioned by forces within the specific situation however. Demarcations and antagonisms may be intensified by the way in which certain styles are taken up and presented as new. The fullest available account of this process operating in practice is Cohen's pioneering study of the imagery surrounding the mods and rockers (S. Cohen, 1973).

The subcultural styles of the mods and the rockers represented two solutions to the shared contradictions in the situation of working-class youth. Initially, Cohen argues, these solutions were simply different; they were not opposed. On the Easter Sunday of 1964 many East End adolescents made the traditional day trip to Clacton. Faced with abnormally cold and wet weather, they were thrown on the town in search of amusements, and finding very few facilities some attempted to create their own diversions. Those with motorbikes rode up and down the Front; there was some vandalism and some minor scuffles. The subsequent news coverage greatly exaggerated the amount and scale of the damage and disturbances, and interpreted the clashes between different youth groups in terms of an image of warring 'gangs' of mods and rockers based on the scenario familiar from *West Side Story*. In fact initially the main division was between the local youths and the day trippers from London. Once established by the original news stories, however, this imagery of mods versus rockers was amplified as subsequent coverage consistently presented acts of vandalism and violence within this basic framework. The imagery was taken up and further elaborated by commercial entrepreneurs who applied the label 'mod' to a wide range of entertainment goods, dances and dress styles. Not surprisingly, this imagery of polarization permeated the self-image of group members, with the result that elements of style which had previously been neutral became foci of intergroup antagonism and conflict. This conflict in turn served to confirm and further amplify the original image.

For the sake of convenience I have discussed news and entertainment separately in this essay. However, as the mods-and-rockers example makes clear, in actuality there is a constant interchange of imagery and symbolization between the two spheres. Consequently, instead of continuing to concentrate on the reception of particular 'messages' as most research to date has done, future work should seek to do justice to the complexity of people's total experience of media-relayed meanings.

Conclusion

In a letter written towards the end of his life, Engels argued that although 'men make their history themselves, they do so in a given environment which conditions it, and on the basis of actual relations already existing' (Marx and Engels, 1968, p. 705). Taking this general proposition as a starting point, this brief paper has attempted to explore the relationship between situational choices and contextual constraints, drawing concrete illustrations from the field of mass-media studies. Obviously, given the relatively sparse and fragmented nature of the evidence currently available, the arguments outlined here must be regarded as tentative. Nevertheless, if social psychology is to reconstitute itself as a comprehensive and genuinely social study of everyday life, it must necessarily take the issues raised in this paper as a central topic for further investigation. That is, starting from the premise that a man is never totally conditioned and constrained by the social situation in which he finds himself, and 'can always make something out of what is made of him' (Sartre, 1969, p. 45), social psychology must explore the complex and multi-layered interplay between intentional social actions and their conditioning contexts. More particularly it must examine the circumstances in which people cease to act within these contexts and begin to act against them.

References

Cohen, P. (1972) Subcultural conflict and working-class community. *Working Papers in Cultural Studies*, No. 2, Birmingham: University of Birmingham.
Cohen, S. (1973) *Folk Devils and Moral Panics*, St. Albans: Paladin.
Davis, F. and Muroz, L. (1970) Heads and freaks: patterns and meanings of drug use among hippies. In Douglas, J. D. (ed.) *Observations of Deviance*, New York: Random House.

Filmer, P. *et al.* (1972) *New Directions in Sociological Theory*, London: Collier-Macmillan.

Goldthorpe, J. H. (1973) A revolution in sociology? *Sociology*, 7(3), 449–62.

Hall, S. (1972) The external–internal dialectic in broadcasting. Paper to the Manchester Broadcasting Seminar, University of Manchester.

Halloran, J. D. *et al.* (1970) *Demonstrations and Communication: A Case Study*, Harmondsworth: Penguin.

Hartmann, P. and Husband, C. (1971) The mass media and racial conflict. In McQuail, D. (ed.) *Sociology of Mass Communications*. Harmondsworth: Penguin.

Hartmann, P. and Husband, C. (1974) *Racism and the Mass Media*, London: Davis-Poynter.

Katz, E. *et al.* (1973) Utilization of mass communication by the individual. Paper to the Conference on Directions in Mass Communications Research, New York; Arden House.

Marx, K. and Engels, F. (1968) *Selected Works: In One Volume*, London: Lawrence & Wishart.

McQuail, D. *et al.* (1972) The television audience: a revised perspective. In McQuail, D. (ed.) *Sociology of Mass Communications*, Harmondsworth; Penguin.

Monod, J. (1967) Juvenile gangs in Paris: toward a structural analysis. *J. Research in Crime and Delinquency*, 4, 142–64.

Murdock, G. (1973a) Political deviance: the press presentation of a militant mass demonstration. In Cohen, S. and Young, J. (eds) *The Manufacture of News*, London: Constable.

Murdock, G. (1973b) Culture and classlessness: the making and unmaking of a contemporary myth. Paper to the Symposium on Work and Leisure, University of Salford.

Murdock, G. and McCron, R. (1973) Scoobies, skins and contemporary pop. *New Society*, 23(547).

Murdock, G. and Golding, P. (1974) For a political economy of mass communications. In R. Miliband and J. Savile (eds) *Socialist Register 1973*, London: Merlin Press.

Parkin, F. (1972) *Class Inequality and Political Order*, St Albans: Paladin (especially Ch. 3).

Rock, P. (1973) News as eternal recurrence. In Cohen, S. and Young, J. (eds) *The Manufacture of News*, London: Constable.

Sartre, J. P. (1969) Itinerary of a thought. *New Left Review*, 58, 43–66.

Tuchman, G. (1973) Making news by doing work: routinizing the unexpected. *American Journal of Sociology*, 79(1), 110–31.

18

On looking into Bourdieu's black box

Martin Barker and Kate Brooks

Consider the following quotations, all of them from a group of young males talking about going to the cinema:

Interviewer (I): *Where do you normally go?*
L: Showcase, and the Odeon sometimes cos it's cheaper.
I: *Why the Showcase and not the Odeon?*
L: Cos they got seats you can rock ... it's cool.
M: I know why I'd be there ... CHICKS! There's loads of em, they hang around in the lobby.

I: *What's better about the cinema [than video]?*
M: Sound, quality, picture.
L: Bigger screen.
M: Better atmosphere, more females ... Cos you got like, Surround Sound and all that in there, and just say someone's about to stab someone and you hear screaming, and it comes from behind, you think, oooh shit! And it's a bigger screen so you can see like, more of what's going on. I prefer them sort of things.

I: *What sorts of things would you put in [a putative sequel to the film being discussed]?*
M: Lots of scary things ... Things that made you jump ... yeah, things that get your adrenalin rushing!
J: An adrenalin rush off a film!
M: Do you get 'em?
J: Not very often, no.

What might we learn from these very ordinary quotations? For these young men, going to the cinema is as much about the event and its other (sexual) possibilities as it is about the film. They're effectively inseparable. And they like films that head-butt you, make you jump out of your skin. The pleasure is in being 'done to'. An 'action' film should have a reaction: it should make you laugh, make you jump, turn you on, shock you, or it hasn't 'worked'. But truth to say, at least for one of them, though this is what they like, they don't often get it.

Something of the same is perhaps being said here:

I: *Right ... so there are certain films you'd say were like, 'Showcase' films?*

R: Definitely ... in their main screen obviously with the sound system they've got there, uh, to get the best out of the technicians in Hollywood, I think you've got to see [a film] with state-of-the-art projection and sound equipment and it really does make a big difference.

It is, of course, said in a different way. While recognisably the same idea is being referenced, there's a more 'knowing' manner of talking. This person finds it natural to refer to Hollywood as a mediating entity, to the processes of making a film, and to a 'proper' relationship almost owed to their skills. This interviewee was in fact a long-standing fan of Sylvester Stallone (about one of whose films the interview was being conducted), and for him the choice of right cinema had other connections than 'Chicks!':

R: I follow the films from a very early stage - pre-production ... A loyal fan will go and see him in whatever film he's made ... I love seeing who's going to do the music, who's director of photography, because I know these people and their work, so you can automatically work out what type, what look the film is gonna have ... So I look at literally every aspect of it, and try to obtain as much information about it as possible, except I mean I don't like to know too much, I like to know the basic story but I don't like to know too much about the plot, because in the past I think you can read too much into a film ... too many things spoiled.

This is all about preparing properly, getting knowledge adequate to being a proper fan of Stallone, but keeping that margin of ignorance so that he can walk into a cinema and be pleasurably boggled. This was his experience with *Rambo: First Blood*:

R: There was just something about that film ... I mean I've seen it probably 30 or 40 times all the way through and it still is my all-time favourite film ... I can watch it and still get excited by it.

To watch something and get excited by it at the 41st viewing is simply not the same as the very sensory, explosive and immediate pleasure that the group of males gained from, perhaps, the same film. Though they can share a sense of the rightness of a particular kind of cinema, even that takes on different meanings. For the Stallone fan, the experience is a matter of properly acknowledging the technical skills of a film's makers. For the young males, it is a social experience: meeting your mates, meeting girls, enjoying the unpredictability of a film and experiencing the 'roller coaster' of reactions this uncontrolled aspect of cinema-going should bring. There is an element of uncontrolledness for the Stallone fan, too – he wants to take the risk of seeing a film for the first time without knowing it fully. But it is structured quite differently, and the rest is very calculated and controlled.

What would it mean to call either of these viewing responses 'active' or 'passive'? These two words have become key terms in recent writing about audiences, but as Roger Silverstone has admirably argued, their meaning is notoriously unclear.[1] In these cases, it seems to us that the most interesting thing about the responses of both the young males and the Stallone fan is their strategic combinations of activity and passivity, and conscious swings between them.

Bearing this in mind, compare the above quotations with the following ones:

A: My local's a multiplex ... I don't like this type of place ... A brand new independent cinema has just opened ... with little gems on all the time that the general populace doesn't get to know about. This is more my kind of place ... A lot of the time we go on my recommendation because I do generally know more about cinema and I've got a good idea for what's bogus and what's not ... I tend to go with what certain film critics say ... anything really opinionated I can dismiss out of hand ... I get most of my information through my brother who's a massive film buff and I respect his opinion ... I think the popularity of some films puts me off because they've usually been designed and built to be popular and tend to have no worth of their own. I've no respect for what the general public find appealing.

S: I have a rule that I won't go on my own ... I think it's particularly sad [laughter in the group]
I: *You've only got to sit there in the dark, though.*
S: Yeah, I know, but you're on your own, I mean, you go to the cinema to share it with people. You hear about a film at work ... whatever the most fashionable films are

B: The idea of being part of a group is you go and share the experience.
M: You just pick up on lines, if it's got a good script.
G: The prime example was *Dumb and Dumber*, wasn't it?
All: Yeah!
G: We'd only just got into the transit van and it was like 'aaah!'
H: Yeah, picking up on one-liners straightaway, something like that ...

P: I was hoping it would just be entertaining and stay faithfulish to Dredd ... I tried to make a conscious effort to leave my Dredd-head outside the cinema ... I've been waiting since 1981 for a Dredd film and I wanted to enjoy it, and I did.

M: My instant reaction was 'No!' Don't let the Americans get hold of our British Dredd and you know, turn him into some bland boring character, but after I knew it was definitely going to happen I thought, well, I'm definitely going to go and see it because I have to see it.

A great deal could be said about each of these separately, but we would rather ask the question: what do all these, and the earlier quotations, have in common?

Researching *Judge Dredd*

These quotations are all taken from interviews gathered during an 18-month project, funded by the ESRC, to investigate the audiences of the 1995 film *Judge Dredd*.[2] The research had as its fundamental question the issue: how do audiences' prior orientations to a film (their existing knowledges, hopes, fears, expectations, involvements) relate to the ways they respond to and use it (their preparations for seeing it, modes of attention to it, criteria for judging it, pleasures or dislikes, recall and subsequent use, and categorization of it)? The research arose from an acute sense of dissatisfaction with the directions taken by a good deal of recent work.

When we surveyed the field, we found it oriented by three broad tendencies.[3] First, inasmuch as people wished to retain an interest in media as texts, it was likely to be done through one of two approaches: either a half-acknowledged adherence to the 'Hall Model' of encoding and decoding, and preferred reading.[4] A revealing example is Liebes and Katz's important study of audiences for *Dallas*.[5] A study of this showed that the idea of 'decoding' is overtly used 45 times in the course of the book, yet not once is it defined or justified. This can surely only be because the word is not seen to be theory-laden, but to be a neutral descriptor. In another place, we aim to show how much this disables and damages their investigation.

Alternatively, there is the psychoanalytic approach. The hold of such approaches on film studies, in particular, is fierce. The recent debate in *Screen* about Jane Campion's *The Piano* is a glaring example. Four essays have so far appeared, all of which take for granted a broad psychoanalytic approach. They simply disagree about the application. What is remarkable is the number of occasions, in the course of the essays, in which moves are made which make assumptions – untested, and untestable – about audience responses.[6] This seems to us to typify the relationship between psychoanalytic work, and the investigation of audiences.[7]

But recently, there has been a strong tendency by audience researchers and theorists away altogether from textual issues. The move in many ways begins with David Morley's Postscript to his (1980) *The 'Nationwide' Audience*, in which he very honestly critiqued his own commitment to the encoding model.[8] His argument that there needed to be a turn to more contextualized, perhaps ethnographic methods, was echoed in Janice Radway's *Reading The Romance*. A fair characterization of the state of play of the field would be to say that it is currently pulled between the following poles:

- residual but not strong textual determinism, particularly from those still adhering to the strong psychoanalytic programme proposed by 'gaze' theorists, following Laura Mulvey's (1974) essay;[10]
- at the other extreme, an effortless freeing of audiences into multiple 'readings', as proposed in his less guarded moments by John Fiske;

- in between, two main compromise accounts, one stressing the dominance of contextual factors over 'reading' processes, to account for the range of kinds of response to media materials which people display – but commonly with the caveat that these responses are limited, and that there still is a 'preferred reading';
- the other attempting to use the concept of 'interpretive communities' as a way of preserving a role for the text while at the same time preserving the social nature of responses.

What does need saying, in all cases, is that these positions are largely derived from perceived theoretical needs, and only in rare cases have been empirically tested. Psychoanalytic claims about audience responses have rarely if ever been tested, if indeed they have ever been elaborated to a point where we could know what would count as testing them. Fiske's extreme position is not so much a testable claim as a gesture to populism. The first compromise position, with its limit of a preferred reading, has yet to our knowledge pointed to such a limit and shown it at work. The fourth position may seem the one closest to empirical research, but as has recently been argued by Schrøder among others, uses ambiguous and largely rhetorical concepts of 'interpretive community'.[11]

One consequence of this theory-drivenness of audience research is that it encourages a blindness to materials and data which are awkward, and resist the approach being favoured; or at best, turn them into defeating puzzles. It leads to a clinging to languages for discussing audiences which may mislead in significant ways.[12] We have to acknowledge that in fact, despite our scepticism about many of these positions, some of their assumptions affected our own thinking: in two ways. They infected the way we asked questions of our audiences; and they made it difficult for us to understand the answers we got, when they defied our expectations.

The following seem to us the central untested assumptions common to many positions in the field:

- insisting on narrative as the central feature of films;
- processes of identification as the key link between films and audiences, along with an emphasis on visual 'spectatorship';
- a stress on mental/cognitive modes of responding to films;
- an opposition between 'active' and 'passive' viewing, with 'decoding' (the dominant metaphor for audience activity) depicted as an external, distancing response;
- and a notion of media power which uses the 'figure' of a vulnerable viewer.

In conflict with these, we found evidence in different groups of the following:

- a disregard for plot or narrative, sometimes to the extent that complex narrative was a barrier to the filmic pleasures being sought;
- a great emphasis on the sensory pleasures of cinema, which included comfort, sound, pace, rhythm, and a celebration of the spectacular;
- an acute awareness of others also viewing whose co-presence (real or

imagined) was a condition of many viewing styles – this was often associated with an evident awareness of a social geography of cinemas and
their audiences;
- in some cases, a powerful assertion of rights over the entire cinematic
experience;
- sharp shifts between activity and passivity as part of strategically
adapted audience patterns.

Most important of all, in all but the most 'casual' viewers, we found strong
evidence of ideals of film and cinema-going guiding and prompting individuals' and groups' responses. It is these which we would argue constitute the common element in the quotations we introduced earlier. In each
case, an element of a hoped-for ideal, or of a to-be-avoided contra-ideal,
provides a potential measure for the success of a cinematic experience.
There are, of course, a number of quite different ones; and the core of our
research into the audiences for *Judge Dredd* has been an attempt to separate and identify, and then model in detail the specific ideals. They are
ideal in the sense that, if met, they offer the conditions for real pleasure
and satisfaction. Also, the way the ideal is understood sets up a set of
practical conditions for its realisation. For instance, take the idea of being
'sad': if going with a big group of friends is the 'ideal' – because it places
film-going as an activity which confirms one's membership of on-going
cultural groups, and provides new resources for their continuation – then
one has to justify why one went alone, or risk pity or mockery. 'I know it's
a bit sad but ... I like going on my own/my friends had seen it/I work
shifts so ...' Being 'sad' was indeed the contra-ideal of a number of our
groups.

If on the other hand you want (the ideal) to do proper honour to
Stallone, find out as much as you can in advance that is consistent with
still being able to be astonished and experience admiration at your first
viewing of his new film. If you want (the ideal of) good conversational
swaps, in-jokes and shared cultural references, make sure your film
viewing is followed by an appropriate get-together (pizza, beer,
whatever) that sustains a reaffirmation of your belongingness. And so on.
These 'practical logics' provide a bridge between what particular
audiences want, their resources, and their access to such things as
knowledge.

Several ideals of film-going share, but use differently, a clear understanding of the social geography of cinemas. This is part of a whole recon-
figuration of film and cinema.[13] From the late 1940s until 1985 cinema
audiences fell overall, and underwent a change with a greater dependence
on young viewers; after 1985, audience figures began at last to climb
again, and this was in association with the arrival and conscious promotion of the blockbuster film. The 1980s also saw the birth of a new kind of
cinema, the multiplex, which presented itself as a new, American-style
entertainment mall where cinema, pizza house, and bowling alley can lie
cheek-by-jowl. These new cinemas quickly became a mecca and a magnet
for working-class boys and girls to parade and enjoy themselves in an
environment they felt to be theirs.

Of course, film-goers of all kinds know very well that their ideal conditions may not be met. Then it becomes a question of how much you care and are committed to your ideal. Each person and group evidences an orientation to the ideal conditions which they postulate. In a few cases, we met considerable anger when an ideal was seen to be threatened. In most cases, such failures are just accepted as a price to be paid. Compare the quotation from P, earlier, with the following from a series of interviews at the 1995 UK Comic Art Convention, in which two people debate the 'reality' of Dredd:

I   *So who could play Judge Anderson?*
3   Erm ...
I   *Come on, Clint Eastwood's everybody's favourite for Dredd, though he can't do it cos he's probably too old now.*
3   Well, he could do a modern-day Dredd, I mean, Dredd's about 55 now, isn't he, in the comic?
4   Yeah. Mind, he's been through so many ...
I   *He could do the Dead Man but who could play Anderson?*
3   Oh. She'd have to be blonde ...
4   ... Why?
3   Well, she is, I think, in the comic.
4   Well, like, they can't change the colour of an actress's hair??
3   Well, no, but then you'd complain, oh heck, that woman hasn't got blonde hair ...
4   ... no, no, the actress's hair ...
I   *You'd prefer a blonde, OK ...*
3   Well, I mean, if, if you're going to, you check all the uniforms and everything on Dredd, you know, so you want characters that people do come I think from the comic background will recognize. Erm. Erm. I don't know, erm, she might be a bit old but Sharon Stone, erm ...
I   *[laughs]*
4   FOR GOD'S SAKE!! Why can't you (a) choose some woman who can act, (b) someone who can enunciate, and (c) someone who actually captures something of Anderson, which is a street-smart person who has actually got some personality? Not a cardboard fucking cut-out!

This explosive retort reverses the 'real' situation: Judge Anderson, a two-dimensional fictional character whose material existence has been marks on paper is now sufficiently 'real' to set the rules for who can play her – and Sharon Stone is judged a 'cardboard cut-out' insufficiently 'real' to play her. This, we believe, demonstrates one of the aspects of strong investment. Such extremes of commitment may often be momentary, even tactical, but they do constitute a limit and measure against which more negotiable positions set themselves. People are aware of making concessions.

The ideals against which people measure their possible pleasures are socially-generated and socially-defined relations to film. But each references and depends on a different kind of sociality. The man avoiding 'looking sad' is defending himself against those – real and imagined – who would judge him as such. Real, because they could well be his friends, or the others in the focus group, or the cultural group of which he perceives us as interviewers to be part; imagined, in that it might come from an imaginary 'community' in relation to which his sense of identity is partly formed. The Stallone fan can only be such because of the publicity regime which has accompanied Stallone's rise to stardom, a regime which has stressed the way he will always bounce back from defeat; hurt, scarred, in the end he will not be defeated. Stallone embodies a 'surviving-ness', and each film is assessed for its ability to add a new dimension to his demonstration of this quality.

These ideals, then, are the outcome of dense historical and social processes. In orienting to them with more or less commitment, individuals are doing far more than simply being 'audiences'. They are choosing the extent to which they will participate in forms and fields of their culture. We've chosen to name this dimension of caring and committing oneself to a particular orientation, the process of investment. This concept of 'invest-ment' is a key one for us; it is intended to summarize all the ways in which audiences demonstrate strength and depth of involvement to a social ideal of cinema. One linkage which we have found strongly evidenced is that depth of investment associates strongly with singularity of preferred ideal. While those with relatively low investment in a film or a kind of cinematic event will happily mix modes of orientation, high investors will tend to adhere closely to a single and consistent orientation. There are of course many people who see films with no significant investment at all – those who see a film by accident, for instance, or because they are dragged along by someone else, or because they had nothing better to do. Interestingly, these people seem to lack any reference to ideals of cinematic experience at all. They do not care, they do not invest, they do not remember – and they have almost nothing to say in interviews, a fact which makes them hard to investigate, and therefore poses real problems for research.[14]

Pierre Bourdieu's black box

The concept of 'investment' is a key one for us. In the space of this chapter, we cannot do more than follow its consequences into one area. If we are right, then our empirical findings must constitute a significant challenge to a number of currently popular models for thinking about text/audience relations. The widespread use of psychoanalytic, and of 'preferred reading' models look at least vulnerable. But one approach, that of Pierre Bourdieu, looks useful; in particular, his concepts of 'field' and 'habitus' seem to relate to what we have found.

We understand Bourdieu to be arguing that a culture comprises a series of relatively autonomous areas of production: these are his 'fields'. Together these constitute a system in which some are privileged as offering cultural and symbolic capital to their cognoscenti; others are dismissed as 'popular' and 'merely' participative. To take one of Bourdieu's own examples, the field of sports – originally made up of games which genuinely belonged to 'the people' – has been seized and organized as a controlled field of cultural production, and returned to the people in the form of a spectacle. To the extent that they emphasize participation in the spectacular, sports are of 'low' taste. 'High' taste is associated with the contemplative and the aesthetic – these being virtually terms of abuse for Bourdieu.[15]

Fields, according to Bourdieu, develop historically, and their cultural position can change. But most important to him is that each work within a field has to be understood in terms of its relations with its predecessors and contemporaries – not in terms of some presumed direct relation with 'class interests' or 'representativeness'. This is the basis of his critique of Sartre's analysis of Flaubert as an artist.[16]

Audiences have to be trained how to respond, and to participate. They have to learn the 'rules' (of efficacy, of success, of aesthetics). They have to learn to participate 'properly', that is, with a proper orientation of both mind and body. This takes us to Bourdieu's concept of 'habitus'. 'Habitus' constitutes an internalized system of relatively stable predispositions which operate across all cultural fields that a person encounters. A habitus is learnt, but becomes the self, which is a social self, since the predispositions are organized and distributed according to class.

Bourdieu is opposed to Marxist accounts of class (which he met largely in their Stalinist and post-Stalinist versions via Louis Althusser and his followers); his main modification is to distinguish three kinds of 'capital': economic, cultural and symbolic. Economic capital refers to access to and control over the means of production; cultural capital refers to distributed power over knowledge, repertoires of response, and hierarchies of taste; and symbolic power refers to accrued personal prestige, gained through the acquisition of appropriate economic and cultural capitals. Bourdieu's point is that these do not exactly coincide, although they do collaborate in building and maintaining a system of domination.[17]

His enormous work *Distinction*[18] offers a body of evidence to substantiate his broad claims. Using questionnaires, he claimed to identify two stable patterns of preferences which operate consistently across many cultural fields (for example, clothing, furniture, music, art, and so on). He identifies these two as the dominant and subordinate cultural taste system.[19] In work conducted largely by colleagues of his, on photography, a third and strategic intermediate has also been identified.[20]

In a number of important respects, our work seems to confirm Bourdieu's approach, at the least in the following respects:

- our emphasis on the social nature of ideal cinematic experiences, especially inasmuch as we derive them from the historical processes of a 'field' of film;
- our recognition that Hollywood, undergoing the changes between 1948–85, has had to train its viewers into distinct modes of response;
- our realization (not developed here, but important to our overall picture) that these ideals have different cultural status, and constitute a hierarchy of discourses, which relate closely to class;
- our investigation of the ways that people's responses to film interconnect with their modes of response to other phenomena.

But we want to argue that our account challenges Bourdieu's theory of culture at some crucial points.

Bourdieu developed his account of 'habitus' for two main reasons. First, rather like Anthony Giddens within British sociology, he wanted a way to resolve a perceived epistemological difficulty between 'structure' and 'agency'. Disliking the tendency in structuralist accounts to reduce human responses to mere ciphers of structuralist processes, he none the less rejected ideas of free agency – the social world is just too predictable to permit notions of free human individuality. The second, more specific reason was his own revolt against structuralism on empirical grounds. This grew from his discovery that, for instance, the Berber peoples of Algeria would claim adherence to highly specific rules about marriage and kinship, yet almost totally ignore those rules in practice. This gap between rules and practices, between structures and actions, led Bourdieu to reformulate his own early accounts of culture. In the cultural field, there are oppositions between how structures demand we behave, and how we respond. His notions of 'field' and 'habitus' are intended to meet both the epistemological and the empirical needs here.

The trouble is that they don't. The following seem to us the key problems in his account. First, there is a real tension between two uses he makes of his concept. In *Distinction* (and indeed in his general statement of the theory of 'habitus' in *The Logic of Practice*), Bourdieu stresses its involuntary, relatively stable and transferable nature. These are the implications of his famous, tortured but memorable definition of habitus as 'systems of durable, transposable dispositions, structured structures predisposed to function as structuring structures, that is, as principles which generate and organize practices and representations that can be objectively adapted to their outcomes without presupposing a conscious aiming at ends or an express mastery of the operations necessary in order to attain them'.[21] This explains why recipients of cultural forms respond quite consistently in what they enjoy, what constitutes pleasure for them, how they involve themselves (both mentally and physically), and what constitutes experience and expertise. 'Habitus' explains how people intersect with their class taste, without having to be 'told' what to do.

The crucial thing here is that though tastes may feel like free and motivated choices, they are actually the expression of acquired predispositions. As such, 'habitus' are almost uninvestigable. We may observe their consistent operation, but in themselves they are simply the mediating steps between structure and agency. Thus it makes no difference whether they are regarded as analysts' constructs – convenient shorthand for our means of explaining events – or as claims to real ontologically existent entities or processes. Either way, they are in principle unobservable, Skinnerian black boxes.[22] They also operate 'averagely' within all people who fall within their domain – there is a connection here with Bourdieu's faith in statistical modes of discovering their operations, which by virtue of their methodology do average responses.

But Bourdieu bends his own rules. In his essays on Flaubert, he defines 'habitus' as the 'feel for the game' through which writers – the producers of a form of culture – produce their output. How does an artist know how to respond to previous and contemporary works in his/her field? S/he has a palette of kinds of response which are produced in relation to those other instances within the field. In one essay, Bourdieu produces a telling example to illustrate the potential power of his method of analysis, as applied to the field of novels:

> Just one example: within the 'popular' novel which, more than any other category of novel, is abandoned to writers issuing from dominated classes and women writers, we find yet another hierarchy: literary treatments that distance themselves most from the genre or that are semi-parodic ... are the work of relatively more privileged writers.[23]

There are some important but unacknowledged differences between these two accounts of 'habitus': between a generalizing disposition, prompting and shaping responses across cultural fields, and a much more localized and field-specific response-system. How has the difference come about? In the first account, a person is simply living out the consequences of his or her culture-class position. Although by the nature of 'habitus' it isn't mechanical, it might as well be, since it has become the self. We are as we respond. On this version of 'habitus', it becomes quite hard to conceive how change or development might take place, unless it be through personal change of class circumstances or through structural reorientation of a taste-system. But the fact is that Bourdieu's theory, whatever its intentions, is a theory of overwhelming determinants which masquerade as agency.

In the second account, however, Bourdieu's author is driven by a need to achieve a response. This particularizes their orientation and response. Here, then, 'habitus' provides the very mechanism for explaining change and development. This is possible because an author is conceived as inhabiting one field with more commitment, more investment, than other fields; indeed, their relationship to other fields and human activities generally is likely to be shaped by the requirements of their life-as-author.

On this second account, the meaning of 'habitus' starts to change more generally. For a start, his kind of 'author' is a special case. Most cultural production is not individualized in the ways that novel-writing is. Films, television, theatre, shows, bands and orchestras, sports: all are highly collectivized. And if we extended the examples to forms of unofficial cultural production, the picture would become even more complicated: what about the products of fan cultures, alternative productions, fanzines, amateur arts and non-professional sports activities? Frequently these only continue because of a collective will either to try consciously to change the way a field operates, or to step outside it and find an alternative space. This is a different sense of agency than Bourdieu's epistemological polarity. This is agency as an achievement. It doesn't matter (for purposes of analysis) whether people achieve their goals or not. The point is that their collective investment in a situation generates possibilities of action otherwise not available.

'Investment', we wish to argue, looks to be the dimension that unlocks the black box of Bourdieu's concept of 'habitus'. People do not 'belong' within a habitus in some mechanical, even manner. Fields generate possibilities of, even genres of, responses to which people orient themselves.

The manner of their orientation will be a function of their history and class situation, of course, but also of their individual and collective investments in the situation. How important is it to them, and why? What do they hope to achieve through their participation (and that notion of 'hope' reintroduces our idea of ideals)? In what kinds of organization (informal, formal; narrow, wide) do they embody the manner of their participation?

Put at its simplest, 'investment' references the differences that are made according to how much people care about their participation or involvement in a leisure activity. High investment, in our research, associated with greater and more detailed preparation for the activity, with a more concentrated but selective manner of attending and participating, and with a greater capacity for disappointment. Low investment, on the other hand, is associated with less focused and less retentive ways of participating. And people who are low investors seem to have very much less to say about their involvement – a point which has tricky implications for any research process. This concept of 'investment', and the differences it draws attention to, seems to us quite fundamental. Yet we can find almost no writing on it, other than work on fans as a distinctive group.

Finally, we would point to one other limit which our work proposes to Bourdieu's still-useful concepts of 'field' and 'habitus'. Perhaps because both of his chosen examples and of his (statistical) manner of studying, Bourdieu is able to portray fields as essentially autonomous. They may blur at the edges, but the motors of development, and the repertoires of response are largely internally generated. We want to suggest that this is a potentially quite misleading picture. Rather, we would argue that under capitalist modes of production cultural fields fight to preserve an illusion of autonomy, which is frequently punctured. The punctures can take many forms. When football spills over into regionalist or nationalist conflict, the authorities desperately distinguish between 'real' supporters and others -'real' ones being those who are 'just there to enjoy the football'.[24] When black music has offended against various rules (delighting in anti-police attacks, or denigrating women), their publishers either play down the offence, declaring for instance that this is 'part of the music game'; or they punish a 'breach of the rules' by, perhaps, blocking releases or demanding changes. In all-such cases, the agreed agenda is to try to tidy up the boundaries, to insist that art is art, culture is culture, sport is sport, and that offending items should be pushed properly to one side of the fence or the other.

But what seems to us important is that high investors do not willingly accept these limits and boundaries. A high level of commitment to an activity can be linked with a claim that it has a significance which breaks boundaries. And this returns us to work one of us has previously done. An earlier study of the audiences for the comic-book version of Judge Dredd found that there are, among its followers, some for whom the story is important in an apparently paradoxical way – its very dystopic bleakness provides a resource for hope in the future. In giving scope for imaging the future, even a dark and fearful one, the comic made a space within which they could keep social and political hopes alive.[25] We need to remind ourselves that policing boundaries within culture may not be just or simply a 'protective' act. It can be positively debilitating for those who grasp a chance to use them 'subversively'. But that, as they say, is perhaps another essay.

Notes

1. Silverstone, R. (1994) *Television and Everyday Life*, London: Routledge, especially Chapter 6.
2. ESRC Project No. R000221446. We wish to express our thanks to the ESRC in more than the required formal way. Audience research is expensive of time and money, and is very difficult to conduct without this kind of financial backing. There has recently been a flowering of writing about audiences, built on the back of too little solid research. Without doubt, one of the reasons for this is the time and financial commitments it involves. Far easier, unfortunately, either to do a textual analysis which will make assumptions or claims about the audience, or to write an essay on the idea of audiences.
3. There has recently been a flurry of books and articles surveying the state of audience research, and each has tended to provide its own list of kinds of research. For instance, Rowland Lorimer's *Mass Communications: A Comparative Introduction* (Manchester University Press, 1994) finds seven groups ('effects', uses and gratifications, cultural studies (subdivided into Frankfurt and British), feminist, reception analysis, structuration, and institutional). Unfortunately, these groups are not all of the same order: some are based on methodological postulates; some on intellectual sources; one – structuration – is almost entirely a proposal, with hardly an exemplar.
4. Stuart Hall (1981) Encoding/decoding the TV message. In Hall, S. *et al.* (eds) *Culture, Media, Language*, London: Comedia.
5. Liebes, T. and Katz, E. (1990) *The Export of Meaning: Cross-Cultural Readings of 'Dallas'* (Oxford: OUP).
6. The debate seems to us a juicy example of the arbitrary nature of this sort of textual work which David Bordwell has attacked in his under-examined *Making Meaning* (Cambridge MA: Harvard University Press, 1989).
7. Two interesting exceptions would be Jackie Stacey's *Star Gazing* (London: Routledge, 1993), and Valerie Walkerdine's 'Video Replay', in V. Burgin, J. Donald and C. Kaplan (eds) *Formations of Fantasy* (London: Routledge, 1985).
8. Morley, D. (1981) The 'Nationwide' Audience: a critical postscript, *Screen Education*, **39**, 3–18.
9. Radway, J. (1984) *Reading the Romance*, Chapel Hill: University of North Carolina Press.
10. Laura Mulvey (1975) Visual pleasure and narrative cinema, *Screen*, **16**(3), 16–18.
11. Schrøder, K. C. (1994) Audience semiotics, interpretive communities and the 'ethnographic turn' in media research, *Media, Culture and Society*, **16**, 337–47.
12. A good example of this is to be found in Jackie Stacey's *Star Gazing*, which we mentioned above, when she discusses the concept of 'identification'. She had found that, contrary to theoretical expectations, there were multiple and complex relations between women and romantic movies. Asked why this did not lead her to question, if not to reject, that concept, she wrote that she kept it among other reasons because it was a concept some of her respondents themselves used. We would argue that it is inevitable that there will be what we would call 'folk theories of the media' among audiences, analogous to the folk theories of crime which Hall *et al.* delineated and discussed in their *Policing The Crisis: Mugging, the State, and Law and Order* (Basingstoke:

Macmillan, 1979), see chapter 6, especially; and the 'folk theories of language' identified by Deborah Cameron in her essay 'Demythologising sociolinguistics: why language doesn't reflect society' in John E. Joseph and Talbot J. Taylor, *Ideologies of Language* (London: Routledge, 1990), pp. 79–93. For an example of a more problematic way of addressing these matters, see Michael Banton, 'Analytical and folk concepts of race and ethnicity', *Ethnic and Racial Studies*, 2(2), 1979, 127–38. Banton's interesting discussion of 'folk theories of race' is marred by his inability to see either that 'academic' thinking about 'race' might easily be penetrated by folk concepts. On the other hand, he does usefully explore some of the consequences of such folk theorizations for those who are their 'object'. It is surprising how little attention has been given to this by those working within cultural studies, for whom the development of the concept of 'commonsense' has been so critical. We would argue that there is an important research task to study how people who are effectively derogated by them live with the omnipresence of such folk theories – often, half-accepting them themselves. For example, what does it mean to a person to be a fan of 'violent' movies while knowing that this pleasure is widely condemned? How is this managed, and what does it do to the very possibilities of pleasure?

13. The best summary of all these changes that we know, is Thomas Schatz's superb, measured essay 'The new Hollywood' in Jim Collins *et al.* (eds), *Film Theory Goes To The Movies* (New York: American Film Institute, 1993) pp. 8–36. See also the opening chapter of Jim Hillier's excellent *The New Hollywood* (New York: Continuum, 1992). Sadly, neither Schatz nor Hillier attempts to address the implications of their picture for film audiences.

14. It has worried and puzzled us that so few audience researchers acknowledge the existence of these groups – a fact which has led us to doubt the 'representativeness' of many pieces of research. One researcher who does note these problems very interestingly is Joke Hermes, *Reading Women's Magazines*, (Cambridge: Polity Press, 1995), see in particular Appendix 4.

15. We note in passing an important error in John Codd's essay on Bourdieu's account of distinction and taste. Codd repeatedly talks of working class (dominated) taste in terms of its 'lacks' and 'absences', as if Bourdieu in some way regarded it as deficient or failing. This is absolutely the opposite of Bourdieu's intent, who was on the contrary deeply hostile to the pretensions of dominant cultural taste. See John Codd, 'Making distinctions: the eye of the beholder', in Richard Harker, Cheleen Mahar and Chris Wilkes (eds), *An Introduction to the Work of Pierre Bourdieu: the Practice of Theory*, (Basingstoke: Macmillan, 1990).

16. See his essays on Flaubert in the collection of his work, *The Field of Cultural Production*, edited by Randal Johnson (Cambridge: Polity Press, 1993).

17. Bourdieu simply lacks any notion of labour power, alienation and collective workplace organization, concepts which would be central to what we would understand to be a Marxist account of the capitalist process. The result is a curiously one-sided account of workers under capitalism, in which workers suffer economic domination and exploitation, but seem only able to respond at the level of culture.

18. Bourdieu, P. (1986) *Distinction: A Social Critique of the Judgement of Taste*, London: Routledge & Kegan Paul.

19. It is questionable whether his evidence can sustain this notion of two taste systems. Using his own data, it would not be difficult to break the two down into a larger number of taste systems. We have not pursued this point here, as it has only tangential relevance to the argument of this essay.

20. See Pierre Bourdieu (1990) *Photography, A Middlebrow Art*, Cambridge: Polity Press.

21. Bourdieu, P. (1990) Structures, habitus, practices, *The Logic of Practice*, Cambridge: Polity Press, 53.
22. It is interesting to ask in what ways Bourdieu's account of cultural taste systems could be used by members of a culture-class, to review and perhaps reconstruct their own relations to the world through gaining a wider understanding of their own position. British cultural studies, at least in the early days, tried hard to examine its own role and potential in this respect. To our knowledge this is not an issue Bourdieu or his followers have ever posed perhaps because it is simply conceptually unimaginable on his account.
23. Bourdieu, P. (1993) Principles for a sociology of literary works. In Johnson, R. (ed.) *The Field of Cultural Production*, Cambridge: Polity Press, 189–90.
24. For one among many recent useful books on the inevitability of politics in football, see Simon Kuper's (1994) *Football Against The Enemy*, London: Orion.
25. Barker, M. (1993) Seeing how far you can see: on being a 'fan' of 2000AD. In Buckingham, D. (ed.) *Reading Audiences: Young People and the Media*, Manchester: Manchester University Press, 159–83.

19

Domestic relations: the framework of family viewing in Great Britain

David Morley

From Lull, J. (ed.) (1988) *World Families Watch Television*, Newbury Park, CA: Sage Publications, pp. 22–48.

Investigating family viewing in Britain

The research reported below concerns two different types of research questions regarding, on the one hand, how television is interpreted by its audiences and, on the other, how TV material is used in different families. [...]

The central thesis was that the changing patterns of television viewing could be understood only in the overall context of family leisure activity. Previous work in this area has tended to focus too narrowly on one or another side of a pair of interlinked issues that need, in fact, to be considered together: these are the issues of how viewers make sense of the materials they view, and the social (and primarily familial) relations within which viewing is conducted. [...]

In this research, I took the premise that one should consider the basic unit of consumption of TV to be the family/household rather than the individual viewer. This is done to raise questions about how the television set is handled in the home, how viewing decisions are made – by which family members, at what times, what is watched – and how responses to different kinds of materials are discussed within the family, and so on. In short, this represents an attempt to analyse individual viewing activity within the household/familial relations in which it commonly operates.

Audience research that ignores this context cannot comprehend a number of key determinations relating to both viewing 'choices' and responses – those involving questions of differential power, responsibility, and control within the family at different time of the day and night.

My further premise is that the use of the television set has to be understood in the wider context of other competing and complementary leisure activities (hobbies, interests, pastimes) in which viewers engage. Television clearly is primary leisure activity, but previous research has tended merely to investigate leisure options as separate and unrelated activities to be listed, rather than to be studied in relation in each other.

Investigating how television is used: reviewing some key strands of the relevant research literature

What does it mean to 'watch television'?

'Watching television' cannot be assumed to be a one-dimensional activity of equivalent meaning or significance at all time for all who perform it. I was, therefore, interested in identifying and investigating differences hidden behind the description 'watching television' – both the differences between choices made by various kinds of viewers in relation to different viewing options, and differences of attention and comprehension between and among viewers' responses to the same viewing materials. One important set of differences explored in the project concerns the different levels of attention given to different programs by different viewers – differences that are typically masked by the finding that they all 'watched' a given program.

I wanted to explore both differences between families in different social and cultural contexts. I would argue that it is only in this context – that of the wider fields of social and cultural determinations that frame the practices of viewing – that individual choices and responses can be understood.

In particular, this project was designed to explore in detail within a deliberately limited universe the 'how' and 'why' of questions that lie unexplained behind patterns of viewing behavior revealed by large survey work. I aimed to produce a more developed conceptual model of viewing behavior in the context of family leisure by investigating now such factors as program type, family position, and cultural background interrelate to produce the dynamics of family viewing.

We are, in short, discussing television viewing in the context of domestic life, which, as we all know, is a complex matter. To expect that we could treat the individual viewer making program choices as if he or she were the rational consumer in a free and perfect market is surely the height of absurdity when we are talking about people living in families. For most people, viewing takes place within the context of what Sean Cubitt (1985) calls 'the politics of the living room', where, as he puts it, 'if the camera pulls us in, the family pulls us out', and where the people you live with are likely to disrupt, if not shatter, your communion with the 'box in the corner'.

Let us consider the problem from another angle:

> Early in the evening we watch very little TV. Only when my husband is in a real rage. He comes home, hardly says anything and switches on the TV.
> (Bausinger, 1984, p. 344)

As Bausinger notes, in this case 'pushing the button doesn't signify "I would like to watch this", but "I want to see and hear nothing"'.

How much space, and of what types, is available to which family members in the context of television viewing activity? How is that space organized, and how are the television set(s) and other communication technologies inserted into that space? Is the living room organized around the TV set? Do different family members have characteristic viewing positions within that space? All of these may appear at first to be banal questions. But they do indeed have great significance in understanding how television 'works' within a family. As Lindlof and Traudt (1983) note, for instance, 'in higher density families . . . TV viewing may function as a way of avoiding conflicts or lessening tensions in lieu of spatial privacy'. [. . .]

Research objectives

The particular research project reported here was designed to investigate the changing uses of television among a sample of families of different types drawn from a range of social positions. It was designed to investigate differences between families of different social positions and between families with children of different ages in terms of:

- the increasingly varied use of household television set(s) for receiving broadcast television, video games, teletext, and so on
- patterns of differential commitment and response to particular types of programming
- the dynamics of television use within the family; how viewing choices are expressed and negotiated within the family; the differential power of particular family members in relation to viewing choices at different times of the day; the ways in which television material is discussed within the family
- 'the relations between television watching and other dimensions of family life – television as a source of information on leisure choices and how leisure interests and work obligations (both inside and outside the home) influence viewing choices.

The project was designed to identify and investigate the differences hidden behind the catch-all phrase, 'watching television'. We all watch television, but with how much attention and with what degrees of commitment and response, in relation to which types of shows, at what times?

Moreover, as argued earlier, we are now in situation in which watching broadcast television is only one among various possible uses of the domestic television set. Among the questions I set out to explore were the following ones. Which family members, in which types of families, use their televisions for which purpose at which points in the day? What are the factors that give rise to different patterns and how are they understood by respondents themselves? Further, how are the priorities and preferences of family members negotiated and resolved in relation to conflicting demands on the use of the television in general and of viewing preferences in particular? In short, how do family dynamics interact with viewing behavior?

Methodology

The methodology adopted was a qualitative one, whereby each family was interviewed in depth in order to elucidate their various accounts of how they understand the role of television in their overall leisure activities. The aim was to gain insight into the terms within which respondents themselves defined their viewing activities. Centrally, I wanted to generate insights into the criteria used by viewers in making choices and in responding (positively or negatively) to different types of programming and scheduling. I believed that this approach would produce some insights into the criteria lying behind (and generating) particular viewing choices and responses. Thus it was hoped that the project would provide a useful complement to the results of survey work that itself, while usefully detailing the overall pattern of viewing choices that are made, cannot hope to explain why and how these choices and responses take place.

The families were interviewed in their own home during the spring of 1985. Initially the two parents were interviewed, then later in each interview their children were invited to take part in the discussion along with their parents. The interviews lasted between one and two hours and were audiotape recorded and later transcribed in full for analysis. [...]

Sample design

The sample consisted of 18 families. All were drawn from one area of South London. All possessed a video recorder. All consisted of households of two adults living together with two or more dependent children, up to the age of 18. All were white.

Because of the nature of the area where respondents were recruited, my sample contains a high proportion of working-class/lower middle-class families – not necessarily in terms of income (my sample includes quite a wide range of income) but in terms of all the other aspects of class (cultural capital, education, etc.) [...]

Television and gender: the framework for analysis

The following major themes were identified in the interviews. They recur frequently enough with the different families that I can point to a reasonable degree of consistency of response. Clearly, one structural principle working across all the families interviewed is that of gender. These interviews raise important questions about the effects of gender in terms of

1. power and control over program choice
2. styles of viewing
3. planned and unplanned viewing
4. television-related talk
5. use of video
6. 'solo' viewing and guilty pleasures
7. program type preferences
8. national versus local news programming

Before describing the findings under these particular headings, I would first like to make some general points about the significance of the empirical differences that my research revealed between the viewing habits of the men and the women in the sample. As will be seen, men and women offer clearly contrasting accounts of their viewing habits in terms of their differential power to choose what they view, how much they view, their viewing styles, and their choice of particular viewing material. However, I am not suggesting that these empirical differences are attributes of their essential biological characteristics as men and women. Rather, I am trying to argue that these differences are the effects of the particular social roles that these men and women occupy within the home. Moreover, I am not suggesting that the particular pattern of gender relations within the home found here (with all the consequences that that pattern has for viewing behavior) would necessarily be replicated either in nuclear families from a different class or ethnic background or in households of different types with the same class and ethnic backgrounds. Rather, it is always a case of how gender relations interact with, and are formed differently within, these different contexts.

Aside from these qualifications, there is one fundamental point that needs to be made concerning the basically different positioning of men and women within the domestic sphere. The dominant model of gender relations within this society (and certainly within that subsection of it represented in my sample) is one in which the home is primarily defined for means a site of leisure – by distinction from the 'industrial time' of their employment outside the home – while the home is primarily defined for women as a site of work, whether or not they also work outside the home. This simply means that, in investigating television viewing in the home, one is by definition investigating something that men are better placed to do wholeheartedly, and that women seem only to be able to do distractedly and guiltily, because of their continuing sense of domestic responsibility. Moreover, this differential positioning is given a greater significance as the home becomes increasingly defined as the prime sphere of leisure.

When considering the empirical findings that follow, care must be taken to hold in view this structuring of the domestic environment by gender relations as the backdrop against which these particular patterns of viewing behavior have developed. Otherwise, we risk seeing these patterns a somehow the direct result of 'essential' or biological characteristics of men and women *per se*. Ang (1987) extends the argument:

> Women's viewing patterns can only be understood in relation to men's patterns: the two are in a sense constitutive of each other. What we call 'viewing habits' are thus not more or less static set of characteristics inhabited by an individual or group of individuals; rather they are the temporary result of a . . . dynamic . . . process . . . male/female relationships are always informed by power, contradiction, and struggle.
>
> (pp. 18–19)

So, as Ang argues, male and female modes of watching TV are not two separate, discrete types of experience, clearly defined and static 'objects' of study or expressions of essential natures. Rather than taking differences between male and female relations to TV as an empirical given, one must look to how the structure of domestic power relations works to constitute these differences.

Power and control over program choice

Masculine power is evident in a number of the families as the ultimate determinant on occasions of conflict over viewing choices ('We discuss what we all want to watch and the biggest wins. That's me, I'm the biggest.'). It is even more apparent in the case of those families that have a remote control device. None of the women in any of the families use the remote control device regularly. A number of them complain that their husbands use the device obsessively, channel-flicking across programs when their wives are trying to watch something else. Characteristically, the remote control device is the symbolic possession of the father (or of the son, in the father's absence) that sits 'on the arm of Daddy's chair' and is used almost exclusively by him. It is a highly visible method of condensed power relations:

> *Daughter: Dad keeps both of the automatic controls – one on each side of his chair.
> *Woman: Well, I don't get much chance, because he sits there with the automatic control beside him and that's it. I get annoyed because I can be watching a program and he's flicking channels to see if a program on the other side is finished so he can record something. So the television's flickering all the time, while he's flicking the timer. I just say. 'For goodness' sake, leave it alone.' I don't get the chance to use the control. I don't get near it.
> *Woman: No, not really, I don't get the chance to use the automatic control. I leave that down to him. It is aggravating, because I can be watching something and all of a sudden he turns it over to get the football result.
> *Daughter: The control's always next to Dad's chair. It doesn't come away when Dad's here. It stays right there.

Interestingly, the main exceptions to this overall pattern are those families in which the man is unemployed while his wife is working. In these cases it is slightly more common for the man to be expected to let other family members watch what they want to when it is broadcast while he video-tapes what he would like to see in order to watch that later at night or the following day. His timetable of commitments is more flexible than those of the working members of the family. Here we begin to see the way in which the position of power held by most of the men in the sample (and which their wives concede) is based not simply on the biological fact of being men but rather on a social definition of a masculinity of which employment (that is, the 'breadwinner' role) is a necessary and constituent part. When that condition is not met, the pattern of power relations within the home can change noticeably. […]

Styles of viewing

One major finding is the consistency of the distinction made between the characteristic ways in which men and women describe their viewing activity. Essentially, men state a clear preference for viewing attentively, in silence, without interruption 'in order not to miss anything'. Moreover, they display puzzlement at the way their wives and daughters watch television. The women describe viewing as a fundamentally social activity, involving ongoing conversation, and usually the performance of at least one other domestic activity (ironing, etc.) at the same time. Indeed, many women feel that to just watch television without doing anything else at the same time would be an indefensible waste of time, given their sense of their domestic obligations. To watch in this way is something they rarely do, except occasionally, when alone or with other women friends and when they have managed to construct a situation in which to watch their favorite program or video. The women note that their husbands are always 'on at them' to shut up, and the men can't really understand how their wives can follow the programs if they are doing something else at the same time. [...]

Planned and unplanned viewing

It is men, on the whole, who speak of checking through the paper (or the teletext) to plan their evening's viewing. Very few women seem to do this at all, except in terms of already knowing which evenings and times their favorite series are on and thus not needing to check the schedule. This is also an indication of a different attitude to viewing as a whole. Many of the women have a much more take-it-or-leave-it attitude, not caring much if they miss things (except for their favorite serials):

> *Man: Normally I look through the paper because you (his wife) tend to just put on ITV, but sometimes there is something good on the other channels, so I make a note – things like films and sport.
> *Woman: I don't read newspapers. If I know what's going to be on, I'll watch it. He tends to look in the paper. I don't actually look in the paper to see what's on. [...]

Television-related talk

Women show much less reluctance to 'admit' that they talk about television with their friends and workmates. Very few men [...] say they do this. It is as if they feel that to admit that they watch too much television (especially with the degree of involvement that would be implied by finding it important enough to talk about) would be to put their very masculinity in question (see the section on program type preference below). The only standard exception is where the men say that they talk about sports on television. Some part of this has simply to do with the fact that femininity is a more expressive cultural mode than is masculinity. Thus even if women watch less, with less intent viewing styles, they are nonetheless inclined to talk about television more than men, despite the fact that men watch it more attentively. [...]

Use of video

The women didn't operate the video recorder themselves to any great extent, but relied on their husbands or children to work it for them.

Videos, like remote control devices, are largely the possessions of fathers and sons:

> *Woman: There's been things I've wanted to watch and I didn't under-stand the video enough. She (the daughter) used to understand it more than us.
> *Woman: I'm happy with what I see, so I don't use the video much. I mean lots of the films he records I don't even watch. He watches them after we've gone to bed.
> *Man: I use it most – me and the boys more than anything – mostly to tape racing and pool, programs we can't watch when they (the women) are watching.
> *Woman: I can't use the video. I tried to tape 'Widows' for him and I done it wrong. He went barmy. I don't know what went wrong . . . I always ask him to do it for me because I can't. I always do it wrong. I've never bothered with it. [...]

'Solo' viewing and guilty pleasures

A number of the women in the sample explain that their greatest pleasure is to be able to watch 'a nice weepie' or their favorite serial when the rest of the family isn't there. Only then do they feel free enough of their domestic responsibilities to 'indulge' themselves in the kind of attentive viewing in which their husbands routinely engage. Here we enter the territory identified by Brodie and Stoneman (1983), who found that mothers tended to maintain their role as 'domestic manager' across program types, as opposed to their husbands' tendency to abandon their manager/parent role when viewing materials of particular interest to them. The point is expressed most clearly by the woman who explains that she particularly enjoys watching early morning television on the weekends because these are the only occasions when her husband and sons 'sleep in', providing a chance to watch television attentively without keeping half an eye on the needs of others. [...]

What is at issue here is the guilt that most of these women feel about their own pleasures. They are, on the whole, prepared to concede that the dramas and soap operas they like are 'silly' or 'badly acted' or inconsequential. They accept the terms of a masculine hegemony that defines their preferences as having low status. Having accepted those terms, they then find it hard to argue for their preferences in a conflict because, by definition, what their husbands want to watch is more prestigious. They then deal with this by watching their programs, when possible, on their own, or only with their women friends, and will fit such arrangements into the crevices of their domestic timetables:

> *Woman: What I really like is typical American trash, I suppose, but I love it . . . all the American rubbish, really. And I love those Australian films. I think they're really good, those.
> *Woman: When the children go to bed he has the ultimate choice. I feel guilty if I push for what I want to see because he and the boys want to see the same thing, rather than what a mere woman would want to watch. . . . If there was a love film on, I'd be happy to see it and they wouldn't. It's like

when you go to pick up a video, instead of getting a nice sloppy love story, I think I can't get that because of the others. I'd feel guilty watching it because I think I'm getting my pleasure while the others aren't getting any pleasure, because they're not interested.

Program type preferences

My respondents displayed a notable consistency in this area, whereby masculinity was primarily identified with a strong preference for 'factual' programs (news, current affairs, documentaries) and femininity identified with a preference for fictional programs. The observation may be banal, but the strength of the consistency displayed here was remarkable whenever respondents were asked about program preferences, and especially when asked which programs they would make a point of watching and doing so attentively:

> *Man: I like all documentaries. . . . I like watching stuff like that. . . . I can watch fiction but I am not great lover of it.
> *Woman: He don't like a lot of serials.
> *Man: It's not my type of stuff. I do like the news, current affairs, all that type of stuff.
> *Woman: Me and the girls love our serials.
> *Man: I watch the news all the time, I like the news, current affairs and all that.
> *Woman: I don't like to so much.
> *Man: I watch the news every time, 5.40 p.m., 6.00 p.m., 9.00 p.m., 10.00 p.m., I try to watch.
> *Woman: I just watch the main news so I know what's going on. Once is enough. Then I'm not interested in it.

These responses seem to fit fairly readily into a kind of syllogism of masculine/feminine relationships to television:

MASCULINE	FEMININE
Activity	Watching television
Factual programs	Fictional programs
Realist fiction	Romance

It could be claimed that my findings in this respect exaggerate the 'real' differences between men's and women's viewing and underestimate the extent of 'overlap' viewing between men and women. Certainly my respondents offer a more sharply differentiated picture of men's and women's viewing than is ordinarily reported in survey work, which shows substantial numbers of men watching fictional programs and equally substantial numbers of women watching factual programs. However, this apparent contradiction largely rests on the conflation of 'viewing' with 'viewing attentively and with enjoyment'. Moreover, even if it could be demonstrated that my respondents had systematically misrepresented their behavior to me (offering classical masculine and feminine stereotypes that belie the complexity of their actual behavior), it would remain as a social fact of considerable interest that these were the particular forms of misrepresentation that respondents felt constrained to offer of themselves. Further, these tendencies – for the men to be unable to admit to watching fiction – themselves have real effects in their social lives.

National versus local news programming

As has been noted, it is men and not women who tend to claim in interest in news programming. Interestingly, this pattern varies when we consider local news programming, which a number of women claim to like. In several cases they give very cogent reasons for this. For instance, they say that they don't understand what international economic news is about and, as it has no experiential bearing on their lives, they're not interested in it. However, if there has been crime in their local area, they feel they need to know about it, both for their own sake and their children's sakes. This connects directly to their expressed interest in programs like 'Police Five', or programs warning of domestic dangers. In both these kinds of cases the program material has a practical value to them in terms of their domestic responsibilities, and thus they will make a point of watching it. Conversely, they frequently see themselves as having no practical relation to the area of national and international politics presented in the main news and therefore don't watch it. [...]

Roads (and potholes) ahead – the prospect of empirical research

Some years ago, in the conclusion to my study of the *Nationwide* Audience (Morley, 1980), I argued that the relation of audiences to television's ideological operations had always, in principle, to be formulated as an empirical question and that the challenge was to try to develop appropriate methods for empirical investigation of these relations. Whatever difficulties might be raised about the status of the knowledge produced as a result of this complex process, it seems to me to be a fundamentally more appropriate way to attempt to understand what audiences do when they watch TV than if I were simply to stay home and try to imagine the possible implications of how people might conceivably watch TV.

I would accept that in the absence of any significant element of participant observation of actual behavior beyond the interview situation, I am left only with the stories that respondents choose to tell me. These stories are themselves obviously limited by the cultural and linguistic frames of reference that respondents have available to them through which to articulate their responses.

However, a number of other points need to be made. The first concerns the supposedly lesser validity of respondents' accounts of behaviour as opposed to observations of actual behavior. The problem here is that observing always leaves open the question of interpretation. I may be observed to be sitting staring at the TV screen, but this behaviour could be equally compatible with a sense of total fascination or total boredom on my part – and the distinction may not be readily accessible from observed behavioral clues. Moreover, should you wish to understand what I am doing it would probably be as well to ask me. I may well, of course, lie to you or otherwise misrepresent my thoughts and feelings, for any number of purposes, but at least you will then begin to get some access to the language, criteria of distinction, and types of categorizations through which I construct my (conscious) world. Without these clues my TV viewing (or other behavior) will necessarily remain more opaque.

The interview method then is to be defended, in my view, not simply for the access it gives the researcher to the respondents' conscious opinions and statements, but also for the access that it gives to the linguistic terms and categories – the 'logical scaffolding' in Wittgenstein's terms – through which respondents construct their worlds and their own understanding of their activities.

I would like to argue here that we need to broaden the framework of our analyses to focus on the contexts in which processes of communication occur, including especially those instances in which class and gender considerations are articulated. Among other things, I wish to argue that the broader frame required also involves analysis of the physical as well as the social contexts in which television is consumed. This argument can perhaps usefully be made in the first instance, by reference to the development of film theory.

Predominantly, within film theory, the subject addressed has been the subject of the text – the film. At its simplest, I want to argue that it is necessary to consider the *context of viewing* as much as the *object of viewing*. Simply put, films traditionally had to be seen in certain places, and the understanding of such places has to be central to any analysis of what 'going to the pictures' has meant. I want to suggest that the whole notion of the 'picture palace' is as significant as the question of 'film'. This is to introduce the question of the phenomenology of 'going to the pictures', which involves the 'social-architecture' – in terms of decor and ambience – of the context in which films have predominantly been seen. Quite simply, there is more to cinema-going than seeing films. There is going out at night and the sense of relaxation combined with the sense of fun and excitement. The very name 'picture palace', by which cinemas were known for a long time, captures an important part of that experience. Rather than selling individual films, cinema is best understood as having sold a habit, or a certain type of socialized experience. This experience involves a whole flavour of romance and glamour, warmth and color. This is to point to the phenomenology of the whole 'moment' of going to the pictures – the queue (line), the entrance stalls, the foyer, cash desk, stairs, corridor entering the cinema, the gangway, the seats, the music, the lights fading, darkness, the screen, which begins to glow as the silk curtains are opening (Corrigan, 1983). Any analysis of the film subject that does not take on board these issues of the context in which the film is consumed is, to my mind, insufficient. Unfortunately, an awful lot of film theory has operated without reference to these issues, given the effect of the literary tradition in prioritizing the status of the text itself, abstracted from the viewing context.

My further point is that this argument applies with equal force to the study of television. Just as we need to understand the phenomenology of 'going to the pictures', so we need equally to understand the phenomenology of domestic television viewing – that is, the significance of various modes of physical and social organization of the domestic environment as the context in which TV viewing is conducted. There is more to watching TV than what's on the screen – and that 'more' is, centrally, the domestic context in which viewing is conducted.

References

Ang, I. (1987) On the politics of empirical audience studies. Paper presented to Rethinking the Audience symposium, Blaubeuren, West Germany.

Bausinger, H. (1984) Media, technology and daily life. *Media, Culture, Society*, **6**, 340–52.

Brodie, J. and Stoneman, L. (1983) A contextualist framework for studying the influence of TV viewing in family interaction. *Journal of Family Issues*, **4**, 329–48.

Corrigan, P. (1983) Film entertainment as ideology and pleasure. In Curran, J. and Porter , V. (eds) *British Cinema History*. Totowa, NJ: Barnes & Noble.

Cubitt, S. (1985) The politics of the living room. In Masterman, L. (ed) *TV Mythologies*, London: Comedia.

Lindlof, T. and Traudt, P. (1983) Mediated communications in families. In Mander, M. (ed.) *Communications in Transition*, New York: Praeger.

Morley, D. (1980) *The 'Nationwide' Audience*, London: British Film Institute.

20

Television and everyday life: towards an anthropology of the television audience[1]

Roger Silverstone

From Ferguson, M. (ed.) (1990) *Public Communication: The New Imperatives*, London: Sage Publications, pp. 173–90.

No consideration of public communication can reasonably ignore the audience: the readers, viewers, consumers of the content of the mass media. Indeed, the history of mass communication research has been continuously sustained and informed by concerns with its effects on audiences – on their moral, political and economic lives. That history has been an uneven one. It has been dominated by a concern with effects, effectiveness and power, but judgements on each of these, and of the relative weight to be attached to the overall capacity of the media to influence its audiences in significant ways, has, as countless observers have noted, produced little convincing evidence of the media's potency one way or the other. The problems are substantial. The media operate in an already complex world. Audiences live in a complex world. Both are rapidly changing. The belief that the media can affect an audience in some direct or measurable ways has passed, despite commonsensical view to the contrary. […]

In this chapter I would like to offer an approach to some of the questions posed for the study of the television audience, not so much in the hope of providing conclusive answers as marking out a territory for future exploration. I will argue for a broadly anthropological conceptualization of the audience and for a methodological approach, or a set of approaches, which sets the audience for television in a context of the world of everyday life: the daily experiences of home, technologies and neighbourhood, and of the public and private mythologies and rituals which define the basic patterns of our cultural experience. […]

Towards a framework for the analysis of the television audience

[…] I intend to explore a number of possible avenues for the pursuit of the television audience, and to argue for a naturalistic methodology – a critical ethnography – as the appropriate way to proceed. There are three elements to the argument. The first is the status of television as technology. The second concerns the nature of mass and mass-mediated consumption. The third focuses on the principles of rhetoric as a way of approaching the relationship between medium and content (technology and text) and its receivers. I will conclude by considering the methodological consequences of perceiving the audience through the various lenses I have offered, in the hope of defining an approach to the study of the television audience which takes into account the rapidly changing context of its embedding.

Television as technology

Television is a technology, a machine, and as such it as much socially shaped as socially shaping (MacKenzie and Wacjman, 1985; Williams, 1974). Inscribed in its design and creation (and crucially, also in its marketing) is a model of the viewer, the audience, the household (Boddy, 1985; Spigel, 1986; Keen, 1987). Its inscription as a social object and its ability, in turn, to inscribe its audience (its users) is a feature it shares with all technologies. In this sense television as technology can be compared to a text, which embodies intentions (however contradictory) and rhetorical claims for attention in the same way that all inscriptions do. Television as technology creates a space for the user, a space of operation and the creation of meaning, a space of possibility and indeterminacy. What distinguishes television (and other information and communication technologies) from non-communicating domestic appliances, though by no absolute divide, is its double articulation: it is both meaningful in itself and it is the transmitter of meanings.[2]

Television, then, has been constructed as domestic, for the family and the household. As such it takes and holds its places alongside other technologies; it takes its place and necessarily alters the technological environment of the household. And as Lynn Spigel has pointed out, this domestic occupation was neither straightforward nor uncontested (Spigel, 1986). Television is, relatively speaking, an open technology; its double articulation creates an enormous space (as compared, for example, to a washing machine or an iron, but in a similar way to other mediating and informing technologies) for variations in use – hence, among other things, the problem of meaning, the problem of the audience. Television is potentially meaningful and therefore open to the constructive work of the consumer-viewer both in terms of how it is used, or placed, in the household – in what rooms, where, associated with what other furniture or machines, the subject of what kinds of discourses inside and outside the home – and in terms of how the meanings it makes available through the content of its programmes are in turn worked with by the individuals and household groups who receive them.

So, even though I have major reservations about the notion of television as text (with the implication that the audience must be understood as reader), I want now to suggest an extension of the metaphor in relation to television as technology. However the relationship between television and its audience comes finally to be understood, it will need to take into account two kinds of mutually interdependent 'textualities': that of the content and that of the technology – the textuality both of message and of medium. Audiences, as I argue below, consume both, and the processes of consumption, while quite specific in relation to each, are nevertheless of a piece.

However, there is a further context to be taken into account, of course, and that is the social one. Technologies and meanings appear in a social environment – initially, but not solely, the household (the household itself is further contextualized by the wider political-economic environment). The status of television as technology and as the transmitter of meanings is in turn vulnerable to the exigencies, the social structuring, the conflicts and the rituals of domestic life. Television is a shared and gendered medium (Morley, 1986); so is video (Gray, 1987); it is also an age-related one.

It is in these senses, therefore, that I want to suggest that the technological aspects of television must intrude into our understanding of its relationship to its audience, especially if by 'audience' we assume some kind of listener and viewer rather than reader. Two things follow from this. The first is a perception of the place of television as embedded in a dialectic of domestic technology and culture; and the second is a requirement to get to grips with the dynamics of that dialectic as it works itself out in specific settings. The dynamics are multiple and increasingly problematic, for not only do they involve changes in families and households, but, and crucially, they involve major technological changes, involving convergence of video and telecommunication technologies and a potentially explosive increase in the range of moods and services available to the domestic consumer (Miles, 1988). These are questions to which I shall return, but they are also very much the preoccupation of those who have concerned themselves recently with the nature of consumption in contemporary society (Morley and Silverstone, 1988). The quality of the domestic use of television, and of the particular characteristics of 'audiencing', is a function of the negotiation of consumer choices within the market.

Television and consumption

The purchase of a television set or a cable subscription or a video cassette or even a satellite dish (or their rental) buys the purchaser into complex economy of meanings, a cultural economy. The subsequent use of these technologies, their incorporation into the daily lives of their users, as technologies and as carriers of meanings, transforms their status as commodities into objects of consumption. This transformative work is active, and powerful. The shift from production through marketing to consumption is dynamic. The goods bought, the meanings appropriated and transformed, are embedded in a social web of distinctions and claims for identity and status (Bourdieu, 1986). If we are to make sense of the ways in which television is and might be used, then we need to understand better than we appear to do now the nature and consequences of the choices that are daily made in the public and private acts of consumption.

There is not a great deal to go on. John Fiske (1987), towards the end of his discussion of television culture, addresses these problems directly, arguing for a distinction between the financial and cultural economies, and ascribing consumer power principally to those involved in the latter. It is in the selection and 'reading' of films or programmes that consumers exert their power, and the producers of such commodities cannot ever be certain of success, hence the production of what Nicholas Garnham (1987) calls 'repertoires of products'. Of course viewers and listeners have significant freedoms to reconstruct and redefine the meanings generated in their favourite (or least favourite) programmes, but Fiske's assumption that this is sufficient to distinguish the cultural from the economic is wide of the mark. Goods too, are meaningful, and the meanings we attach to them circulate just as do those associated with the consumption of programmes. The consumption of meaningful technologies and the consumption of technologically transmitted meanings are not, one assumes, identical (meanings are not finite, for example), but I would like to suggest that they differ only relatively, not absolutely. And I would like to suggest that it is in what they share (as well as in what distinguishes them) that the key to their significance in contemporary society might be found. If we are interested in the quality of television culture and in the pivotal role of the audience in articulating this culture, then we have to understand the relationship between goods and meanings in a more dialectical way.

Consumption, of course, has as one of its bases utility, and as one of its foundations human need, but neither utility nor need exhaust it. Consumption, following Mary Douglas and Baron Isherwood (1979), Marshall Sahlins (1976) and Daniel Miller (1987), is a general process of the construction of meaning; it is 'concerned with the internalization of culture in everyday life' (Miller, 1987; 212), the result of 'a positive recontextualization' of the alienating possibilities of the commodity (Miller, 1987: 175).

Daniel Miller's (1987) argument, beginning with a discussion of Hegel, Marx and Simmel, develops and deepens two anthropological approaches to the problem of consumption; the first that of Douglas and Isherwood (1979), and the second that of Pierre Bourdieu (1986). From the critical juxtaposition of these two views Miller offers an analysis of consumption which attempts to place it within both a subjective and an objective frame, and to characterize goods, correlatively, as both symbolic and material. The key to understanding consumption is the interactive possibilities in play. The social differentiation of objects through consumption need not (indeed, in a world of mass consumption will not) simply be an expression of social divisions or the power of the producer to define how a product will be used, nor indeed will it be necessarily defined or determined by the intrinsic properties of the object in itself. Miller, like Michel de Certeau (1984; cf. Silverstone, 1989) draws attention to the possibilities for the transformative work of consumption, but equally to the limits of that work in particular circumstances:

> All . . . objects . . . are the direct product of commercial concerns and industrial processes. Taken together, they appear to imply that in certain circumstances segments of the population are able to appropriate such industrial objects and utilize them in the creation of their own image. In other cases, people are forced to live in and through objects which are created through the images held of them by a different and dominant section of the population. The possibilities of recontextualization may vary for any given object according to its historical power, or for one particular individual according to his or her changing social environment.
>
> (Miller, 1987: 175)

And not just material objects. There is a precise parallel here with the arguments offered by Stuart Hall in what has now become a classic paper (Hall, 1980). In discussing the (always analytic) distinction between denotative and connotative levels of television's signification he draws attention to its polysemy, a polysemy which 'must not be confused with pluralism' and to the existence of 'a dominant cultural order though it is neither univocal nor uncontested' (p. 134).

I have dwelt on Miller's argument because I think that it provides an important route not only into an understanding of the nature of consumption, but also into the nature of the television audience. We are already aware of the audience's capacity to work creatively with the meanings generated by their involvement with the medium. We also know how important the communication of those meanings is for the creation and maintenance of the group and of individual identities within it. Miller's argument allows us to recognize the same processes at work in all acts of consumption, and it seems to suggest that we can now look at the audience as multiply embedded in a consumer culture in which technologies and messages are juxtaposed, both implicated in the creation of meaning, and in what Michel de Certeau calls the 'perambulatory rhetorics' (de Certeau, 1984: 100ff.) of everyday life. Consumption, from this point of view, is a rhetorical activity.

The rhetorics of technologies, 'texts' and consumption

Rhetoric (like myth) is usually identified as pejorative: the phrase 'mere rhetoric' signifies that a particular communication is distorting and aimed to deceive. Television is often charged with such deception. I wish to use the notion of rhetoric in three different but compatible senses. The first is the traditional and perhaps most familiar sense: rhetoric as persuasion (Burke, 1955). The second is rhetoric as argument (Billig, 1987) and the third is what Richard McKeon (1987) described as architectonic: 'an art of structuring all principles and products of knowing, doing and making' (p. 2). These notions of rhetoric offer, I would like to suggest, a major route into the study of contemporary culture. To apply them both to 'texts' and technology, and to the processes of their appropriation through consumption, involves the consideration not just of persuasion and appeal, but also of the mutual involvement by producer and consumer, addresser and addressee, in the structuring of experience.

The point about identifying this process of communication and consumption, therefore, in terms of rhetoric is first of all to see it as a bid or a claim for attention and action, more or less open to resistance or negotiation; second to see that the relative success or otherwise of rhetorical appeal depends significantly on an *a priori* sharing of interests between the addresser and addressee; and third it is to bring to the fore a requirement to focus on, and analyse, the mechanisms, the strategies and tactics, of rhetorical address and response, and to identify the creativity and invention that is possible in both. By implication, what follows is the possibility of a methodology which insists on an examination of the processes of communication as situated, motivated, textual, interactive, politically asymmetrical and skilful. The goal is to understand not just the generality of rhetorical appeal which articulates consumption, but also the specific rhetorics of different texts, technologies and arguments as they bid for attention and action. At issue, therefore, is the need to produce a semiological and a sociological analysis which generates a view of the audience both as the focus of these various rhetorical appeals and more or less imaginatively responsive to them within the domestic rhetorics of their own lives and culture. There is a great deal to be said about all of these dimensions of rhetorical analysis. I can only hope, in this chapter, to sketch out a few of them.

Situation   The first requirement of any rhetorical claim is shared experience or culture. Rhetoric operates within a taken for granted world, the world of the 'commonplace'. The 'commonplace' is both, within rhetoric, a statement of something entirely familiar and understood and the basis for creativity, a spur to novelty and invention. The commonplace is the place of memory and invention. The 'texts' of television are entirely understood, predictable, shared and familiar, almost inert, yet they can spark an audience into creative work, to new thoughts, into a recontextualization of meanings, indeed into the new commonplaces of daily life.[3] Technologies are marketed through the commonplaces of advertising, the basis for a continuous invention of image and idea; and indeed advertising, as many writers have noted (Barthes, McLuhan and others), is the source of many of the commonplaces of everyday life. The domestic technologies themselves are built to fit into common places, as gadgetty or user-friendly, and then appropriated more or less inventively in households where they become part of domestic consumer rhetoric, a private or sub-cultural textuality of style and status (de Certeau, 1984; Hebdige, 1979).

A shared situation is therefore a precondition for effective rhetorical address, but effective rhetorical address also creates, even within the 'as-if' culture of mass communication, a shared situation. The 15 or 17 million people who regularly have their sets tuned to *EastEnders* or *Neighbours* are an audience who, for that time, become a community engaged in some measure with a community. The programmes' rhetoric of character and narrative provides the stuff, the commonplaces, for the sustenance of community in the talk at work, in the canteen or in the school playground. The purchase of a new television set or domestic technology is articulated into a consuming rhetoric in a similar way, as it provides the basis often, not just of individual display, but also as the effective entry into 'insider talk', the rhetoric of a bid for membership into a particular sub-culture or group.

The schedule is another dimension of this, as far as broadcast television is concerned (Paterson, 1980): a bid for mass regulation through the management of texts and time, though vulnerable increasingly to the effects of new communication technologies which release the viewers from its grip. The art of scheduling is, however, a rhetorical art in a strict sense. It is dependent on the effective management of commonplaces and common times to create and hold an audience.

Textuality   Television audiences occupy a site of overlapping, competing and sometimes overdetermining textualities: the 'primary texts' of television; the 'secondary texts' of their embedding in the ephemera of newspaper and magazine discussions; the 'texts' of consumption, of advertising and marketing; the 'texts' of the technologies, of the goods consumed; and the 'texts' of their audience's own reworking, their own perambulations and displays, their identities, their histories and their geographies. These textualities are predominantly of a secondary oral kind: framed and to some extent dependent on literary and literacy skills, they nevertheless do not necessarily require them. They are persistent, ubiquitous, insistent, yet ephemeral and fragmentary.

The 'rhetoricization' of these textualities is simply to invite a concern with both a universalization and particularization of the strategies and tactics of public and private meaning creation: to focus attention on the dynamic processes of communication through the analysis of specific acts and contexts. The history of rhetoric itself, which is a history of just such analysis (Todorov, 1977), is entirely instructive in this regard, for its offers a whole world of work on the analysis of the coincidence of meaning and action.

I want to suggest that it is precisely in the formal and dynamic relationship between 'text' and audience that rhetorical theory can prove instructive. This ought to be the case at a general level – that is, in the identification of those processes: homology (Ricoeur, 1984), identification (Burke, 1955), amplification and suppression (Group μ, 1981), which can be seen to define the quality of the links between 'texts' and the discourses of everyday life. It ought also to be the case at a specific level where the particularities of individuals', households' and groups' responses to the figure and tropes of images, sounds and narratives of technologies and 'texts' (either programmes or flows) can be assessed and understood. Here what is involved is the identification and analysis of narrative and rhetorical structures in such a way as to demonstrate their effectiveness and their reincorporation in the activities of audiences: the identification of the tropes, metaphors, ironies and commonplaces that stud our public 'texts' and our private discourses (Lakoff and Johnson, 1980); and the analysis of different levels of meaning – image, sound, voice, music, titles – unevenly present and unevenly significant in (for the present argument at least) the television 'text' (Silverstone, 1981, 1984, 1986; cf. Mercer, 1986; Masterman, 1988).

Motivation and resistance   Both Michel de Certeau (1984) and Claude Lévi-Strauss (1966) identify the rhetorical work of daily life as motivated, but motivated in the spaces and cracks (de Certeau) or with the flotsam and jetsam (Lévi-Strauss) of contemporary culture. Their concepts of 'la perruque' and 'bricolage' focus on the creative possibilities for individual and collective rhetorical work which become available within hegemonic culture, without any prejudgement about the likelihood of major transformations of that culture: 'Here order is *tricked* by an art' (de Certeau, 1984; 26). The world of everyday life is constituted by these tricks and turns, the figures of conversation and of daily ritual and display, which are meaningful not only for themselves (and within 'popular' discourse), but also as visible transformations and recontextualizations of the dominant in contemporary culture. This play of power and the clash of intentions and motivations which mark it, defines the limits and possibilities of pleasurable participation in daily life: the successes and failures in the construction and assertion of individual, domestic and collective identities.

I am suggesting that we ought to be interested in these relationships between public and private 'texts', in the parallel and competing rhetorics (and mythologies) of the relatively powerful and the relatively powerless; in the cultural stratification of everyday life. And in this stratified world we need to establish how much room there is for doing what and by whom, in the transformations of fashion into style, commodities into objects, and broadcasts into action and gossip. It is in these transformations that we can gain a measure of the strengths and weaknesses of contemporary culture and of its asymmetrics. And it is this formulation rather than the classic 'who says what in which channel to whom and with what effect' (Lasswell, 1948) which should now orient our research into the television audience.

The audience and the consumer are, for all their activity and creativity, still at the end of a process of production, even though in many circumstances (Miller, 1987; Fiske, 1987) their activities work back to redefine the product and challenge the producer. It is tempting to romanticize audience freedoms, significant though they may increasingly be as mass communication fragments and becomes increasingly demand-led. It is also tempting to make a fetish of the idea of consumer choice, of programmes and software as much as of the technologies that we must continue to consume. Choices are constantly being made, perhaps increasingly narrow ones as cable and satellite offer the possibility of much more focused consumption. But the questions of what those choices might mean, and how they work their way into the lives of those who make them, separating those lives from others perhaps who share everything but locality; these questions remain.

Towards an anthropology of the television audience

Television as 'text' and television as technology are united by their construction, their recontextualization, within the practices of our daily lives – behind and beyond the closed doors of our houses – in our display of goods and cultural competences, both in private and in public. If we are to make sense of the significance of these activities, which after all, are the primary ones for any understanding of the dynamics of the pervasiveness and power of the mass media in contemporary culture, then we have to take seriously the varied and detailed ways in which they are undertaken. This is the basis for the case for an anthropology of the television audience, and for a commitment to ethnography as an empirical method.[4]

The starting-point for any such study is the household or the family, for it is here that the primary involvement with television is created, and where the primary articulation of meanings is undertaken. The household or family, itself embedded in a wider social and cultural environment, provides through its patterns of daily interaction, through its own internal system of relationships, and its own culture of legitimation and identity formation, a laboratory for the naturalistic investigation of the consumption and production of meaning (Anderson, 1988).

The empirical questions raised are many and various. Significantly, they revolve around three sets of issues. First, description: we need to know about the different patterns of consumption in different families and households in different areas at different stages of their life cycles. We can hardly hope to ask more sophisticated questions of the processes of consumption and reception, or provide more enlightened suggestions for policy, until we have some knowledge of the what and the how and the who of audience involvement with their television in the context defined by their involvements with other technologies and other things and people.

Such a requirement in turn suggests another: an ethnographic approach to family and household use of television. Observation and detailed and specific interviewing, at least as a first step, must ground any attempt to understand the embedded practices of the audience in the domestic setting. In short, we need to provide substance to the notion of the embedded audience by a consideration of the particular patterns of family and household life. This is a problem of the place of the household or family in the wider context of society, culture and technology – a problem which suggests the need for an integration of ethnography and political economy (Marcus and Fischer, 1986: 85) – but it is also a problem of the dynamics of the household and the family itself as the specificity of social and cultural and technology relations are negotiated within its own domestic space and time.

Second, *dynamics*: we need to understand the differences between the active and the passive viewer and to define these terms (or reject them entirely) within context of the differential practices of different individuals, and in relation to different family and household 'techno-cultures' (Giner, 1985). We ought to be in a position to distinguish both within families and households and comparatively between families and households the various kinds of relationships that audiences generate with television and other communication and information technologies, beginning, for example, with the distinction between primary and secondary viewing or between referentiality and poeticality (Katz and Liebes, 1985). We also need to know who is involved and in what kinds of ways with television and to identify gender-, age- and class-based differences where they occur and where they seem to be significant.

The argument that new technologies based on the computer and telephone are interactive in way that the older ones based on the television and the video are not, needs to be tested against such assessments as I have suggested in relation to the activities surrounding the television set. We also, finally, need a sense of changing patterns of use, particularly in so far as technological developments are offering a more complex and varied communication culture to the domestic consumer, who in turn is being offered more choices and more encouragement to make them. 'More choice' is itself a problematic notion in this context.

Third, *consequences*: there is a whole series of question to be asked about the consequences, both for individuals within the household or family and for the household and in particular for the family as a whole, of their involvement with television. These are important questions, of course, having major implications for policies, not just for the future of television but also for the future of the family.

The key issues, I would suggest, revolve around questions of isolation and integration. What are the consequences of differential involvement with television for individual and family identity and social and cultural involvement? How does the differential pattern of use and consumption affect the boundary around the household? This question itself fragments into a number of separate but necessarily interrelated further questions: questions to do with the separation of the public and the private; the existence or absence of different networks (social, technical or information) along which different family or household members might find routes to the community; the links between home and school, home and work, home and leisure opportunities, and the question of to what extent they are affected by the household's use of television and an increasingly wide range of television-based services.

It has also been suggested that the incorporation of television (and of television-based technologies and services) into the household is likely not to be without consequence also for the daily lives of family members, for their material and moral identities. The use of television and video can integrate or separate not just the family as a whole from its neighbours or wider society, but can integrate or separate the individuals within the family, as age and gender groups form and reform around particular activities that centre on the use of the screen or screens in the family home (Lull, 1980a and b; Morley, 1986). Here the questions have to do with the placing of the television in the micro-geography of the home (cf. Palmer, 1986; ch. 4), its articulation with other information and communication technologies, its role in defining age and gender identities, its significance as an ameliorator or prompter of conflict.

In making such sweeping suggestions and in framing them, as I have done here within the triangle of technology, consumption and rhetoric, I am not for one moment suggesting that research has to start from scratch. There is a wealth of literature and work already undertaken to draw upon, and I have referred to some of it. The key challenge lies in our ability to construct the audience as both a social and a semiological (a cultural) phenomenon, and in our ability to recognize the relationship between viewers and the television set as one powerfully mediated by the determinacies and indeterminacies of everyday life – by the audience's daily involvement with its daily medium. This is certainly not a new idea, but it is one which we have barely begun to take seriously.

Notes

1. This chapter arises out of work carried out under an ESRC (PICT) project into the household and communication and information technologies. It has benefited from the enormously helpful comments of David Morley, Sonia Livingstone, Virginia Valentine and Marjorie Ferguson.

2. The notion of television and other mass media as being 'doubly articulated' is derived from models of language, especially from the work of André Martinet (1969), though the parallel is not an exact one. The intention is to identify the double and interdependent character of the meaningfulness of the mass media: the first articulation is the 'meaning' of the technology as an object of consumption, and the second is the 'meaning' that communicating and informing technologies carry. In other words, there is meaning in the texts of both hardware and software.

3. Billig (1987: 199) 'On the one hand these [common] places of argument were frequently visited by orators. These common-places were the stock phrases of oratorical production, to be used time and time again. One the other hand, the commonness of the common-places related to the fact that these bits of folk wisdom were commonly shared by members of the audience, and also by the speaker. Thus, the common-places were assumed to be both commonly used by orators and commonly held by their audiences.'

4. This is not quite as straightfoward as it might seem, for enthnography as a method of empirical investigation is currently the subject of considerable interest and interrogation. It is not possible, within the scope of the present chapter, to pursue this issue, fascinating as it is (cf. Marcus and Fischer, 1986).

References

Anderson, J. A. (1988) Commentary on qualitative research and mediated communication in the family. In Lindlof, T. R. (ed.) *National Audiences*, Beverly Hills: Sage.

Billig, M. (1987) *Arguing and Thinking: A Rhetorical Approach to Social Psychology*, Cambridge: Cambridge University Press.

Boddy, W. (1985) The shining centre of the home: ontologies of television in the 'Golden Age'. In Drummond, P. and Paterson, R. (eds) *Television in Transition*, London: British Film Institute, 125–34.

Bourdieu, P. (1986) *Distinction: A Social Critique of the Judgement of Taste*, London: Routledge & Kegan Paul.

Burke, K. (1955) *A Rhetoric of Motives*, New York: George Brazillier.

Certeau, M. de (1984) *The Practice of Everyday Life*, Berkeley, CA: University of California Press.

Douglas, M. and Isherwood, B. (1979) *The World of Goods: Towards an Anthropology of Consumption*, Harmondsworth: Penguin.

Fiske, J. (1987) *Television Culture*, London: Methuen.

Garnham, N. (1987) Concepts of culture: public policy and the cultural industries. *Cultural Studies*, 1, 23–7.

Giner, S. (1985) *Communio, Domini, Innovacio: per una Teoria de la Cultura*, Barcelona: Editorial Laia.

Gray, A. (1987) Behind closed doors: women and video recorders in the home. In Bache, H. and Dyer, G. (eds) *Boxed In: Women in Television*, London: Routledge & Kegan Paul, 38–54.

Group μ (1981) *A General Rhetoric*, Baltimore, MD: Johns Hopkins University Press.

Hall, S. (1980) Coding and encoding in the television discourse. In Hall, S., Hobson, D., Lowe, A. and Willis, P. (eds) *Culture, Media, Language*, London: Hutchinson, 128–38 .

Hebdige, D. (1979) *Subculture: The Meaning of Style*, London: Methuen.

Katz, E. and Liebes, T. (1985) Mutual aid in the decoding of *Dallas*: preliminary notes from a cross-cultural study. In Drummond, P. and Paterson, R. (eds) *Television in Transition*, London: British Film Institute, 187–98 .

Keen, B. (1987) 'Play it again, Sony': the double life of home video technology. *Science as Culture*, 1, 7–42.
Lakoff, G. and Johnson, M. (1980) *Metaphors We Live By*, Chicago: Chicago University Press.
Lasswell, H. D. (1948) The structure and function of communication in society. In Bryson, N. (ed.) *The Communication of Ideas*, New York: Harper/ Cooper Square Publishers Inc. (1964), 31–51.
Lévi-Strauss, C. (1966) *The Savage Mind*, London: Weidenfeld & Nicolson.
Lull, J. (1980a) The social uses of television. *Human Communication Research*, 6(3), 197–209.
Lull, J. (1980b) Family communication patterns and the social uses of television. *Communication Research*, 7(3), 319–34.
Marcus, G. E. and Fischer, M. M. J. (1986) *Anthropology as Cultural Critique: An Experimental Moment in the Human Sciences*, Chicago: Chicago University Press.
Martinet, A. (1969) *Elements of General Linguistics*, London: Faber & Faber.
Masterman, L. (1988) *Teaching the Media*, London: Comedia.
MacKenzie, D. and Wajcman, J. (eds) (1985) *The Social Shaping of Technology: How the Refrigerator Got its Hum*, Milton Keynes: Open University Press.
McKeon, R. (1987) *Rhetoric: Essays in Invention and Discovery*, Woodbridge, CT: Ox Bow Press.
Mercer, C. (1986) That's entertainment: the resilience of popular forms. In Bennett, T., Mercer, C. and Woollacott, J. (eds) *Popular Culture and Social Relations*, Milton Keynes: Open University Press, 177–95.
Miles, I. (1988) *Home Informatics: Information Technology and the Transformation of Everyday Life*, London: Frances Pinter.
Miller, D. (1987) *Material Culture and Mass Consumption*, Oxford: Basil Blackwell.
Morley, D. (1986) *Family Television*, London: Comedia.
Morley, D. and Silverstone, R. (1988) Domestic communication: technologies and meanings. Paper presented to the International Television Studies Conference, London, 1988.
Palmer, P. (1986) *The Lively Audience: A Study of Children Around the TV Set*, London: George Allen & Unwin.
Paterson, R. (1980) Planning the family: the art of the TV schedule. *Screen Education*, 35, 79–85.
Ricoeur, P. (1984) *Time and Narrative*, Vol. 1, Chicago and London: University of Chicago Press.
Sahlins, M. (1976) *Culture and Practical Reason*, Chicago: University of Chicago Press.
Silverstone, R. (1981) *The Message of Television: Myth and Narrative in Contemporary Culture*, London: Heinemann Educational Books.
Silverstone, R. (1984) Narrative strategies in television science: a case study. *Media, Culture and Society*, 6(4), 377–410.
Silverstone, R. (1986) The agonistic narratives of television science. In Corner, J. (ed.) *Documentary and the Mass Media*, London: Edward Arnold, 81–106.
Silverstone, R. (1989) Let us then return to the murmuring of everyday practices: a note on Michel de Certeau, television and everyday life. *Theory, Culture and Society*, 6(1), 77–94.
Spigel, L. (1986) Ambiguity and hesitation: discourses on television and the housewife in women's home magazines 1948–55. Paper presented to the International Television Studies Conference, London.
Todorov, T. (1977) *Theories of the Symbol*, Oxford: Basil Blackwell.
Williams, R. (1974) *Television, Technology and Cultural Form*, London: Collins.

21

Modernity, consumption and anxiety: television audiences and food choice[1]

Roger Dickinson

Introduction

Some years ago Michael Schudson argued that because culture 'works' on a number of levels at different degrees of intensity it is one of the tasks of the sociology of culture to find a way of describing the 'influence of culture in the everyday world where culture reminds more often than it informs, and highlights more often than it galvanizes' (Schudson, 1989: 175). Thus, he suggested, the small but widely experienced effects of media messages are as worthy of investigation as dramatic but isolated incidents of influence.

In this chapter I take up this suggestion and argue further that to understand television's role in representing a social issue or topic, rather than thinking in terms of its impact, influence or effects, it is more helpful to think of television as a source of possibilities, guides, or recommendations for social behaviour. The basis for this claim lies in the findings of some research recently carried out on television as an agent of 'public knowledge'. I hope to demonstrate the value of this approach by exploring television's role in the processes of household decision-making about food and eating. Following the logic developed within a current research project I argue that television contributes to decision-making about food by offering solutions to the dilemmas viewers confront as a result of their confusion over which foods might be a benefit or which might be a danger to their health, which foods may be a source of pleasure or which they may dislike. For this reason in this context, but perhaps also in others, I propose that television is best thought of as a *resource*.[2]

Recent themes in audience research

A number of themes which have been circulating recently in the field of audience research can be brought together to address specific questions regarding television's contribution to daily life. These themes, however, also have wider relevance for our understanding of television and its influence on social practices more generally. So, although my immediate objective in this chapter is to explore the role of television in the highly specific area of food choice, the broader aim in bringing these themes together is to construct a theoretical framework which can make sense of the wider role that television plays in people's lives.

The themes I have in mind – 'consumption', 'everyday life', 'the domestic', and 'the family' – are obviously central to any consideration of the nature and formation of food habits, but, as other chapters in the present volume show, these themes have assumed some importance in recent theoretical discussions of audiences.

The topic of food is especially interesting for two reasons. First, although food is an object of consumption in the most obvious sense, food consumption can also be seen as reflecting and expressing different identities and different lifestyles (Narayan, 1995; James, 1996). In this sense food and eating are thus bound up with the communication of meaning. Second, because most food consumption takes place in the home, interest in it draws our attention to the home as a site for other forms of consumption, here, most notably, the consumption of *culture* in the form of television viewing. Although some more recent studies of television audiences have identified viewing as an act of consumption (e.g. Moores, 1997) they have tended to concentrate on the *act* (in fact, most often, the context of viewing) at the expense of the *object* of consumption. Those studies which have taken content to be central, on the other hand, have tried to explore audience decodings of individual programmes or of particular types of programmes – news, soap operas, current affairs or documentary programmes (see Corner *et al.*, 1990, for an example of the latter) – to a large extent leaving the everyday context of viewing to one side. While both strands of work have been fruitful and have drawn attention to key processes in audience reception, the impact of television's message for specific areas of social life and specific issues of public concern has received relatively little attention. I suggest that we need research which first, acknowledges the fact that television can carry meanings about specific areas of personal and social life across several genres and thus makes these its explicit object of study, and second, explores the decoding of these meanings by studying people's beliefs, practices and ways of talking about these specific areas. By taking food as the focus for a study of content *and* a study of reception we can further develop our understanding of the role of television in the formation of public knowledge.

Modernity, consumption and anxiety

Recent social theory has drawn attention to the increasing uncertainty and anxiety felt by people in modern society and the heightened sense of risk associated with everyday decision-making. The notions of anxiety and risk have been explored in a wide range of studies, particularly those concerned with questions of consumption, in their authors' attempts to identify and explain the sources of variation in lifestyles and patterns of behaviour in modern life. Some theories of consumption identify an increasing fragmentation of social life, an erosion of group strengths and constraints and a growth of 'individualization' (Beck, 1992; Giddens, 1991). As a result of these processes acts of consumption have become important ways of expressing personal identity. It is a matter of continuing debate whether consumption in the late twentieth century can be said to have led to a degree of cultural fragmentation symptomatic of a 'postmodern world' or whether, instead of displaying cultural disorganization, variations in consumption are patterned, reflecting materially-based distinctions between social groups. None the less, consumption's growing importance for self-expression seems to be widely accepted. Because consumption has this importance in defining identity, decision-making regarding a wide range of ordinary everyday acts of consumption is thought to be a potential cause of anxiety, the latter being seen by Giddens (1991), among others, as a distinguishing feature of 'high modernity'.

The recent scares about the food supply in the UK and abroad – salmonella bacteria in eggs and chicken, listeria in cheese, BSE in cattle – make this thinking particularly attractive for an analysis of the contemporary situation, but the stresses of food choice have in fact been the subject of academic debate among sociologists of food and eating for some time.

Several years ago the prominent French sociologist Claude Fischler (1980) argued that in contemporary society social norms and behaviour regarding food have been eroded and food has become a source of increased discomfort, anxiety and confusion. Whereas in the past, when patterns of consumption were related much more closely to social class and food choices were thus linked securely to collective identities, in the contemporary world food choices have gradually become ways of expressing individuality. The search for new food norms and dietary goals, according to Fischler, explains the rising popularity of cooking, the appearance of so-called 'fashionable foods' and the promotion of various slimming or health-enhancing diets. However, Fischler argues, the contradictory advice of experts, food manufacturers and suppliers regarding which foods are best to choose leads to a 'dietetic cacophony' creating the anomie of 'arbitrary individual diversity and hence widespread public anxiety – a state of gastro-anomie'.

> One view is that this process began in the nineteenth century with the emergence of modern nutritional science, the main aim of which was to optimize the relationship between food and income and to spread consumer information [in] an endeavour to improve life management. One of the most crucial points in the attempt to improve life management in the working class was to condemn irrational food habits – irrational from an economic point of view – and foster healthy ones.
>
> (Ilmonen, 1990: 34)

In the twentieth century, Ilmonen argues, the cultural codes of 'healthy' and 'unhealthy' food practices began to receive more attention than ever before. Today, he suggests, the tension between the 'healthy' and the 'unhealthy' is a fundamental feature of modern life.

The picture of the increasingly confused and worried consumer receiving ever larger amounts of information and ideas which influence his or her consumer choices in various ways, serves as a further backdrop to the research reported in this chapter. By examining a specific issue (food choice) and a specific medium (television), it will be argued, it should be possible to begin to show more precisely how, through the consumption of their messages, the mass media contribute to the pattern of material consumption in modern life.

The media and everyday life

The importance of the concept of 'everyday life' for the study of audiences and media reception has been asserted by several writers over the past decade or so. Bausinger (1984), for example, is frequently quoted as influential in this respect. His main point is that people make technology a part of the routines of their life and in order to understand technology's impacts or effects one has to examine the patterns of daily life in which it is used. As far as the media are concerned, Bausinger argues, we must recognize that through their regular use they become integral to the daily routine. To understand their role the focus of study should not be media content or reception/impact alone, although these are important, but should be the mode of media use as part of the everyday.

This line of enquiry has been pursued by several researchers. Morley (1986), for example, in his study of television viewing in the family drew from and connected Bausinger's ideas on the routines of domestic technology use with studies of the family (Goodman, 1983), work on the social uses of television (Lull, 1980) and feminist studies of media use (e.g. Radway, 1984; Gray, 1987). This interest in the social context of media consumption has gradually led audience studies away from a concern with media content towards issues of domestic relations, the 'ecology of viewing' and an ever tighter focus on the impact of television and other communication technologies seen chiefly as 'technologies' rather than as sources of images, meanings and understandings (Silverstone *et al.*, 1992).[3]

Concerned with the way media use is integrated with the routines of daily existence, Silverstone has suggested (Chapter 20, this volume) that the role of television may be understood more fully if we can chart its contribution to what he calls, following de Certeau (1984), 'the practice of everyday life'. In a development of this idea and drawing also on Giddens's work (Giddens, 1991), Silverstone views people's everyday lives as something built around the search for ontological security – the search for a sense of trust and continuity in the world around them. The content of television's message is important because television provides some of the material – the meanings and understandings it conveys – through which we build a sense of self. Television viewing, then, can be seen as another, albeit extremely significant, form of consumption. Through the consumption of television output and an 'engagement' with its meanings people find the means to understand their social roles, their obligations, their relations to others and the possibilities for social action.

The idea that television-viewing and audiences' engagement with its meanings are in this way implicated in the 'practices of everyday life' seems plausible enough, and Silverstone has pursued this theoretically in his later work (Silverstone, 1994), but to take his case further, I want to suggest, we need to make more progress in examining these practices empirically, not by focusing only on everyday media use as social behaviour, but also by refocusing our attention on the consequences of the process of engagement within the context of the home. This is where all or most viewing occurs, but it is also the site where most material goods are consumed.

To test Silverstone's argument about television as an agent for the reduction of anxiety and the creation of trust we must address a specific aspect of television's output and explore viewers' everyday engagement with it. An obvious example, then, is that most ordinary, everyday, but, if Fischler's arguments are accepted, increasingly anxiety-filled practice of food consumption. By examining this particular source of anxiety we may then explore how or whether television actually functions in the way Silverstone's theorizing suggests. To do this we must look at content to see what television is saying about food, what its messages are, how it represents food and eating, and at audience interpretations of that content and how this is woven into people's daily lives. The question whether television is a source either of anxiety-reducing or anxiety-raising meanings and understandings then becomes amenable to empirical study.

Television influence

Before going any further with the argument, a few observations about the question of television influence need to be made. This is partly because it is important to be clear about why research of this kind needs to be carried out, and partly because it gives further justification for choosing the home as a research site. It has been pointed out several times in the past (most recently by Livingstone, 1996) that although it is frequently only rather obliquely implied in many studies of media reception, the notion of television influence lies at the centre of most research on audiences. Although many researchers have recently wished to steer clear of questions of 'effects' on the usual grounds that it betrays a simplistic, perhaps even behaviourist style of theorizing, media effects, influences, or, to use a perhaps less loaded term, *consequences* are still something that audience researchers need to take seriously, even though, as research on viewing contexts and domestic relations has quite rightly shown, the scope of debate about the significance of the media in the modern world needs to be broadened to see television use, for example, as but one social practice amongst a large number of others. This is because outside the confines of academic debate public discussion of social issues and social problems continues to hypothesize a (mostly malign) causal role for the media (especially television) and if audience research is to be worthwhile we should try to study issues which are at least relevant to the questions that this kind of discussion poses.

Consumption

Because television can be thought of as a 'doubly articulated' technology – 'it is an object of consumption and it facilitates consumption in its circulation of meanings' (Silverstone and Hirsch, 1992: 9) – a fruitful way of thinking about its role in food choice is to consider the way in which both the consumption of television and the consumption of food fit into the 'moral economy' of the household. Silverstone *et al.* (1992) use the idea of the moral economy to explain the different ways in which households (generally families in their study) incorporate information and communication technologies into their patterns of day-to-day living. This entails an 'active engagement' with the technologies and what they offer, according to the norms and values of the home. Silverstone and his colleagues suggest that information and communication technologies pose a number of control problems for the family which makes the project of creating ontological security particularly problematic. Television, for example, poses problems of regulation: who should watch, how much, and when? In addition to the act of watching (considered perhaps as displacing or distracting from other activities) an obvious focus of concern is the content of television – the 'what' of television consumption. My point here is that if that content is about or contains references to food and eating then the control problems posed by television combine with those posed by food: 'what to watch and when to watch' become linked to 'what to eat and when to eat'.

Audience research and the 'public knowledge project'

John Corner has identified two strands of work in academic audience research: that concerned with the media as bearers of 'public knowledge', interested in their power to define and limit the terms of public debate about certain issues, and that concerned with the media as popular culture, interested in them as sources of pleasure and their implications for social consciousness (Corner, 1990). The 'public knowledge project' has enabled audience researchers to relate their analyses to wider issues of power and citizenship. This justifies an emphasis in research on television news and current affairs genres rather than other forms of output, and a focus on these programmes as bearers of meaning regarding a given social issue. As with Silverstone's work, this seems to be preferable to the emphasis on *context* to the exclusion of *content* prevalent in other studies, but at the same time it appears that in practice research on television and public knowledge has focused rather too much on non-fictional forms of output, as if news and current affairs programmes were the only sources of public knowledge on television. This compartmentalizes television content too firmly and assumes that the processes of reception can be similarly compartmentalized.

It seems to make more sense, on the contrary, to recognize that public knowledge about some issues will be transmitted across the range of television's output, and is also, in the case of commercial television, very likely to be relayed through the advertising that accompanies that output. Our own experience as viewers tells us, surely, that public knowledge can just as easily (perhaps, in some cases, more easily) be borne by fiction and persuasive forms as by non-fiction forms of output. In fact some fictional genres (soap opera, for example – see Dickinson, 1995) assume an explicit knowledge-giving role. To understand television's role as a bearer of public knowledge then we need to look at the way the *whole* of its output contributes to the construction of meaning and forms of consciousness about a given topic.

Reception research which has focused on audience interpretations of specific texts or genres has had to ignore the fact that programmes and genres are parts of the much larger whole of television output. While specific programmes or genres may be bearers of 'preferred meanings' which detailed textual analysis may be able to reveal, the messages and meanings encoded in the different genres of television are likely to be uneven, inconsistent, and probably contradictory. This only becomes obvious – as an analytical and methodological issue – when we consider television's role as a bearer of meanings about a specific topic or a particular aspect of social life such as food and eating.

But what are the implications for audience interpretation when there are contradictory meanings in the television text? To understand television's contribution to audience understandings about a given issue, we must assume that audience interpretation involves the evaluation or the weighing up of the different frameworks, interpretive schemes or ways of thinking about that issue that television makes available. To the extent that these frameworks have a role in structuring audience interpretations, they will help to inform decision-making, and may guide actions regarding the specific area of social life under consideration. Research on the 'active audience' has established that audiences have the power to construct meanings from media texts, but it is important to remember that they do not exercise that power freely. Media texts clearly are not open to an infinite range of readings, audiences can only interpret those texts which they are offered (television offers limited and limiting choices), and they make their interpretations in specific personal, social, cultural and material circumstances. I shall return to these points shortly. First, however, it will be necessary to outline the approach adopted in the present research project.

Television and food

The main objective in the research reported here was to try to determine what contribution, if any, television makes to family food choices. A little of the background to this project will help to explain its significance.

Despite a very large measure of public concern about the influence of television on children's, young people's and adult's diets, little work has been done on the wider depiction of food and eating on television. Until now little was known about the role that television as a whole plays alongside other influences in shaping food choices.

Most public and official concern about television's influence on food habits seems to be centred on television advertising. This concern has stimulated a great deal of research interest over the years both in the UK and abroad, and most notably the US. There is now quite a large body of research on television food advertising and its impact on children (see Young and Hetherington, 1996 for a review), but there is a contrasting *lack* of research on food-related television output *as a whole*, although there have been a few studies focusing on specific programmes or genres (e.g. Kaufman, 1980; Story and Faulkner, 1990; see Signorielli, 1993, for a review). The fact that food and eating do not just appear on our television screens during the commercial breaks seems to have escaped attention. Depictions of food choice, purchase, preparation and consumption appear on television in a variety of settings and situations.

Food is used in television fiction, for example, as a prop, a plot device, or a focus for action or dialogue. The Rover's Return in *Coronation Street*, or the café in *EastEnders*, for example, offer both sources and sites of dialogue and action – the nature of the food depicted is sometimes commented on, sometimes not, but it is unmistakably *there*. Food is also widely used in television drama as a mood-creating, scene-setting vehicle for images and ideas. This use of food as a symbol was evident, for example, in the early 1990s Yorkshire Television drama series *The Darling Buds of May*. Set in the 1950s the use of food in this programme was placed explicitly against the modern trend towards the bland, boring, low-fat/high-nutrition, 'healthy' diet, and was widely celebrated, particularly in the popular press, for returning to 'old' food and health values. Use was made of alcohol and fried and fatty food in the series at least partly to lend it period 'flavour' – as a way of marking off the dramatic context from the contemporary world – but there was also a sense in which the idea of 'a healthy appetite' and the notion that 'a little of what you fancy does you good' were used to symbolize ideals for family life as well as ideals for nutritious eating. The equations of 'proper' meal = 'proper' parenting = 'proper' – i.e. stable – family life were quite clear. These images, to judge by the viewing figures for this programme, seemed to resonate with the values and attitudes of a large section of the British public.

Interestingly, this juxtaposition of the 'healthy' with the 'tasty' on television is also evident in programmes where food is the main object of focus. Consider the contrasting approaches of programmes such as BBC2's *Food & Drink* on the one hand, which displays a clear 'health and consumer' consciousness, and *Rhodes Around Britain* on the other, which features the successful chef Gary Rhodes whose concerns seem primarily to be to rediscover and resurrect 'traditional British cooking' – not noted by today's nutritionists as especially 'healthy'. These programmes are located at two polls in the continuum of the television diet, with 'healthy eating' at one end and what one might call 'food-as-culture' at the other. Both of these programmes are very popular, each regularly drawing audiences of between 2 and 5 million.

Food, as a topic, also appears frequently in television news and current affairs programmes where it is presented as a cause for concern: about either the lack or over-abundance of different foodstuffs in different national and regional contexts; about the issues of weight loss and eating disorders; about the risks of food contamination; about issues of diet, nutrition and health; and about methods of food production.

Television, then, presents a very wide range of images of food on a daily basis. In general, these images, and the ideas and values they embody, are likely to make significant contributions to the social environment in which food choices are made by providing models, reference points, indicators of the acceptable and unacceptable, and, at the simplest level, by offering information which may lead to action over food use. It would seem that the *context* of daily programming into which *food adverts* are placed is at least as important an object of study as the adverts themselves. To understand television's role in relation to a specific topic it is perhaps more helpful to think of its output not as a system of ordered meanings but rather as one of *disorderly* meanings, appearing across different genres and formats, both fiction and non-fiction.

In fact this is borne out by the results of an analysis of two weeks of British terrestrial television output (Dickinson, 1998). These results showed, among other things, the predominantly 'unhealthy' messages of television adverts contrasting with overtly 'healthy' messages in programmes; 'healthy' messages in factual output contrasting with 'unhealthy' messages in fictional output. These findings confirm that television does in fact convey *contradictory* messages about food and food use; the study failed to detect a single dominant or *ordered* meaning but rather a number of contradictory meanings about food choice and food use. Television content about food therefore appears, on detailed analysis, to be somewhat *disorderly*.

Researching reception

How, then, are these varied and contradictory images of food received, interpreted and acted upon by the audience? If there is no single dominant meaning available in television content about food and eating, but a number of contradictory meanings, how do viewers react to, make sense of and resolve these contradictions? To what extent do television's discourses contribute to and circulate within daily family discourse about food and eating and, if they do, what part do they play? To try to answer these questions, 12 households, each containing at least two adults (in most cases male and female parents) and at least one child between the ages of 11 and 18 years, were chosen to take part in a series of interviews and group discussions.

Interviews, which took place in our respondents' homes, were unstructured but made use of an *aide mémoire* so that a number of themes could be pursued in all cases. At the first interview, which involved parents only, the aim was to discuss how the research would proceed and to obtain data about household eating habits, attitudes to food and eating, the household's use of television and their daily patterns of viewing. The second and third interviews involved the whole household and used a VCR and television monitor to show excerpts from television programmes and advertisements selected from the sample of television output previously analysed. During each interview these excerpts (chosen from programmes for the second visit; advertisements for the third) were used in a series of exercises designed to generate data on viewer interpretations. The interviews and discussions resulted in a total of more than 40 hours of recorded material.

Group interviews in households are not new to television audience research (for examples see Lull, 1990) and a number of researchers (e.g.

Philo, 1990) have used still photographs as a way of prompting viewers to recall their viewing experiences and reveal the extent to which their knowledge and beliefs about a given issue are shaped by what they see on television. The innovation here was to use soundless videotaped extracts from television programmes and advertisements for this purpose. The aim was to discover how well families 'know' the television discourses about food, to uncover the frameworks family members use to interpret television content and to see how these relate to family discourses about food. From previous studies of family and household food use (e.g. Brannen *et al.*, 1994) it was anticipated that there could be several competing discourses in play in some households, with evidence, for example, of conflict over family roles, over likes and dislikes, over vegetarianism vs. meat-eating, or over weight gain and weight loss, and so on.

The research sought to explore the extent to which television discourses contributed to these conflicts, ran parallel with them, or offered a means of conflict resolution, say, by acting as a reference point for different family members at different times. The objective was to use the programme excerpts to encourage parents and children to articulate their views on food and its portrayal on television and reveal the extent to which their frameworks of interpretation arise from television content. Were they aware of and able to recall television's food narratives and how far did this mode of interpretation coincide with their own modes of food use? Did they accept or reject the different interpretive frameworks television offers about food?

The reason for conducting at least some of the research as a group exercise was that the discussion and conversation would also help to reveal the gender, power and inter-generational relationships that exist in each family, especially as these are played out in relation to food and eating behaviour. These themes helped to frame the questions and prompts for discussion designed to explore whether and how the divisions and differences of opinion and taste were being articulated through the exercise. For example, it was anticipated that there would be divisions over knowledge between different programme types and genres. Children might possibly be more aware of the characters and plot nuances of tea-time soap operas than their parents, while parents might be more familiar with news and current affairs discourse. But it was recognized also that such distinctions might depend on the topic referred to in programme excerpts. Children might be very well informed about BSE in comparison to their parents, for example; mothers and daughters might know more about anorexia than fathers and sons. The aim was to try to show how these competences related or contributed to individual eating habits and preferences.

Family discussion would also help to answer the question of how far ideas and suggestions were made from a 'television discourse perspective' (i.e. what experienced and knowing viewers would expect the message to be, the characters to be saying, the news story to be about, or the turn the plot will take) and how far this was done from an 'independent' or individual perspective shaped by other factors. In other words, would it be possible to distinguish between what people would expect the television discourse to be about (based on their knowledge of genre conventions) and what they thought based on their knowledge of 'real life' and their personal experiences and beliefs? To an extent this was the difference between viewers' assessments of whether television depicts life realistically and whether it works as 'good TV'. On these grounds did family members accept or reject the different discourses on food? Was it possible to detect some negotiation going on between viewers' perceptions of television discourses and individual or family decodings of them? Did these discourses provide meal ideas, or styles of eating behaviour, or attitudes to food which circulated in the family and contributed to the family's food choices, preferences, and eating behaviours? A way of revealing this was to show programme excerpts which depicted contrasting types of eating behaviour – 'healthy' vs. 'unhealthy', for example – and ask families to respond to these as realistic or not, similar to their lives or not, or appropriate for the family/individual being depicted or not. This, it was felt, would show clearly whether people were accepting or rejecting what they see from these different perspectives.

Audience interpretations: resolving food dilemmas?

A detailed account of the research findings lies outside the scope of the present discussion. Instead just four points will be made.

First, the video exercises showed that in almost every case these households were extremely familiar with television's language, its formats and its style of presentation. In several cases, between them, respondents were able to piece together from their knowledge of characters and plots and their memories of particular pieces of dialogue, remarkably accurate soundtracks for the video excerpts being shown to them. Young people in particular seemed to be especially adept at recalling the voice-overs and jingles from food adverts, for example. Clearly, the language that television uses to 'talk' about food and eating is well known to its audience, but it is equally clear this knowledge does not necessarily lead to action. In the case of food advertising, there appears to be no clear relationship between the ability of respondents to recall the details of a food brand (and its advertising) and their consumption of that brand. There was an awareness of the difference between 'television talk' and everyday language, and a clearly demarcated boundary between what happens on television and what happens in the home.

Second, the data suggest that television can be a source of potential solutions to conflict over choices; innovations in eating patterns and dietary choices; ideas and arguments which contribute to conflict over preferred meal types, preferred meal times, and preferred foods. Thus, while its message may be contradictory, television seems also at times to be a source of conflict resolution for these households. On the present evidence it seems that television can act, on occasion, as a mediating force between household members, particularly between parents and children, in that it offers viewers a readymade set of arguments, justifications, or just simply ideas for food, eating and related choices, regardless of whether these could be described as 'healthy' or 'unhealthy'.

Third, the talk about food choices generated in interviews and household discussions revealed these household members' decision-making to be as contradictory as the images they see on television, and it is certainly difficult to see television as having a direct and clearly discernible impact on food choices in any particular direction.

Fourth, television's contribution to food choices is made through the specific context of household routines, patterns of organization and relationships. Households displayed different patterns of meal-taking according to whether adults were in paid work or not; whether work was full-time or part-time; according to the age and number of children, and the degree of involvement in leisure activities inside and outside the home.

Conclusion

Warde (1997) has suggested recently that discourse about food in popular culture contributes to the anxieties of the modern age by representing the contradictory social pressures that operate on food choice. 'The structural anxieties of our age,' he writes, 'are made manifest in discourse about food.' (1997: 56). There is little in the evidence collected in the present study to suggest that television's contribution can be viewed comfortably in these terms. While it is certainly a source of contradictory images, those images are not consumed in an atmosphere of anxiety, nor do they appear to contribute to one. Television's contribution, on the contrary, is best understood in the way it offers a kind of *repertoire* of different discourses, different meal types, eating patterns, foods, ideas and prescriptions about food use which help to give shape to the patterns of food consumption in the home. The different discourses will have different meanings and values for different household or family types, different social classes, and different household members, and will circulate and contribute in differing degrees depending on role and status differentiation in the home, and on personal tastes and preferences. This, I suggest, is the basis of a theory of television as *resource*, preferable to a theory of 'effects' or 'influences' because it acknowledges an active engagement with television content and places this in a context of choice and decision-making which is subject to a number of other mediating factors, but preferable also to a theory of consumption such as Warde's which sees popular cultural forms as sources of anxiety-provoking, contradictory appeals to which consumers are easy prey.

We know from other research on food and families that food use and food choice are key elements in defining family relationships (DeVault, 1991). In some circumstances food consumption in the form of the family meal serves to maintain the family (physically and socially) – in a sense, to *produce* it by helping to cement the relationships within it. In other words, in some circumstances families come to maintain their identity *as families* by eating together. The present study shows that television's contribution is made through the specific context of family structures and family relationships. This contribution is significant – television may be dominant as a source of food discourse in some households – but there is a good deal of evidence to show that whatever the magnitude of its contribution, television's message is highly mediated and filtered by household and family circumstances. The culture of the home mediates and filters ideas and knowledge about food. Television in turn contributes to this culture in specific ways. The research reported here has begun to show how this works, by showing how, like the research on family meal-making, television contributes to the *social production* of the family. Further research is now underway to explore this in detail, but from the evidence currently available it seems that audiences can and do frequently find the support for their choices in the content they see, whether they are 'healthy' or 'unhealthy'. It may be helpful then to think of television's role as a supplier of different explanatory and supporting frameworks accounting for and offering possible food choices. Television can supply *post hoc* justifications for some unhealthy choices, and recommendations for some healthy choices. If, as I am suggesting, the recurring themes appearing in television content reproduce the symbolic context in which people make food choices, then by supplying frameworks of explanation or models of practice they may at the same time help to resolve the contradictions that those choices create between the healthy (but not always appealing or stimulating) and the unhealthy (but tasty and satisfying).

Finally, however, it is important to remember that even if people find meanings in television content which help to reduce their confusion about food choices, decisions about food have a material as a well as a symbolic dimension. In other words, food choices are likely to be influenced by taste preferences, economics, and practicalities such as convenience or ease of preparation. Whatever understandings viewers derive from television's portrayal of food and eating, they are always made from positions which are materially, personally and practically determined.

To conclude, my argument in this chapter has been that the influence of television on people's food habits is an instance of the widely-experienced, everyday 'influence of culture' described by Schudson (1989). The research reported here has attempted to examine this process in some detail. The findings indicate that while the level of intensity of television's influence appears to be low, it appears also that it has a high level of significance as a *resource* on which people can draw to find support for their food choices, whether they are defined as 'healthy' or 'unhealthy'. This, then, is an important example of television's influence not only on the formation of public knowledge about food, but also on the practice of food consumption.

Research of this kind is essential if we are to develop a greater understanding of television's role in the home and the implications of the viewing experience for everyday life. While the claim that television's impact on people's everyday lives should be the proper focus for audience research is not new, this study suggests that far more work needs to be done to combine a study of television with a detailed analysis of the culture of the home.

Notes

1. I would like to thank my colleague Simon Leader for his assistance in the research on which this chapter is based; Eamonn Forde and Catherine Sansom

for help with content coding; Russell George for data preparation, and
Samantha Collin for transcribing the household interviews. The research was
supported by the Ministry of Agriculture, Fisheries and Food (Grant No.
AN0913).
2. Lull (1980) in his account of the social uses of television in family settings refers
to television as an 'environmental resource' to explain its significance in giving
structure to various family activities, the emphasis being on the routines of
viewing and non-viewing and the physical presence of the technology in the
home. Here, in a similar way to Jensen (1988) who uses the term in relation to
news comprehension and the idea of the 'viewer citizen', I am referring instead
to the content of television and its messages and meanings.
3. Corner makes a similar point in making his case for text- or genre-specific
studies of 'text–viewer interaction' in a more broadly conceived 'public knowledge project' (Corner 1991: 279), although, as I suggest below, text- or genre-
specific studies, have rather limited value for a study of television and public
knowledge.

References

Bausinger, H. (1984) Media, technology and daily life. *Media, Culture and Society*,
6(4), 343–52.
Beck, U. (1992) *Risk Society: Towards a New Modernity*, London: Sage Publications.
Brannen, J., Dodd, K., Oakley, A. and Story, P. (1994) *Young People, Health and
Family Life*, Buckingham: Open University Press.
Certeau, M. de (1984) *The Practice of Everyday Life*, Berkeley, CA: University of
California Press.
Corner, J. (1991) Meaning, genre and context: the problematics of 'public knowl-
edge' in the new audience studies. In Curran, J and Gurevitch, M. (eds) *Mass
Media and Society*, London: Arnold, 267–84.
Corner, J, Richardson, K and Fenton, N. (1990) *Nuclear Reactions: Form and Response
in 'Public Issue' Television*, London: John Libbey.
DeVault, M. (1991) *Feeding the Family: The Social Organisation of Caring as Gendered
Work*, Chicago: University of Chicago Press.
Dickinson, R. (1995) Two cultures, one voice? Problems in broadcaster/health
educator co-operation. *Health Education Research: Theory & Practice*, 10(4), 421–30.
Dickinson, R. (1998) Food in the media. In Bas, J. (ed.) *Perspectives on Food
Advertising in the UK*, London: The Advertising Association.
Fischler, C. (1980) Food habits, social change and the nature/culture dilemma.
Social Science Information, 19(6), 937–53.
Giddens, A. (1991) *Modernity and self-identity*, Cambridge: Polity Press.
Goodman, I. (1983) Television's role in family interactions: a family systems
perspective. *Journal of Family Issues*, 4(2), 405–24.
Gray, A. (1987) Behind closed doors: women and video. In Baehr, H. and Dyer, G.
(eds) *Boxed In: Women on and in Television*, London: Tavistock Books, 38–54.
Ilmonen, K. (1990) Food choice in modern society. In Somogyi, J. C. and Koskinen,
E. H. (eds) *Nutritional Adaptation to New Life-styles. Biblioteca Nutritio et Dieta*, 45,
30–51.
James, A. (1996) Cooking the books: global or local identities in contemporary
British food cultures? In Howes, D. (ed.) *Cross Cultural Consumption: Global
Markets, Local Realities*, London: Routledge, 77–92.
Jensen, K. B. (1988) News as social resource: a qualitative empirical study of the
reception of Danish television news. *European Journal of Communication*, 3,
275–301.

Kaufman, L. (1980) Prime time nutrition. *Journal of Communication*, **30**(3), 37–46.

Livingstone, S. (1996) On the continuing problem of media effects. In Curran, J. and Gurevitch, M. (eds) *Mass Media and Society*, London: Arnold (second edition) 305–24.

Lull, J. (1980) Family communication patterns and the social uses of television. *Communication Research*, **7**(3), 319–34.

Lull, J. (1990) *Inside Family Viewing*, London: Routledge.

Moores, S. (1997) Broadcasting and its audiences. In MacKay, H. (ed.) *Consumption and Everyday Life*, London: Sage Publications

Morley, D. (1986) *Family Television: Cultural Power and Domestic Leisure*, London: Comedia.

Narayan, U. 1995: Eating cultures: incorporation, identity and Indian food. *Social Identities* **1**(1), 63–86.

Philo, G. (1990) *Seeing and Believing: The Influence of Television*, London: Routledge.

Radway, J. (1984) *Reading the Romance: Women, Patriarchy and Popular Literature*, Chapel Hill: University of North Carolina Press.

Schudson, M. (1989) How culture works: Perspectives from media studies on the efficacy of symbols. *Theory and Society*, **18**, 153–80.

Signorielli, N. (1993) *Mass Media Images and Impact on Health*, Westport, CT: Greenwood Press.

Silverstone, R. (1994) *Television and Everyday Life*, London: Routledge.

Silverstone, R. and Hirsch, E. (eds) (1992) *Consuming Technologies: Media and Information in Domestic Spaces*, London: Routledge.

Silverstone, R., Hirsch, E. and Morley, D. (1992) Information and communication technologies and the moral economy of the household. In Silverstone, R. and Hirsch, E. (eds) *Consuming Technologies: Media and Information in Domestic Spaces*, London: Routledge, 15–31.

Story, M. and Faulkner, P. (1990) The prime time diet: a content analysis of eating behavior and food messages in television programme content and commercials. *American Journal of Public Health*, **80**(6), 738–40.

Warde, A. (1997) *Consumption, Food and Taste: Culinary Antinomies and Commodity Culture*, London: Sage Publications.

Young, B. and Hetherington, M. (1996) The literature on advertising and children's food choice. *Nutrition and Food Science*, **99**(5), 15–19.

22

Cultural differences in the retelling
of television fiction

Tamar Liebes

From *Critical Studies in Mass Communication*, 5(4) 1988, Annandale, VA: Speech Communication Association, pp. 277–92.

[...] If understanding is in fact a process of negotiation between the text and the viewer, each anchored in a different culture, then retellings ought to reveal the negotiation process at work. And if the model of negotiation is correct, equal attention should be paid to what viewers bring to the program, not only how they use it or what they get from it. In this article, therefore, I examine how viewers apply their own narrative forms and their own explanatory schemes to their 'editings' of the story.

This study assembled 54 groups of five to six members in Israel and the United States to view and discuss an episode of *Dallas*. As a first question, the discussion leader asked the group, collectively, 'How would you retell the episode you just saw to somebody who has not seen it?' We chose *Dallas* because it was the most popular program in the world at the time and because, contrary to common belief, its meaning is not self-evident from the action; quite the contrary, it is not understandable without its words, and in some ways (kinship structure and the several strands of interwoven subplots) it is quite complex.

Groups were chosen from four widely different subcultures in Israel (Arabs, Moroccan Jews, new immigrants from Russia, second-generation Israelis living in a kibbutz) and from second-generation Americans in Los Angeles. Approximately 10 groups were assembled within each cultural community, each group consisting of three couples of like ethnicity. Age, education, and regular viewing of the program were essentially homogeneous for all participants.[1] Group members were recruited by asking a host couple to invite two more couples to meet in the living room of the host family. The hosts were recruited informally by a field supervisor and ethnic interviewers from within known ethnic neighbourhoods and suburban communities around Jerusalem and Los Angeles. Obviously, we cannot make a claim of formal randomness or representativeness, but, on the other hand, we have no reason to suspect any systematic bias. Because the hosts typically invited others from among their circle of family, friends, and neighbors, these others were demographically alike for reasons of relatedness and propinquity.[2]

By viewing the episode off the air and in a home, we attempted to simulate the normal viewing situation as much as possible, since we had established from the questionnaire completed by each participant that the program is both viewed and later discussed with others. All groups viewed one of four consecutive episodes of *Dallas* and participated afterward in a one-hour guided discussion (Kaboolian and Gamson, 1983); Morgan and Spanish, 1984): the first half consisted of relatively open questions and the second half of more closed questions.

The ethnic communities which we chose are thought to differ widely, both in the popular image and in the social science literature (Peres, 1987), by virtue of mother tongue, media literacy, socio-historical experience, and location in the social structure. While we did not formulate specific hypotheses concerning the differences that might be expected among the groups, we were aware of the differences between the foreign groups and the native Americans for whom the program was originally intended, between the Eastern groups (Arabs, Moroccan Jews) and the Western ones (second-generation Americans and Israelis, Russians), between those socialized in more or less collectivistic ideologies (from which Russian Jews, of course, demur), and between less and more peripheral groups (Arabs in Israel and Russian newcomers vs. the others). All of these overlapping identities might have bearing, we thought, on differences in decoding and retelling. […]

This article is based on the replies of each of the 54 groups to the opening question of the questionnaire, which asks group members to retell the episode they have just seen. The unit of coding is the whole of the collective retellings (some two to five pages of typescript). […]

Our retellings

Formally speaking, we proceeded as follows: one of us read through a subsample of discussions of an episode 'The Sweet Smell of Revenge'. Each of the ethnic groups was represented in the sample. On the basis of this reading, and with Barthes' classifactory scheme (1977) in mind, three types of retellings seemed to apply, each with its own idiosyncratic form and content. We call them 'linear', 'segmented', and 'thematic', where the linear form describes a sequential story line, the segmented form dwells on the characters, and the thematic form focuses on messages, virtually ignoring events and characters. Our linear mode corresponds to Barthes' 'distributive functions' (1977), which, like Propp's functions (1968), are the units of meaning that advance the story. Barthes' 'indexical functions', which operate at the level of characters, attributes, and the general atmosphere of the story, are similar to our segmented mode. However, whereas his emphasis is primarily on contribution to the story, ours is more psychological in emphasis, even if there is a straying away from the narrative. Our thematic retellings correspond to Barthes' 'paradigmatic' level.[3]

Using these three rough categories, a second reader then ranked the three narrative forms according to the degree of their applicability to each of the 54 discussions in our corpus.[4] This coding was done 'blind', in that the reader did not know the ethnic identity of the group (though the reader could perhaps guess) and, more important, the reader did not know the research hypotheses connecting these forms of retelling to ethnic differences.

At the same time, we went back to the script and videotape of the first of the episodes in order to retell the story for ourselves, using each of the three forms. We wanted to see how much the story lends itself to each form, or, stated otherwise, how much and what kind of 'editing' needs to be done to transform the story-as-shown to the three types of story-as-retold.

Our analysis reveals that there are two main plots which run parallel and are interwoven over the four acts and some 30 scenes of the episode. The two stories deal with the two brothers (J.R. and Bobby), each of whom is trying to 'produce' an heir ahead of the other: one by means of regaining a child who may or may not be his own, the other by means of adoption.[5] Their wives are punished for their efforts to act independently (Sue Ellen for leaving with the child and Pam for attempting suicide) and end up more dependent on their men than before (Swanson, 1982). In turn, both brothers move from acting, and failing, according to the rules, to illegal actions: the one from the law court to kidnapping, the other from legal adoption to illegal purchase. Both brothers act to 'save' their wives from themselves, that is, to rescue them from individualism and emotion and restore them to family and obligation, again revealing similarity between the 'good' and the 'bad' brother.[6] In addition, some five subsidiary plots are sprinkled over the 30-odd scenes of one- or two-minute duration.[7] Each scene typically consists of two people, usually a man and a woman, exchanging intimacies that are in themselves often more compelling than the plot line they serve, inasmuch as the plot is alternately predictable or reversible but always unending (Thorburn, 1987) [...]

Viewer retellings

I am now in a position to ask of the viewers we studied (1) whether there is a correlation between cultural background and the choice among the forms of retelling, (2) how closely these forms of retelling correspond to our own textual analysis,[8] and (3) what can be inferred from the choice of form about the chooser's perception of the relationship of the program to real life.

The coding of the 54 discussions in terms of the three forms of retelling reveals correlation between ethnicity and narrative form. The Arab and Moroccan groups specialized in linear retellings; in two-thirds of the groups from these communities, linear retellings were ranked first among the three forms of retelling. On the other hand, the kibbutz and American groups offered segmented retellings, emphasizing not the sequence of events but the expression of personalities over and above changing situations. For their part, the Russians put aside the story, in both linear and segmented forms, in favor of a thematic (or paradigmatic) retelling that typically concerned the moral or the message.

Thus, there is confirmation for the suggestion that readings of *Dallas* fit the three forms of retelling and that each form characterizes one or another of the ethnic groups. This does not mean, however, that the three forms, as told, correspond to our own attempt to provide an optimal fit between the story and each of the forms. Instead of the complex fittings, which seem correct to us, the discussions tend toward much simpler retellings with selective perception playing an important part. Whereas we perceive two linear strands moving parallel throughout the story, the linear retellings of Arabs and Moroccans tend to focus on only one of the two. They choose to note not Pam's suicide attempt but J.R.'s kidnapping operation, perhaps because the latter is a more obvious story of action. The story is retold in great detail, often invoking direct quotations for the high melodramatic moments:

> Interviewer: First of all, I would like to ask you to retell the story of the episode you have just seen as if you were telling it to a friend who has missed it today.
> William: J. R. is trying to get Sue Ellen and the child back home. So he goes off to try to get a monopoly of 25,000 barrels of oil, or maybe it is 50,000, I don't remember the exact number.
> Hyam: Yes, it was 25,000 barrels.
> George: To get his son back. He's trying to get a monopoly on the oil wells.
> Marinetti: Yes, he told him . . .
> George: So he takes [control of] all the oil in order to empty all of the refineries.
> William: It's in order to provoke [them] and organize an exchange. And he [Farlow?] said to him, 'Others, bigger than you, weren't able to break me.' After J.R.'s father was in South America on business, he [J.R.] talked to him and told him 'Come back'.
> Hyam: Jack phones J.R. and said, 'Your wife and the child will be . . .'
> William: J.R. called his father and said to him, 'When you come home next week, Sue Ellen and the child will be back home.'
>
> (Arab group #46)

Just as the Arabs and Moroccans select between the possible linear retellings, so the American and kibbutz groups select among the characters for their segmented retellings. It is no wonder that the most popular choice for this kind of character-based reporting is Pam, whose story is presented as possessing deep psychological roots. Indeed, these segmented retellers are often aware that their focus on character abstracted from the large context of the story is the result of their own psychological interests or emotional involvement.

> Sandy: The main thing I would tell them would be about [laugh]. . . . I'm trying to think of a character in the picture, Victoria Principal.
> Greg: Pam.
> Others: Pam.
> Sandy: That she was, you know, upset about a lot of things inside herself and that she wanted to kill herself and that her husband was trying to talk her into committing herself to the hospital to help her. That is the main thing that got to me in this episode because, emotionally, that's what got to me, that she would want to kill herself. And that is the strongest point in this episode.
>
> (American group #3)

Within the segmented readings, there is another retelling which speaks not of a particular character but about the interaction between two characters, who are often connected in some primordial way. It may be the relationship between J.R. and Sue Ellen, Bobby and Pam, Miss Ellie and J.R., and so on. For example, in retelling the story, a kibbutz group proceeds as follows:

> Hillel: There was Lucy and her husband with their problems, and there was Bobby and Pam and their crisis, and J.R. and his son.
> Orly: There was a crisis in the marriage of Bobby and Pam. Until now, they were the ideal couple, and suddenly they have these problems.
> Igal: Sue Ellen is beginning to get discouraged by her what's-his-name, and with Pam and Bobby it simply exploded. They were always the ideal couple. They knew between them that it wasn't so. But at least externally. . . . But that's it. It just exploded. You can't bluff the whole way.
>
> (Kibbutz group #85)

But neither of these forms coincides fully with the sorts of problems that may be said to constitute a fully segmented reading. In particular, the viewers' segmented retellings ignore nuances and changes that writers ascribe to the characters, apparently in order to make identification easier. This is not a very 'serious' misreading, of course. More serious, perhaps, is the extreme selectivity in focusing on one or two evocative characters at the expense of all the others who make up the story. The fuller versions of the segmented retellings, those which account for most of the characters, probably represent the best fit between the story as presented and the story as retold. The following is an example of a relatively full retelling in the segmented form:

> Don: You have Pam trying to commit suicide because of her mother. You had J.R. being his typical self, scheming. . . .
> Beverly: Cliff Barnes, his sister, his stepsister, whatever, I think was a little upset that the mother gave him the business or gave the running of the business.
> Don: Then you have the little gal and her husband split. What's her name? Oh, Charlene Tilton and her husband split up – Lucy, yeah, and him being offered a job that he really doesn't want.
> Linda: Then Bobby got a picture of what's-her-name's baby, and he's got hope again.
> Don: Kristen's baby. Kristen.
> Beverly: Which is really his brother's.
> Don: The gentleman called on the phone and said he wanted money for more information regarding the baby.
>
> (American group #7)

I wish to suggest at this point that there appears to be a correlation not only between ethnicity and forms of retelling but that this may be equally true of sex differences; indeed, it is possible that the ethnic differences themselves may be explained in the linear retellings, on the one hand, and in the segmented retellings, on the other. Thus, the Arab women are very reticent to enter the conversation; they appear to enter it when they have something 'expert' to add. It is certainly true that the opening of the discussion is dominated by men. By contrast, the American and the kibbutz groups, who specialize in segmented retellings, are egalitarian; it may be that kibbutz women speak even more than the men although this has not been studied formally. [...]

Unlike the *ad hoc* character of the segmented retellings, the linear and, even more, the thematic or paradigmatic retellings impose an organizing principle on the story as a whole that attempts to put the pieces together in a kind of cognitive map. In the case of the paradigmatic, note the way a general principle is applied deductively to construct a story. Here, for example, is the beginning of a discussion in a Russian group:

> Misha: The program reflects the reality in America.
> Interviewer: Let's get back to the last episode: What is it about?
> Sima: The financial problem plays an important role; J.R. wants to revenge himself using his economic background. Through the oil well. In this particular episode, the financial problem plays an important role.
> Interviewer: Rosa, did you want to add something?
> Rosa: That's it?
> Interviewer: That's what?
> Rosa: That the oil is the main theme.
> Interviewer: Can you go back to the story?
> Rosa: The oil is the main problem in the program.
>
> (Russian group #63)

The exchange reveals three unsuccessful attempts of the interviewer to get beyond the thematic level and into the details of the story. This refusal to get into details reflects not only a reluctance on the part of the Russians to show involvement in a television program, which is defined as trivial, but is also a statement of concern over the threat of a program like *Dallas* as capitalist propaganda. This can be seen repeatedly in numerous examples from the Russian groups, where the program is retold paradigmatically in terms of a message. Moreover, the message is not considered innocent but one that serves the hegemonic interests of the producers or of American society. The Russians, it should be recalled, are the only ones who respond in this way to the request to retell the episode.[9] Consider the following examples from three different Russian groups:

> Hona: I started to ask myself what is the secret of the popularity of the series. Why does it attract the middle class to such an extent? It is comforting for them to know that the millionaires are more miserable than themselves. Well, a poor millionaire is beautiful. Deep down, everyone would very much want a millionaire to be miserable, and, on the other hand, they themselves would like to be millionaires. In the program, they see millionaires as if they really were that way.
>
> (Russian group #62)

> Hanna: The program praises the American way of life. It shows the America of the rich, and, at the same time, it shows the American middle-class viewer that our country is beautiful and rich. We have everything, and those rich people of course, have their problems.
>
> (Russian group #67)

> Misha: The progam is propaganda for the American way of life. They show American characters. The progam deals with the dilemma of life in America.

It is actually advertising – or, more accurately, propaganda – for the American way of life. They show the average person, in an interesting way, the ideal he should be striving towards.

(Russian group #63)

Thus, it may be said that the Russians are not interested in the paradigm *per se* but, beyond it, in the relationship among the message, the motives of encoders, and themselves as audience. Perceived in this context, the message far overshadows the details of the narrative in its importance because it is perceived as a social and political strategy, with an ulterior and destructive aim. Like the critical theorists, the Russians who read the story paradigmatically focus on the macro level, and their analysis, therefore, is on a different level than the analysis of any episode. It is at a political level; their message, in fact, corresponds to one of the two conflicting messages that Thomas and Callahan (1982) attribute to television's high-class family drama: the message of solace for those who are not invited to move to the top.

Characteristics of the forms

Each of the three patterns of retelling implies an orientation to time and different degrees of openness or inevitability. Whereas linear and thematic retellings are deterministic and closed, the segmented retellings are more open. Linear retellings are closed because they relate to a story that has mostly happened in the past, even if it is not altogether concluded, and thematic retellings are closed because they treat the continuing story as timeless repetitions of the same narrative principle. Thus, the Arabs and Moroccans, in their linear retellings, tend to tell an almost completed sequence which is presented as inevitable: J.R. has lost his baby, but he is getting him back, and the family is going to be reunited in the ancestral estate .[…]

The paradigmatic retellings, for their part, treat the series, on the whole, as a constant and monolithic message, regarding any individual episode as a manifestation of the ruling principle. Any variation has to be dictated by this principle.

Put differently, it can be argued that the linear and paradigmatic forms employ inductive and deductive reasoning to attribute inevitability, or closedness, to the story.Thus, the paradigmatic story is closed because it is thought to derive from an ideological formula which is applied by the producers to the various subplots and episodes. The linear stories proceed inductively, not from a principle but from the presumed reality of the characters, […]

It is an obvious step to the conclusion that the linear retelling, anchored, as it is, in the referential, correlates with a 'hegemonic' reading in which the reality of the story is unquestioned and its message is presumably unchallenged. The paradigmatic retelling, on the other hand, is more likely to accompany an 'oppositional' reading (Hall, 1980; Morley, 1980), whereby critical awareness of an overall message surely sounds an alarm that the message may be manipulative. […]

Unlike the linear and paradigmatic forms, the segmented retellings are more open or future oriented. Armed with the knowledge of the characters and their motivations, the segmented retellings treat the story prospectively, using what has already happened to speculate on possible continuations. Thus, rather than looking for deterministic principles in the plot, either in the lives of the characters or the ideology of the producers, the Americans and kibbutzniks (who specialize in segmented retellings) search creatively for new complications which might emerge. [...]

The three forms of retellings also can be considered in terms of the epistemological perspectives with which they are associated. The linear retellings explain the story in sociological terms; the segmented retellings tend toward a psychological or psychoanalytic explanation; and the paradigmatic patterns are mostly ideological. These epistemological perspectives help to explain why the different forms of retelling choose to focus on different subplots or characters and prefer particular forms of labeling the characters. Thus, the linear stories are told from the perspective of kinship, where the characters are motivated by social and normative consideration having to do with the hierarchical order within the family and the continuity of the dynasty. [...]

Conclusion

In order to analyze how popular American family drama is perceived in other cultures, we asked viewers, organized into intimate focus groups, to retell an episode of *Dallas*. The viewer retellings are fitted into the three levels of narrative structure deriving from Barthes' 'actions', 'characters', and 'themes', which take forms that we call 'linear', 'segmented', and 'paradigmatic', respectively. More generally, these types of retelling invoke 'sociological', 'psychological', and 'ideological' perspectives.

The two more traditional groups, Arabs and Moroccan Jews, prefer linearity. They select the action-oriented subplot for attention, defining the hero's goals and adventures in trying to achieve them. They tell the story in 'closed' form, as if it were an inevitable progression, and the characters they describe are rigidly stereotyped; indeed, they are often referred to by family role rather than by name. The perspective is sociological: that is, the story is of the recognized reality of extended family, in an ancestral house (Lévi-Strauss, 1983), holding itself together in the face of contests of power, both within and without. The cultural proximity of these groups to the *Dallas* story may seem surprising in view of the ostensible modernity of *Dallas*. But there is considerable support for the argument that *Dallas* is, in fact, an old-fashioned family saga (Herzog-Massing, 1986; Swanson, 1982), less like the stripped-down mobile nuclear family of the West and more like the premodern clan in which economic, political, and religious functions still inhere and the division of labor by age and sex is still prescribed. A study of the reception of *Dallas* in Algeria (Stolz, 1983) gives strong support to this argument. The concern of these two ethnic groups with power and relative position in family and society may be related to their social position in Israel: the one a politically suspect minority and the other an ethnic minority with experience of status deprivation.

The Russians speak of the episode in themes or messages. They ignore the story in favor of exposing the overall principle which is repeated relentlessly and which, in their opinion, has a manipulative intent. Like the Arabs and Moroccans, their story is closed and deterministic, but the determining force is ideological rather than referential. Unlike the Arabs and Moroccans, they perceive the story as being a false picture of reality. They are also aware that their illustrations from the story are chosen, self-consciously, to highlight the potential persuasive power of the program. Their interest is in the story as a product of hegemonic control. This suspiciousness on the part of the Russians seems overdetermined; it is almost too easy to explain. Dmitri Segal (personal communication, summer 1985) suggests that the Russians, especially Russian Jews, learn early to scan their environment for signs of where true power is hidden: they learn to read between the lines (Inkeles, 1950). Their literary training is another determining factor: unlike the Arabs or the Moroccans, Russians are steeped in a tradition of literary criticism which they apply relentlessly and with flaunted superiority to the texts and images they encounter in their new environment. What is more, these are refugees who are well trained in applying ideological criticism to other people's ideologies as well as their own. As we noted in connection with their suspiciousness of the interview situation, they are also continually alert to sources of potential danger.

If the Russians invoke ideological theory, Americans and kibbutzniks tell the story psychoanalytically. They are not concerned with the linearity of the narrative but with analyzing the problems of characters intrapersonally and interpersonally. Their retellings are 'open', future oriented, and take account of the never-ending genre of the soap opera. One version of these psychological retelling relates to the business constraints and interpersonal problems on the level of actors and producers. In these keyings, the drama behind the scenes appears to be the real story of *Dallas*. Segmented retellings label the characters in terms of their on-screen or off-screen personae. Their illustrations from the story are chosen in terms of emotional effect, rather then the cognitive effects of the thematic retellings. These comparatively secure, second-generation viewers are fascinated by psychology and group dynamics and can afford the luxury of interest in the individual (i.e., in themselves). They have no illusions about the reality of the story; they allow themselves to dive into the psyches of the characters, oblivious to those aspects of the ideology, the morality, and aesthetics of the program that occupy others. Their definition of both the viewing and the retelling as liminal (Turner, 1985) permits a playful subjunctivity in their negotiations with the program, with fellow viewers, and with the discussion leaders.

Notes

1. The Russians, on the whole, are somewhat better educated, inasmuch as many Russian immigrants in Israel tend to have had some higher education. The Arab groups also have a somewhat higher proportion of persons with some university training.

2. We did occasionally request the hosts to limit invitations to acquaintances of like age, education, and ethnicity, and in three or four cases we disqualified discussions whose membership was too disparate. [...]
3. Barthes (1977) distinguishes between the syntagmatic and the paradigmatic levels in the structure of narrative. The syntagm consists of narrative functions, defined as the smallest units of meaning out of which the story is constructed. There are two types of functions the 'distributive' ones, which are functions in Propp's sense (1968), corresponding to our linear model, and the indexical ones, which operate at the level of characters' attributes and the general atmosphere of the story. These indexes of personality and atmosphere make their appearance repeatedly, in the segments of parallel and intersected subplots, which describe the segmented model out of which *Dallas* is constructed.
4. We wish to thank Nahum Gelber for his coding.
5. We have tried to compare these themes with Biblical ones (Liebes and Katz, 1988).
6. This fits Gerbner and his colleagues' description (1979) of the diminishing difference between heroes and villains in television fiction. The good and the bad are not different in their aims or in the methods they use. The criterion, rather, is the degree of efficiency in achieving their aims. Thus, the evil J.R. can qualify as a hero more than the chaste Bobby.
7. These plots on the side burners of the episode include crises in the marriage of other Ewing couples (that of Mitch and Lucy and that of Ray and Donna) and mounting tension in the competing dynasties (between Cliff and his mother and between Mitch and his sister Afton).
8. I here make the assumption that the other three episodes of Dallas seen by our discussion groups are constructed along the same principles as the episode that we analyzed in detail. This must be true almost by definition (i.e., the linear story must have at least the J.R. and Bobby strands; the segmented discussion must be distorted by the writers' intentional inconsistencies of character portrayal; and, similarly, the thematic or paradigmatic must be constant across episodes). I therefore move directly to the total of all retellings of the four episodes, rather than treating each one separately.
9. The Russians' inclination to get to the message of the program can also be seen in an analysis of statements which deal explicitly with the message or 'moral' of the progam (i.e., 'What the progam/the producers/the writers want to tell us is . . .'). In this analysis, the Russians are the only ones who point to messages when asked to retell the story. [...]

References

Barthes, R. (1977) Introduction to the structural analysis of the narrative. In *Image, Music, Text*, London: Hill & Wang, 79–124.

Gerbner, G., Gross, J., Signorielli, N., Morgan, M. and Jackson-Beeck, M. (1979) The demonstration of power: Violence profile No. 10. *Journal of Communication*, 29(3), 177–96.

Hall, S. (1980) Encoding/decoding. In Hall, S., Hobson, D., Lowe, A. and Willis, P. (eds) *Culture, Media, Language: Working Papers in Cultural Studies, 1972–79*, London: Hutchinson, 128–38.

Herzog-Massing, J. (1986) Decoding 'Dallas'. *Society*, 24(1), 74–7.

Inkeles, A. (1950) *Public opinion in Soviet Russia*. Cambridge, MA: Harvard University Press.

Kaboolian, F. and Gamson, W. (1983, May) New strategies for the use of focus groups for social science and survey research. Paper presented at an annual meeting of the American Association for Public Opinion Research, Buck Hill Falls, PA.

Lévi-Strauss, C. (1983) Histoire et ethnologie [History and ethnology], *Annales*, **18**, 1217–31.

Liebes, T. and Katz, E. (1988) *Dallas* and Genesis: Primordiality and seriality in popular culture. In J. Carey (ed.) *Media, Myths, and Narratives*, Newbury Park, CA: Sage , 113–35.

Mander, M. (1983) *Dallas:* The methodology of crime and the moral occult. *Journal of Popular Culture*, 17, 44–51.

Morgan, D. L. and Spanish, M. T. (1984) Focus groups: A new tool for qualitative research. *Qualitative Sociology*, **7**, 253–70.

Morley, D. (1980) *The 'Nationwide' Audience*. London: British Film Institute.

Newcomb, H. (1987) Texas: A giant state of mind. In Newcomb, H. (ed.) *Television: The Critical View*, New York: Oxford University Press, 221–8.

Peres, Y. (1987) Etsem el atsma bitsrima [The dissonant reunion of the dry bones]. *Politika*, **14/15**, 20–3.

Propp, V. (1968) *Morphology of a Folk Tale*, Austin: University of Texas Press.

Stolz, J. (1983) Les Algériens regardent *Dallas* [Algerians view Dallas]. In *Les nouvelles chaines*, Paris: University of France Press, 223–43.

Swanson, G. (1982) *Dallas. Framework*, **14**, 32–5; **15**, 81–5.

Thomas, S. and Callahan, B. (1982) Allocating happiness: TV families and social class. *Journal of Communication*, **32** (3), 184–90.

Thorburn, D. (1987) Television melodrama. In Newcomb, H. (ed.) *Television: The Critical View*, New York: Oxford University Press, 628–44.

Turner, V. (1985) Liminality, kabbalah, and the media. *Religion*, **15**, 201–3.

23

Documentary meanings and interpretive contexts: observations on Indian 'repertoires'

Ramaswami Harindranath

My main concern in this chapter is to elaborate on a particular aspect of a larger project examining the interpretation of environmental documentaries by audiences in India and Britain, the empirical part of which was designed to illustrate/substantiate theoretical interventions aiming to rectify a perceived lacuna in the attempts in communication research to make a connection between the socially culturally situated audiences and their interpretive practices.[1] In this chapter, I isolate for closer inspection a specific strand from the web of data, with the intention of demonstrating both the presence of different interpretive repertoires in India, as well as the role of higher education as a relevant factor in the creation of these repertoires.[2] This chapter examines the possible links between cultural contexts and the reception of documentaries, and interrogates *en route* the idea of culture as context. What is postulated here is a conceptualization of context based on phenomenological hermeneutics, which it is argued, accommodates the complexity and diversity of collectivities within 'national cultures'.

Documentary interpretations

The empirical part of the study involved four films, two by an Indian and the others by Western film-makers, of which I showed each respondent two films. The subject matter of these films was broadly environmental, but dealt with different topics – global warming, the effects of war on children in Angola and Mozambique, child labour in India, and the impact of development on tribal communities in India. Both in India and in Britain the respondents were selected from three communities within a university setting: teachers, students (both undergraduate and postgraduate), and non-academics (technicians, lab assistants, administrative staff).[3] Initially my intention was to compare interpretation of the films by audiences from one national culture (Indian) with those of another (British), and not between various sections within the same national culture. This intention was based on the assumption that firstly, different cultural contexts generated different interpretive practices, and secondly, that the national cultures of India and Britain were sufficiently distinct as to engender different interpretations.

One of the significant outcomes of this study, which is of particular relevance to this chapter, is that there was little systematic difference in interpretation of the films *across cultures* to form a recognizable pattern. The respondents, apart from a particular group, generally utilized framings and interpretive procedures in a manner which was far from uniform or sustained. Many of them moved freely between 'transparent' and 'mediated' frames, and between 'critical' and 'referential' readings.[4] Identifying statements for easy positioning of responses therefore would be a spurious exercise. While it is possible to locate statements with which to mark off a particular respondent's account as either 'critical' or 'transparent', as in Liebes and Katz (1990), such a strategy would eliminate the possibility of taking the responses in their entirety. Moreover, it would belie the complexity of the respondents' accounts, substituting instead an easily categorizable set of frameworks which could provide a totally false impression of the responses.

The motif that emerges clearly from the data – the one this chapter is concerned with – is at once simple and unsurprising as well as complex and less straightforward. On the simplest level, it is hardly surprising, given the characteristics of the documentary text, especially its rhetorical strategies and its logic of information, that the films posed few significant problems to the respondents' understanding of them, whatever the 'framings' or interpretive strategies that were mobilized. Given the direct form of address of documentaries, a basic level of comprehension among those with at least a passing knowledge of the English language was more or less guaranteed (see Corner, 1995: 152). Nor is it startling, given the documentary's truth claims and its relatively high position in the hierarchy of truth among moving image genres (Winston, 1978, 1993), that many of the readings utilized a 'transparent' framing, even while some were critical of the argument being proffered in the films. The textual cues inherent in documentary call for a processing of the text different from that of fiction; intrinsic in this difference is the acceptance that documentary representation (metonymic) is different from the fictional (metaphorical). On the other hand, given the implicit assumptions on which were based the categories underpinning the gathering of data – selecting respondents from 'Indian' and 'British' cultures implied an expectation of these categories performing a normative function, generating interpretations significantly different from each other – the results which emerged on analysing the data were unexpected, making any explanation of this 'discrepancy' more complex than a monolithic conception of culture would suggest.

The group which emerges as markedly different from all the others in both cultures in its consistent use of 'transparent-uncritical' framings is the one comprising Indian non-academics, forming an interpretive 'repertoire' which is in itself deeply instructive. Fundamentally, this interpretive community or 'repertoire' undermines the easy, relatively straightforward classification of all Indian viewers as belonging to one 'culture'.

The interpretation of television is linked to the concept of 'the horizon of expectations' (following Gadamer, 1975) in specific ways. Genre recognition is crucial, as is familiarity with the mode of moving image representation in general. An audience's visual and generic expectations combine to give the impression of veridicality to the moving image. In the case of documentary, however, this veridicality is further compounded by its truth claims and its socially accepted position at the top of the hierarchy of truth in cinematic representation. The horizon of expectations generated by the documentary genre therefore, necessarily involves either accepting or rejecting its claims to authenticity and truthful depiction.

Nearly all of those respondents who either accepted the generic claim or were at least ambivalent about it utilized largely transparent frames. There appeared to be a link between those (the Indian non-academics) who concurred most strongly with the idea that documentary as non-fiction depicted 'reality' and their interpretation of the films as representations of profilmic reality. While this might seem an obvious outcome of their horizon of expectation, what is interesting is the difference between this interpretive repertoire and the others who were less certain about documentary authenticity, and whose readings indicated a level of 'critical' framing. What distinguishes the Indian non-academics from the rest of the respondents is their relatively consistent transparent–uncritical reading of all four films.

In other words, the Indian non-academics, unlike the other respondents, accepted all three 'proofs' (Nichols, 1981) contained in the films' rhetoric. In doing so, these viewers acknowledged the authority of documentary, both in general as well as in the case of the particular films. The distance between the modalities of filmic representation and historical reality were, as a consequence, collapsed, making the viewers react to the images as if they were real. On a more semantic level, their acknowledgement of textual authority positioned them in the role of 'the desire to know', which, as Nichols observes, is part of the viewer-documentary contractual arrangement (p. 205). These respondents' uncritical framing accepted the texts as the locus of He-Who-Knows, correspondingly positioning themselves as willing subjects, accepting the films' arguments as reflections of 'that is the way it is'.

Critical frames used by most respondents (from both cultures) themselves were varied in their treatment of the images as veridical. While there were only rare instances of a sustained mediation-critical reading which recognized the films as constructions, and at times projected an authorial intent behind sequences, most critical responses contained a variety of positions on the transparent-mediation continuum: at some points in their responses the viewers appeared to treat the films as depicting reality in an unmediated fashion, and their criticism came in the form of questioning the objectivity of the producer; on other occasions, the same viewers employed a type of syntactic criticism which acknowledged the films as mediated.

The degree of semantic criticism was again, varied. While with most respondents (from both cultures) who adopted a critical frame this amounted to a questioning of the film's argument as possibly partial (thereby doubting its demonstrative proof), indicating a level of transparent framing inherent in their critical frames, a few respondents (especially one Indian postgraduate student) demonstrated a more sustained mediation-critical frame which occasionally moved into a manipulation frame, identifying in the films' argument authorial intentions which they considered politically unacceptable. While these readings did not form a sufficiently systematic pattern, their presence is itself interesting, since it suggests a horizon of expectation which includes a level of scepticism about documentary representation and its truth claims. In this specific instance, their scepticism was manifested in their rejection of the ethical and demonstrative proofs in the films. Witness accounts were estimated as specially incorporated in the text, while others were specially left out, in order to support the film maker's particular ideological leanings.

On the whole, the pattern which does remain posits the Indian non-academics as uncritically accepting the veridicality of the films, acknowledging documentary's logic of information and the didactic intent inscribed in it. Opposed to this position are the other respondents, Indian as well as British, whose readings combined a variety of critical and uncritical, transparent as well as mediation frames.

Theorizing 'context'

In relation to the category of 'context' the data and results of their analysis are instructive in broadly two ways: first, they underline the crucial flaw in the implicit assumption, while dividing the respondents into two mutually exclusive camps ('Indian' and 'British'), that these categories would generate significantly different interpretive procedures; and second, the results from the data which indicate the presence of an interpretive repertoire *within* the 'Indian' category suggests a re-assessment of my initial classification. I would argue, following Gadamerian hermeneutics (Gadamer, 1976), that understanding occurs only within 'tradition' or 'effective history', which proscribes any effort at 'objective' understanding. Interpretations are not made in a social vacuum but, on the contrary, are the *consequences* of socio-cultural contexts of the interpreters. In this formulation, interpretation of texts is an extension of the general understanding which is a fundamental characteristic of human being-in-the-world, ineluctably circumscribed by historicity.[5] The reverse of this argument, is of course, that different interpretive practices are symptomatic of different socio-cultural contexts. By this argument, the Indian non-academics appear to constitute a 'world' separate from other groups from both cultures, while at the same time, the rest of the Indian respondents must co-exist with their British counterparts in the same or at least similar 'world'.

The first of these issues, the unthinking utilization of the classical notion of culture as corresponding with geographical space, amounts to an unconscious acknowledgement of the colonial practice of dividing the world into the West and the Other, a position which is neither politically desirable nor intellectually fertile. Traditionally, anthropology opposed the West to the Other, participating 'in a significant way in the establishment of Western selfhood via its otherness; modern versus traditional, developed versus undeveloped, civilised versus primitive.' (Lash and Friedman, 1992: 27). From this position were drawn power and authority, the anthropologist or ethnographer supplying details of an alien life-style – often inscribed in the 'ethnographic present' tense, law-like and 'objective' which Rosaldo (1993) parodies brilliantly and with telling effect in 'After Objectivism' – to be better governed by the colonial power, while simultaneously supporting its increasingly precarious bulwark of moral authority by positing the Other as primitive, child-like, and pre-modern, needing the guiding hand of 'progress' of the Western industrial civilization. Rosaldo's quintessential pre-1960s anthropologist, 'the Lone Ethnographer' was 'willy-nilly complicit with the imperialist domination of his epoch. [His] mask of innocence (or, as he put it, his "detached impartiality") barely concealed his ideological role in perpetuating the colonial control of "distant" peoples and places.' (Rosaldo, 1993: 30).

Needless to say, my original proposal contained no such intention. As already mentioned, the objective of my case study – the comparison of interpretations of documentaries *across* cultures – was based on the assumption that the culturally different spaces inhabited by audiences in India and Britain would generate diverse interpretations. Yet, my conception of Indianness and Britishness as monolithic amounted to a tacit subscription to the Victorian divide, with its implicit hierarchy in which occidental culture held the privileged position; and in which any 'study' of non-occidental culture implied an unspoken evaluation of it using Western norms.[6] Morley and Silverstone (1991) refer to the need for reflexivity which recent debates concerning ethnographic research call for in order to counter what Edward Said has called 'Orientalization': 'the process of imaginative geography which produces a fictionalised Other as the exotic object of knowledge' (Morley and Silverstone, 1991: 161). The questionable politics intrinsic in the data collected from an assumed 'value-neutral' position is suspect, since such a position overlooks the important fact that these data are the result of particular discursive practices generating culturally informed knowledge. To pretend otherwise is to be either disingenuous, or naïvely blind to the politics inherent in the researcher's position. Said's argument linking knowledge to power is pertinent in this context. The seemingly 'neutral' observations of the ethnographer, riding on objectivist conceptions of social science, posits a generalized Orient as a homogeneous entity. 'Under such descriptions, the Orient appears to be both a benchmark against which to measure Western European "progress" and an inert terrain on which to impose imperialist schemes of "development".' (Rosaldo, 1993: 42). The notion of progress and development are tied in with the project of modernity, whose juggernaut-like inevitability (as Giddens, 1990, conceives it) is likewise connected to debates concerning globalization. Such debates fall outside the scope of this chapter, but it is worth noting that my initial conception of 'Indian' and 'British' as hermetically sealed, independent cultures is questionable on these grounds.

More importantly (and perhaps from a less overtly political posture), the conception of cultures, especially national cultures, as discrete compartments is becoming increasingly rated as invalid. In the context of this study this is crucial, since in dividing the respondents thus, and expecting each 'culture' to then be represented in the form of different interpretive repertoires, I was guilty of a degree of determinism inherent in, for example, Morley's (1980) conception of the audience. Geographical space does not necessarily correspond to cultural space, as if such spaces existed within confining, protective boundaries which excluded any 'outside' influence. Moreover, to assume a nation to possess a monolithic culture, the inhabitants of which exhibited a certain measure of uniformity in their behaviour is both grossly simplistic and patently erroneous. Therefore, the 'discrepancies' which the data produced were more or less inevitable given the simplicity of the framework I had used to categorize the audiences. To conceive of a culture, national or otherwise, to be a determining factor in individual behaviour presupposes a causal link between conventional structural elements and behaviour which this study has been arguing against. The notion of culture as elaborated here embodies an attempt at formulating it as the site *shaping* individual behaviour (including media use and interpretation), while avoiding the reductionist idea of culture or any other social variable *controlling* such behaviour.

This raises two significant issues: one, a thematic consideration with regard to cultural differences across geographical space on a broad scale, and the other concerning the data generated in my case study, particularly the decodings of the Indian non-academics. The first concern involves a balancing act: denying the presence of different cultures is difficult, and yet conceiving this difference as based on static, timeless, and homogeneous cultures is clearly wrong. In some ways, this is linked to the conception of what culture is – culture as a system of values, tradition, or a way of life is at once dynamic and evolving as well as linked with 'traditional' beliefs, that is, the conception that national culture is inherently dynamic. Using such broad brush strokes it is possible to describe the Japanese notion of honour, the Indian belief in fate and destiny, or oppose American bonhomie to British reserve, and so on, as characteristic features of these cultures, thereby emphasizing the difference between them on a *general* level. The forces of modernity and the realities of international trade and politics have produced a thin veneer of uniformity across twentieth-century international life, bringing disparate cultures closer in time and space in an effort to create one cosmopolitan culture. In a sense these attempts at minimizing pluralism lie at the heart of debates concerning normative international regulations based on an allegedly universal moral discourse, whose origins in Western (Enlightenment) thought has been a source of disagreement and dissent from cultures and nations of the South.[7]

In this context philosophical hermeneutics provides a useful platform from which to overcome the apparent incommensurability of cultures, leading to conversation and agreement. Shapcott's (1994) intriguing analysis linking Gadamer's hermeneutics to the study of 'the place of culture in international society' suggests that in order to arrive at universal principles while recognizing differences in perspective inherent in disparate cultures, 'hermeneutics, with its celebratory attitude to difference, may provide the orientation' (p. 78). Shapcott interprets Gadamer's 'fusion of horizons' as presuming a genuine desire to understand, a desire which overcomes the problem of relativism contained in Gadamer's notion of historicity and tradition.

> It is important to remember that we only know ourselves by contact with the other [...] If cultures, peoples, traditions are not hermetically sealed, if our cultures are, in part, constituted by cultural interaction, then relativism becomes less problematic. Gadamer argues that in such circumstances we must be open to genuine discussion and interpretation to really know each other.
>
> (Shapcott, 1994: 76)

This recognition and accommodation of difference means that moral claims cannot be assumed to be self-evident; they have to be acknowledged as based on certain philosophies, whose legitimacy arises from certain interpretations. What is called for, in other words, is the awareness 'that before we can judge and pontificate, we are obliged to engage in critical dialogue.' (Shapcott, 1994: 82).

This chapter, however, is concerned with issues on a more micro-sociological level, where the primary sphere of interest lies with the data generated. As we saw earlier, the interpretive strategies employed by the Indian non-academics stand out as anomalies precisely because the framework used to create audience categories was based on the classic notion of culture. In this context, it is useful to recast the idea of culture within phenomenological sociology, and especially Schutz's (1964, 1972, 1973) reconception of the life-world: culture in this formulation forms the pregiven, 'handed-down' part of an individual's knowledge-at-hand with which he/she engages in daily life. Formulated thus, it does not differ greatly from the normative notion of culture as the determining factor in behaviour. But Schutz's conceptualization of the life-world contains two factors which set it apart from deterministic notions. The first of these is the idea that the individual's stock of knowledge consists of not just passively received elements from his/her existential condition of 'thrown-ness', but also elements of a more experiential sort – an idea which allows the individual to escape the confines of his existential world into other 'worlds'. While the individual's 'paramount reality' remains anchored to that of everyday life, his/her social reality also derives from other 'provinces of meaning' or 'multiple realities' – the second factor which distinguishes this formulation of collectivity from uni-dimensional conceptions. Schutz's idea of multiple realities brings to the individual other socializing agents such as religion, education, and so on, providing a richer, multi-dimensional notion of the life-world. Instead of a deterministic strait-jacket in the form of a unitary sociological variable which the individual is expected to 'inhabit', this posits the individual at the intersection of various possible realms of 'reality', which while still socially contextualized, are not unitary or normative.[8] The argument proposed by hermeneutics identifies understanding not as the methodological reconstitution of the author's intentions, nor an empathic unity with the author's mind, but as, following Gadamer, inevitably and insurmountably linked to the interpreter's 'horizon' or socio-cultural context.

Combining the insights of Schutz and Gadamer therefore, it follows that understanding and interpretation, while an intrinsic part of everyday life, ensues from the individual's life-world.

Education, hybridity, and 'third' culture

To return to the data, the responses of the Indian group of respondents are indicative of first, the role of education in the formation of a particular life-world, and second, the presence of a 'third', hybrid culture whose members retain their Indian identities within some aspects of their life-worlds which simultaneously possess 'modern' or Westernized attributes in others. Let me examine these two issues one by one.

At the end of their study examining the different interpretations of *Dallas* by different ethnic groups, Liebes and Katz (1986; 1990) conclude that 'the more "modern" groups are less involved in the programme, knowing the mechanisms of distancing and discount, while the more traditional groups are more "involved"' (1986: 169). It is tempting to concur with this conclusion since it offers a seemingly straightforward explanation of the different interpretations. However, while *prima facie* feasible, on reflection their modern–traditional dichotomy appears simplistic and politically loaded. Primarily, Liebes and Katz's conclusion that the degrees of involvement in and distanciation from mediated communication correspond to degrees of modernity reinforces the perception of the West (on whose terms modernity is conceptualized) as the repository of modernity and 'progress', as well as all its positive connotations. Their finding that the Russian viewers were more critical than the other groups is interesting, but their conclusion which suggests that Russians were somehow innately critical seems tautological, and certainly begs the question. Arraying the different 'cultures' which their respondents were assumed to represent along a 'multidimensional plane' (p. 169) indicating patterns of involvement and distancing, and by implication, referential and critical readings, appears to call out for a more complex theorizing, not only of the process of diverse decodings, but also of the nature of the 'cultures' which encourage such readings. Without such detail, their rich findings remain unexplained, and open to critiques such as that offered by Corner (1991) that question the critical potential of such studies.

In the present context, for instance, to take the Indian non-academics' reading of the films simply as an indication of the 'traditional' culture to which they belong, in relation to the 'modern' critical reading of the Indian academics, postgraduates and some of the undergraduates, as well as the British group of respondents, would be to examine the results only superficially. This group's 'horizon of expectation' deriving from their obvious acceptance of the documentary's truth claims, effects uniformly transparent–uncritical decodings which positions them differently from other Indian groups. Among the variables encountered in the study, this group is also distinguished from the others by the respondents' lack of university higher education. The question arises therefore, as to whether education could be assumed to create a prominently different 'culture' among Indians, both generally as well as with regard to this particular case study involving interpretation of documentaries.

Education as a major socializing factor has been discussed often enough in sociological, especially phenomenological literature, exemplified in Berger and Luckmann (1966), and Berger *et al.* (1974). Berger and Luckmann address the issue of education as one of the factors involved in the process of 'secondary socialization' (1966, Part 3, *passim*) in the creation and maintenance of social constructions of reality, as well as arguing the case of education (particularly formal education) as creating 'modern' consciousness. Thus, in this conception education emerges not merely as a question of heuristics, but also as one of the 'secondary carriers' (Berger *et al.*, 1974, Chapter 4, *passim*) of modern consciousness: 'Mass education, while it certainly cannot be considered an important factor in the creation of the modern world historically, is today a modernizing force of very great importance indeed.' (1974: 105).[9] In the 'plurality' of life-worlds that characterizes modern consciousness, religion has been to a certain extent replaced by education and mass communication (a feature of mass media and contemporary life developed by Gerbner) in its role as the provider of meaning in everyday life. This is a complex argument and of only tangential interest here. However, the notion of education as contributing to the creation of one aspect of the 'multiple realities', or to a 'sub-world', which make up a person's life-world, is crucial. The relative uniformity of formalized education creates a potential for homogeneity (as suggested by the term 'formal') among its subscribers. This homogeneity might appear to paradoxically contain within itself the possibility of dissonance, but even this is subsumed under the general orientation of the 'reality' or 'sub-world' engendered by formalized education. In other words, education provides a preconstituted system of values and typifications with which a person makes sense of and exists in everyday life; formal education helps promote a common conception of at least some elements of the 'world' of its members. It should be noted that a classical, deterministic version of culture would prevent any attempt at examining such 'sub-worlds'. Indeed, it can be argued that such conceptualizations are possible only from the perspective of Schutz's formulation of the 'multiple realities' which make up a person's life-world. While being socially derived, these multiple realities transcend normative categorizations to take into account the sheer variety which makes a life-world unique. In the present context, what is pertinent is the presence of two distinct sub-worlds characterized by formal higher education and the lack of it, existing under the rubric of 'Indian national culture', which, from the perspective of classical notions, would be considered a normative whole.

Whether this system of relevances and typification created by formal education engenders a 'distancing' from the mediated text is arguable. However, while there is no evidence to prove a causal link between education and critical distancing in the reception of media, the data from this case study indicate a possible connection in the Indian context. A possible question to consider here is whether the difference in framings between the Indian non-academics and the other Indian groups can be attributed to differing degrees of familiarity with the moving image and its mode of representing reality. This seems unlikely, since India produces the highest number of films, and cinema-going has long been a favourite pastime both in rural as well as urban areas. While the arrival of television has to some extent dented cinema attendance in some sections of the population, it could still be said that watching television has perhaps replaced visiting cinemas. The seductive power of and the fascination with the moving image are as yet undimmed.[10] However, the interpretation of documentary television and film requires the recognition of its truth claims and the consequent rejection or acceptance of it. In other words, the documentary genre calls for a slightly varied set of expectations from the fiction film. This is where education and/or a relative familiarity with the genre itself could perhaps be significant with regard to different expectations from and interpretations of documentary films.

In the Indian context the difference created by higher education is particularly germane. The notion of India's 'national' identity, which is under constant threat from the sheer diversity which the political nation-state encompasses, has been questioned elsewhere (Das and Harindranath, 1996). The multi-lingual, multi-ethnic, multi-religious nature of the population suggests a multi-cultural state. Among the forces instilling a sense of national integration education, particularly formal, higher education, should rate as one of the most important. In order to appreciate the force of higher education in India, however, it is necessary to be familiar with some of the features of its history.

Two of these features are particularly pertinent to this discussion. First, the social value accorded to higher education among certain sections of the population, which has been exploited for political gain by the powers that be, especially in terms of appeasing an economically significant, politically active minority. The sudden spurt in enrolment during the five years preceding 1966–69 (see Table 23.1) was a direct response to, as Rudolph and Rudolph (1987) claim, 'demand politics'.

Table 23.1 Enrolment growth rates for primary, secondary, and higher education

	Primary		Secondary		Higher	
Year	Enrolment	% Increase	Enrolment	% Increase	Enrolment	% Increase
1950–51	18,677,642	—	4,817,011	—	423,326	—
1955–56	24,511,331	31	6,826,605	42	736,124	74
1960–61	33,631,391	37	10,942,293	60	1,094,991	49
1965–66	48,912,678	45	17,132,945	57	2,095,217	91
1970–71	55,167,533	12	21,773,019	46	3,502,357	67
1975–76	63,108,492	14	25,999,227	19	4,615,992	32
1978–79	72,390,000	14	27,090,000	4	4,192,934	–9
					(5,049,957)	(+4)

Source: Rudolph and Rudolph (1987: 298).

Ignoring the advice of the central government, state governments across the country 'responded to the insistent demands of the urban middle-class and rural notable constituents for more college seats by creating intellectually and physically jerrybuilt institutions or underfunding existing ones' (p. 296).

This politically expedient state of affairs resulted in 'skewed' funding allocations favouring higher education. One of the consequences of this is the neglect of primary and secondary education, especially in the rural areas, although the constitution guarantees free education up to the secondary level for all. The share of funds assigned to each level of formal education is illuminating:

> Of the funds allocated to education under the fourth [five year] plan (1969–70 to 1973–74), only 30 percent went to the elementary level, which accounted for 68 million enrolled students, while 18 per cent and 25 per cent went to secondary and higher levels, respectively with enrolments of only 22 and 3.5 million. [...] Fifth-plan allocations followed a similar pattern.

(Rudolph and Rudolph, 1987, p. 297)

In this way, the political and social elite continue to exert their dispropor-tionate influence while the majority uneducated, semi-literate population remain in the wilderness. As shown in the table above, the number of students entering higher education is considerably less when compared to the number enrolling for primary and secondary education. In other words, despite growing student numbers higher education remains acces-sible only to a relative minority. Thus an elite group has become the chief beneficiary of formal higher education and the resulting social and economic gains. 'In an hierarchical society such as India, education has always been accepted as the preserve and prerogative of a small class of people. [...] The ancient Brahminical values were replaced by the modern educated middle class values' which were 'transmitted' by the education system. (Pattnayak, 1981: 67). Sociologically, this development can be viewed from a variety of perspectives. From within the conception of 'culture' advanced in this thesis, this signifies the presence of a category of persons possessing the norms and values of the 'sub-world' created by higher education, existing within the population of the state but differing from the majority.

Another important factor to be noted with regard to higher education in India is its colonial legacy. Most university education is Western oriented, which is reflected in course design, syllabuses, reading lists, but most importantly by the fact that the medium of instruction in universities is English. The consequence of this has been profound, creating and sustaining a politically influential, Westernised, hybrid culture signifi-cantly different from the majority indigenous one. According to Pattnayak (1981), the advent of English has had a negative implication for local cultures:

> English engendered among its speakers an attitude of indifference to the local languages and cultures and thus created a communication gap between the elite and the masses and between innumerable islands of cultural and linguistic minorities. [...] The middle class elite [for whom English represents

their culture] who consider themselves the repository of all values and who expect others to emulate their values have failed to recognize difference as having a different perspective and ethos.

(p. 68)

Thus higher education in India has generated a 'culture' significantly different from others within the country. Not only does the minority who occupy this cultural space possess values inherent in the educational 'sub-world' that are denied to the majority, but the essentially Western orientation of these values and norms sets this group or category apart from the rest to an even greater degree. Even at the level of education, therefore, India's claim to a cultural unity is weakened. The 'modern consciousness' provided by higher education is markedly Western and therefore inimical to the indigenous 'sub-worlds'. In essence, formal higher education effectively creates 'two nations' in India: those who are 'Westernized', English-speaking, and 'modern' and those who are not.

However, it would be wrong to assume that this divide in contemporary Indian life creates an insurmountable dichotomy, or that indigenous life-worlds are completely alien to the educated minority. Certain spheres, 'sub-worlds', or 'realities' of their lives are bound to coincide or cross each other. Normative claims suggesting mutually exclusive, watertight compartments are as erroneous as the simplistic West–Other divide, and as unproductive, apart from being unacceptable from the point of view of the phenomenological conception of the collective that has been proffered in this chapter. The two 'worlds' described here, therefore, are neither unchanging nor incontrovertible wholes, and cannot be expected to perform a law-giving function as in a physical property. Again, such conceptions are more the norm in demarcations generated by classical anthropology discussed earlier. A more constructive approach would be to conceive of the Indian with formal higher education as residing in a 'cultural borderland', a notion in which 'the fiction of the uniformly shared culture increasingly seems more tenuous than useful. Although most metropolitan typifications continue to suppress border zones, human cultures are neither necessarily coherent nor always homogeneous.' (Rosaldo, 1993: 207). Such a conception coincides with the new ethnographic move from 'closed communities' to the idea of 'open borders' (Rosaldo, 1993, *passim*), reconstituting the task of social analysis from that of discovering law-like intractable variables to exploring heterogeneity, change, and the way culture changes and is changed by human behaviour.

From this notion it is possible to conceive of the persons inhabiting the 'borderland' between indigenous Indian culture and Western 'modernity' as a cultural hybrid. The concept of hybridity in culture has recently been highlighted in post-colonial cultural theory, as in Bhabha (1994) for whom,

A contingent, borderline experience opens up *in-between* colonizer and colonized. This is a space of cultural and interpretive undecidability produced in the 'present' of colonial moment. [...] The margin of hybridity, where cultural differences 'contingently' and conceptually touch, becomes the moment of panic which reveals the borderline experience. It resists binary opposition of

racial and cultural groups, sipahis and sahibs, as homogeneous polarized
political consciousness.

(pp. 206–7; emphasis in the original)

The political stance evident in this quote is not of concern here; what is
pertinent is the invocation of the notion of hybridity as the 'in-between'
space between the West and the Other. The existence of Western-oriented
higher education, I would argue, lends a handle with which to grasp the
otherwise 'undecidable' bridge touching both cultural monoliths at once.
In the middle of this divide is the university-educated Indian, retaining
within his/her life-world the 'realities' of Indian existence as well as
Western-oriented norms adopted through the socializing force of higher
education.

From a prominently micro-sociological project it is difficult to make
generalizations. A relatively small percentage of the respondents in this
study can be said to represent an interpretive repertoire of their own,
which, according to the data, is more different from that of other Indian
respondents' than are the differences between the interpretive practices of
the latter Indians and the British respondents. While there is no *conclusive*
evidence to suggest that these two Indian 'cultures' generate different
interpretive practices, from the perspective of Gadamerian hermeneutics,
it appears that the 'tradition' or the sub-world which the Indian groups
other than the non-academics operated from was the one created by
education. The responses of the Indian non-academics could have been
influenced by their desire to provide me with the responses which they
assumed I expected from them. From the data, however, the less educated
appear to assume a subject position posited by documentary and less
likely to challenge the authority of He-Who-Knows. Is it then possible to
argue that a critical attitude is *necessarily* correlated with education?
Answering this question requires a study formulated differently from the
one reported here.

Notes

1. There have been several studies exemplifying the link between social position
   and interpretive practice, the most prominent of which are Morley (1980),
   Liebes and Katz (1986, 1990). But while they *demonstrate* this link, their attempts
   at theorizing it are relatively inadequate.
2. I borrow this term from Jensen (1991), since it signifies a concept which 'implies
   that audiences are not formal groups or communities, but contextually defined
   agents who employ such repertoires to make preliminary sense' (p. 42).
3. Crucially, few of the Indian 'non-academics' had had any *formal* education
   beyond the school level, although some had diplomas and other vocational
   qualifications.
4. These analytic categories follow the framework used by Corner and Richardson
   (1986) and Liebes and Katz (1990).
5. Gadamer's ideas and their relevance to audience research are discussed in
   greater detail in Harindranath (1996).
6. My use of the past tense here must not be taken to mean that I believe such
   norms to be no longer in currency. They are very much in evidence, even in the
   popular media, where the 'us' and 'them' opposition is invoked from time to

time. In academic anthropology however, the tide seems to be turning. As Rosaldo (1993) observes,

> When people play 'ethnographer and natives', it is ever more difficult to predict who will put on the loincloth and who will pick up the pencil and paper [...] One increasingly finds North American Tewas, South Asian Sinhalese, and Chicanoes are among those who read and write ethnographies.

(p. 45)

7. The issue of human rights is a particularly contentious example, based as it is on Western notions of individual rights which many countries from the South see as subsumed under collective responsibility.
8. Harindranath (1996) contains an elaboration of Schutz's ideas and their pertinence to theorizing the 'situatedness' of audiences.
9. Berger *et al.* (1974) conceive of 'modernity' and industrialization more in historical terms than in terms of 'development', as attested by the section on 'demodernization' in the book which emphasizes counter culture movements within the West as well as the 'demodernization consciousness' in other cultures.
10. The number of film actors and actresses who have successfully entered political careers is indicative of their enduring popularity with the 'masses'. Conversely, this fact is also suggestive of the lack of political acumen in the majority of the (rural) population.

References:

Berger, P. and Luckmann, T. (1966) *The Social Construction of Reality: A Treatise on the Sociology of Knowledge*. Harmondsworth: Penguin.

Berger, P. *et al.* (1974) *The Homeless Mind: Modernization and Consciousness*. New York: Vintage Books.

Bhabha, H. (1994) *The Location of Culture*. London: Routledge.

Corner, J. (1991) Meaning, genre and context: the problematics of 'public knowledge' in the New Audience Studies. In Curran, J. and Gurevitch, M. (eds) *Mass Media and Society*. London: Arnold.

Corner, J. (1995) *Television Form and Public Address*. London: Arnold.

Corner, J. and Richardson, K. (1986) Documentary meanings and the discourse of interpretation. In Corner, J. (ed.) *Documentary and the Mass Media*. London: Arnold, 141–60.

Das, S. and Harindranath, R. (1996) Nation-state, identity, and the media. Unit XX of MA Mass Communication by Distance Learning, Centre for Mass Communication Research, University of Leicester.

Gadamer, H-G. (1975) *Truth and Method*. New York: Continuum.

Gadamer, H-G. (1976) *Philosophical Hermeneutics*. Berkeley, CA: University of California Press.

Geertz, C. (1973) *The Interpretation of Cultures*. New York: Basic Books.

Giddens, A. (1990) *The Consequences of Modernity*. Cambridge: Polity Press.

Harindranath, R. (1996) Audience interpretations and cultural contexts: a reappraisal using hermeneutics and post-colonial theory. Paper presented at the IAMCR conference, Sydney.

Jensen, K. (1991) Humanistic scholarship as qualitative science: contributions to mass communication scholarship. In Jensen, K.B. and Jankowski, N.W. (eds) *A Handbook of Qualitative Methodologies for Mass Communication Research*. London: Routledge, 17–43.

Lash, S. and Friedman, J. (1992) Introduction: subjectivity and modernity's other. In Lash, S. and Friedman, J. (eds) *Modernity and Identity*. Oxford: Blackwell.

Liebes, T. and Katz, E. (1986) Patterns of involvement in television fiction: a comparative analysis. *European Journal of Communication*, **1**(2), 151–71.

Liebes, T. and Katz, E. (1990) *The Export of Meaning: Cross-Cultural Readings of 'Dallas'*. Oxford: Oxford University Press.

Morley, D. (1980) *The 'Nationwide' Audience*. London: British Film Institute.

Morley, D. and Silverstone, R. (1991) Communication and context: ethnographic perspectives on media audiences. In Jensen, K.B. and Jankowski, J.W. (eds.) *A Handbook of Qualitative Methodologies for Mass Communication Research*, London: Routledge.

Nichols, B. (1981) *Ideology and the Image: Social Representation in the Cinema and Other Media*. Bloomington: Indiana University Press.

Pattnayak, D. P. (1981) *Multilingualism and Mother-Tongue Education*. Delhi: Oxford University Press.

Rosaldo, R. (1993) *Culture and Truth: The Remaking of Social Analysis*. London: Routledge.

Rudolph, L. and Rudolph, S. (1987) *The Pursuit of Lakshmi: The Political Economy of the Indian State*. Chicago: Chicago University Press.

Schutz, A. (1964) *Collected Papers, Vol. II: Studies in Social Theory*. The Hague: Martinus Nijhoff.

Schutz A. (1972) *The Phenomenology of the Social World*. London: Heinemann.

Schutz, A. (1973) *Collected Papers, Vol. I: The Problem of Social Reality*. The Hague: Martinus Nijhoff.

Shapcott, R. (1994) Conversation and co-existence: Gadamer and the interpretation of international society. *Millennium: Journal of International Studies*, **23**(1).

Winston, B. (1978/79) Documentary. *Sight and Sound*, Winter.

Winston, B. (1993) The documentary film as scientific inscription. In Renov, M. (ed.) *Theorizing Documentary*. London: Routledge.

24

Critique: elusive audiences

Peter Dahlgren

In some slightly mythic recent past – of no more than a few decades ago – 'audiences' used to be a rather unproblematic notion. They may have been seen at times as difficult (and expensive) to research, but the concept and the empirical reality it referred to had a fairly common-sense quality. Audiences could be studied in terms of their size, their composition, their responses to media output, and even how they evolved over time. Research interests varied, of course, and commercial, public service and academic concerns were not always of one piece. Also, most researchers would admit, at least privately, that the methods used to study audiences had some shortcomings, but these would hopefully be reduced as research techniques improved. The status – ontological and epistemological – of 'audiences' was generally not in itself a topic which engaged researchers. Today we find ourselves in a very different situation. While the traditions of empirical quantitative audience research established in the post-war years are still very much with us – as are its close and older kin, public opinion surveys – the contemporary research landscape has become quite heterogeneous. Newer strands of inquiry have not only challenged the established social scientific perspectives, but they have also disputed and realigned amongst themselves. In the present situation, we are not just dealing with issues of how to get better knowledge of audiences, but even questions such as what kind of knowledge of audiences is possible/desirable, what is the nature/definition of audiences, and, indeed, is it even meaningful to use the concept of 'audience': to what exactly does it refer?

Each of the chapters in this section makes a particular contribution to the ongoing rethinking of audiences in recent years (and even not-so-recent years, as in the case of Graham Murdock's piece). They all move us further from the established social scientific tradition; with a bit of shoe-horning, one could argue that they all to varying degrees belong to the polymorphous Cultural Studies tradition – though for the ever-expanding Cultural Studies of today, the media and their audiences seem to have become a marginal concern (Dahlgren, 1997). Though sharing a good degree of premises, these chapters reflect a diversity of approach and do not speak as a unified chorus. Space does not permit a full engagement with each of these texts, nor with all the possible topics which are of importance to audience research. In this presentation my aim is to take up a limited number of key themes – conceptual issues – which all are touched upon by at least some of the contributions. For the sake of coherence in this discussion, my focus will be on television audiences. Yet even such a move is of course not wholly unproblematic, given the structural evolution of the industry, the technical developments of the medium and the growing interface and integration of television with other domestic media technologies and leisure patterns (e.g., videos, computers and home shopping).

I begin with the tension between the interpretive freedom of audiences and the determining power of the media. From there I take up the theme of contextualization and how this has come more and more to the fore in our understanding of audiences. Yet, as I suggest, as our sense of context expands, empirical research becomes all the more problematic. I then move on to the idea of 'active audiences' and the notion of sense-making itself and take up the theme of the heterogeneous state of audience research.

Balancing acts

In the narrative history of audience research, we find that the behavioural effects tradition – i.e. the mainstream social science approach – encompassed considerable debate precisely about effects: some researchers argued for a 'strong' view of the media, while others emphasized that the actual measurable effects were not so great. When versions of a critical paradigm – critical in the sense of critiquing what was perceived to be the ideological dimensions of the media – began to emerge within media studies during the late 1960s and early 1970s, another interpretation of strong media was put forth: the media, as bearers of ideology, were seen by these researchers as having an enormous impact on the way people think and act. The actual processes of the transfer of ideology were rarely examined empirically: this school of thought tended to take media texts as their point of departure, from which audience responses were extrapolated. John Fiske's interventions during the 1980s can be understood as an attempt to forcefully modify this notion of the powerful media by theorizing the processes of sense-making, while at the same time maintaining a basically critical stance towards the prevailing power structure. Fiske (and many others associated with Cultural Studies) reacted in particular against two features of the critique of ideology school: the overly deterministic treatment of how meaning is generated in people's encounter with the media, and what he saw to be an exaggeration of the media's – especially television's – homogenizing character.

He proposes the idea of polysemy, that is, the notion that media texts (for our purposes, television) are potentially open, even contradictory, which makes them available for a variety of interpretations. Indeed, according to Fiske, this is what makes them 'popular': different social groups (subcultures, in Fiske's terms) can generate different meanings from the same text, thus the broad appeal of such media output. Moreover, Fiske emphasizes the pleasure involved in this sense-making, i.e. that meaning making *per se* is not merely a rational/cognitive operation but also has affective dimensions. This too can be seen as a corrective of the critical trajectory, which had for the most part been operating with a rather rationalistic psychology model. This now invites inquiry of the irrational features of sense-making, which are especially operative in the case of television, as I argue elsewhere (Dahlgren, 1995). In tandem with the polysemic text, Fiske emphasizes the active audience, sense-making viewers who watch programmes and enjoy responding to them, and talk with each other about what they see on television: in the home, in the neighbourhood, in school, at work. In this way, Fiske underscores the social character of meaning and the way in which it circulates in society, yet is never fully stable in that it is forever being reinterpreted.

Thus, on both sides – in the media output and among the audience – we have a non-deterministic situation. Fiske does not see the potential range of meanings that can be generated from any TV output as random or unlimited, but bounded by the particular interpretive frames of specific subcultures. There is also a political pay-off here, in the sense that Fiske sees meaning as contested, as a site of ongoing struggle: meaning-making is equivalent to the social struggles for power. The hegemony of the power elite can never be taken for granted but must always be reaccomplished and can always potentially be contested. And finally, in attributing different subcultures different horizons of meaning, Fiske helps to open the concept of ideology itself up to a larger range of possible themes. It is now no longer a question of one over-arching dominant ideology – understood as supporting capitalism – but rather a plurality of social domination which includes the economic sphere but also not least gender and race. Ideological resistance by definition must then be understood as having a plural character.

Fiske's views elicited much favourable response, but even a good deal of criticism from people who were basically in sympathy with his project. A number of issues were raised, but for my purposes here, the most central are, first, that he at times tends to exaggerates the degree of interpretive freedom of audiences as well as the extent of polysemy of media texts, and second, he makes too much of the 'resistance' to hegemony that alternative interpretation of popular programmes might entail. In advocating an active audience, according to some critics, Fiske ends up with a hyperactive audience, one which is heavily engaged in the pleasures of making sense of popular media, and indeed, making alternative or even oppositional sense. And while critics could acknowledge that media texts were polysemic, the point of contention became to what degree: how significantly alternative could readings of popular TV programmes actually be? And others asked, what differences in readings would actual make any social difference? To what extent does some variant interpretation of a soap opera constitute ideological resistance in any significant way? Particularly in the case of women and soap operas, some feminists were making a Fiskean case that women could use television dramas not only in ways which resist dominant (male) ideology, but also empower them psychologically (cf. Brown, 1990); such claims were of course contested.

While I basically agree with those who pointed out there are some excessive tendencies in Fiske's views from this period, I would still argue that his interventions were productive and that there is still something valuable to be retained from such perspectives today. It becomes a question of modifying the excesses, but just how much is 'excessive'? In other words, just *how* interpretively active are audiences, under what circumstances should the interpretations be deemed an instance of resistance, and further, just how polysemic is television output? Clearly the answers to such questions have to be worked out in relation to our developing understandings of the complex attributes of television, audiences, and the larger societal landscape. And that of course is part of the dilemma of audience studies: finding a secure position in relation to these large issues. In the past decade, conventional wisdom has tended to swing back from Fiske's claims, but his contributions helped to define a set of thematics which qualitative audience research has continued to find relevant. What we have today is a sort of conceptual polarity which in practice becomes an analytical and empirical force-field, a set of terms and debates which organizes a good deal of our research attention. Researchers will of course position themselves in this regard, and the spectrum of interpretations appears to be narrowing. Yet, given our current awareness of the contingencies of knowledge, militant certitude seems ill-advised.

It is interesting to compare the text by Graham Murdock. It was written more than a decade before Fiske's, in a different context. It was not part of a debate within Cultural Studies, but instead was a response to what Murdock perceived to be a growing subjectivist tendency within certain circles of social psychology and sociology in the early 1970s. There was a danger, he saw, in that these developments leaned towards cancelling any impact of the larger social structure because these structures could not be incorporated within people's subjective horizons. With an anchoring in an historical materialist view of society, Murdock argues that we must acknowledge that there are certain 'objective' factors which impinge on how we make sense, even if these factors are not a part of our own subjectivity or in some way accessible to us in our everyday lives. Further, he makes a distinction between situated and media-relayed meaning systems. Though this point is not developed in his text, it suggests that he would argue that the factors of social structure do not impact directly on the individual, but instead are mediated and modified via the domain of social interaction as well as mass communication. Murdock takes what he has later come to call a realist position, which in simple terms assumes that there is an external social reality 'out there' which impacts on us. At the same time, in keeping with the historical materialist view, our actions can give shape to this reality, modify and even alter it. While we can have some, though never full access to social reality, the task of research is to illuminate it as well as possible. A pivotal feature of this social reality that shapes us is its class character, and that the practices and interaction of specific subcultures are an important key for charting the impact of class.

From these premises, Murdock deduces that the media should be understood as powerful in their impact. Their role in 'relaying dominant meanings' is indisputable: they serve as the

> main source of information about, and explanations of, social and political processes, and also a major fund of images and suggestions concerning modes of self-presentation and general life styles. The mass media therefore represent a key repository of available meanings which people draw upon in

their continuing attempts to make sense of their situation and find ways of
acting within or against it.

(p. 206)

It is important to note that what Murdock expresses – in this articulate
rendering of the neoMarxian position – is a set of premises. He does not
make any deterministic claims, but leaves the question of actual impact
open for investigation. He establishes a framework for possible research.
It could be argued that this framework has a built-in way of looking which
would colour the research strategy and the findings, but on the other
hand, all approaches must of necessity commence from sets of premises,
theoretic orientations, and so on. No research is without its *a prioris*, but all
research must handle them in a suitable and self-reflective manner; there
are no fail-safe formulas.

None the less, it is clear that Murdock's points of departure differ from
Fiske's; indeed, his views can be seen as belonging to those voices who
(later) found Fiske's claims exaggerated. Murdock's emphasis here is on
the power of the social structure generally, and the media specifically –
their structures and their output – rather than on the subjectivity or the
activity of the audience. Today, almost a quarter of a century after this
piece was written, some readers may question the centrality of class,
which no longer has quite such a prominent place in the concerns of
media researchers. Without pursuing this particular thought very far, I
would just say that there are certainly an array of factors which we must
attend to if we are to critically investigate the prevailing social order
(and the media and their audiences), and class may analytically no
longer be privileged; gender and race/ethnicity, for example, certainly
have been shown to play key roles in the shaping and circulation of
meaning and power. However, it would be a severe mistake to simply
dismiss class. Rather, we may have to rethink what class means in the
era of late modernism and a global capitalism which at present has no
serious political opposition. But Murdock's basic assumptions about
powerful media and their role in shaping our semiotic environment, and,
by implication, our subjectivity, are in my view still highly compelling
today.

Can we have it both ways? If we juxtapose Fiske and Murdock, can we
analytically have both an active (though not hyperactive) audience with a
considerable degree of interpretive freedom and at the same time
powerful, yet non-deterministic media? Can we allow for emphasis on
both audiences' subjectivities as social actors and the media's objective
structures and outputs? At this point in the discussion, without clarifying
the terms in more detail, I would simply say: Yes. We must. The tension at
work here is but a version of the classical force-field within sociology
between the perspectives of actors and structures. Sociologists tend to
work within one perspective or the other, and some, like Bourdieu (with
his notion of habitus) and Giddens (with his structuration) even attempt
to theoretically link them, but very few would contemplate calling one of
the perspectives irrelevant. If firm and final knowledge about audiences
remains elusive, we can at least specify the analytic and empirical horizons of the particular research with which we are involved. That is, as

researchers we have to be aware of the theoretic context of any given work we do and the claims we make for it.

I believe we have strong consensus for rejecting the two extremes positions: few today would advocate full media determinism, where the audience is deemed wholly inert or passive and where the consequences of media could thus merely be determined by looking at the output. Likewise, few would support the idea of total 'interpretive freedom', or, expressed differently, media irrelevance: that the audience can make any sense whatsoever out of any output, regardless of what it looks like. Thus we end up somewhere between these poles, where some mix of the specifics of the output and the interpretive practices of the media both have bearing. We can assume that the balance between them will vary considerably between people, social circumstances, and media output. Even for the same person watching a weekly series on TV there is no guarantee that the ratio of media output to interpretive freedom will remain constant. What can become significant for research in this regard is specifying as best we can the relevant contexts of viewing.

In part, the issue has to do with the level of analysis with which one is engaged, and perhaps, an analytic perspective on what kinds of differences actually make a difference, and in which contexts. Thus, at the macro societal level, I take the view that television as a media institution, its output, and the practices of audiencing, all meet up with social structure and power relations. Such a view of course immediately cries out for nuance: I am not suggesting that we are confronted by a hermetically sealed, media-driven social system – on the contrary, I see many stresses and tensions in a complex social formation which is in transition. Also, if we assume that television offers frameworks of collective perception and serves as producer/reproducer of implicit sociocultural common sense, this position must confront such modifying facts as the large number of channels available today and the growth of genre hybrids. In the present situation where television is decentralizing, the collective common sense may be on its way to becoming more plural and fragmented, which could well have a bearing on the issues of power.

Yet the centrality of television to cultural, political and economic power strikes me as indisputable. But 'centrality' at this macro-level does not always translate neatly in mid-range and micro-settings: variations and permutations arise everywhere. The phenomena of audiencing are intricately interwoven into mutual reciprocity with an array of other sociocultural, political and economic fields. It is via such interplay that television in its present forms is both made possible by, and makes possible, these other fields. 'Power' in the classic sense may not always be the central or most relevant feature in every situation, and audiencing may offer a wide array of other themes which are of relevance for our understanding of television and society and highly meaningful for audience members.

The protean contexts of audiencing

One of the criticisms of Fiske's work was that it was largely theoretical, with very little systematic research on audiences. David Morley, on the other hand provided an important empirical grounding for our under-standing of the interpretive processes related to television viewing. His qualitative studies of television viewing during the 1980s had an immense impact on the evolution of audience research (see Moores, 1993 for an overview of the research that emerged during the 1980s). In the text included in this volume, he describes some of the main considerations in his research of TV viewing in the family. The reader quickly comes to realize the importance of context here. Morley situates viewing in the family, but is careful to point out that 'the family' not only varies consider-ably within British society, but that its overall profile has been in marked evolution in recent decades. Thus, his first context is still further contextu-alized. Moreover, he situates television viewing in relation to other leisure activities and also notes how these have been evolving, most notably the decline in cinema attendance and the increase in leisure activities in the home. Further, he reflexively contextualizes his own work in the light of previous research traditions on audiences, distinguishing his premises and intentions from both quantitative effects studies and the text-based critical/theoretical strands of inquiry.

His empirical findings tell him that the context of television viewing is as significant as the object of viewing. In the family context, gender relations loom large in importance, especially with regard to the power and control over programme choice. Though even here, he 'meta-contexts': gender patterns are not universal but rather specific to class and subculture. Further, Morley focuses on a number of other topics, including different styles of viewing, the distinction between planned and unplanned viewing, talk in the home that relates to television, the use of video, and solo viewing and what he calls 'guilty pleasure'. Thus, even from this brief overview, we understand that television viewing is a multidimensional activity, which encompasses a range of social interaction, purposes, and patterns. The contexts of viewing include an array of factors which stretch from fairly stable patterns shaped by overall social structure to middle range factors of daily domestic patterns to specific conditions which may shift from moment to moment. Viewers themselves can to some degree define the circumstances of viewing and the mind-set with which they approach it.

Thus, Morley's deep empirical probe seems to both confirm and slightly modify Fiske's and Murdock's positions. Morley acknowledges the factors of social structure which Murdock emphasizes. However, the distinction between what Murdock calls 'situated and media-relayed meaning systems' would appear to be empirically quite problematic: Morley's work (and of course that of others as well) suggests that they are inexorably entwined. At the site of reception, there seems to be a whole lot going on which potentially may be of relevance for sense-making: so much is going on, and it manifests such diversity, that we may feel compelled to problematize the smoothness of ideological integration that Murdock implies. Yet, against Fiske, the picture which Morley presents suggests that 'textual readings' are only a small part of what is involved in television watching. Television is much more than just a text; it is utilized for a variety of purposes, not all of which make the actual audio-visual output the primary focus. Moreover, the readings which are done would

seem to be filtered by an array of specific circumstances which can fluc-
tuate from day to day.

The utilization of television for purposes beyond that of the (traditionally understood) consumption of the audio-visual texts is the starting
point for Roger Dickinson's chapter. He emphasizes the idea of television
as a multifaceted resource, in this particular case as a resource for guiding
household choices about food and eating. This perspective links up with
John Corner's notions of public knowledge; seen in that light, television
can contribute to the construction of meanings which are pertinent to
specific domains of the social and personal world, and can do so via a
variety of different programme genres. Research about television's role in
the area of public knowledge requires analysis of both output and reception, with careful attention not least to possible contradictory messages
from different genres or programme formats.

In the case of food, Dickinson finds that British television programming
as a whole does not produce a dominant, orderly discourse about food
and eating, but a variety of discourses, at times even contradictory in
nature. Yet the really interesting angle in his research is on the reception
side. His results show, among other things, that in the households interviewed, people are not only very familiar with television's discourses
about food, but also can use these discourses to potentially resolve
conflicts over choices about food and eating. And at a more general level,
he finds this domain of public knowledge is very much mediated by the
context of the household: its daily routines, patterns of interaction, social
relationships, etc. A number of key social variables about households
impacted on the ways in which televisual discourses about food were
filtered by the household context. Here we see the commanding presence
of the household as a micro-context - and by consequence - the methodological limitations of focusing exclusively on the individual in studying
television reception. The domestic character of most television consumption demands that attention be paid to the social ecology of the household,
the prime micro-context for most viewing.

There are of course many possible kinds of contexts that may be relevant in understanding reception. Harindranath's chapter begins with the
notions of national cultures (Indian and British) and higher education,
and seeks to probe how these factors may serve as contexts which can
shape the interpretation of films (both Indian and British). In an interesting display of critical self-reflection in regard to methods, politics and
epistemology, Harindranath comes to see not least the problematics of
retaining national cultures as analytic contexts which impact on reception.
Recalling the phenomenological tradition's insistence that we inhabit
multiple realities, he finds rather that higher education, which in India is
largely Western-inspired via the colonial legacy, sets up a form of cultural
partition. Educated Indians demonstrate more resemblance to educated
Westerners in the use of conceptual frames and in their readings of the
films than to Indians without higher education. Education seemingly
contributes to profoundly altering the life worlds of these Indians, generating a 'third', 'hybrid' culture, one that is Westernized, English-speaking
and 'modern'. The argument here is that it is not so much education as a

variable which shapes how the interpretation of these films proceeds, rather that education has altered the horizons and life worlds of these individuals (what Bourdieu would call their habitus), to such a degree that the conceptual co-ordinates of their everyday lives no longer mesh well with those of the indigenous culture. The sociocultural contexts of the sense-making processes of these educated Indians are now different from that of the majority in their country.

The theoretical reflections in this chapter are stimulating and the empirical evidence suggestive; the next logical step would be to further explore the respective everyday realities of the different groups to ascertain how and to what degree the different micro-contexts have bearing on sense-making in different domains. A general micro-sociology of everyday life, while conceptually compelling, lies beyond the terrain most media researchers have defined for themselves. However, translating this thought into terms relevant for audience research would lead us largely in the direction which Roger Silverstone argues for. He shares Graham Murdock's sense of the ubiquity of the media in our everyday lives, and from that perception he advocates an anthropology of television audiences. The anthropological view emphasizes our daily, routine encounters with television output – the forms and contents of its programming. Television is a central part of our daily lived reality; it is interpreted by viewers, and enters their social worlds via interaction, being re-interpreted and recast within a variety of discourses. Further, television's modes of discourse, its themes, styles of humour, etc. – are intertextually circulated through other media. Silverstone is also an advocate of contextualization: we must be cognisant of the sociocultural situatedness of audiences. Moreover, he too reminds us that audience practices are fragmented and dispersed; indeed, the same viewer can shift his or her subjective dispositions and utilize different viewing styles under different circumstances. But all these contexts can become inhibiting. The social and cultural embeddness of audiences risks spilling out over the whole terrain of everyday life, and the variation of contexts even for one individual can become myriad. And television viewing as such interlaces with other media consumption linking it to the larger 'mediascape' of late modern society.

Conceptualizing audiences and their sense-making

It is at this point that we can begin to question the very concept of 'audience', as a number of researchers have done in recent years (see for example the collection by Hay *et al.*, 1997 for recent discussions on this theme). Audiencing is a set of practices which is truly protean; it can take many forms and its mercurial moves can be quite capricious. How do we conceptually and empirically pin it down? What, concretely, is the object that audience research studies? When is one an audience, or when is one audiencing? There are different answers to these questions; one could no doubt make an inventory and map a range of positions on these questions. Rather than pursue that task, which lies beyond the bounds of this presentation, I would underscore that the various answers relate to different sets of interests and horizons. To say this is to invoke a constructivist position, which suggests that 'audiences' are always *at least in part* discursive constructs, shaped by specific institutional needs and discursive domains.

There are in other words different 'audiences' for different sets of concerns: we turn the prism on the audiences partly in accordance with the kind of knowledge we want or need about people and their relationships to television. Emancipatory projects will emphasize interpretive freedom and resistance to domination; to make arguments about media and the power elite, one needs 'audiences' who are at least in some way 'victims'. Upholders of liberal individualism will underscore viewers' free and active choices. Seen from the perspective of the television industry, 'audiences' become basically statistical objects, used as a symbolic currency for the instrumental/economic ends of the industry. An interest in identity processes in late modern culture may well tend to emphasize the power of viewers over the power of the medium. In other words, one's point of departure and interests shape to some extent the notion of 'audiences', and one thus conceptualizes 'audiences' within particular discursive settings. Further, one also takes some position – cognisant of it or not – on the politics of audience research. Given the current state of scientific self-reflection, we must consequently acknowledge that different kinds premises can give different kinds of knowledge, and that knowledge about audiences has different kinds of uses and implications. This cognitive relativism, however, does not necessitate an ethical relativism: I would not suggest that all kinds research 'interests' in audiences are equal contributors to the 'good life'.

But do not audiences simply and actually exist as raw empirical stuff that we can grasp and measure? Or is it the case that audience research merely constructs its object, which has no empirical reality? The constructivist argument (to which I adhere) clearly has a point to make: different 'audiences' are indeed constructed within different discursive and institutional contingencies. Yet we must be careful not to push this line of reasoning to the point of pure idealism. Constructivism suggests that all knowledge is contingent, but this does not mean that all claims about social phenomena are equally valid or beyond improvement with reference to some external social reality. Here more difficulty arises, of course, since *how* – i.e. via which methodological strategies – we actually refer to an external social reality also varies and has varying legitimacy in different circles. Most researchers would posit that some perspectives (namely, their own), are superior to others, but we would be wise to recall that every perspective/tradition has its limitations, its blind spots. I do not find that it is meaningless to speak about 'audiences' as social phenomena, but I have a lot of respect for the conceptual and empirical problems of researching them, whether from the horizons of behavioural analysis or Cultural Studies. In practical terms, the trick is to be reflexively aware of the constructivist dimension of our research and the implicit (or even explicit) politics in our research, and see how that colours the kind of results we generate.

Further, it is important not be closed to different kinds of empirical evidence, even if they are problematic and derived from other points of departure. For example, the notion of 'active audiences' sits well with me; it is congruent with a variety of my social and political perspectives. Yet, traditional empirical research about viewing patterns, and not least the massive extent of viewing, especially in North America, forces me to at least consider such notions as 'TV dependence' and passivity (see Kubey, 1997 for a discussion along these lines). Even if I may have deep differences with such research at the conceptual, theoretical and methodological level and may take the rhetoric about its scientific precision with a grain of salt, I cannot simply dismiss it. In the face of such research, the notion of 'active' becomes somewhat problematic, though I am by no means ready to jettison it. By 'active' must we mean that audiences are always fully 'free' in their decisions to watch or not? Further, do we mean that they are always actively and consciously interpreting? Is it not possible to make sense of television in ways which are indeed 'passive', i.e. that follow the paths of least resistance, that flow in the already established channels of ideological patterns? The semantic space of 'active' could reasonably hover close to that of 'work', yet television is notorious for avoiding placing any demands on viewers. To come back to Fiske's arguments about pleasure for a moment, it seems that one could just as easily posit that much sense-making in relation to television is pleasurable precisely because one does *not* have to be very 'active'.

To pursue this line of thought for just another moment, it could be the case that these dilemmas have not only to do with the conceptual dimensions we attach to 'active', but also with deeper philosophical issues about 'freedom'. The notion of 'active audiences' is grounded in a sense of people's agency, their free will to choose and act (i.e., to view television and make sense of it in their own way). Yet 'free will' today is inescapably coloured by contingency: our actions and decisions are always 'relatively' free, never absolutely. Psychological categories which depict the subjective states of audiences will never be able to fully extract themselves from ambiguity and indeterminacy. Our apparent inability to resolve the nature of audiences may thus in part be due to an even more fundamental indeterminacy about ourselves as subjects. This is no cause to give up research as a pursuit, but it does suggest (once again) that we have to learn to be comfortable with the contingent character of all our knowledge. Thus, to return to the research about TV dependency/passivity, I retain a certain scepticism and am aware of its premises and horizons, for example, it will most likely not tell me much in depth about the subjective realities of viewers. However, it also prompts me to reflect that 'active' needs to be further nuanced, and that it may well be the case, for example, that not all people are 'active' all the time when they view. 'Active' may turn out to be one of several possible modes of viewing we could conceptualize.

In this regard I find Barker and Brooks' critical interrogation of the 'active audience' thesis productive. Their arguments could have been all the stronger if they did not allow a certain slippage to creep into their discussion: I sense a certain shifting between the media of television and film in the first part of their presentation, which is not always made explicit. Yet there is a nice conceptual pay-off in their encounter with

Bourdieu's work and the notion of 'investment' as a way to avoid some of the problematics of 'active'. They use investment to refer to the degree to which 'people *care* about their participation or involvement in a leisure activity'. I won't recap their entire argument, but only say that the differences that can emerge between, say, high and low investment in the viewing of a particular programme could help elucidate not only the issue of what constitutes 'active', but also help to specify more about the sense-making process generally.

Qualitative audience studies tends to use the concepts of 'meaning' and 'sense-making' quite routinely these days, only occasionally pausing to consider the semantic space thereby included. This is not the place for an extensive analysis of these terms, but I would briefly note that we can readily specify a number of levels or dimensions, and that we could no doubt enhance our clarity by keeping in mind and specifying. Thus, one could identify (in semiotic terms) denotational and connotational dimensions of meaning-making; cognitive perspectives would include associational dimension, i.e., how we relate new media experiences to our pre-existing knowledge and frames of reference. Meaning can also be said have an existential dimension ('my life doesn't make much sense') which in various ways may touch upon the grounds of our being. It could well be that we could enhance some audience research by specifying/identifying which dimensions of sense-making are relevant in particular cases. It is in this light that the notion of 'investment' may prove to be a useful concept: the extent that viewers care about the meaning they may or not be making. In other words, the intensity of involvement seems potentially to be an important dimension of the sense we make of television, a way of differentiating engagement during different programmes and viewing contexts.

Further, sense-making varies conceptually among researchers, depending on what view of the psyche is assumed. This is of course hardly news, but we have to accept that researchers working with, say, psychoanalytic horizons have a different notion of sense-making than those with a cognitive psychological background. Some sense-making proceeds along rational, cognitive lines. Some may be subconscious, merely below our active awareness. If we introduce some notion of the unconscious, we take a big step into the realm of the extra-rational or the irrational. How can we relate findings predicated on such premises to ones anchored in other psychological traditions or in linguistics? Can 'pleasure' be a form of meaning or is it another form of experience? We can of course answer these questions, but we do so in different ways. All this is not to argue that differing perspectives are always totally incommensurable, but just to remind ourselves that at present consensus on even such a fundamental term as 'meaning' is less than total, since it is predicated on differing theoretic traditions.

No guarantees

Research from all traditions over the years has contributed to our knowledge of audiences, and it could be argued that we actually today know quite a bit about television viewing. Yet today our knowledge also includes an awareness of our extensive (and growing?) ignorance. Of course this development can be said to colour all gains in knowledge, but one cannot but feel frustration here, not least given the pervasiveness of the medium and the importance it has in modern society. We want to know *more* about audiences (for a variety of reasons) but that knowledge, it seems, will have to have an increasingly conditional or provisional character. The certitudes of the past are gone. There will be no unified 'theory of the audience'; there will not even be a consensus on what we mean by 'audiences' or what methods we should use to study them. And within whatever particular tradition or theoretic framework we do our research, we are confronted by the multidimensional quality of audiences' practices and the mutable contextual factors which can impinge on viewing – and presumably on the sense viewers make of it. This suggests that we would be prudent to maintain a degree of modesty in our expectations, especially if we are researching television audiences from the horizons of the post-empiricist traditions. (Traditional social science approaches seem to have a less developed appreciation for ambiguity.) Yet such a view does not promote despair. On the contrary, it signals a step forward in our knowledge and understanding. It may mean that some things we thought we knew are no longer valid or may have to be greatly modified, but even that must be seen as progress.

It may be some consolation that this state of affairs is not unique to audience research. Increasingly in the humanities and social sciences, epistemological self-reflection has come to emphasize the contingencies of our knowing, while methodological thinking has come to underscore the situatedness of the phenomena we study. While the waves of postmodernism in the past two decades have given impetus to such thinking, these themes in fact have been gradually flowering within key post-positivist strands of twentieth-century philosophy, such as hermeneutics. The Enlightenment ideal has not been eclipsed, but we have today perhaps a renewed respect for the difficulties inherent within it. We have been so clever that we have unmasked features of our own knowledge; we should be clever enough to figure out what to do next.

References

Brown, H. (ed.) (1990) *Television and Women's Culture*, London: Sage.

Dahlgren, P. (1995) *Television and the Public Sphere: Citizenship, Democracy and the Media*, London: Sage.

Dahlgren, P. (1997) Cultural studies as a research perspective: themes and tensions. In Corner, J., Schlesinger, P. and Silverstone, R. (eds) *An International Handbook of Media Research*, London: Routledge.

Hay, J., Grossberg, L. and Wartella, E. (eds) (1997) *The Audience and its Landscape*, Boulder, CO: Westview Press.

Kubey, Robert (1997) On not finding media effects: conceptual problems in the notion of an 'active' audience. In Hay, J., Grossberg, L. and Wartella, E. (eds) *The Audience and its Landscape*, Boulder, CO: Westview Press, 187–205.

Moores, S. (1993) *Interpreting Audiences*, London: Sage.

Author index

Adorno, T. 42, 46, 48
Ahern, D. 143
Alasuutari, P. 166, 176, 178, 180
Alley, R. 202, 204
Altheide, D. L. 39, 47
Althusser, L. 39, 40, 44, 47, 81, 226
Anderson, D. R. 138, 142
Anderson, J. A. 132, 139, 141, 142, 253, 255
Andison, F. S. 113, 117
Andrews, E. S. 12
Ang, I. 166, 180, 237, 244
Ariès, P. 129, 131, 143
Aristotle 94, 100
Armstrong, G. M. 143
Asamen, J. K. 136, 143
Asp, K. 32, 34
Atkin, C. K. 134, 143, 154, 163

Bagdikian, B. 13, 38, 47
Baker, C. E. 13
Ball-Rokeach, S. 105, 117
Bandura, A. 105, 113, 114, 117, 124
Banton, M. 231
Barber, B. 43, 47
Barker, M. 104, 111, 117, 123, 129, 132, 133, 136, 143, 184–91, 218–32, 308–9
Barnouw, E. 37, 47
Barthes, R. 273, 279, 281
Bartlett, F. C. 173, 180
Bauer, R. A. 153, 163
Bausinger, H. 234, 244, 260, 270
Beck, U. 258, 270
Becker, L. B. 154, 164
Bell, D. 38, 47
Belson, W. A. 109, 117, 168, 179, 180
Bennett, T. 200, 203
Berelson, B. 25, 34, 78, 86, 152, 163, 164
Berg, H. 93, 99, 100
Berger, C. R. 168, 180
Berger, P. 291, 296
Berkowitz, L. 105, 113, 114, 117
Berry, G. L. 136, 143
Best, S. 47
Bettelheim, B. 94, 100
Bhabha, H. 294–5, 296
Billig, M. 178, 179, 180, 249, 255
Björkqvist, K. 100
Blumler, J. G. 33, 35, 141, 143, 153, 154, 163, 164
Boddy, W. 246, 256
Bogart, L. 36, 47
Boggs, C. 47
Borden, R. J. 124, 129
Bordwell, D. 230
Bøthun, 99, 101
Bouthilet, L. 102
Bower, R. T. 46, 47

Boyanowski, E. O. 66, 72
Boyd-Bowman, S. 203
Brand, J. E. 134, 144
Brannen, J. 266, 270
Brantlinger, P. 47
Brewin, C. R. 175, 180
Brodie, J. 240, 244
Brooks, Kate 218–32, 308–9
Brosius, H.-B. 73
Brown, A. 14–24, 76–7
Brown, H. 300, 310
Brown, J. R. 154, 163, 164
Brown, N. 117
Brown, R. L. 101
Brucks, M. 135, 143
Bruner, J. 172, 180
Bruun Pedersen, J. 107, 117
Bryant, J. 25, 96, 103
Buchanan, P. 38
Buckingham, D. 104, 111, 117, 122, 127, 129, 131–42, 143, 190
Burke, K. 249, 251, 255
Burns, T. 61, 72

Calder, B. J. 67, 72
Callahan, B. 278, 282
Cameron, D. 231
Cantril, H. 167, 180
Carey, J. W. 39, 47, 97, 101, 154, 158, 163
Chaffee, S. H. 125, 129, 135, 143
Chaney, D. C. 101, 154, 163
Charlton, T. 128
Chomsky, N. 39, 47, 48, 81
Christiansen, K. O. 89, 101
Codd, J. 231
Cohen, B. C. 27, 34
Cohen, P. 213, 216
Cohen, S. 215, 216
Collins, R. 61, 72
Collins, W. A. 138, 143
Comstock, G. 105, 110, 113, 117
Connell, I. 133, 143
Conway, M. M. 135, 143
Corner, J. 66, 72, 168, 174, 180, 258, 262, 270, 284, 290, 295, 296, 305
Corrigan, P. 243, 244
Crawford, A. 47
Cressey, P. G. 167, 180
Cronholm, M. 106, 117
Cronström, J. 99, 101, 170, 180
Crozier, M. 38, 48
Cubitt, S. 234, 244
Cumberbatch, G. 64, 72, 104, 111, 112–13, 117, 118, 189, 191
Cummings, C. 15, 24
Curran, J. 167, 168, 180

Dahlgren, P. 172, 180, 298–310

Das, S. 292, 296
Daun, Å. 170, 180
David, K. 128
Davies, B. 136, 143
Davies, M. M. 14, 141, 143
Davis, F. 214, 216
Davis, H. 203
de Certeau, M. 71, 248, 249, 250, 251, 252, 255, 260, 270
De Fleur, M.L. 98, 101, 105, 117, 167, 182
De Palma, A. 12
de Sola Pool, I. 101
De Vault, M. 268, 270
Dickinson, R. 257–70, 305
Diedrich, T. 72
Dobash, R. E. 102, 130
Dobash, R. P. 102, 130
Dodd, K. 270
Donaldson, M. 139, 143
Donnerstein, E. 114, 117, 118
Dorr, A. 135, 137, 139, 143, 144
Doubleday, C. 144
Douglas, M. 248, 255
Douglas, W. 64, 72
Drabman, R. S. 113–14, 117
Dreier, P. 38, 48
Durkheim, E. 85
Durkin, K. 136, 144

Eaton, H. Jr. 34
Eco, U. 194, 199, 202, 203
Efron, E. 37, 38, 46, 48
Elliott, P. 101, 102, 154, 163
Ellis, J. 199, 203
Emery, M. C. 37, 48
Emmett, B. 153, 164
Engelhardt, T. 141, 144
Engels, F. 216, 217
Epstein, E. 39, 48
Eron, L. D. 89, 101, 105, 113, 117, 118, 124, 129, 130
Esserman, J. F. 135, 144
Eyal, C. H. 30, 34, 35
Eysenck, H. 111, 117

Fairchild, H. 118
Faulkner, P. 264, 271
Featherstone, M. 12
Feilitzen, C. von 88–100, 101, 107, 117
Feldbaum, E. 143
Fenton, N. 72, 270
Ferguson, D. A. 72
Feshbach, S. 94, 101
Feshback, W. D. 118
Festinger, L. A. 178, 180
Filipson, C. 117
Filmer, P. 205, 217
Findahl, O. 168, 172, 180, 181
Finsrud, E. 101
Fischer, M. M. J. 253, 255, 256
Fischler, C. 259, 261, 270

Fiske, J. 141, 144, 166, 180, 194–203, 204, 221, 222, 247, 248, 252, 255, 299–301, 302, 303, 304
Fiske, S. T. 166, 173, 178, 181
Foucault, M. 45, 48
Freedman, J. L. 114, 117
Freeman, N. 167, 181
Friedman, J. 287, 297
Friendly, F. 38, 48
Funkhouser, G. R. 28, 34
Furu, T. 154, 164

Gadamer, H.-G. 284, 286, 288–90, 295, 296
Gaines, L. 135, 144
Gamson, W. 273, 281
Gans, H. 39, 48
Garnham, N. 248, 255
Garrow, K. 72
Gaudet, H. 25, 34, 164
Gauntlett, D. 104, 111, 117, 120–8, 129
Geertz, C. 296
Gerbner, G. 12, 13, 39, 48, 61–71 *passim*, 72, 83, 92, 98, 101, 105, 112, 117, 118, 123, 126, 129, 197, 203, 281, 291
Giddens, A. 227, 258, 259, 260, 270, 287, 296, 302
Gilberg, S. 34
Gilbert, D. 46, 48
Gillespie, M. E. 142, 144
Giner, S. 253, 255
Gitlin, T. 47, 48, 203
Glasgow University Media Group 128
Gleich, U. 170, 181
Goldberg, M. E. 134, 143, 144
Golding, P. 99, 101, 206, 217
Goldthorpe, J. H. 205, 217
Goodman, I. 260, 270
Gorn, G. J. 134, 144
Graber, D. A. 30, 35
Gramsci, A. 44, 47, 48, 84, 91
Graves, S. B. 135, 144
Gray, A. 247, 255, 260, 270
Gray, H. 55, 127, 129
Gray, K. 73
Greenberg, B. G. 154, 164
Greenberg, B. S. 64, 68, 72, 134, 144
Greenfield, P. 203
Griffin, C. 122, 129
Gripsrud, J. 95, 101
Gross, L. 65, 72, 101, 118, 129, 281
Grossberg, L. 195, 203, 310
Gunter, B. 62, 73, 92, 95, 101, 103, 122–3, 136, 145, 168, 172, 181
Gurevitch, M. 33, 35, 154, 164

Haas, H. 164
Hagell, A. 121, 129
Hagen, I. 166, 170, 178, 181
Hagiwara, S. 101

Hall, S. 45, 74, 95, 101, 179, 181, 197, 202, 203, 209, 217, 221, 230–1, 249, 255, 278, 281
Halloran, J. D. 91, 92, 101, 104, 107, 110–11, 118, 208, 217
Hamelink, C. J. 100
Hansen, A. 61, 72
Hardy, G. 117
Harindranath, R. 283–96, 305–6
Hartley, J. 200, 203, 204
Hartmann, P. 208, 209–11, 217
Hartwig, H. 95, 101
Hawkins, R. P. 139, 144
Hay, J. 306, 310
Hebdige, D. 250, 255
Hedinsson, E. 92, 101, 154, 164
Hellbom, B. 99, 101
Henriques, J. 145
Herman, E. 39, 48, 81
Herman, E.S. 4–5, 12, 13
Hermes, J. 231
Herschensohn, B. 46, 48
Herzog, H. 167, 181
Herzog-Massing, J. 279, 281
Hesjedal, O. 101
Hetherington, M. 263, 271
Hexamer, A. 142
Hill, A. 127, 129
Hillier, J. 231
Himmelweit, H. T. 109, 118, 151, 154, 156, 159, 164
Hirsch, P. 39, 48, 204, 261, 271
Hobson, D. 202, 203
Hodge, B. 142, 144, 146–50, 188, 191, 200, 201, 202, 203
Hoggart, R. 105, 118
Holmberg, O. 96, 101
Home, A. 140, 144
Horkheimer, M. 42, 46, 48
Howitt, D. 104, 111, 118, 189, 191
Höijer, B. 99, 101, 166–79, 180, 181
Huesmann, L. R. 89, 101, 105, 113, 114, 117, 118, 124–5, 129, 130
Huntington, S. 38, 48
Hurwitz, S. 89, 102
Husband, C. 208, 209–11, 217
Huston, A. 112, 118
Hyman, H. H. 34

IIC 61, 72
Ilmonen, K. 259, 270
Inkeles, A. 280, 281
Isherwood, B. 248, 255
Isrenn, K. 101
Iwao, S. 98, 102
Iyengar, S. 28, 29, 33, 34

Jackson-Beeck, M. 281
Jaeger, M. F. 164
James, A. 131, 144, 258, 270
James, C. L. R. 15–16, 24
Jenks, C. 121, 122, 129
Jensen, J. F. 96, 102
Jensen, K. B. 166, 168, 172, 181, 270, 295, 296

Jhally, S. 50–60, 81–3, 144
Johnson, M. 251, 256
Johnson, R. 140, 144
Johnsson-Smaragdi, D. 154, 164
Jones, C. 72
Jones, I. 117
Jones, M. 111–12, 118

Kaboolian, F. 273, 281
Katz, E. 152, 154, 157, 158, 163, 164, 166, 182, 212, 217, 221, 230, 253, 255, 281, 282, 284, 290, 295, 297
Katz, P. A. 118
Kaufman, L. 264, 271
Keen, B. 246, 256
Kellner, D. 36–47, 48, 81
Kenny, D. A. 125, 129
Kessler, R. C. 102, 118, 125, 130
Kinder, D. R. 28, 29, 33, 34
Kippax, S. 154, 164
Klapper, J. T. 151, 153, 156, 164, 167, 181
Kline, G. 154, 164
Kline, S. 141, 144
Kovaric, P. 135, 144
Kreiling, A. L. 154, 158, 163
Kubey, R. 308, 310
Kunkel, D. 141, 144
Kuper, S. 232

Lacan, J. 201, 203
Lagerspetz, K. 118, 129
Lakoff, G. 251, 256
Lang, G. E. 25, 34
Lang, K. 25, 34
Lapham, L. H. 12
Lash, S. 287, 297
Lasswell, H. D. 252, 256
Lawrence, J. 48
Lawrence, P. A. 96, 102
Laybourne, G. 140, 144
Lazar, J. 102
Lazarsfeld, P. F. 25, 34, 153, 164
Lee, M. 117
Lefever, E. 37, 46, 48
Leffler, B. J. 176, 182
Lefkowitz, M. N. 117, 118, 124–5, 129, 130
Leiss, W. 134, 144
Leonard, D. 129
Lévi-Strauss, C. 251, 256, 279, 282
Levy, M. R. 64, 72, 154, 164
Lewis, G. H. 160, 164
Lewis, J. 50–60, 81–3, 166, 172, 182
Liblik, M. 99, 102
Lichter, L. S. 38, 46, 48
Lichter, S. R. 37, 46, 48
Liebes, T. 166, 182, 221, 230, 253, 255, 272–81, 282, 284, 290, 295, 297
Lindlof, T. 142, 144, 235, 244
Linné, O. 100, 104–17, 118, 168, 182
Lintz, D. 117

Lippmann, W. 25–6, 29, 32, 33, 35, 78, 86
Livingstone, S. M. 141, 144, 166, 168, 176, 182, 261, 271
Lorch, E. P. 138, 142
Lorimer, R. 230
Lowery, S. A. 167, 182
Luckmann, T. 291, 296
Lull, J. 166, 182, 254, 256, 260, 265, 270, 271
Luria, A. R. 174–5, 182
Lusted, D. 132, 144
Lyle, J. 164

MacCabe, C. 199, 203
Maccoby, E. 154, 164
Mackay, R. W. 147, 150
MacKenzie, D. 246, 256
Madson, M. N. 73
Mander, M. 282
Mandler, J. M. 173, 182
Marc, D. 202, 203
Marcus, G. E. 253, 255, 256
Marcuse, H. 42
Marks, A. M. 67, 72
Marosi, K. 168, 182
Marqusee, M. 15, 22, 24
Martinet, A. 255, 256
Marx, K. 84, 216, 217
Masterman, L. 251, 256
May, R. 175, 182
McCombs, M. E. 25–34, 35, 77–81, 94, 102
McCron, R. 104, 110, 111, 118, 214, 217
McKeon, R. 249, 256
McLeod, D. M. 72
McLeod, J. 154, 164
McQuail, D. 151–63, 164, 212, 217
Mediascope, Inc. 123, 128, 130
Medved, M. 123, 130
Melody, W. 132, 140, 144
Mendelsohn, H. 154, 164
Mercer, C. 203, 251, 256
Meyer, M. 138, 144
Meyer, T. 142
Middleton, S. 99, 101
Milavsky, J. R. 89, 102, 113, 115, 118, 125, 130
Miles, I. 247, 256
Miller, A. 56
Miller, D. 128, 130, 248, 249, 252, 256
Miller, P. V. 164
Mills, C. W. 84, 86
Monod, J. 215, 217
Moores, S. 142, 144, 258, 271, 304, 310
Morgan, D. L. 273, 282
Morgan, M. 62, 72, 73, 92, 101, 102, 118, 129, 135, 144, 281
Morley, D. 66, 72, 166, 174, 182, 189, 191, 203, 221, 230, 233–44, 247, 254, 256, 260, 271, 278, 282, 287, 288, 295, 297, 303–4
Morrison, A. J. 164

Mowlana, H. 12, 13
Moynihan, D. 38, 48
Mullen, L. J. 72
Mulvey, L. 221, 230
Murdock, G. 98, 101, 102, 104, 110, 111, 118, 205–16, 217, 298, 301–3, 304
Muroz, L. 214, 216
Murray, J. P. 118, 135, 144, 154, 164

Narayan, U. 258, 271
Nash, N. C. 12
Negrine, R. 64, 72
Newburn, T. 121, 129
Newcomb, H. 39, 48, 202, 204, 282
Newson, E. 111
Newtson, D. 72
Nias, D. K. 111, 117
Nicholas, D. 34
Nichols, B. 285, 297
Nisbet, R. 38
Noble, G. 139, 141, 144, 154, 164
Nordahl Svendsen, E. 106, 118
Nordenstreng, K. 99, 102
Nordlund, R. 99, 102

Oakley, A. 270
Oestbye, H. 106, 118
Ogles, R.M. 67, 72
O'Guinn, T.C. 68, 73
Oliveira, O.S. 12
Olson, B. 67
Olson, B. M. 64, 72
Oppenheim, A. N. 118, 154, 164
Ostry, B. 13
Ostry, S. 12
O'Sullivan, T. 200, 204
Oswell, D. 132, 145

Paik, H. 110, 113, 117
Palmer, E. 136, 140, 145
Palmer, P. 127, 130, 142, 145, 254, 256
Palmgreen, P. C. 96, 102
Parenti, M. 39, 44, 48, 81
Parker, E. B. 164
Parkin, F. 189, 206, 217
Paterson, R. 250, 256
Pattnayak, D. P. 293, 297
Pearl, D. 93, 102
Penrod, S. 117
Pereira-Norrman, L. 171, 182
Peres, Y. 273, 282
Perse, E. M. 69, 72
Petley, J. 104, 111, 117
Pfau, M. 72
Phillips, K. 38, 46, 48
Philo, G. 128, 130, 266, 271
Piaget, J. 122, 130, 139, 172, 182
Pietilä, V. 99, 102
Plato 132
Postman, N. 133, 145
Poulsen, I. 168, 182
Preston, W. Jr. 13

Propp, V. 273, 281, 282

Radway, J. 203, 204, 221, 230, 260, 271
Rapping, E. 39, 47, 48
Rawlings, F. 113, 117
Reeves, B. 105, 119
Reimer, B. 62, 72
Reith, M. 66, 73
Richards, C. 142, 145
Richardson, K. 72, 270, 295, 296
Ricoeur, P. 251, 256
Riggs, M. 55, 60
Riley, J. W. 154, 164
Riley, M. W. 154, 164
Risenberg, B. 164
Roach, C. 12
Rock, P. 208, 217
Roe, K. 96, 102
Rönnberg, M. 97, 102
Roper, B. 46, 48
Rosaldo, R. 287, 294, 296, 297
Rose, J. 141, 145
Rosenberg, B. 39, 48
Rosengren, K. E. 62, 72, 137, 145, 166, 168, 181
Rothman, S. 37, 46, 48
Rowell, E. 129
Rowland, W. 102, 204
Rubens, W. S. 102, 118, 125, 130
Rubinstein, E. A. 118
Rudolph, L. 292, 297
Rudolph, S. 292, 297
Ryan, M. 47, 48

Sahlins, M. 248, 256
Salomon, G. 138, 145
Samuel, R. 204
Sarnecki, J. 91, 102
Sartre, J. P. 216, 217, 226
Saunders, D. 200, 204
Schatz, T. 231
Schiller, H. I. 1–12, 13, 39, 48, 74–6, 77, 81, 98, 102
Schlesinger, P. 95, 98, 102, 127, 130
Schmidt, W. E. 12
Schramm, W. 151, 154, 164, 167, 182
Schrøder, K. C. 166, 182, 222, 230
Schudson, M. 257, 269, 271
Schutz, A. 289–90, 291, 296, 297
Schyller, I. 117
Seiter, E. 141, 145
Semetko, H. A. 33, 35
Shanahan, J. 69, 70, 73
Shapcott, R. 288–9, 297
Shaw, D. L. 28, 29, 30, 35, 94, 102
Sheatsley, P. B. 34
Shore, B. 169–70, 171, 172, 178, 179, 182
Shrum, L. J. 66, 68, 71, 73
Siepmann, C. A. 38, 48, 49
Sigal, L. V. 32, 35
Signorielli, N. 92, 102, 103, 118, 129, 135, 145, 271, 274, 281
Silj, A. 166, 182

Silverstone, R. 220, 230, 245–55,
    256, 260–2, 271, 287, 297,
    306
Simmel, G. 85
Singer, D. G. 91, 103
Singer, J. L. 91, 103
Singer, R. D. 94, 101
Sjögren, O. 95, 103
Sklair, L. 12
Skornia, H. 38, 48
Slater, J. W. 30, 35
Smith, K. 35
Smith, K. T. 145
Smythe, D. W. 153, 165
Smythe, T. Curtis 37, 48
Sonesson, I. 89, 102
Spanish, M. T. 273, 282
Sparks, C. W. 66, 72
Sparks, G. G. 66, 67, 73
Spigel, L. 132, 145, 246, 256
Spinoza, B. 93, 103
Stacey, J. 230
Staiger, J. 189, 191
Stein, B. 38, 49
Stephenson, M. A. 35
Stephenson, W. 167, 182
Stern, D. N. 172, 182
Stevenson, R. L. *et al.* 38, 49
Stipp, H. H. 102, 118, 125, 130
Stolz, J. 279, 282
Stoneman, L. 240, 244
Story, M. 264, 271
Story, P. 270
Strawser, K. S. 145
Sullivan, D. 13
Svensson, B. 91, 103
Swanson, D. L. 155, 165, 168,
    183
Swanson, G. 274, 279, 282
Swift, B. 164

Swingewood, A. 47, 49

Tan, A. S. 136, 145
Tannenbaum, P. H. 91, 103, 154,
    165, 167
Tapper, J. 66, 73
Taylor, S. E. 166, 173, 178, 181
Thomas, M. H. 113–14, 117
Thomas, S. 278, 282
Thorburn, D. 274, 282
Timberg, B. 48
Todorov, T. 251, 256
Tracey, M. 74–86
Traudt, P. 235, 244
Trenaman, J. M. 168, 179, 183
Tripp, D. 142, 144, 146–50, 188,
    191, 200, 201, 202, 203
Tuchman, G. 39, 49, 209, 217
Turk, J. V. 32 35
Turner, P. 55
Turner, V. 280, 282
Turow, J. 140, 145

UNESCO 99, 103

Vaagland, O. 99, 103, 107–8, 118
Van Evra, J. 125, 130
Varis, T. 99, 102, 103
Vernon, P. E. 168, 179, 183
Viemerö, V. 89, 103
Vince, P. 118, 154, 164
Volosinov, V. 198, 204
von Feilitzen, C. *see* Feilitzen, C.
    von
Voort, T. H.van der 189, 191
Vygotsky, L. 172, 183

Wajcman, J. 246, 256
Walder, L. O. 117, 118, 129, 130
Walkerdine, V. 139, 145, 230

Wall, J. 92, 103
Walster, E. 72
Walton, P. 203
Wanta, W. 35
Warde, A. 268, 271
Wartella, E. 104, 105, 116, 119,
    134, 145, 310
Watanuki, J. 48
Watkins, B. 141, 144, 204
Weaver, C. K. 102, 130
Weaver, D. 30, 33, 35
Weber, M. 85
Weimann, G. 73
White, D. 39, 48
White, D. M. 164
Wilcox, B. 118
Williams, G. 63, 73
Williams, R. 63, 91, 103, 246, 256
Willis, P. 142, 145
Wilson, W. J. 54, 55, 60
Windahl, S. 137, 145, 154, 165
Winnicott, D. W. 176, 183
Winston, B. 284, 297
Winter, J. P. 30, 35
Wober, M. 61–71, 73, 83–4, 92,
    95, 101, 103, 110, 112, 119, 136,
    145
Wood, J. 142, 145
Woollacott, J. 200, 203
Wriston, W. B. 3, 4, 12
Wyckoff, M.L. 143

Yang, S.-M. 135, 143
Young, B. M. 134–5, 145, 263,
    271

Zillmann, D. 25, 96, 103, 113–14,
    119
Zucker, H. G. 30, 35
Zuckerman, D. 118

Subject index

accumulation, of audiences and
capital 40–1
adolescents and children
see also audiences; childhood
active viewing 95–6, 136–40,
146–50
aggression 88–90, 107–8, 113,
125, 211
hyperactivity 91
as media audience 131–42,
146–50
media violence and 104–17,
149
parental influence 107, 108,
146, 147
political socialization 135–6
social behaviour 88–90, 105,
106–8, 110, 113, 124
advertising
aspiration and 57–9
effect on children 134–5, 211
food 264, 265
in radio and television 6, 41,
63, 148, 250
of television equipment 132
transnational 4, 5, 8
affirmative action 53, 82
African Americans
see also ethnic minorities
media stereotypes 55–6, 59
representation on television
50–60, 81–3
Against All Odds 179
agenda setting
news media and 27–34,
77–81, 94, 207–11
aggression
causal effects 88–91, 94, 95,
105–6, 108, 110, 112–14,
133–6
children and adolescents
88–90, 107–8, 113, 125, 211
on screen 64, 124
Aids, government announce-
ments 79–80
American dream 52, 56–9
Änglans boningar, TV film 179
Annenberg group, Cultural
Indicators project 61–2, 63, 64,
66–7, 68, 70, 71
attorneys, perceptions of
through television 68–9
audiences
see also adolescents and children; television; violence
accumulation of 40–1
active viewing 94–7, 136–40,
153, 187, 220–30, 238–9,
263, 300, 302, 308, 309
anthropology of 245–55, 306
comprehension 168, 173–9,
234, 267, 272–81
food choices 257–69, 305

interpretive freedom 302,
303
news media 26–7, 33, 77–81,
167, 170–8
passive viewing 230, 308
patterns of viewing 65–7, 69
pleasure 167, 197, 200,
218–30, 308–9
response to programmes
66–9
self-defining or duped 74
by social grouping 142
for sport 16, 19–21, 24, 76
VCR owners 69

banking, electronic 3
BBC *see* British Broadcasting
Corporation
Beavis and Butt-Head 123, 124
Bond, James, polysemy in 200
Breaking The Waves, a response
184–7
British Broadcasting
Corporation
comprehension studies 179
World Television Service 3
broadcasting
commercial 5–7, 8, 99, 106,
141
economic expansion 5
international 3, 4–5
public service 5, 6, 83, 99,
106, 108, 115, 132, 141
social regulation of 70, 71
technological change 116
Broadcasting Standards Council
123
Bulger, James, murder case
132

Cable News Network (CNN) 3
cable television 6–7
audiences 69, 106, 115
Canada, impact of US culture 11
capitalism
accumulation of capital 40–1
media control 40–6, 97–9,
116
racism and 51
society and 40–1, 43–4, 194,
198–9
Capra, Frank, war documentaries 167
cartoons 149
catharsis, media violence and
94, 105–6
censorship 109, 115, 132
childhood
see also adolescents and
children
definition 131–2
innocent 'golden' age 133
psychology of 121–2

cinema
see also Hollywood
audiences 218–30, 243, 308–9
and investment 225–30, 309
Civil Rights movement 51
cognitive research 30, 137,
138–40, 171–5, 178
see also audiences, reception
analysis; research
cold war, role of television 36
colonialism, and the spread of
cricket 15–16, 23, 76
comics, reality and 224
commercialization, of sport 18
communication technologies,
globalization of 2–3, 16, 18, 19
community, and TV viewing
250
computer games, violence and
90, 96, 108
consciousness, Schiller's view of
74, 76, 77–8
consumption
see also uses and gratifications
of television culture 186,
247–52, 253, 258–60, 304
content analysis 92–3, 98, 112
critique of 121–2, 126–7,
141
Coronation Street 264
corporations, legal standing of
in America 6
Cosby Show, The
see also family dramas; soap
operas
marxist critique 50–60, 81–3
Crash, controversy 185
creativity, corporate produced
culture and 11
cricket
commentaries 22
effects of media technologies
14–24, 76
criminal behaviour
and media violence 89, 91,
110, 113
TV viewing and 121
cultivation analysis 63, 92, 136
particular studies 67–70
underlying assumptions
65–7
cultural apparatus, understanding and 94
cultural context, and documentary reception 283–96
cultural democracy 43
cultural environment, and
media violence 91–4, 105
cultural experiences 170–3,
175–8
Cultural Indicators 61–71, 83,
92, 112

cultural industries
   manipulation of viewers
      197, 286
   television 41, 45
   transnational 4
Cultural Studies, children's television 140–2
culture
   see also subcultures
   Bourdieu's theory of 225–9
   cost of privatization 11
   mind and 168–9
   national differences 287–95,
      305–6
   pluralism and dissent 288,
      296
   technology and 14–24

Dallas 179, 221
   retelling of 272–81, 290
Darling Buds of May, The 264
Death of a Salesman 56
deconstruction, televisual texts
   198–201
democracy, in the US 42–3
Denmark, television 106
developmental studies 139
disinhibitory effects of television 113–14
dissent
   exclusion of 41–2
   and pluralism 288, 296
   stifled by broadcast media
      6–7
documentaries, reception of
   283–96
dramas
   see also Cosby Show, The
   family dramas 64
   Greek tragedy 94
   situation comedy 112
   soap opera 67–8, 112, 167,
      240, 272–81

EastEnders 264
economic activity, affected by
   global communications 3,
   85–6
education, as socializing agent
   290–5, 305
emotional excitement, violence
   and 91, 93, 96
emphases, in news media *see*
   agenda setting
entertainment media, subcultures and 212–16, 272–81
environmental concern, viewing
   and 69–70, 71
environmental documentaries,
   contrasting audiences 283–96
equal opportunities 51, 53, 54,
   111
ESRC projects 230, 255
ethnic minorities
   see also African Americans;
      social class
   in British television 64–5

news media and 208,
   209–11
response to media violence
   95
ethnicity
   documentary reception 284,
      286–7
   and identification 201
   retelling of fiction 272–81,
      290
EU *see* European Community
European Community 10, 86

Falcon Crest 179
families
   active viewing and 94, 137,
      142, 147–50, 234, 238–9,
      304
   aggression and 89, 121
   and culture of the home
      268–9
   patterns of consumption
      253, 304
   screen violence and 109
   television research and 109,
      233–44, 252, 304
   viewing choices and 233–44,
      257–69
family dramas 64, 279
   *see also Cosby Show, The;
      Dallas*
fantasy programmes 149
fear
   children and 93
   result of screen violence
      61–2, 67, 68, 69–70, 71, 92,
      93–4
fiction viewing 172, 176–7
   retelling of 272–81
fields, Bourdieu's concept of
   225–6, 229
film *see* cinema
food, in TV fiction 264
Food & Drink 264
food choice 257–69, 305
food scares, role of television
   259, 264
Frankfurt School 42, 91, 194,
   195, 197
Freud, S., Pleasure and Reality
   principles 167

gender
   perspectives 172–3, 175–6
   relations in families 237–42,
      266
   retelling of fiction 276–7
   stereotyping 134, 135, 136

habitus, Bourdieu's concept
   226–9, 302, 306
Hart to Hart, TV drama 195–7
hegemony theories 43–5, 47, 84,
   91
Hollywood
   see also cinema
   racial inequality themes 54

homosexuals
   Aids and 79–80
   representation on television
      65

Independent Television
   Commission (ITC) 64–5
India
   education and culture 291–5
   interpretive repertoires
      283–96
   television versus cinema 292
inflation, price of gasoline
   29–30, 78
infocom technologies, impact on
   cricket 17–24, 76
information
   effect of global monopoly
      3
   free flow of 10
information technologies, globalization of 2–6
infrastructures, institutional 4
institutional process analysis
   61–2, 63–4, 70
instrumentalist theories 43–4
International Cricket Council
   (ICC) 22
international media organizations 9–10
Internet 5–6
   violence and 90

journalists
   see also news media
   agenda-setting role 27–33,
      34, 207–11, 285–6
   objectivity of 26, 34, 285–6
   personnel vetting and
      control of 10
   political reporting 25, 32–3,
      34
Judge Dredd 221–5, 229

Kennedy, J.F. news of assassination 25, 68
Kids, controversy 185

laboratory studies 107, 113, 115,
   116, 122, 124
   altered behaviour response
      124
lawyers *see* attorneys
leisure activity
   competing leisure activities
      233, 304
   the home and 237, 304
   the media and 206, 211–16
liberal left, defined 46–7
life-style, and food choices
   258
life-style expectations, frustration and 91
longitudinal studies 89–90, 113,
   115, 124–5, 128

market forces 9, 64

materialism
advertising and 134
and the American dream
57–9
meaning
layers of 194–202, 249,
299–301
mass communication and
205–16, 246–7, 253, 258,
260–1, 302
media content
coding and decoding 95, 221
myths 92, 94
satisfaction and 160–1
media effects, research critiqued
120–8, 133–40
media experiences 184–8
media industries, political role
of 3–6
media technologies, effect of on
cricket 14–24, 76
media violence *see* violence
media–cultural conglomerates
3–4, 9–10, 74
message system analysis 62–3,
64–5, 70, 83
message transferral 26–7, 77
Mexico, economic collapse 8
Ministry of Agriculture,
Fisheries and Food 270
'moral panics' 108, 132
multinational companies *see*
transnational companies
music
popular 137, 213
violent images 90, 96, 108,
137
myths
media contents 92, 94
of public relations 32
of violence 175–7

national power, erosion of 2–3,
38, 62
New Left, television and the 38
New Right, critique of television
37–8, 46, 47
news, sources of 31–2
news agenda, shaping of 31–3,
34, 77–8
news media
see also journalists; television
adversarial function of 38
audiences 26–7, 33, 77–81,
167, 170–8
conservative critiques 37–8,
40, 46, 47
dependence upon for information 25–6, 29–30, 77–8,
206–7, 258–69, 308
economic pressures 209
emphases *see* agenda setting
gatekeeping 27, 39
impact on daily life 25–6,
77–81, 167
meaning and dominant
group control 207–11

political influence of 25–6
presentation of civil distur-
bance 208, 215–16
presentation of violence 92,
98, 99, 110, 125–6, 127,
170–1, 175–7, 178
racial issues 208, 209–11
scare stories 77–81, 259, 264
news viewing 170–8
Newson Report 111, 115
newspapers
agenda setting 27–31
cricket reporting 15–16
political ownership 32–3
political reporting 25, 32–3
sources of news 32–3, 79–81
non-governmental organizations (NGOs) 4, 5
North American Free Trade
Agreement (NAFTA) 4, 86
Norway, television 106

orientation, voter behaviour
30–1, 34

Packer, Kerry 17, 22, 23
peer groups
active viewing and 94, 137,
142, 150
aggression and 89
Persian Gulf War 3, 10, 62
Piano, The, psychoanalytic
debate 221
political analysis, voter behaviour 20, 25, 26, 28, 29, 30–1, 34
polysemy
layers of meaning in television 194–202, 249, 299–301
social class and 195, 198–9,
249
popular culture 95, 97, 98
Popular Culture Association 39
pornography 108, 149
poverty, culture of 54–5
power relationships
in families 266, 303
polysemy and 195
presidential elections
role of news media 25, 28, 29
role of television 36, 37
presidential power, erosion of
38
privatization, and the arts 11
propaganda
hegemony and 45
World War I 26
psycho-dynamic processes, TV
viewing 175–7
public agenda *see* agenda
setting
public opinion 28, 31
public relations
source of news 32, 33, 209
television industry 140

Quantum Leap, portrayal of
racial divisions 53

racial issues, news media and
208, 209–11
racism, on US television 41,
50–60, 149
radical left, defined 47
radio
cricket commentaries 16
news reading 167
Rambo: First Blood 219
Ramsey, JonBenet murder,
statements to the media 80–1
reception analysis 166–79, 263,
265–9, 283–96, 305
remote control devices 238
research
see also cognitive research;
surveys
agenda setting 28–30, 33
cinema audiences 218–30,
243, 308–9
critiques of media effects
research 120–8, 133–40
Cultural Indicators 61–71,
83, 92, 112
family viewing 109, 233–44,
253, 304
media violence 88–100,
105–16, 137
public knowledge project
262–3
voter behaviour studies 25,
26, 28, 29, 30–1, 34
rhetoric, of television 249–52
Rhodes Around Britain 264

Said, Edward, on
'Orientalization' 287
satellite communication 3–4
satellite TV channels 106, 115
Save the Children Fund,
campaign against TV violence
106–7
school
active viewing and 94, 137,
150
aggression and 89
sexually related behaviour, on
screen 61, 64, 67–8
Simpson, O.J., trial, viewer
responses 66
Simpsons, The 58
single-issue pressure groups 6
slimming diets 259
soap opera
see also Cosby Show, The;
Dallas
radio 167
television 67–8, 240
social class
see also ethnic minorities;
subcultures
aggression and 90, 91
cinematic experience 226
comprehension of TV texts
168
meaning and 195, 198–9,
205–6, 207, 212–16, 302

response to media violence
   95, 111, 126
   in the US 51–60
   viewing choices and 96,
   236–44
social learning 113, 114, 135–6
social sciences
   behaviourism 109, 133, 135,
   186
   constructivism 135, 137–40
   folk theories 230–1
   functionalism 152, 153–4
   positivist methods 152,
   153–4
   structuralist theory 227
   variable analysis 153
society
   economic control and media
   violence 97–100, 116
   globalization and 84–6
socio-cultural impact, of
   media–cultural companies 5
sponsorship
   cricket 18
   in cultural industries 57–9
   of public service broadcasting 6
sport
   audiences and 16, 19–21, 24,
   76
   commentaries 22
   commercialization of 18
   infocom technologies and
   17–24
Stallone, Sylvester, a fan's view
   219, 223, 225
stereotyping
   the elderly 135
   ethnic/racial 55–6, 59, 135,
   149
   gender 134, 135, 136
   negative 135–6
subcultures
   see also culture; social class
   and entertainment media
   212–16, 272–81
surveys
   see also research
   audience surveys 4, 50, 52,
   54, 55
   false responses to questionnaires 124
Sweden
   crime levels 91
   media violence research 92,
   105, 107, 137
   television 106

taste, individual and cultural
   160–2
technocapitalism 42, 47
technology
   culture and 14–24
   and daily life 260

television as 246–7
telecommunications industry 2,
   9
television
   see also audiences; news
   media
   African Americans and
   50–60, 64, 81–3
   conservative critiques 37–8,
   40, 46, 47
   corporate control of 39, 40–2,
   45–6, 97–100, 116
   Cultural Indicators 61–71
   deregulation 64, 71
   exclusion of radical views
   40–2, 208
   exploitation of audiences 41
   exploitation of labour 40–1
   exposure versus consumption 185–6
   gender roles 64, 197
   hegemony theories 43–5, 47,
   84, 91
   ideological criticism 195–7
   impact on cricket 17–24
   impact on individual lives
   36, 46
   influence of and food
   choices 257–69, 305
   interactivity and 253–4
   interpretation of 267–8,
   284–5
   liberal critiques 38–40
   marxist analysis 50–60, 62
   planned viewing 239, 304
   polysemy of 194–202, 249,
   299–301
   popularity and profitability
   59, 194–202
   programming 7, 40–1, 82
   racial inequality and 51–60,
   64, 82–3
   reality factor 148
   regulation of 262
   as resource 268, 305
   and societal conflict 42–6
   sociopolitical functions
   39–40, 81
   as technology 246–7
   theory of 36–46
   white heterosexual male
   dominance 62, 64
television news
   adversarial function 38
   agenda setting 29, 94
   audience view 159–60,
   170–1, 172, 175–7, 178
   family viewing 241–2
   presentation of violence 92,
   125–6, 127, 170–1, 175–7,
   178
   production 39
textual analysis, television 141,
   246–52, 263, 274

Thatcher, M.
   resignation of 68
   and trades unions 78
Three Loves 179
trade unionism 78
transnational companies 2, 3–4,
   7–10, 47, 86
   and political processes 62

unemployment
   television viewing and 66
   understanding of 30, 78
United States
   corporate voice in society 6,
   7
   domination of world information sources 5, 9, 75, 99,
   107, 112–13, 115–16
   global cultural influence 4–6,
   7–8, 75–6
US National Television Violence
   Study 123
uses and gratifications 137,
   151–63, 154–63, 168, 187, 212
   see also consumption

VCR ownership 69
video
   as technology 247
   use of 239–40
   violence and 90, 95, 96, 108,
   132
*Video Violence and the Protection
   of Children* (Newson) 111
Vietnam War, television and
   36–7, 41
violence
   see also audiences; research,
   media violence; television
   arousal and 113–14, 187
   desensitization 113–14,
   175–6, 187
   differing national treatment
   of 98–9, 122–3
   effects on audiences 61–2,
   64–5, 69, 104–17, 133–40,
   149, 170–1, 175–7, 178
   power hierarchies 61–2,
   92–3, 98
   victims' response to media
   violence 95, 122

Welles, Orson, *Invasion from
   Mars* radio play 167
women
   response to media violence
   95
   television viewing 237–42,
   300
   in TV drama 197
World Series Cricket 17–18, 22
World War I, mass communication and propaganda 26